EDUCATING EXCEPTIONAL CHILDREN

Fifth Edition

Editor

Karen L. Freiberg
University of Maryland, Baltimore

Dr. Karen Freiberg has an interdisciplinary educational and employment background in nursing, education, and developmental psychology. She received her B.S. from the State University of New York at Plattsburgh, her M.S. from Cornell University, and her Ph.D. from Syracuse University. She has worked as a school nurse, a pediatric nurse, a public health nurse for the Navajo Indians, an associate project director for a child development clinic, a researcher in several areas of child development, and a university professor. She is the author of an award-winning textbook, *Human Development: A Life-Span Approach*, which is now in its third edition. She is currently on the faculty at the University of Maryland, Baltimore County.

Cover illustration by Mike Eagle

The Dushkin Publishing Group, Inc.
Sluice Dock, Guilford, Connecticut 06437

The Annual Editions Series

Annual Editions is a series of over fifty volumes designed to provide the reader with convenient, low-cost access to a wide range of current, carefully selected articles from some of the most important magazines, newspapers, and journals published today. Annual Editions are updated on an annual basis through a continuous monitoring of over 200 periodical sources. All Annual Editions have a number of features designed to make them particularly useful, including topic guides, annotated tables of contents, unit overviews, and indexes. For the teacher using Annual Editions in the classroom, an Instructor's Resource Guide with test questions is available for each volume.

VOLUMES AVAILABLE

Africa
Aging
American Government
American History, Pre-Civil War
American History, Post-Civil War
Anthropology
Biology
Business and Management
Business Ethics
Canadian Politics
China
Comparative Politics
Computers in Education
Computers in Business
Computers in Society
Criminal Justice
Drugs, Society, and Behavior
Early Childhood Education
Economics
Educating Exceptional Children
Education
Educational Psychology
Environment
Geography
Global Issues
Health
Human Development
Human Resources
Human Sexuality
Latin America
Macroeconomics
Marketing
Marriage and Family
Middle East and the Islamic World
Money and Banking
Nutrition
Personal Growth and Behavior
Psychology
Public Administration
Social Problems
Sociology
Soviet Union and Eastern Europe
State and Local Government
Third World
Urban Society
Violence and Terrorism
Western Civilization, Pre-Reformation
Western Civilization, Post-Reformation
Western Europe
World History, Pre-Modern
World History, Modern
World Politics

Library of Congress Cataloging in Publication Data
Main entry under title: Annual editions: Educating exceptional children.
1. Exceptional children—Education—United States—Periodicals. 2. Educational innovations—United States—Periodicals. I. Freiberg, Karen, *comp.* II. Title: Educating exceptional children.
371.9′05 76–644171
ISBN 0–87967–824–0

Fifth Edition

Manufactured by The Banta Company, Harrisonburg, Virginia 22801

Editors/ Advisory Board

Members of the Advisory Board are instrumental in the final selection of articles for each edition of Annual Editions. Their review of articles for content, level, currency, and appropriateness provides critical direction to the editor and staff. We think you'll find their careful consideration well reflected in this volume.

To The Reader

In publishing ANNUAL EDITIONS we recognize the enormous role played by the magazines, newspapers, and journals of the *public press* in providing current, first-rate educational information in a broad spectrum of interest areas. Within the articles, the best scientists, practitioners, researchers, and commentators draw issues into new perspective as accepted theories and viewpoints are called into account by new events, recent discoveries change old facts, and fresh debate breaks out over important controversies.
Many of the articles resulting from this enormous editorial effort are appropriate for students, researchers, and professionals seeking accurate, current material to help bridge the gap between principles and theories and the real world. These articles, however, become more useful for study when those of lasting value are carefully *collected, organized, indexed,* and *reproduced* in a *low-cost format*, which provides easy and permanent access when the material is needed. That is the role played by *Annual Editions*. Under the direction of each volume's *Editor*, who is an expert in the subject area, and with the guidance of an *Advisory Board*, we seek each year to provide in each *ANNUAL EDITION* a current, well-balanced, carefully selected collection of the best of the public press for your study and enjoyment. We think you'll find this volume useful, and we hope you'll take a moment to let us know what you think.

Applying oneself to the study of the exceptional child is similar to studying the atmosphere and its phenomena (e.g., heat, moisture, winds). The phenomenon of exceptionality, like heat, moisture, and wind velocity, can be described and assessed. However, each exceptional child has his or her own degree of "difference." Even in the same child, the degree of "difference" changes with maturation and environmental input. Predicting the future course of any exceptional condition, under different family, school, community, and developmental forces, is as difficult as predicting the weather.

With the passage of the Education for All Handicapped Children Act (PL 94-142) in 1975, and its amendments (PL 99-457) in 1986, the education of children with exceptional conditions has been turned upside down. No longer can "different" children be hidden in residential institutions, special schools, or special classes. They are entitled to free and "appropriate" education, and related services to meet their special needs, in the "least restrictive" environment, from ages 3 to 21 inclusive. While education in a regular classroom is not mandated, clear cause must be shown why any exceptional child should be restricted to educational programming apart from nonhandicapped peers. Not all exceptional children welcome the idea of integrated schooling with nonhandicapped peers. Not all parents, teachers, and administrators support the idea either. However, it is the law. Educational facilities are currently in a state of flux, as more exceptional students with extraordinarily diverse conditions are being placed in regular classroom settings.

A major reason for a continually updated reader such as *Annual Editions: Educating Exceptional Children* is to keep all persons involved with exceptional children apprised of new legislation (e.g., PL 99-457, which will be enacted in school year 1990-91) and legal interpretations of old legislation (e.g., the Supreme Court ruling in *Honig v. Doe*, 1988, dealing with disciplining handicapped students). A second reason for frequently providing new, up-to-date articles is to share ideas with persons working with exceptional children on how to modify existing programs to maximize their effectiveness. As changes occur, new challenges arrive in their wake. Reading about the recent experiences and programs of others, in an anthology such as this, can provide helpful hints on how to meet these new challenges successfully.

In the selection of new articles, considerable attention was given to readers' needs for information on changing conditions and on ways to meet new challenges. An attempt was made to balance pedagogical articles with maximum relevancy for teaching of exceptional children, articles focusing on legal changes, articles presenting new knowledge about assessing and intervening in exceptionalities, and articles focusing on attitudinal changes.

The anthology begins with two units discussing issues surrounding the regular education initiative and the integration of handicapped and nonhandicapped children. It then proceeds to discuss each of the different classifications of exceptionality covered by the Education for All Handicapped Children Act, and also includes a unit on gifted and talented children.

It is hoped that each reader will find articles in this anthology that enrich him or her. Beyond this, it is hoped that the information provided herein will prove beneficial to all exceptional children, their families, their teachers, and their friends. In order to continue to increase this anthology's usefulness, readers are encouraged to complete and return the article rating form on the last page of the book.

Karen Freiberg

Karen Freiberg
Editor

Contents

Unit 1

Mainstreaming: Basic Concepts and Issues

Five articles examine the status of special education programs and services for the nation's exceptional children.

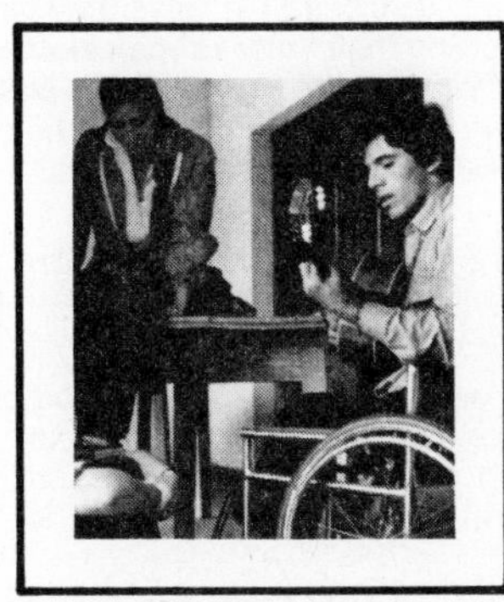

Unit 2

Attitude Change: Integration of Handicapped and Nonhandicapped Children

Four articles discuss the need for developing strategies for establishing interaction between handicapped and nonhandicapped persons.

Unit 3

Teaching the Learning Disabled Child

Six selections discuss the need to accurately assess children with learning disabilities and develop strategies for addressing the special needs of these students.

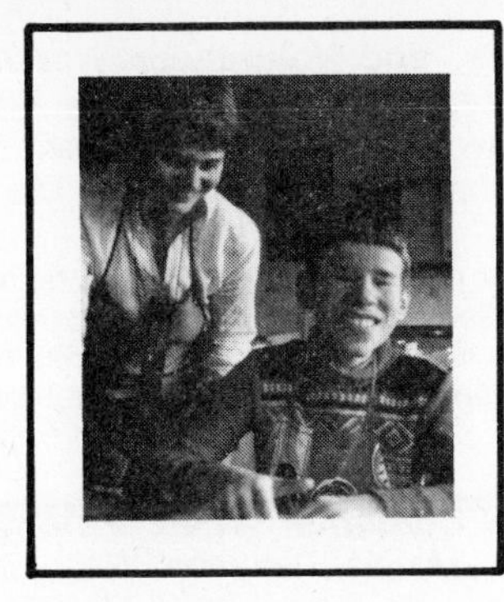

Unit 4

Teaching the Mentally Retarded Child

Six selections discuss the identification, incidence, and prevalence of mental retardation, special learning programs, and the attitudes of mentally retarded individuals.

Unit 5

Teaching the Gifted and Talented Child

Five articles examine the problems inherent in teaching the gifted and talented child. The current status of gifted educational programs is also discussed.

Unit 6

Teaching the Emotionally Disturbed and Behaviorally Disordered Child

Five articles discuss strategies for mainstreaming and teaching children with emotional and behavioral problems.

The concepts in bold italics are developed in the article. For further expansion please refer to the Topic Guide and the Index.

Unit 7

Teaching the Communication Disordered Child

Five selections discuss children with communication disorders and some of the ways in which teachers can assist in these students' learning and development.

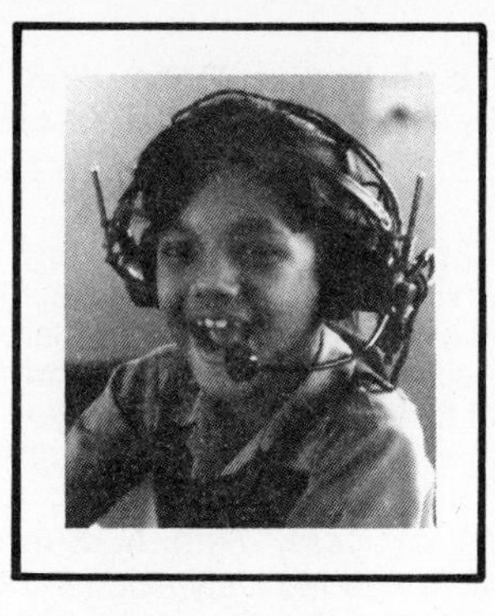

Teaching the Hearing Impaired Child

Five articles examine hearing impairments, special needs of the hearing impaired, and teacher strategies.

Teaching the Visually Impaired Child

Five selections discuss mainstreaming and the special needs of visually impaired children.

Teaching the Physically or Health Impaired Child

Four selections examine the educational implications of physical impairment, the effects of medication on learning, and the value of using microcomputers in helping the severely handicapped child.

The concepts in bold italics are developed in the article. For further expansion please refer to the Topic Guide and the Index.

Topic Guide

This topic guide suggests how the selections in this book relate to topics of traditional concern to students and professionals involved with educating exceptional children. It is very useful in locating articles which relate to each other for reading and research. The guide is arranged alphabetically according to topic. Articles may, of course, treat topics that do not appear in the topic guide. In turn, entries in the topic guide do not necessarily constitute a comprehensive listing of all the contents of each selection.

TOPIC AREA	KNOWLEDGE (These articles provide information about a handicap or about a special education concept.)	ATTITUDES (These articles contain personal experiences of exceptional persons or discussions about changing children's attitudes toward handicaps.)	TEACHING (These articles contain practical suggestions about how to apply special education principles to the teaching of exceptional children.)
Assessment of Handicaps	10. Learning Disabilities 11. The Learning Disabled Preschool Child 18. Autism: The Child Within 23. Meeting the Needs of Gifted Preschoolers 42. The Visually Handicapped Child 44. A Model for Integrating Low Vision Services Into Educational Programs	12. The Masks Students Wear 16. Changes in Mild Mental Retardation 24. Gifted/Learning Disabled Students 25. Creative Underachievers 29. Meeting the Mental Health Needs of Minority Children and Adolescents 33. Culturally and Linguistically Diverse Children	26. Training for Staff, Parents, and Volunteers Working With Gifted Young Children 28. Suicide and Depression 34. Some Ways to Help the Language-Deficient Child 37. Poor Learning Ability . . . or Poor Hearing? 45. Appropriate Education for Visually Handicapped Students
Communication Disorders	32. See Me, Help Me 36. Functional Aphonia in the Child and Adolescent	33. Culturally and Linguistically Diverse Children	34. Some Ways to Help the Language-Deficient Child in the Classroom 35. A Model for Training and Using Communication Assistants
Computers and Other Technological Aids	39. Hearing for Success in the Classroom 45. Appropriate Education for Visually Handicapped Students 46. Evaluating Microcomputer Access Technology for Use by Visually Impaired Students	38. Teachers' Knowledge of, Exposure to, and Attitudes Toward Hearing Aids and Hearing Aid Wearers	48. Students With Special Health Care Needs 50. Comprehensive Microcomputer Applications
Due Process (PL 94–142)	1. The Necessary Restructuring of Special and Regular Education 3. A Social Observation Checklist for Preschoolers 30. Human Rights Review of Intrusive Treatments	2. The Regular Education Initiative Debate	5. Parent Participation by Ethnicity 38. Teachers' Knowledge of, Exposure to, and Attitudes Toward Hearing Aids and Hearing Aid Wearers 48. Students With Special Health Care Needs
Due Process (PL 99–457)	3. A Social Observation Checklist for Preschoolers	4. The IFSP and the Early Intervention Team	48. Students With Special Health Care Needs
Effects of the Disorder on Learning and Development	36. Functional Aphonia in the Child and Adolescent	12. The Masks Students Wear 32. See Me, Help Me	20. Increasing Independence Through Community Learning 43. The Parent and Toddler Training Project 47. Including Young Children With "New" Chronic Illnesses in an ECE Setting
Emotional and Behavioral Disorders	28. Suicide and Depression 30. Human Rights Review of Intrusive Treatments	27. Educator Perceptions of Behavior Problems of Mainstreamed Students 29. Meeting the Mental Health Needs of Minority Children and Adolescents	31. Principles for a System of Care
Gifted and Talented	22. Our Most Neglected Resource 24. Gifted/Learning Disabled Students	25. Creative Underachievers	23. Meeting the Needs of Gifted Preschoolers 26. Training for Staff, Parents, and Volunteers Working With Gifted Young Children
Hearing Impairments	39. Hearing for Success in the Classroom	38. Teacher's Knowledge of, Exposure to, and Attitudes Toward Hearing Aids and Hearing Aid Wearers 41. Reducing Ethnocentrism	37. Poor Learning Ability . . . or Poor Hearing? 40. Service Delivery Alternatives for the Mainstreamed Hearing-Impaired Child

TOPIC AREA	KNOWLEDGE (These articles provide information about a handicap or about a special education concept.)	ATTITUDES (These articles contain personal experiences of exceptional persons or discussions about changing children's attitudes toward handicaps.)	TEACHING (These articles contain practical suggestions about how to apply special education principles to the teaching of exceptional children.)
Individualized Education Programs (IEPs) and Individualized Family Service Plans (IFSPs)	30. Human Rights Review of Intrusive Treatments 45. Appropriate Education for Visually Handicapped Students	4. The IFSP and the Early Intervention Team	5. Parent Participation by Ethnicity 31. Principles for a System of Care
Interaction Between Handicapped and Nonhandicapped	50. Project PAIRS	6. Special Class Placements as Labels 41. Reducing Ethnocentrism	7. Promoting Handicap Awareness in Preschool Children 20. Increasing Independence Through Community Learning
Learning Disabilites	10. Learning Disabilities 11. The Learning Disabled Preschool Child 15. Learning Disabled Students Make the Transition	12. The Masks Students Wear 24. Gifted/Learning Disabled Students	13. Teaching Organizational Skills to Students With Learning Disabilities 14. Helping Disabled Readers in the Regular Classroom
Least Restrictive Environment	16. Changes in Mild Mental Retardation 30. Human Rights Review of Intrusive Treatments	6. Special Class Placements as Labels 29. Meeting the Mental Health Needs of Minority Children and Adolescents	31. Principles for a System of Care 48. Students With Special Health Care Needs
Mainstreaming	3. A Social Observation Checklist for Preschoolers 38. Teachers' Knowledge of, Exposure to, and Attitudes Toward Hearing Aids, and Hearing Aid Wearers	6. Special Class Placements as Labels 17. Special Talents	14. Helping Disabled Readers in the Regular Classroom 27. Educator Perceptions of Behavior Problems of Mainstreamed Students 40. Service Delivery Alternatives for the Mainstreamed Hearing-Impaired Children
Mental Retardation	17. Special Talents 18. Autism: The Child Within	16. Changes in Mild Mental Retardation	19. Using Task Variation to Motivate Handicapped Students 20. Increasing Independence Through Community Learning 21. Sexuality and Students With Mental Retardation
Physical and Health Impairments	48. Students With Special Health Care Needs	49. Project PAIRS	47. Including Young Children With "New" Chronic Illnesses in an ECE Setting 50. Comprehensive Microcomputer Applications
Special Education Programs/Services	10. Learning Disabilities 18. Autism: The Child Within 35. A Model for Training and Using Communication Assistants	1. The Necessary Restructuring of Special Education 2. The Regular Education Initiative Debate 4. The IFSP and the Early Intervention Team 6. Special Class Placements as Labels 33. Culturally and Linguistically Diverse Children	5. Parent Participation by Ethnicity 15. Learning Disabled Students Make the Transition 19. Using Task Variation to Motivate Handicapped Students 20. Increasing Independence Through Community Learning 50. Project PAIRS
Testing/Labeling	1. The Necessary Restructuring of Special and Regular Education 3. A Social Observation Checklist for Preschoolers	6. Special Class Placements as Labels 16. Changes in Mild Mental Retardation	24. Gifted/Learning Disabled Students
Visual Impairments	42. The Visually Handicapped Child 46. Evaluating Microcomputer Access Technology for Use by Visually Impaired Students	45. Appropriate Education for Visually Handicapped Students	43. The Parent and Toddler Training Project 44. A Model for Integrating Low Vision Services Into Educational Programs

Mainstreaming: Basic Concepts and Issues

Public Law 94-142, the Education for All Handicapped Children Act, passed into law in 1975, had four major provisions. It guaranteed the availability of free special education to children who require it, assured that decisions about special education would be fair and appropriate, required clear management procedures for special education at all levels, and provided federal funds to supplement the costs of state and local governments' special education programs. Handicapped children, as defined by PL 94-142, include children with specific learning disabilities, mental retardation, serious emotional disturbances, speech and language impairments, hearing impairments, visual impairments, orthopedic impairments, and other health impairments. Public law 99-457, the Education of the Handicapped Act Amendments, signed in 1986 to be implemented by school year 1990-91, had three major amendments. It extended the rights of PL 94-142 to handicapped children ages 3 through 5, provided a state grant program to provide early intervention services for handicapped infants ages birth through 2, and refined the early education authority to maximize early intervention and preschool initiatives.

Fair and appropriate education, as defined by PL 94-142, requires a comprehensive educational assessment of every handicapped child, an annually updated, written, individualized education plan (IEP), and education in the least restrictive educational environment compatible with the child's handicap. The law does not mandate mainstreaming: i.e, not every disabled child must be educated in a regular classroom. Furthermore, the law does not abolish any particular educational settings, even education within a residential institution. It does, however, require that public education agencies "show cause" if and when a child is moved from the least restrictive environment to a more restrictive one, and provide a written statement describing the extent to which the child will be able to participate in regular educational programs. Any handicapped child who is placed in a parochial or other private school by a public education agency is to be afforded all the rights and protections of PL 94-142 and PL 99-457. If, however, the parent rather than the agency places the child in a private school, the rights and protections may be surrendered.

Mainstreaming, the term used to describe the provision of a free and appropriate education for all handicapped children in the least restrictive educational environment, has been fraught with problems. It has resulted in dissatisfaction among educators unprepared for mainstreamed classes, some incorrect labeling, some inappropriate programming, and many additional expenses. Some parents have fought to get their children out of regular classes and into special programs, special schools, or even residential institutions. Yet PL 94-142 and PL 99-457 are laws passed by the United States Congress which must be enforced. Educators, administrators, and parents must work together to resolve problems, obey the laws, and make mainstreamed education a happier situation for everyone concerned with it.

The articles in this section address the basic concepts and issues surrounding the practice of mainstreaming. They begin this anthology on educating exceptional children because they represent the foundation upon which the programs and services for each category of exceptionality must be constructed.

The first article considers the numbers of children who are deemed to be qualified for special education services, and the areas of exceptionality in which most children are served. The controversy about appropriate education, mainstreaming versus education in a more restricted setting, is addressed in the second article. This question has come to be known as the Regular Education Initiative (REI). Advocates and opponents each have problems concerning compliance with PL 94-142 and PL 99-457. The last three articles give educators and administrators materials to help them bridge the gap between principles and practice. Article 3 provides a social observation

Unit 1

checklist which can be used to assess handicapped children ages 3 through 5 in order to comply with PL 99-457. The next selection recommends procedures for implementation of PL 99-457's mandate for Individualized Family Service Plans (IFSPs) for young children receiving early intervention services. The final article in this section suggests ways in which educators and administrators can involve families from diverse linguistic and cultural backgrounds in planning for their handicapped children's free and appropriate education in the least restrictive educational setting.

Looking Ahead: Challenge Questions

In what areas of exceptionality are children most commonly served in schools today? In what areas are fewer students being served? Do percentages of students served in each area of exceptionality reflect prevalence of the condition or problems with testing and labeling?

Should regular education assume responsibility for all children who need special education? Should students have a voice in decisions about their own educational settings?

How will the amendments of PL 99-457 affect public education? Will agencies be able to develop a systematic plan for integrating handicapped preschoolers into regular day-care or nursery school settings? Who will establish and manage early intervention services for handicapped infants?

Who will collaborate to write Individualized Family Service Plans (IFSPs) mandated by PL 99-457 for handicapped infants and young children? Should parents participate in such planning?

What can be done to increase the participation of families from diverse linguistic and cultural backgrounds in planning for the free and appropriate education of their handicapped children?

The Necessary Restructuring of Special and Regular Education

MAYNARD C. REYNOLDS
MARGARET C. WANG
HERBERT J. WALBERG

MAYNARD C. REYNOLDS *is Professor of Special Education, University of Minnesota, Minneapolis.* MARGARET C. WANG *is Director, Temple University Center for Research in Human Development and Education, Philadelphia, Pennsylvania.* HERBERT J. WALBERG *is Research Professor, College of Education, University of Illinois at Chicago.*

ABSTRACT: The categories used in special education for mildly handicapped students are not reliable nor valid as indicators of particular forms of education. Their use is expensive and inefficient; they cause much disjointedness in school programs. It is recommended that a program of pilot projects be initiated in conjunction with regular educators to redesign categorical programs and policies.

■ Unless major structural changes are made, the field of special education is destined to become more of a problem, and less of a solution, in providing education for children who have special needs. This is our conclusion following a broad review of research in special education. Our remarks refer to programs for "mildly" or "judgmentally" handicapped children, more than three-fourths of the clients of special educators, and to other similar categorical programs (e.g., Chapter I programs as originally provided under the Elementary and Secondary Education Act of 1965 for economically disadvantaged children, migrant education, low English proficiency programs, etc.), but not to programs for children who are deaf, blind, severely disturbed, or deeply retarded in cognitive development. The major flaw is in the way special education has been "categorized." The restructuring we propose would involve both categorical and "regular" education.

PROBLEMS AND TRENDS

Imagine this situation in a large elementary school: The principal has proposed that all of the specialists in the building try a coordinated approach in services to children. A great deal of money and effort are going into "special" programs: One out of six teachers in the building is a specialist; most of the itinerant staff who come to the building part-time (e.g., school psychologist, social worker, vision specialist, English as a Second Language supervisor) work on special problems; a disproportionate number of the paraprofessionals, mainly teachers' aides, and volunteers work in specialized programs. The principal reports that growing numbers of children with problems are being referred to her office, possibly because the existing specialized programs have been organized into a set of little"boxes" that leave many children "falling through the cracks."

No overall system is in place for meeting the needs of these students. For example, the learning disability (LD) program is supposed to serve only children showing a very wide "discrepancy" between "ability" and "achievement"; the Chapter I program is supposed to serve only students who have a sufficient number of eligibility "points" according to an increasingly more selective statewide eligibility system; and the migrant education program serves only children whose parents moved recently to secure agricultural employment. The services of the school psychologist and social worker are consumed almost totally by children enrolled in special education because their salaries are reimbursed through that program. No one is in a position to serve the many poorly motivated children whose achievement falls just beyond the various categorical program boundaries, children in grief because of family problems and the myriad of children suffering neglect and abuse, often associated with alcohol or drug problems in the family and community.

Many schools are better coordinated than the hypothetical one described above, but many others are not; as a result, they find themselves in a losing battle with what might be termed "disjointed incrementalism" (Reynolds & Wang, 1983). This term refers to what happens when a series of narrowly framed programs is launched one by one, each program well-justified in its own time and way, but based on the assumption that it does not interact with others. Each program has its own eligibility, accountability, funding, and advocacy systems. The result is extreme disjointedness, which also leads to excesses of *proceduralism*, including the tedious, costly, and scientifically questionable categorizing of students and programs.

We believe that the field of special education and closely related categorical programs now represent an extreme case of these twin problems: disjointedness and proceduralism. One researcher puts it this way, mainly in terms of inefficiency:

> The amount of time and energy now devoted to preplacement and reevaluations [in special education], which are dominated by determination of eligibility, represents excessively costly and ineffective use of resources. (Reschly, in press, a)

As we look to the future, such inefficiencies will present increasing problems. Every indicator shows that the number and the proportion of children having "special needs" are rising and will continue to rise over at least the next several years. For example, the numbers and percentages of children living in poverty have increased steadily in recent years. The fertility rate among women at low income levels is higher than that for women at average or higher income levels. The rates at which children are judged by teachers to need remedial or special education are much higher for children in poverty than for children from families with greater economic resources. The data on children in poverty tend to correlate highly with the data on children from minority families and the birth rate in minority families is relatively high (Reynolds & Lakin, in press).

More than 1 infant in 20 in the United States is now placed in an intensive, neonatal care unit at birth or soon thereafter, with low birthweight being a frequent factor in such placements. Survival rates for such children have increased dramatically, but so have disability rates.

> Data from the Collaborative Perinatal Study (Broman, Nicholas, & Kennedy, 1975), and other major studies (Wiener, 1968), suggests that special education services are required perhaps 2.5 times more frequently by [low birthweight] children when compared to a group of normal birthweight children. (Scott & Carran, in press)

An added factor is the clearly predictable general increase in the school-age population. From 1975 to 1985, the school-age population decreased from about 51 to 44 million, but now a reversal is underway with expectations that the number will approximate 50 million by the year 2000. Thus we face a general increase in numbers of children, an increasing proportion of them likely to have special needs, and a new and negative climate with respect to competitiveness with regular education for funds to support special programs.

THE RESEARCH BASE

There is little research to justify present practices in the categorizing of children and programs in the domains considered here. Lloyd Dunn made that point memorably in 1968, referring mainly to so-called educable mentally retarded children. Reflecting on the major review of research and practice (Hobbs, 1975) in special education which he led in the early 1970's, the late Nicholas Hobbs said that the present classification system for exceptional children is "a major barrier to the efficient and effective delivery of services to them and their families and thereby impedes efforts to help them" (1980, p. 274).

The very important review of special education placement practices undertaken in the early 1980's by the National Academy of Science (Heller, Holtzman, & Messick, 1982) resulted in similar conclusions. Consider the following three statements from the report of the distinguished panel assembled by the National Academy of Science.

> It is the responsibility of the placement team that labels and places a child in a special program to demonstrate that any differential label used is related to a distinctive prescription for educational practices . . . that lead to improved outcomes. (p. 94)

Present practices in special education fall woefully short of the standard implied by that prescription. " We can find little empirical justification for categorical labeling that discriminates mildly mentally retarded children from other children with academic difficulties" (p. 87); "similar instructional processes appear to be effective with EMR, learning disabled, and compensatory educational populations" (p. 102). It is past time for special educators to hold themselves accountable to research findings of these kinds.

Our own recent research review covered most areas of special education (Wang, Reynolds, & Walberg, in press a). Nearly 70 scholars from across the nation participated in this work. Following we present some of the summary results, especially those relating to the disjointedness problem.

One sign of the problem in the structuring of present practices is the lack of consistency in defining categories of children.

> Discrepancies in state eligibility have resulted in large disparities among states in the percentages of students classified as EMR (from 0.49% in Alaska to 4.14% in Alabama); LD (from 0.83% in New York to 5.20% in Maryland); and ED (from 0.04% in Mississippi to 3.09% in Utah). (Morsink, Thomas, & Smith-Davis, in press)

"Efforts to instill practical, instructional, or programming guidance from research are severely hampered by . . . persistent variability in characteristics of school identified samples of students classified under the various categories of mild handicap" (Gerber, in press). A related point noted by many researchers is that:

> Decisions about special education classification are not only functions of child characteristics but rather involve powerful organizational influences. Number of programs, availability of space, incentives for identification, range and kind of competing programs and services, number of professionals, and federal, state, and community pressures all affect classification decisions. (Keogh, in press)

Services for learning disabled students showed the largest growth in recent years and now present the greatest challenge. Keogh (in press) cites Edgar and Hayden's (1984-85) finding that the number of individuals in all handicapping conditions has increased 16% since 1976-77, but that LD increased 119%. It is noteworthy that the LD category, which arguably is the least well-defined of all special education categories, should have grown so rapidly. Ysseldyke (in press) reports that "more than 80% of normal students could be classified as learning disabled by one or more definitions now in use." Even within states, the LD area presents major difficulties, as indicated, for example, in the following summary statement by Smith, Wood, and Grimes (in press).

> More than 45% of the students enrolled in Colorado's LD programs did not meet the state criteria for placement (Shepard & Smith, 1981). This result is in agreement with Algozzine and Ysseldyke's (1981) who found no significant difference between low achievers and identified LD students . . . [These studies] suggest the lack of consistency in decisions made by special education MDT's [multi-disciplinary teams].

The emotional disabilities category also presents major problems. Smith et al. cite the findings from Lakin's (1983) analysis of randomly selected studies related to emotionally disturbed children published over a 10-year period up to 1978. Lakin found that "over 80% of the studies reviewed selected subjects by presence in a setting . . . or by soliciting and accepting nominations of subjects without any attempts to substantiate, quantify, or qualify the cases of those nominations" (Lakin, 1983, pp. 130-131). Similarly, Nelson and Rutherford (in press) observed that "who is or is not labeled behaviorally disordered for a given educational program or research investigation is likely to depend as much on political and subjective factors as an objective, behavioral criteria."

Sometimes there is a kind of hydraulic relationship across categories. A major court finding, for example, may cause a downturn in use of one category in favor of another. Reschly (in press a) notes recent reports to Congress that indicate a decline of 300,000 in the number of students classified as mentally retarded in the period from 1976 to 1983, contrasted with an increase of 1 million for students classified as LD. Reschly (in press b) also points out that the decline in numbers of students classified as mildly mentally retarded (MMR) can almost certainly be interpreted to mean "substantial changes in the population of MMR students which, in turn, constitute a change in the overall diagnostic construct."

The research syntheses make it clear that the present structure of many special programs, particularly those for mildly and moderately handicapped children, cannot be justified. Children are not "carved by nature" into the various categories now used in the schools. There are major problems in assembling the research base as well as in the practical organization of the programs. As Gerber (in press) summarizes, "for practical purposes, there is increasingly convergent belief that these subgroups of learning problems represent a continuum of cognitive and adaptive inefficiency and ineffectiveness in classroom learning situations, and not discretely different disabilities." The change required may be quite radical, that is, "to cease the current classification system, which focuses on within-child categories, and to begin funding programs based on the need for resources" (Epps & Tindal, in press). That proposal seems less radical when one considers that Hobbs recommended it more than a decade ago.

In offering these comments about the classification of students, we do not deny that the students have serious problems; it is the flawed system for addressing those problems—how the children, and even the teachers and programs, are categorized—that is in doubt. And we note that to the extent that classification systems are unreliable and inconsistent, the accountability to children so fervently desired and fought for by advocacy groups simply goes awry.

A PROPOSAL

As an outcome of reflection on these several research reviews we have recommended (Wang, Reynolds, & Walberg, in press b) specific action in the form of a two-part initiative that would involve coordinated efforts of federal, state, and local levels. The first part of the initiative involves the joining of demonstrably effective practices from special, compensatory, and general education to establish a general education system that is more inclusive and that better serves all students, particularly those who require greater-than-usual educational support. The second part of the initiative calls for the federal government to collaborate with a number of states and local school districts in encouraging and supporting experimental trials of integrated forms of education for students who are currently segregated for service in separate special, remedial, and compensatory education programs.

The second part of the initiative may require a "waiver for performance" strategy, though much can be done, we believe, under flexible interpretations of existing rules and regulations. According to this strategy, selected local educational agencies (LEAs) within several states would be given time-limited waivers of certain rules and regulations by government agencies when this is possible under existing laws. For example, waivers would ensure no categorical funding losses for the LEAs during their experimentation with more coordinated programs. In return, LEAs would be required to provide data on student outcomes or performance during the experimental period, thus the term, waivers *for performance*.

The kind of waiver strategy which we propose is not new. The "Medicaid waiver" program, for example, has had tremendous impact in recent years on programs for handicapped persons. This approach began with the case of Katie Becket ("Katie Finds a Friend with Clout," 1985), who was hospitalized for treatment at great expense, even though she could have been treated adequately at home—where everyone preferred her to be. However, the "rules and regulations" would have required the family to impoverish itself to pay for the necessary treatments if she came home. A Medicaid waiver was subsequently designed to facilitate at-home treatment for Katie Beckett.

It is notable that Madeleine C. Will, Assistant Secretary for Special Education and Rehabilitative Services, the U.S. Department of Education, has spoken and written recently of the need to remove the barriers that exclude students with special needs from full integration into the life of the school and the larger society (Will, 1986). To this end, she has called for the establishment of new partnerships in education—partnerships between states and the federal government, between states and local districts, between regular and special educators, and between educators and parents. She notes in particular the need to empower building-level school administrators to assemble all resources necessary for delivery of coordinated educational services in regular school settings for all students, including those with special needs who currently are served by a variety of segregated programs.

Many varieties of experimental programs can be envisioned for trial. Indeed, a variety of programs are already under way and they could be extended. For example, Sage and Fenson (1985) have reported on "mixed category" programs in Pennsylvania. Their findings suggest that broader groupings of children can be successful unless there is neglect of obviously limiting factors such as class size. The Pennsylvania approach could be extended beyond special education to include Chapter 1 and other special programs, if flexible supporting systems were created. Other approaches might well involve the use of broad instructional systems such as curriculum-based identification systems (Tucker, 1985); the Adaptive Learning Environments Model (Wang & Birch, 1984a, b); building-based collaborative models such as teacher assistance teams (Chalfont, Pysh, & Moultrie, 1979); and studies of the relative costs of various instructional models for serving students with special needs (see descriptions of exemplary programs in Cantalician Foundation, Inc., 1983; Epps & Tindal, in press; and Nevin & Thousand, in press).

RIGHTS WITHOUT LABELS

Legal rights of handicapped students and parents are established in connection with education, and there is understandable concern that these rights might be diminished by any attempts to modify the categories. One of the most challenging aspects of the revisions which we see as necessary in special school programs will be to assure parents and other advocates that legal rights, such as rights to due process and to Individualized Educational Plans (IEPs), need not be lost. In our view, such rights ought to be extended to all students as rapidly as is feasible, thus avoiding the problem of having to specify the particular categories of students to which such rights shall pertain.

Leaders of several of the national advocacy groups, including several lawyers who have had prominent roles in special education litigation, have drafted a statement entitled, "Rights Without Labels" which proposes in detail how the kinds of experiments which we propose can go forward while also offering all legal protections to children and parents. (A copy of the "Rights Without Labels" statement can be obtained by writing to Advocacy Center for the Elderly and Disabled, 1001 Howard Avenue, Suite 300A, New Orleans, LA 70113.)

The "Rights Without Labels" guidelines are based on a three-step approach to ensuring effective services for students: first, the use of pre-referral screening and intervention to ensure that further evaluation is limited to only those students with clearly identifiable handicapping conditions; second, the inclusion of curriculum-based assessment procedures in the identification and evaluation of students with special needs to ensure the design of appropriate educational programming; and, third, the reallocation of some special education resources to facilitate the provision of effective services for students with special needs in regular classroom settings.

OTHER ADVOCATES FOR CHANGE

Several other developments add force to the movement for redesign of programs for students with special needs. For example, the National Coalition of Advocates for Students (NCAS) and the National Association of School Psychologists (NASP) have issued a joint statement entitled, "Position Statement: Advocacy for Appropriate Educational Services for All Children" (1986). (Copies available from National Coalition of Advocates for Students, 76 Summer St., Suite 350, Boston, MA 02110.) It says in part

> We propose the development and piloting of alternatives to the current categorical system. This requires reevaluation of funding mechanisms, and advocacy for policy and funding waivers needed for the piloting of alternative service delivery models. ("Position Statement," 1986, p. 2)

A recent policy statement by the Association for Children with Learning Disabilities, while urging multiple protections for children now classified as LD, also expresses support for new approaches: "We endorse continued efforts to fulfill the intent of the law [PL 94-142], while recognizing that new approaches need to be explored to meet the needs of all students" (Association of Children with Learning Disabilities, 1986, p. 4).

CONCLUSION

Special educators and advocates are rightly proud of the progress made in recent decades in serving students with special needs. Wave after wave of students in various categories have been designated for attention and given rights to appropriate, individualized education. Yet basic problems have been rising as well, and we think they are likely to grow more rapidly in the near future if efforts for solutions are not accelerated now. In particular, we believe that the problem centers on the practice of partitioning mildly and moderately handicapped students into various categories which lack evidence of validity. It would be less troublesome if only the students were categorized, but, instead, a whole pattern of related categorization has occurred for teachers, advocacy groups, and funding systems.

It has not been possible to construct a distinct research base for the categorical programs of special education, because the categories have been ill-defined and unreliable. The boundaries of the categories have shifted so markedly in response to legal, economic, and political forces as to make diagnosis largely meaningless and inconsistent. Accountability is unclear because the categories are scientifically indefensible. Special education has contributed to an increasing disjointedness in school programs and an inability to meet the needs of "new morbidities" such as child depression and grief, drug use, teenage pregnancy, poor academic motivation, and school absence.

We propose a new wave of innovation in which special educators would join with others to advance a broad program of adaptive education for all students, including intensive efforts on behalf of children who have not progressed well under current programs. We believe new models can be tried without undermining the hard-won rights of handicapped children (Wang, Reynolds, & Walberg, in press b). This is a great challenge, but one that fits well into the history of special education and that we believe is timely for the second decade of development in the new era heralded in the United States by P.L. 94-142.

REFERENCES

Advocacy Center for the Elderly and Disabled. (1986). *Rights without labels*. New Orleans, LA: Authors.

Algozzine, B., & Ysseldyke, J. E. (1981). Special education services for normal children: Better safe than sorry? *Exceptional Children, 48*, 238-243.

Association for Children with Learning Disabilities. (1986). *Position statement on a regular education/special education initiative*. Pittsburgh, PA: Author.

Broman, S. H., Nicholas, P. L., & Kennedy, W. A. (1975). *Preschool IQ: Prenatal and early development correlates*. New York: Wiley.

Cantalician Foundation, Inc. (1983). *Technical assistance and alternative practices related to the problem of the overrepresentation of Black and other minority students in classes for the educable mentally retarded*. Buffalo, NY: Author.

Chalfont, J., Pysh, M., & Moultrie, R. (1979). Teacher assistance teams: A model for within building problem solving. *Learning Disabilities Quarterly, 2*, 85-86.

Dunn, L. (1968). Special education for the mildly retarded—Is much of it justifiable? *Exceptional Children, 35*, 5-22.

Edgar, E., & Hayden, A. H. (1984-85). Who are the children special education should serve and how many children are there? *The Journal of Special Education, 18*(4), 523-539.

Epps, S., & Tindal, G. (in press). The effectiveness of differential programming in serving mildly handicapped students: Placement options and instructional programming. In M. C. Wang, M. C. Reynolds, & H. J. Walberg (Eds.), *The handbook of special education: Research and practice*. Oxford, England: Pergamon.

Gerber, M. M. (in press). Application of cognitive-behavioral training methods to teaching basic skills to mildly handicapped elementary school students. In M. C. Wang, M. C. Reynolds, & H. J. Walberg (Eds.), *The handbook of special education: Research and practice*. Oxford, England: Pergamon.

Heller, K., Holtzman, W., & Merrick, S. (Eds.) (1982). *Placing children in special education: A strategy for equity*. Washington, DC: National Academy Press.

Hobbs, N. (1975). *The futures of children*. San Francisco: Jossey-Bass.

Hobbs, N. (1980). An ecologically oriented service-based system for classification of handicapped children. In E. Salzmeyer, J. Antrobus, & J. Gliak (Eds.), *The ecosystem of the "risk" child*. New York: Academic Press.

Katie finds a friend with clout. (1985, November 23). *U. S. News and World Report*, pp. 10-11.

Keogh, B. K. (in press). Learning disabilities: Diversity in search of order. In M. C. Wang, M. C. Reynolds, & H. J. Walberg (Eds.), *The handbook of special education: Research and practice*. Oxford, England: Pergamon.

Lakin, K. C. (1983). Research-based knowledge and professional practices in special education for emotionally disturbed students. *Behavioral Disorders, 8*, 128-137.

Lloyd, J. W. (in press). Direct academic interventions in learning disabilities. In M. C. Wang, M. C. Reynolds, & H. J. Walberg (Eds.), *The handbook of special education: Research and practice*. Oxford, England: Pergamon.

Morsink, C. V., Thomas, C. C., & Smith-Davis, J. (in press). Noncategorical special education programs: Process and outcomes. In M. C. Wang, M. C. Reynolds, & H. J. Walberg (Eds.), *The handbook of special education: Research and practice*. Oxford, England: Pergamon.

Nelson, C. M., & Rutherford, R. B. (in press). Behavioral interventions with behaviorally disordered students. In M. C. Wang, M. C. Reynolds, & H. J. Walberg (Eds.), *The handbook of special education: Research and practice*. Oxford, England: Pergamon.

Nevin, A., & Thousand, J. (in press). Avoiding or limiting special education referrals: Changes and challenges. In M. C. Wang, M. C. Reynolds, & H. J. Walberg (Eds.), *The handbook of special education: Research and practice*. Oxford, England: Pergamon.

Position statement: Advocacy for appropriate educational services for all children. (1986). Boston, MA: National Coalition of Advocates for Students and the National Association of School Psychologists.

Reschly, D. J. (in press a). Learning characteristics of mildly handicapped students: Implications for classification, placement, and programming. In M. C. Wang, M. C. Reynolds, & H. J. Walberg (Eds.), *The handbook of special education: Research and practice*. Oxford, England: Pergamon.

Reschly, D. J. (in press b). Minority MMR overrepresentation: Legal issues, research findings, and reform trends. In M. C. Wang, M. C. Reynolds, & H. J. Walberg (Eds.), *The handbook of special education: Research and practice*. Oxford, England: Pergamon.

Reynolds, M. C., & Wang, M. C. (1983). Restructuring "special" school programs: A position paper. *Policy Studies Review, 2*(1), 189-212.

Reynolds, M. C., & Lakin, K. C. (in press). Noncategorical special education: Models for research and practice. In M. C. Wang, M. C. Reynolds, & H. J. Walberg (Eds.), *The handbook of special education: Research and practice*. Oxford, England: Pergamon.

Sage, D. D., & Fenson, H. C. (1985). *A study of mixed category special education programs in the Commonwealth of Pennsylvania* (Final report to the Pennsylvania Department of Education Bureau of Special Education). Syracuse, NY: Syracuse University.

Scott, K. G., & Carran, D. T. (in press). Identification and referral of handicapped infants. In M. C. Wang, M. C. Reynolds, & H. J. Walberg (Eds.), *The handbook of special education: Research and practice*. Oxford, England: Pergamon.

Shepard, L. A., & Smith, M. L. (1981). *The identification, assessment, placement, and remediation of perceptual and communicative disordered chil-*

dren in Colorado. Boulder: Laboratory of Education Research, University of Colorado.

Smith, C. R., Wood, F. H., & Grimes, J. (in press). Issues in the identification and placement of behaviorally disordered students. In M. C. Wang, M. C. Reynolds, & H. J. Walberg (Eds.), *The handbook of special education: Research and practice*. Oxford, England: Pergamon.

Tucker, A. (Ed.). (1985). Curriculum-based assessment [Special issue]. *Exceptional Children, 52*(3).

U.S. Department of Education. (1985). *Seventh annual report to Congress on the implementation of Public Law 94-142: The Education for All Handicapped Children Act*. Washington, DC: Author.

Wang, M. C., & Birch, J. W. (1984 a). Comparison of a full-time mainstreaming program and a resource room approach. *Exceptional Children, 51*(1), 33-40.

Wang, M. C., & Birch, J. W. (1984 b). Effective special education in regular classes. *Exceptional Children, 50*(5), 391-398.

Wang, M. C., Reynolds, M. C., & Walberg, H. J. (in press a). *The handbook of special education: Research and practice*. Oxford, England: Pergamon.

Wang, M. C., Reynolds, M. C., & Walberg, H. J. (in press b). Rethinking special education. *Educational Leadership*, in press.

Wiener, G. (1968). *Long-term study of prematures: Summary of published findings*. Washington, DC: Office of Education, Department of Health, Education, and Welfare. (ERIC Document Reproduction Service No. ED 043389, PS003651.)

Will, M. C. (1986). Educating children with learning problems: A shared responsibility. *Exceptional Children, 52*(5), 411-416.

Ysseldyke, J. E. (in press). Classification of handicapped students. In M. C. Wang, M. C. Reynolds, & H. J. Walberg (Eds.), *The handbook of special education: Research and practice*. Oxford, England: Pergamon.

Ysseldyke, J. E., Algozzine, B., Shinn, M., & McGue, A. (1982). Similarities and differences between low achievers and students classified learning disabled. *Journal of Special Education, 16*, 73-85.

Most of the research syntheses were supported through a project funded by the Office of Special Education Programs, U.S. Department of Education. The findings and interpretations reported here do not necessarily reflect the views of the Department of Education nor of any of the individual researchers involved in the project; the authors take full responsibility for the views presented in this article. The work of certain of the research syntheses authors is cited here as "in press" to refer to its publication as part of the three-volume work entitled, *The Handbook of Special Education: Research and Practice*, to be published by Pergamon Press in 1987.

The Regular Education Initiative Debate: Its Promises and Problems

WILLIAM E. DAVIS

WILLIAM E. DAVIS *is Professor of Special Education and Director, Institute for Research and Policy Analysis on the Education of Students with Learning and Adjustment Problems, College of Education, University of Maine, Orono.*

ABSTRACT: The most intense and controversial issue presently receiving attention in the special education professional literature is the Regular Education Initiative (REI) debate. The proposed merger of special and regular education into a unitary system has attracted both strong advocates and critics. This article examines the current parameters of this discourse, identifies specific problems and issues related to this debate, and suggests strategies for overcoming perceived obstacles and improving the overall dialogue. Particular attention is given to key groups, for example, local educators and students themselves, who have been largely excluded from the REI debate. Most of the suggested benefits of the REI movement will never accrue unless its present discourse is expanded to include these groups.

☐ As the current debate involving the proposed merger of special education and regular education intensifies, it appears that many special educators feel compelled to choose sides. Either one is *for* or *against* what has commonly become known as the Regular Education Initiative (REI), the movement advocating that the general education system assume unequivocal, primary responsibility for all students in our public schools—including identified handicapped students as well as those students who have special needs of some type. Thus, most proponents of the REI (e.g., Reynolds, Wang, & Walberg, 1987; Sapon-Shevin, 1987a; Stainback & Stainback, 1984; Will, 1986) call for a dissolution of the present dual system in our public school structure, to be replaced by a unitary educational system, which, if carefully designed and implemented, would allow for a more effective and appropriate education for *all* students.

In brief, REI advocates argue that the current special education delivery system is beset with a multitude of problems. They see it as based on flawed logic, as discriminatory, as programmatically ineffective, and as cost inefficient. Whereas the rallying cry of special education professional and advocacy groups during the 1960s and 1970s was "greater access to the mainstream," today it is being replaced by a much more complex rallying cry: "full access to a restructured mainstream" (Skrtic, 1987a).

Advocates argue that "mere access" to the current general education mainstream is not enough. However, because of the deficiencies in organizational structure of general education, along with its present inability to respond effectively to individual student diversity and difference, general education requires a major reconstitution if it is to meet the needs of handicapped and other special needs students (Edgar, 1987, 1988; Reynolds et al., 1987; Skrtic, 1987a, 1988).

Most writers commonly identified as REI "opponents" (e.g., Gerber, 1988; Hallahan, Keller, McKinney, Lloyd, & Bryan, 1988; Keogh, 1988; Mesinger, 1985) generally attempt to qualify their positions, claiming not to be necessarily opposed to the merger of regular and special education per se, but rather advocating a more cautious approach to the issue. Typically they argue that the REI movement is based on some basic false assumptions and that it lacks a rigorous research base. These opponents maintain that if the REI is adopted too quickly on a widespread basis, it could bring serious harm to the very students it is designed to help. Despite these qualifications, the battle lines increasingly are being drawn and—justifiably or not—scholars and researchers are clearly being identified as being either for or against the REI.

It is not my purpose to pass judgment on or question the motives of anyone who has offered written or verbal commentary on the REI. This would be both presumptious and nonproductive. Yet several critical factors in the present REI controversy have not been given sufficient consideration by most debators. If these issues are not carefully addressed, they will only present major obstacles to the development and implementation of effective educational reform for *all* students. Passing judgment would also fan the fires of controversy and divisiveness that currently exist in American education, with the unfortunate but inevitable result that increasingly larger numbers of students will "fall through the cracks" of this very system.

SPECIAL EDUCATION UNIVERSITY DOMINATION

First, despite a few recent exceptions (Gartner & Lipsky, 1987), the REI debate has largely taken place among researchers and scholars who are affiliated with special education departments at univesities and colleges. Regular educators, for the most part, have had an extremely limited role in these discussions. Certainly others have recognized this situation and have cited this lack of participation as a major reason that the REI movement is unlikely to be effective. For example, in one of the most frequently cited references, Lieberman (1985) criticized Stainback and Stainback's (1984) call for a merger of regular and special education as similar to "a wedding in which we, as special educators, have forgotten to invite the bride [regular educators]" (p. 513).

Carrying the analogy further, Lieberman (1985) stated:

> We cannot drag regular educators kicking and screaming into a merger [wedding] with special education. The daily evidence on mainstreaming attitudes is too overwhelming. This proposed merger is a myth, unless regular educators, for reasons far removed from "it's best for children," decide that such a merger is in their own best interests. This is something that we will never be able to point out to them. They will have to come to it in their own way, on their own terms, in their own time. How about a few millenia? (p. 513).

Obviously, Lieberman sees little, if any, value in truly examining the REI issue, having already concluded a priori that regular education presently is unwilling or unable to change—and that the likelihood of witnessing such change (at least in our reasonably expected lifetimes) is remote. Possibly, Lieberman is right. However, this isn't the point. To make such an assumption as that of Lieberman's only serves to mask the real critical issues and to beg the real questions.

If the REI never had surfaced as a labeled, identified issue in the first place, I strongly suspect that the role of special education within the overall educational structure presently would still be the object of vehement debate. Its ever-increasing visibility would have demanded such. Even its most vocal and severe critics cannot ignore the widespread impact that the identification, instructional, and placement practices of special education since the implementation of P.L. 94-142 have had on American education—sociologically, politically, economically, and educationally.

Therefore, borrowing Lieberman's analogy, I suggest that "the wedding has already taken place." Formal invitations may not have been sent, but this makes no difference. Neither the bride nor the groom may have been willing, enthusiastic participants in the ceremony, but this too makes little difference. Although not currently formally sanctioned, or even necessarily accepted or desired by either party, the impact of P.L. 94-142 has produced a wedding of sorts. Lieberman and others may have missed it, but unmistakably it occurred. Now, the real question is, how do we make this marriage work?

Special educators at intitutions of higher education (IHEs) need to stop debating exclusively among themselves. Faculty representing other areas, especially elementary and secondary education, as well as educational administration, must be brought into the REI debate. Collaborative discussions, presentations, and correspondence between special and regular educators need to be actively pursued.

Vehicles such as the study and research agenda groups organized and facilitated by The National Inquiry into the Future of Education for Students with Special Needs (Skrtic, 1987b) sponsored by the University of Kansas, provide one specific example whereby greater collaboration among IHE personnel can be fostered. Study groups or "think-tanks" can be organized at various levels—university, state, regional, local, and national— to address particular issues and concerns involving at-risk students. Such vehicles have the potential to provide both scholars and practitioners with valuable opportunities to engage in productive discourse and collaborative problem solving.

LACK OF LOCAL INVOLVEMENT

The REI debate must include more substantial involvement of special and regular educators at the local education agency (LEA) level. Both proponents and opponents of the greater merger of regular and special education programs frequently cite issues and concerns directly involving the roles, responsibilities, attitudes, and skill levels of building principals and teachers as being critical to the eventual success or failure of REI efforts. Yet, for the most part, these frontline personnel have been passive participants, at best, in this discourse.

It is understandable why so much skepticism and, in some instances, even outright hostility exist at the LEA level relative to the REI issue. Because of the myriad pressures, confusion reigns. The REI movement often is perceived as still another in a long line of top-down policy attempts to dictate and control program implementation. Many regular educators, already feeling overburdened and unfairly criticized for their perceived lack of response to more broadly based issues (e.g., rising illiteracy, increasing drop-out rates, and declining student achievement test scores), view increased special education mandates as being especially intrusive and unrealistic.

Many of them feel mired and caught in an "excellence versus equity" trap (Sapon-Shevin, 1987b; Shepard, 1987; Toch, 1984; Yudof, 1984). They feel public pressure to improve the overall academic performance levels of their students, but now must also attempt to "accommodate" difficult-to-teach students within their classes—which may result in the overall decrease of student achievement scores (Gersten, Walker, & Darch, 1988; Kauffman, Gerber, & Semmel, 1988).

Similarly, many building-level principals feel overwhelmed and confused by the REI movement. Madeleine Will may be absolutely correct in her recommendation that building-level administrators "must be empowered to assemble appropriate professional and other resources for delivering effective, coordinated, and comprehensive services for all students based on individual educational needs, rather than eligibility for special programs" (Will, 1986, p. 413). However, many principals may feel that they have not received proper training to assume this responsibility—nor, in some cases, consider this added responsibility to be realistic—given the many other demands and pressures currently being placed on them in the educational reform movements.

Of even greater concern to many LEA principals is the special education backlash effect which is taking place within many communities. The current situation in Massachusetts provides a good example. Marantz (1988) cited the growing, and increasingly hostile, arguments that have been taking place in this state between parents of children in regular education and local/state education administrators relative to the perceived favoritism being granted to children with special needs at the financial and programmatic expense of nonhandicapped children.

Principals in Massachusetts, as well as in other states, are faced with a difficult dilemma. On one hand, they are being encouraged (some would suggest, required) to assume much greater responsibility and advocacy for special education programs, while, at the same time, they must defend their positions in this regard to an increasingly larger number of parents who are becoming more vocal and vehement in their protests and criticism of special education. This is not to suggest that what REI advocates are proposing, regarding the necessity for greater principal and regular classroom teacher involvement and ownership, is wrong. Yet, these policy and program implementors at the local level must be much more involved; their concerns must be heard; and, most important, they must be provided with specific help to solve complex and often extremely delicate problems.

The REI debate has produced similarly frustrating dilemmas for many special education administrators and teachers at the LEA level. Confusion reigns here, too. They are being asked to alter some very basic philosophical and educational beliefs—as well as practices. It is not uncommon for some special education directors and teachers to feel guilt, anger, suspicion, and possibly even betrayal by much of what is embodied in the principles of the REI. For some, it clearly may be an issue of feeling threatened or losing an established professional identity.

However, for many others, there appears to exist a genuine concern that regular education still is not ready—in either attitude or instructional capabilities—to adequately meet the needs of students with special needs. Many special educators are skeptical and untrusting of a regular education system they have been taught to suspect. They harbor feelings of guilt for abandoning their students and feel betrayed by former highly respected professors who seem to be suggesting a total "philosophical flip-flop."

Again, the issue is not so much who is right or what is right. Rather, the REI must be an issue of honest, open dialogue that more meaningfully involves practitioners as well as researchers and scholars. Practitioners need to be listened to, their views and ideas valued, and their feelings respected. As suggested by Clark, Lotto, and Astuto (1984) in their studies involving effective schools and school change, "the key for effective schools lies in the people who populate particular schools at particular times and their interaction with these organizations. The search for the excellence in schools is the search for the excellence in people" (p. 50) [as cited in Skrtic, 1987a, p. 18].

Especially *teachers* at the LEA level (both regular and special) must be convinced of the real need and value of changing. Change is always difficult. It is particularly so when one feels left out of the change process. Both personal and professional changes are being called for in the REI movement. There is the tendency for both regular and special education teachers to place blame on each other; to harbor feelings of resentment and distrust; and even to succumb to cynicism. But the most dangerous of all consequences of excluding teachers from meaningful participation in the REI debate is the apathy that likely will occur. If the REI is perceived as nothing more than just another in a long line of bandwagon approaches, bereft of any substance or real value, I fear that its potential to truly improve the quality of schooling and the quality of lives of students will never be realized.

The bottom line in successful education was, is now, and will continue to be the quality of individual teacher-student interactions. Teachers must become more involved in the REI discourse.

LACK OF CONSUMER PARTICIPATION

The widespread absence of *consumers* themselves in the REI debate, if not surprising, is particularly disturbing. Historically, there have been few efforts to directly involve students themselves in the design, implementation, and evaluation components of their own educational programs. Although several observers (e.g., Biklen, 1985; Blatt, 1981; Bogdan & Taylor, 1982; Davis, 1982; McCaul & Davis, 1988; Skrtic, 1988) have argued for greater consumer involvement in the overall special education process, rarely are students' attitudes, feelings, and opinions directly assessed regarding "what is being done to them" under the guise of sound educational policies and practices.

I am not referring to token involvement on the part of consumers. We already witness this all too often in the Individual Education Program (IEP) process (Turnbull, Turnbull, Summers, Brotherson, & Benson, 1986; Ysseldyke, Algozzine, & Thurlow, 1980). Students are provided with general pieces of information about the programs they are about to enter; the appropriate consent forms, where applicable, are signed; even the diagnostic tools to be employed (irrespective of their actual validity and appropriateness) that may eventually label them as "disabled" are briefly explained. Yet, seldom does any real discourse occur. Typically, professionals talk and clients (students and parents) listen.

Few studies have attempted to assess students' perceptions concerning why they have been placed in special education programs, an understanding of their own handicapping condition label, and judgments regarding the efficacy of their own programs. The results of these studies have generally indicated wide differences between consumer and professional judgments and beliefs regarding the specific issues addressed (Davis, 1982; McCaul & Davis, 1988).

I am advocating the real, meaningful involvement of consumers in the REI debate, especially those students at the secondary level. I strongly suspect that students frequently feel "jerked around" by the educational system. They become either benefactors or victims, in varying degree, of philosophical debate, litigation, and legislative mandates that are subsequently transformed into educational policies and practices (e.g., the principles of *least restrictive environment* and *maximum feasible benefit*—policies and practices that directly impact their daily lives). Yet, how often are students really listened to or their opinions truly valued?

Do not misconstrue or overgeneralize the point that I am attempting to make in this plea for greater consumer involvement in the current REI debate. Clearly, federal, state, and local governing bodies have both the right and responsibility to determine and monitor educational policy and practices in our schools. Likewise, professional educators, as well as professionals representing other disciplines, have the responsibility (and, presumably the expertise) for analyzing educational environments and practices. These educators are responsible for making recommendations regarding optimal student learning and adjustment. I am not suggesting that these "adults" be absolved of their responsibilities toward our children and youth, nor that students be expected to make "adult decisions" without a sufficient living and learning base.

Very simply, I am urging that students not be denied access to the REI debate—that deliberate and purposeful efforts be made to both talk with them and listen to them about the issues. Should this not occur with significantly greater frequency, not only will opportunities for valuable input for the shaping of the debate be lost but also many students, both handicapped and nonhandicapped, will continue to labor under totally invalid assumptions about what *others* are trying to do with, for, and to *them*.

INVOLVEMENT OF OTHER DISCIPLINES

It must be recognized that the REI is much broader than a debate about educational issues and concerns. It is rooted in political, economic, and sociological thought and action. Therefore, in total support of Skrtic's recommendation (1988), this debate, to have any real long-range impact, must be expanded to the "voices of scholars in the social sciences and humanities . . . who can help us understand the place of special education in the complex web of social, political, cultural, economic, and organizational interrelationships within which we and our clients live" (p. 475).

The REI debate is really about how our nation's schools can better serve students who require special attention, interventions, and support systems to enjoy a better quality of life—educationally, personally, socially, and vocationally. For many years now, we have given these students, along with their programs, various labels: *disadvantaged, special needs, disaffected, remedial, Chapter I, migrant, underachievers*, and so forth. Although often an extremely heterogeneous group as measured by many variables, these students typically have had one thing in common as judged by educators: They are viewed as differing from the established norm of a particular educational system at a given point in time. Educational programs have been developed for these students based on the assumption, true or false, that they are different; they do not fit the normal mold; they possess deficits and disadvantages of some type and degree that require atypical interventions.

Most educators would agree, however, that for many of these students, their "problems" are not primarily educational in origin. Rather, they are rooted in much deeper societal problems and issues (e.g., lack of health care, inadequate housing, poverty, and dysfunctional family environments). The educational needs possessed by these students often pale in comparison to their other more basic human needs, such as shelter, food, and affection. Thus, school personnel frequently are expected to develop programs that they know full well do not begin to address many students' real needs. This situation has caused countless special education and other remedial teachers to become extremely frustrated, feeling that what they are doing with certain students will likely have minimal meaningful long-range impact. Put simply—the environmental odds are perceived to be too great to overcome via traditional educational interventions alone.

This issue strikes right at the heart of the global question: "What are the purposes of education?" And more to the point, "What should be the parameters of education's responsibility to students?" Education may be perceived as having very broad responsibilities, including promoting positive mental health, developing lifelong leisure time skills, and providing very specific vocational training. On the other hand, others may perceive education's responsibility to be very narrowly and exclusively focused: to teach academics. Unfortunately, the students themselves continue to be the victims of these controversies. It is not the students who have failed. Rather, "the system" has failed the students.

The current REI debate will not likely provide a solution to the far more complex problem of defining the goals of American public school education. However, I suggest that the debate has the potential to help clarify some very critical issues and questions. *What is education's responsibility to students who deviate or differ from the established norm?* The REI debate, if its discourse is sufficiently rigorous, open, and democratized, can provide a vehicle and forum to generate collaborative thinking, problem solving, and action related to many dilemmas that currently exist in our schools.

For example, who is responsible for the education of students who do not qualify for special education programming services under current eligibility criteria but who clearly appear to be in need of some instructional and curricular modifications? Or, what are the legal, programmatic, and ethical responsibilities of schools for students whose "emotional problems" appear to be primarily home related and do not appear to be "significantly interfering with academic performance"—yet who clearly seem to be *at risk* and extremely vulnerable youngsters who are in need of counseling intervention? Is this a special education responsibility? A regular education responsibility? A family responsibility? A combination of all three?

It would be naive to think that the REI debate has the potential for providing definitive, simple solutions to these problems. Nevertheless, it does have the potential to help clarify some of the issues and concerns, as well as to provide some clear direction, relative to the responsibilities of society, in general, and the education community, in particular, to students who are "falling through the cracks." Because the issues and problems are much broader than educational in nature, scholars and thinkers representing other disciplines must be involved in the debate. If not, the issues and problems, as well as the suggested solutions, will be too narrowly focused. The larger questions need to be asked. The broader perspective needs to be sought. As advocated by such writers as Skrtic (1986, 1987a) and Edgar (1988), we must experiment with new paradigms in education—paradigms that may look drastically different from the present and that take into full consideration the social, political, and economic influences on current educational environments.

OTHER CONTEMPORARY DISCOURSES

REI debators and critics must also recognize that "our debate" is not an isolated or independent discourse. It should not, and must not, be separated from other debates on broader societal issues currently taking place in America: homeless children and families, child abuse, chemical abuse, unemployment and underemployment, hunger, poverty, and so forth. The issues involved in these broader discourses often are directly or indirectly related to the REI agenda. The voices of those who are participants in these very debates must be heard and their positions examined in light of their implications for, and relevance to, our REI discourse. Of more importance, they should be formally invited to share their thinking with us.

CONCLUSION

The REI debate must be placed in proper perspective. It is not important which scholars view themselves as, or are perceived by others as, being "winners" or "losers" in this discourse. If any substantial and meaningful benefit is to accrue from REI deliberations, practitioners and consumers must be more directly involved as participants.

Issues and concerns currently being addressed as part of the REI debate are important ones. They provide us with a rare opportunity to rigorously evaluate public education's commitment to serving handicapped and other special needs, at-risk students, as well as to assess its present level of organizational readiness necessary to not only accommodate but also to respect and value individual student differences. Most important, however, the REI debate is focusing, in part, on quality-of-life issues—basic human needs issues that are much more global and significant than simply P.L. 94-142 compliance issues.

REFERENCES

Biklen, D. (Ed.). (1985). *Achieving the complete school: Strategies for effective mainstreaming.* New York: Columbia University.

Blatt, B. (1981). *In and out of mental retardation: Essays on educability, disability, and human policy.* Austin, TX: PRO-ED.

Bogdan, R., & Taylor, S. (1982). *Inside out: The social meaning of mental retardation.* Toronto: University of Toronto Press.

Clark, D. L., Lotto, L. S., & Astuto, T. A. (1984). Effective schools and school improvement: A comparative analysis of two lines of inquiry. *Educational Administration Quarterly, 20*(3), 41-68.

Davis, W. E. (1982, April). *I'm glad you finally asked: Students' reactions to their special education program experiences.* Paper presented at the international conference of The Council for Exceptional Children, Houston, TX.

Edgar, E. (1987). Secondary programs in special education: Are many of them justified? *Exceptional Children, 53,* 535-561.

Edgar, E. (1988, March). *New directions for education as an intervention for quality of life.* Paper presented at the international conference of The Council for Exceptinal Children, Washington, DC.

Gartner, A., & Lipsky, D. K. (1987). Beyond special education: Toward a quality system for all students. *Harvard Educational Review, 57,* 367-395.

Gerber, M. M. (1988). Tolerance and technology of instruction: Implications for special education reform. *Exceptional Children, 54,* 309-314.

Gersten, R., Walker, H., Darch, C. (1988). Relationship between teachers' effectiveness and their tolerance for handicapped students. *Exceptional Children, 54,* 433-438.

Hallahan, D. P., Keller, C. E., McKinney, J. D., Lloyd, J. W., & Bryan, T. (1988). Examining the research base of the regular education initiative: Efficacy studies and the adaptive learning environment model. *Journal of Learning Disabilities, 21*(1), 29-35; 55.

Kauffman, J. M., Gerber, M. M., & Semmel, M. I. (1988). Arguable assumptions underlying the regular education initiative. *Journal of Learning Disabilities, 21*(1), 6-11.

Keogh, B. K. (1988). Improving services for problem learners: Rethinking and restructuring. *Journal of Learning Disabilities, 21*(1), 19-22.

Lieberman, L. M. (1985). Special education and regular education: A merger made in heaven? *Exceptional Children, 51,* 513-516.

Marantz, S. (1988, April 15). Special needs: Advocates twist law, critics say. *The Boston Globe,* pp. 1, 18.

McCaul, E., & Davis, W. E. (1988). *Special ecducation students' perceptions relative to the strengths, weaknesses, and efficacy of their own programs.* Manuscript submitted for publication.

Mesinger, J. F. (1985). Commentary on "A rationale for the merger of special and regular education" or, is it now time for the lamb to lie down with the lion? *Exceptional Children, 51,* 510-512.

Reynolds, M. C., Wang, C., & Walberg, H. J. (1987). The necessary restructuring of special and regular education. *Exceptional Children, 53,* 391-398.

Sapon-Shevin, M. (1987a, April). *Merger: What it is—What it could be—Why we don't agree—Why maybe we better make it work.* Paper presented at the annual meeting of the American Educational Research Association, Washington, DC.

Sapon-Shevin, M. (1987b). The national education reports and special education: Implications for students. *Exceptional Children, 53,* 300-307.

Shepard, L. A. (1987). The new push for excellence: Widening the schism between regular and special education. *Exceptional Children, 53,* 327-329.

Skrtic, T. M. (1986). The crisis in special education knowledge: A perspective on perspective. *Focus on Exceptional Children, 18*(7), 1-16.

Skrtic, T. M. (1987a). An organizational analysis of special educational reform. *Counterpoint, 8*(2), 15-19.

Skrtic, T. M. (1987b). The national inquiry into the future of education for students with special needs. *Counterpoint, 8*(1), 6.

Skrtic, T. M. (1988). Response to the January executive commentary: No more noses to the glass. *Exceptional Children, 54,* 475-476.

Stainback, S., & Stainback, W. (1984). A rationale for the merger of special and regular education. *Exceptional Children, 51,* 102-111.

Toch, T. (1984, November). The dark side of the excellence movement. *Phi Delta Kappan,* 173-176.

Turnbull, A. P., Turnbull, H. R., Summers, J. A., Brotherson, M. J., & Benson, H. A. (1986). *Families, professionals, and exceptionality: A special partnership.* Columbus, OH: Charles E. Merrill.

Will, M. C. (1986). Educating children with learning problems: A shared responsibility. *Exceptional Children, 52,* 411-415.

Ysseldyke, J. E., Algozzine, B., & Thurlow, M. L. (1980). *A naturalistic investigation of special education team meetings* (Research Report No. 40). Minneapolis: University of Minnesota Institute for Research on Learning Disabilities.

Yudof, M. G. (1984, March). Educational policy research and the new consensus for the 1980's. *Phi Delta Kappan,* 456-459.

Preparation of this article was supported in part by the Institute for Research and Policy Analysis on the Education of Students With Learning and Adjustment Problems, which is sponsored by the College of Education, University of Maine, Orono, and the Division of Special Education, Maine Department of Educational and Cultural Services. I wish to thank Tony Chiappone, Ed McCaul, and James Souza for their review and helpful comments on earlier drafts of this article. Readers interested in obtaining information on the Institute or in receiving a monograph related to the Regular Education Initiative should contact: Dr. William E. Davis, 306 Shibles Hall, College of Education, University of Maine, Orono, ME 04469.

A Social Observation Checklist for Preschoolers

Ruth Johnson
Colleen Mandell

Ruth Johnson *is Teacher and Coordinator, Resource Center for Early Childhood & Family Life Programs, Toledo Public Schools, Ohio.* **Colleen Mandell** *is Associate Professor, Department of Special Education, Bowling Green State University, Ohio.*

Successful mainstreaming of young handicapped children requires integration of these children in several different domains, including the temporal, social, and instructional components of an early childhood program (Turnbull & Blacher-Dixon, 1981). A review of the literature suggests that the process for achieving social integration is not clearly defined (Guralnick, 1981), even though deficits in the social domain are considered to be more of a deterrent to success in the mainstream program than academic readiness problems (Gresham, 1984). This article addresses the need for a systematic plan for achieving social integration. Use of an informal assessment tool focusing on the relationship between the nature and expectations of the environment and the social skills and behaviors of the disabled child is suggested as one way to increase the likelihood of a successful mainstreaming experience.

The SOME Checklist

One instrument that may be helpful to professionals in determining whether or not a particular child has the necessary social skills to successfully participate in the mainstream environment is the Social Observation for Mainstreamed Environments (SOME) checklist, presented in Figure 1. It is designed to relate a child's social skill performance to the behavioral expectations in an early childhood classroom. Because the intent is to examine a specific child's performance for a specific classroom, the SOME is not appropriate for group use. However, providing no major changes occur, the data collected on the social expectations within the classroom (items on next page) could be used over a period of time.

Instrument Development

A first draft of the SOME checklist was developed in part from a literature review focusing on what social skills were considered necessary for successful integration of young disabled children in a regular classroom setting. Refinement of the instrument was then accomplished through a critical review process by 12 professionals, including local area Head Start supervisors, teaching personnel, and day care staff. Recommendations resulting from this review dealt primarily with terminology and specificity. Teachers and supervisory personnel suggested that the language used should be very specific and concrete in nature. A number of reviewers were concerned about the tendency for scores on behavioral checklists to reflect subjective opinions rather than accurate assessments of specific behaviors. The SOME checklist was revised to incorporate the suggestions of the review panel.

Pilot Testing

Follow-up pilot testing was conducted in an integrated day care program serving 3 to 5 year-old children. The pilot testing focused on two mildly handicapped children who were being considered for a mainstream placement in this day care setting. A special education teacher, the day care supervisor, two of the regular education teachers, and the parents of the handicapped children were all involved in the pilot testing. A series of systematic observations of the target children were made during a 2-week trial placement of these children in the day care program. During this time, data were collected on the children's performance and the expectations of the day care environment.

Positive results from the pilot study suggest that the SOME checklist can be of value to professionals in making decisions related to placement of young disabled children. Results also suggest that the checklist could be used for developing educational goals and objectives for young handicapped children in a mainstream setting.

Content of the SOME

There are 15 items on the SOME checklist, with space for additional items that may be considered important. The items represent those social behaviors generally considered important to successful integration at the preschool level, including the ability to attend to tasks, complete tasks successfully with a minimum of adult assistance, and initiate interactions appropriately (Walter & Vincent, 1982). Other skills identified as being important for social integration in the preschool classroom include the ability to observe and imitate other children (Allen, 1980; Guralnick, 1976), the ability to consciously effect change (Braun & Lasher, 1978), and the ability to go along with simple classroom rules and routines (Walter & Vincent, 1982). Following is a brief description of the desired behaviors associated with each of these skills.

1. *Asks for help when needed.* The child communicates, either verbally or nonverbally, the need for assistance. The child may do so by pointing to what he or she wants, by actually saying "Help me," or by using other meaningful gestures or sounds to communicate the need for help.
2. *Plays well with others.* The child interacts with others at play time in a socially acceptable way. Such interactions may include taking turns using play materials, asking permission before entering someone else's play activity, and following group rules about the use of materials for the play activity.
3. *Obeys class rules.* The child demonstrates understanding of simple classroom rules by going along with the established daily routine without needing frequent reminders or directives.
4. *Attends to tasks for short periods of time.* The child stays with a learning activity such as putting puzzles together or listening to a story for more than 5 minutes.
5. *Completes tasks with a minimum of adult assistance.* The child works on and completes simple tasks such as removing napkins or cups from the table, wiping up spilled liquids, or putting blocks on a shelf without a great deal of reminding or coaching by an adult.
6. *Initiates interactions with peers.* The child spontaneously greets other children, asks them questions, or communicates some information to them. Such interactions may be accomplished either verbally or nonverbally and may include behaviors such as smiling, waving, or gesturing. This item refers to interactions that are initiated spontaneously by the child rather than being directed by an adult.
7. *Initiates interactions with adults.* This desired behavior is the same as the behavior described in item 6, with the exception that interactions occur with adults rather than with peers.
8. *Observes other children.* The child indicates interest in other children and their activities by watching, imitating, or commenting on what the other children are doing.
9. *Imitates other children.* The child, at least occasionally, copies the behavior of other children using sounds or using words, performing physical activities, and so forth.
10. *Makes simple decisions.* The child demonstrates the ability to make decisions by making choices as to what activities to participate in, what materials to use, and so forth. The child may also demonstrate the ability to make decisions by commenting on what he or she considers to be "right" or "better than" possible alternatives to ways of behaving.
11. *Practices turn taking.* Both spontaneously and when prompted the child demonstrates understanding and willingness to take turns in performing an activity, using materials, or getting someone's attention.
12. *Respects other's belongings.* The child demonstrates respect for the property of others by generally refraining from claiming possession of or using in a destructive manner objects that belong to others.
13. *Respects others' feelings.* The child demonstrates a sensitivity to the feelings of others by generally showing sympathy when someone else gets hurt and refraining from physically hurting others. Sympathy may be shown by gently touching, expressing words of comfort, or extending other gestures of friendship or caring.
14. *Follows simple directions.* The child follows one- and two-part directions, such as "Put the cup on the table" or "Take this book and give it to Mary."
15. *Uses verbal versus non-verbal means to express feelings.* The child generally uses words or signs to communicate frustration, anger, joy, etc. and refrains from use of hitting, screaming, and other socially unacceptable ways of expressing such feelings.

Format of the SOME

Four different columns on the SOME checklist provide space for recording observations, comments, and suggested resolutions for areas of concern. The first column is used for recording whether or not a child demonstrates the desired behaviors. It is usually completed by the special education teacher in consultation with

Two students demonstrate the ability to take turns and respect others' feelings and belongings.

the classroom teacher and child's parents. A plus (+) is used if the child usually exhibits the desired behavior, even though the child may occasionally demonstrate the opposite behavior. A minus (−) is used if the child usually does not exhibit the desired behavior.

The second column is used for indicating which social behaviors are considered important by the classroom teacher. This column can be completed by the classroom teacher. Another way of obtaining the information to complete this column is for the special education teacher to observe the classroom routines and interview the regular education teacher. Pluses or minuses in this column do not carry any type of value judgment; that is, no conclusions are made as to whether or not a particular behavior *should* be expected by the classroom teacher.

The third column provides space for recording concerns or observations related to any of the child's behaviors or classroom expectations. For example, a comment related to "Plays well with others" (item 2) might indicate that the child does well when playing with only one other child but tends to withdraw in large group activities. This would alert anyone working with the child to the importance of arranging small group play activities for him or her.

The fourth column provides space for suggesting resolutions for areas of concern.

Guidelines for Assessment

The SOME checklist is designed to be completed by a team of individuals, including the regular classroom teacher, the special educator, and the parents or guardians. It requires observation of the child in a variety of settings (classroom, bus, home, playground, etc.) and during different types of activities (free play, teacher-directed activities, snack time, etc.). A minimum of 10 to 15 minutes should be allocated for each observation period. Because an adequate assessment requires observations during different types of activities and in a variety of settings, total observation time will usually run 40 to 50 minutes. If a child demonstrates a specific skill in some settings but not in others, it is important to note where, when, and in what circumstances the desired behaviors occur.

Using the Checklist

The SOME checklist can be used for determining educational placement. Jeremy, a 3 year-old visually impaired child, was assessed on the SOME, which revealed that he did not follow rules consistently, did not interact well with others, and showed little respect for the belongings or feelings of others. Since each of these areas represented competencies expected by the classroom teacher to whom he would be assigned, the recommendation of the assessment team was that Jeremy remain in the home-based component of the preschool program while these skills were being developed. In addition it was found that Jeremy was able to take turns (item 11), a behavior that was not expected by the teacher. The placement team identified that as a strength that the mainstream teacher could use as a model for the other children in the classroom.

The SOME checklist also can be used in developing social development goals and objectives for a child's individualized education program (IEP). Once discrepancies between the child's social performance and classroom expectations are identified, a plan can be developed for fostering the desired social behaviors. Teresa, a developmentally delayed 4 year-old, illustrates this point. Her behaviors seemed to be fairly consistent with the expectations of the mainstream classroom, but one discrepancy, identified through use of the SOME checklist, was in the area of turn taking (item 11). The assessment team recommended that one of her annual IEP goals should be, "Teresa will demonstrate improved interactions with peers." A related short-term objective was stated as, "Teresa will demonstrate appropriate turn-taking behaviors in interacting with others."

Conclusion

Assessing a child's social skills in relation to what behaviors will be

Figure 1

SOCIAL OBSERVATION FOR MAINSTREAMED ENVIRONMENTS (SOME)

Child's Name: ______________ Date: ______

Individual(s) Observing the Child: ______________

Individual Observing the Classroom: ______________

Other settings in which child was observed ______________

Directions: In the first column, mark a plus (+) if the child usually exhibits the behavior, a minus (−) if the child tends not to exhibit the behavior. In the second column, mark a plus if the classroom teacher expects the children to exhibit the behavior, a minus if the behavior is not one of the classroom expectations. Use the third column for noting any related observations or concerns. In the fourth column, write in proposed resolutions to areas of concern; that is, in areas where the behaviors are expected but are not exhibited by the child.

Behavior	*Child's Performance*	*Classroom Expectations*	*Comments*	*Resolution*
1. Asks for help when needed				
2. Plays well with others				
3. Obeys class rules				
4. Attends to task for short periods of time				
5. Completes tasks with minimum adult assistance				
6. Initiates interactions with peers				
7. Initiates interactions with adults				
8. Observes other children				
9. Imitates other children				
10. Makes simple decisions				
11. Practices turn taking				
12. Respects others' belongings				
13. Respects others' feelings				
14. Follows simple directions				
15. Uses verbal vs. nonverbal means to express feelings				
Other ______				
Other ______				

Recommendations: ______________

Signatures: ______________

expected in the proposed mainstream setting should be an integral part of the assessment/selection process. Use of the Social Observation for Mainstreamed Environments (SOME) checklist may be helpful in identifying discrepancies between a child's social skill development and the expectations of a particular environment. If a mismatch between these two is likely to present a problem, it may be necessary to consider alternatives or modifications to the proposed mainstream plan. However, this approach is not intended to replace the need for evaluating other aspects of the environment to determine what changes might be made within it versus within the child, to facilitate the mainstream process.

References

Allen, K. E. (1980). *Mainstreaming in early childhood education*. Albany, NY: Delmar Publishers.

Braun, S. J., & Lasher, M. G. (1978). *Are you ready to mainstream?* Columbus, OH: Charles E. Merrill.

Gresham, R. (1984). Social skills and self-efficacy for exceptional children. *Exceptional Children, 51*, 253- 261.

Guralnick, M. (1976). The value of integrating handicapped and nonhandicapped preschool children. *American Journal of Orthopsychiatry, 42*, 236-245.

Guralnick, M. (1981). The efficacy of integrating handicapped children in early education settings: Research implications. *Topics in Early Childhood Special Education, 1*, 57-71

Turnbull, A., & Blacher-Dixon, J. (1981). Preschool mainstreaming: An empirical and conceptual review. In P. Strain and M. Kerr (Eds.), Mainstreaming of children in schools: Research and programmatic issues (pp. 71-100). New York: Academic Press.

The individualized family service plan and the early intervention team: Team and family issues and recommended practices

The Individualized Family Service Plan (IFSP) requirements of Public Law 99-457 challenge early intervention professionals to reexamine models for team interaction. Programs moving toward a family-focused approach will provide families with a menu of program options, including the opportunity to choose the level of team participation that best meets individual family needs.

Mary J. McGonigel, MS
Family-Centered Care Project Coordinator
Association for the Care of Children's Health
Washington, DC

Corinne W. Garland, MA
Executive Director
Child Development Resources, Inc.
Lightfoot, Virginia

WHEN PUBLIC LAW 99-457, the Education of the Handicapped Amendments of 1986, was being developed, there was near unanimity within the field of early intervention regarding several critical issues addressed in the nascent bill. This consensus, evident in a Congressional report[1] and in the testimony provided to Congress by leading early intervention organizations and practitioners, extended to the belief that a team approach was necessary and that families were essential members of the team.

The testimony reflected the commonly held belief that the infant is uniquely dependent on the family. This physical and emotional dependence requires that early intervention services be provided within the context of the family. Legislators were urged to specify the role of families in early intervention as both planners and recipients of services and to require written program plans addressing not only the needs of the infant, but also the strengths and needs of the family.

Now that Public Law 99-457 is a reality, no provision is producing more controversy and anxiety than the individualized family service plan (IFSP). Many families and service providers alike are concerned about the potential for an assessment and planning process that will be intrusive, judgmental, static, or unresponsive to the family's needs. Others, more optimistic, are searching for best practices for defining, encouraging, and supporting the family's role on the early intervention team.

This article will define the concepts of team and team interaction as they relate to early intervention, discuss the evolution of the family's role on the team, and suggest principles and practices for team development of the IFSP that are consistent with this new role. Examples of exemplary family-focused principles and practices will be provided.

Reprinted from *Infants and Young Children,* Vol. 1, No. 1, July 1988, pp. 10-21, with permission of Aspen Publishers, Inc. © July 1988.

THE TEAM IN EARLY INTERVENTION

Prior to the passage of Public Law 99-457, a team approach to organizing services for young children with special needs and their families was becoming widespread and was gaining support among early intervention professionals.[2,3] The support was in part a result of Public Law 94-142 and in part a result of the growing recognition that no one discipline can meet the diverse and complex needs of these young children and their families.[4]

No longer an option, a team process now must be used to provide three services required by the new law: team assessment, IFSP development, and case management. Those programs that had resisted the team approach are now examining established models for team organization. Others, already using a team approach, are reexamining the organization of their teams and the ways in which those teams work together.

There are many definitions of a "team." Fewell provides one of the simplest: A team is at least two persons associated through work or activity.[2] This definition encompasses all forms and types of early intervention teams. Common to most definitions of "team organization," however, is the concept of interdependence. Holm and McCartin describe a team as "an interacting group performing integrated and interdependent activities."[5(p121)] Dyer describes teams as "collections of people who must rely on group collaboration if each member is to experience the optimum of success and goal achievement."[6(p4)] To be effective in serving young children with special needs and their families, early intervention teams must be more than collections of persons pursuing their own interests and tasks. The group, "functioning together, is greater than the sum of its individual parts."[7(p306)]

This notion of the team being an interdependent and collaborative group can be actualized only when there is a structure for interaction among team members. Three models for team interaction have been identified and discussed in the early intervention literature: the multidisciplinary, interdisciplinary, and transdisciplinary models.[2,3,8,9]

Much attention has been paid to distinguishing one model from another. A certain controversy has attended the discussion, particularly with regard to the transdisciplinary model, the newest among the models for early intervention teams. While many find the transdisciplinary approach difficult to accept and implement because of the high level of interaction and working across disciplinary boundaries that it requires, proponents consider the results well worth the effort.

It is unfortunate that so much attention has been given to naming and defending models of team interaction. Faced with the challenge of developing IFSPs that are, in fact, neither judgmental nor intrusive, the team's energy would be better spent on increasing the interaction among team members and improving the quality of that interaction.

Only recently have early intervention teams begun to examine their team's functioning systematically. As Fewell cautions "teams are made, not born."[2(p304)] Early intervention personnel struggling to develop effective teams are experiencing a number of problems that are described in the literature: "differing levels of participation by different occupational groups . . . ; lack of meaningful discussion in team meetings . . . ; problems in implementing team recommendations . . . ; lack of training and guidance in the team process . . . ; and the inability of professionals to work together in a truly integrative fashion."[10(p17)]

Bennett[7] and Healy et al[11] add to the list of team problems the higher status traditionally accorded to team members from certain disciplines, particularly medicine. This difference in status and the related difference in personnel costs may be one reason that many early intervention teams outside hospital settings do not include physicians and psychologists. Many concepts such as team building, group process, and team maintenance can be profitably borrowed from the literature of social work, psychology, and organizational development to help early intervention programs overcome these and other team problems.

Teams examining their own structure and function in light of the provisions of Public Law 99-457 and current best practices will be best served by arriving at a consensus about their team's goals and constraints, and then choosing the model of team interaction that allows these goals to be met.

MODELS FOR TEAM INTERACTION

A review of the three most common models for team interaction and their usual procedures for assessment and program planning will be helpful to teams choosing or reevaluating a model for their work. All three models are based on a team made up of professionals from a variety of disciplines, often including education, social work, medicine, physical therapy, occupational therapy, and speech-language pathology. Families of infants and children with special needs are included on these teams in various ways and degrees.

Early intervention teams share a common task: the assessment of a child's developmental status and the development and implementation of a program of services to meet the child's needs. Public Law 99-457 requires that the individualized program plan also be based on the family's assessed needs.

Although the composition and tasks may be quite similar for multidisciplinary, interdisciplinary, and transdisciplinary teams, the method of operation is quite different. Each team model provides a structure for team communication and interaction.

Multidisciplinary model

The multidisciplinary model was the first attempt to bring together professionals from a variety of disciplines to work as a team. Multidisciplinary team members work independently of one another. Peterson compares the mode of interaction among members of multidisciplinary teams to parallel play in young children—"side by side, but separate."[9(p484)] This comparison captures the spirit of many multidisciplinary teams. The work of each team member is viewed as important, but the team members are primarily concerned with the clinical issues of their own disciplines.

By design, practitioners on these teams operate more as independent specialists than as interactive team members.[2,7] Such independence can contribute to isolated and fragmented services for children and families.[3] Most often, families are not considered to be full members of the multidisciplinary team.

Multidisciplinary team members conduct separate assessments by discipline. Following the assessment, each team member generally writes a separate report, developing and implementing separate goals. Lack of coordination and communication among multidisciplinary team members places the responsibility for case management on the family.

Interdisciplinary model

The interdisciplinary model of team interaction was developed in response to many of the problems experienced by multidisciplinary teams. The interdisciplinary model builds on the strengths of the earlier model, but provides a formal structure for interaction and communication among team members that encourages the sharing of information.[2,9] Most often, the family is considered to be a member of the interdisciplinary team.

Interdisciplinary teams assess children and, sometimes families, independently by discipline. The team members come together to discuss their individual results and to plan cooperatively for intervention. Although the team develops a service plan jointly, each staff member is usually responsible for the part of the plan related to his or her professional discipline. The plan is implemented by one person, often the educator, with scheduled therapy or consultation from the specialists on the team.

Problems in communication and interaction arise when interdisciplinary team members lack a full understanding of the professional training and expertise of the members from other disciplines on the team. Members may be confused about their role on the team, and their interaction may be complicated by issues of professional "turf."[2,8] As Howard states, many interdisciplinary teams have discovered that shared terminology does not always have shared meaning.[12]

Transdisciplinary model

The transdisciplinary model is an attempt to solve some of the problems of role confusion and team interaction that can result when team members from a variety of disciplines work together. The transdisciplinary team crosses disciplinary boundaries so that all team members teach and learn the basic terminology and simple intervention procedures of other disciplines represented on the team.[13] While there are differences in the degree of interaction among team members, the transdisciplinary model is similar in many ways to the interdisciplinary model.

One critical difference between the transdisciplinary approach and the other two models is the central role that families play on the transdisciplinary team. Although families may be part of the multidisciplinary team, and generally are part of the interdisciplinary team, they are full members of the transdisciplinary team. In fact, many transdisciplinary teams provide families with the option of serving as team captains, thus acknowledging their ultimate decision-making power.

The success of the transdisciplinary model depends on a process of formal and informal exchange that the United Cerebral Palsy's National Collaborative Infant Project calls "role release."[14] Role release is a conscious, carefully planned process that allows transdisciplinary team members to exchange information, knowledge, and skills across disciplines and to work as an integrated team.

All members of the transdisciplinary team assess the child together, using a format called the "arena assessment." During the arena assessment, all team members observe and record every aspect of the child's behavior during the arena. Only the family and one other team member, who serves as the assessment facilitator, interact with and handle the child, a factor that reduces the potentially disruptive effect of having many persons present at the arena. While there have been few comparative studies conducted so far, one, by Woolery and Dyk, reports that both parents and professionals have judged the arena assessment to be more beneficial than individual and isolated assessments by each discipline.[15]

The entire transdisciplinary team also develops an integrated service plan and authorizes one person, usually called the "primary service provider" or "case manager," to carry out the plan with the family. All team members share equal responsibility for the success of the plan by providing formal and informal support to the family and the primary service provider. When complicated interventions require specific disciplinary expertise, backup support and therapy are provided by the team member from the appropriate discipline.

THE FAMILY AS TEAM MEMBER

Regardless of the team interaction model chosen by individual programs, Public Law 99-457 clearly directs teams to work together with the family to plan for and provide early intervention services to infants and toddlers with special needs. The requirement that infants and toddlers be provided services in a family context represents an evolution of the family's role in early intervention.

Turnbull and Summers[16] have traced the history of this evolution from an early view of parents as part of the problem to a more recent emphasis on parent "involvement"—the idea that parents should be intervenors or cotherapists with their children. Parent involvement or participation has been a dominant theme in early intervention for more than ten years.

In recognition of the primary influence that families have on their child's development, the best practice until very recently directed early interventionists to involve parents at all costs. This effort typically took the form of obtaining parental approval of program plans, training parents to carry out these plans at home, and providing opportunities for counseling or participation in parent groups. Parents were encouraged to be team members, but their role on the team often was limited to rubber-stamping the recommendations of the professional team members.

The importance of parental participation and involvement was a belief so firmly held that many early intervention programs would not serve children whose parents were unable or unwilling to participate in the program. The goal of these programs was to help children by helping families—to share their information and experience as professionals so that parents could help their children as much as possible.

The flaw in this approach was in the interpretation of "helping" families. Many programs were directive in their interactions with families, firmly believing in the wisdom of their recommendations for children and, by extension, for families. Goals for the child or family were often not shared by the family and, sometimes, were not even consistent with the family's priorities or values. Turnbull and Turnbull[17] and Bailey[18] have documented the frequent incongruence between the family's and professional's priorities and insights.

When families inevitably failed to become involved in programs as expected—participating in program planning meetings, coming to parent groups, or carrying out program plans at home—professionals sometimes became frustrated or angry, labeling such parents as "difficult" or "noncompliant." Parents, in turn, were frustrated with early intervention services that were intrusive, directive, or unrealistic. Turnbull and Summers, reflecting on the demands that many early intervention staff place on parents' time at home, write that "anything is possible to those with no responsibility for implementation."[16(p10)]

As the field of early intervention has matured, however, many parents and professionals alike have come to regard the concept of parental involvement as counterproductive. The early intervention literature recently took a new look at the philosophies and practices relating to families and offered an enabling and empowering approach that recognizes and builds on the strengths and resources present in all families.[11,19-24]

Best practice is shifting from an emphasis on parental involvement or participation to an emphasis on family-focused services. Families are being viewed as competent decision makers who must be allowed to choose their level of involvement with an early intervention program according to their values, resources, strengths, needs, and supports.

Dunst[19] writes that, while early intervention practitioners may always have sensed these ideas to be true, they lacked in the past a conceptual framework to enable them to act on their intuition. Systems theories provide this framework for a family-focused approach to early intervention.[19,25,26]

A family-focused approach requires that early intervention practitioners redefine the family's role on the team and, perhaps, early intervention itself. Dunst and associates[21] define early intervention in a new way that recognizes the strengths of families and encourages a new professional role. Early intervention, then, is "the provision of support (i.e., resources provided by others) by members of a family's informal and formal social network that either directly or indirectly influences child, parent, and family functioning."[21(p7)]

If widely accepted and put into practice, this new view of early intervention as the provision of support to further strengthen, enable, and empower families may change the entire character of the field. The first step for professionals is to recognize behaviors that operate against this enabling principle. Bailey describes common helping behavior by early intervention practitioners as follows:

> we often find that when a problem is mentioned by parents, early interventionists are eager to offer solutions or services to solve the problem. Interventionists view this as a positive professional characteristic since they are responding to parents' needs. Furthermore, it is self-reinforcing and an exercise of power to be able to dispense solutions to families.[18(p64)]

As early intervention professionals seek new ways to interact with families, they must develop new roles and incorporate them into their professional identities. Dunst et al[21] have identified eight nonmutually exclusive roles for early intervention staff: empathetic listener, teacher-therapist, consultant, resource, enabler, mobilizer, mediator, and advocate. Among the activities associated with these roles are "linking people, mobilizing existing resources and support, facilitating the establishment of new support structures, moderating exchanges among network members, (and) consulting with families about problems or concerns."[27(p28)]

Although some of these roles and activities are very familiar to early interventionists, others will require a substantial change in perspective and behavior. The development and implementation of IFSPs provide a unique, timely opportunity for practitioners to make such changes.

THE INDIVIDUALIZED FAMILY SERVICE PLAN

The IFSP, if approached from a family systems perspective, may be a radical change for many early intervention programs. Most practitioners have been developing service plans based on the "IEP model." Whether these plans were called individualized development, habilitation, education, or service plans, they typically were formulated by program staff based on assessment data on the child's developmental status, with varying degrees of family participation in the process.

Although many programs did include "family" goals in their service plans, these goals often were based on the *staff's perceptions* of the family's needs. Goals were frequently written in terms of family compliance with the program's priorities and procedures. The mandated IFSP challenges early intervention teams to develop instruments and practices that allow families to assess their own needs and that encourage collaborative IFSP goal setting.

Public Law 99-457 specifies the content of the IFSP, as well as certain participation requirements and implementation procedures. Part H, section 677, requires that the IFSP be developed by a team made up of professionals from multiple disciplines and the parent or guardian. The IFSP must be in writing and must contain:

- a statement of the child's present levels of physical development, cognitive development, language and speech development, psychosocial development, and self-help skills, based on acceptable, objective criteria;
- a statement of the family's strengths and needs related to enhancing the development of the family's handicapped infant or toddler;
- a statement of the major outcomes expected to be achieved for the child and family; the criteria, procedures, and time lines used to determine the degree to which progress is being made; and whether or not revisions of the outcomes or services are necessary;
- a statement of specific early intervention services necessary to meet the unique needs of the child and family, including the frequency, intensity, and method of delivering services;
- the projected dates for the initiation of services and the anticipated duration of the services;
- the name of case manager (from the profession most immediately relevant to the child's or family's needs) who will be responsible for implementing the plan and coordinating with other agencies and persons; and
- the steps to be taken supporting the child's transition to part B preschool services, to the extent that such services are appropriate.

Some of the above provisions are already being addressed in service plans in programs across the country, while others are new. Many practitioners are confused about what the new requirements mean. How should they assess the family's needs? How will they decide what services programs and agencies should offer families? What should a team do when families identify needs that their program is not able to meet? What happens when the staff and family disagree on priorities for services?

Assessing the family's needs

Assessing the family's needs is a special challenge for early intervention practitioners, many of whom have little or no training in family systems or family-centered approaches to services. Bailey and Simeonsson[28] have provided a helpful discussion of the complicated issues surrounding the assessment of the family's needs in early intervention. Traditionally, psychologists and social workers have accepted the responsibility for family assessment. Program staff from these disciplines were trained to evaluate the family's needs in a number of dimensions, using instruments that frequently focused on deficits, assumed psychopathology, or required sophisticated interpretation and inferential reasoning.[28]

In general, other early intervention team members have had little experience in assessing the family's needs. Now that such assessment is a required part of the IFSP, programs need instruments that can be used by all team members. The instruments should reflect the program's respect for the family's ability to make its own decisions.

Procedures to assess the family's needs must also provide "systematic and multiple opportunities" for families to express their needs and concerns in both open-ended and structured formats.[18(p67)] In addition, family assessment instruments and practices must be flexible because of the diversity of families. As Chandler et al note, "families may vary in their structure, ethnic and cultural backgrounds, economic status, educational resources, ideologies, personal and mental health problems, and coping styles for dealing with problems."[29(p234)]

Many exemplary early intervention programs are choosing a variety of family needs assessments that stress self-reporting on the part of the family. Only when families have the opportunity to identify their own needs and priorities can service plans accurately reflect family goals.

The Family, Infant and Preschool Program (FIPP) in Morganton, NC, has developed a number of family needs assessments from a family enabling perspective. The FIPP provides both home- and center-based early intervention services to approximately 300 families. The needs-based assessment and intervention strategy at FIPP involves the identification of the family's needs and sources of support and resources to meet those needs and specifies staff roles in helping families find and use the resources in their support network.

Among the family assessments developed and used at FIPP are the Family Support Scale, the Family Resource Scale, the Support Functions Scale, and the Family Needs Scale. All of these instruments involve self-reporting by the family. Using information gathered from these and other assessments, FIPP staff and families develop a "map" of the families' social support network that can be used to develop family service plans. Dunst et al have published data on the reliability, validity, and other characteristics of these instruments, as well as a description of the various scales.[21,30]

Child Development Resources (CDR), a private nonprofit agency in Lightfoot, Va, provides early intervention services to infants and toddlers with special needs and their families. CDR uses a team-based assessment process that allows the family to determine their own service needs. The staff members function as consultants to the family, helping them to identify needs of the child and family and discussing the menu of service options. Once families have decided on their service needs, they work with other team members to identify their own strengths and resources relative to meeting those needs.

Families are not asked to provide information that does not directly address the already identified needs, thus reducing the intrusiveness of the information gathering. Families are provided continuing opportunities to identify their needs so that they feel free to choose how much information they want to share or reveal at any given time.

The Family Needs Survey developed by Bailey and Simeonsson at the Frank Porter Graham Center of the University of North Carolina at Chapel Hill is one instrument that gives families an opportunity to tell staff directly what their needs are in six areas: information, support, explanations to others, community services, finances, and family functioning. The instrument consists of 35 statements relating to common needs of families in these six areas. A simple rating scale allows families to clearly state their needs.[28]

Developing IFSP goals

After the family's needs have been assessed, the next step is translating those needs into goals for the IFSP. This is a difficult step for many programs because it requires negotiation, collaboration, and mutual problem solving between the professional members of the team and the family.[18]

It is at this point in the early intervention process that family and staff differences in perspective, values, and priorities most often surface. Practitioners traditionally have focused on the therapeutic and educational needs of the child, often to the exclusion of other family considerations. Perhaps the most controversial aspect of a family systems, enabling approach to early intervention is the principle that, when family and staff perceptions of need differ, the service goals reflect the priorities and values of the family rather than those of the staff.

This principle of family direction does not devalue the perspective and skills of early intervention practitioners.[18] Rather, it recognizes that "a person's perception of what constitutes the most important needs at a particular time will likely assume priority status and guide the person's behavior."[23(p249)]

Acknowledging this principle frees early intervention practitioners from the frustration of developing goals and service plans that are meaningful only when staff members are actually working directly with the child. The challenge for professionals is to learn new ways to negotiate collaborative goals with families that allow practitioners to share their information, skills, and recommendations in a way that supports rather than supplants the family's role.

Bailey lists five basic skills that early intervention staff need to develop goals collaboratively with families: "the ability to (1) view a family from a systems perspective; (2) systematically assess relevant family needs; (3) use effective listening and interviewing techniques; (4) negotiate values and priorities to reach a joint solution; and (5) act as 'case managers' in helping families match needs with available community resources."[18(p64)]

Public Law 99-457 does not state or imply that the IFSP must contain goals that address all of a family's needs. Rather, in section 677 teams are directed to consider the family's strengths and needs related to enhancing the development of their child. This is a critical distinction. It is beyond the scope of most early intervention programs to meet all of the needs of all families. Clearly, some problems are beyond the skills and resources available in many programs. Among these, according to Bailey, are "serious marital discord, unemployment, financial impoverishment, chronic personality problems, and limited parent cognitive abilities."[18(p69)]

When such problems are present and when the family perceives them to be problems, the staff and family can work together to determine desired outcomes and can identify supports and resources in the community. It is particularly important that needs be perceived by the family, rather than by the staff alone. Staff team members should avoid making judgments about family relationships based on their own values. Making such judgments frequently results in a hidden agenda—unacknowledged staff goals for changes in the family.

As teams begin to develop goals, a natural inclination is to turn to their experience in developing goals for the child—the IEP model discussed earlier. Unfortunately, this model does not lend itself readily to developing goals for the family. After years of practice in writing behavioral objectives for children with measurable criteria for child change, early intervention practitioners must redirect their thinking. While teachers set goals for change in children's behavior and are responsible for bringing about this change, early interventionists have a different role and relationship in working with families.

Early interventionists can provide families with the information and support that enables them to direct their own strengths and resources to bring about their desired outcomes. The goal of this type of help is not a behavioral change in the family in the same sense that the goal of therapy with a child is a behavioral change in the child, such as better head control or the elimination of head banging.

If practitioners do not recognize this difference, they are likely to impose goals on the family that are directive, judgmental, or paternalistic, or that meet the needs of the program rather than those of the family. The following is an example of a "family" goal developed by staff in one program who forgot this important distinction: "When the home visitor arrives at the home, Mrs Smith will be up and dressed and will have Travis dressed and fed at least 90% of the time." The staff measured the progress toward meeting this objective by counting the number of times Mrs Smith took more than five minutes after the home visitor arrived to get herself and her son ready for the visit.

Such a goal clearly is not consistent with an enabling and empowering approach to families. Yet, because it was directed at the mother rather than the child, the staff considered it a family goal. If practitioners are to make the most of the IFSP, they must guard against the temptation to use family goals as a means to increase family compliance with program policies and procedures.

• • •

In light of Public Law 99-457, early intervention programs are facing new challenges. The IFSP requirement of part H challenges practitioners to choose new models for team interaction and to develop the skills needed to work in true, collaborative partnerships with families. The current movement toward a family systems, family-centered approach to early intervention suggests that the most appropriate team models are those that are highly interactive and that consider the family to be a full member of the team—in fact, the team member with the final decision-making power.

Many families have expressed concern that a family-focused approach to early intervention may result in yet one more professional expectation of proper family behavior. These families fear that program staff will interpret the new approach to mean that all families should act as their own case managers, make decisions alone, or be active and involved in all aspects of an early intervention program.

A family-focused approach encourages just the opposite. Far from prescribing a required role for all families, family-centered programs give families many options, including the opportunity to choose the level of team participation that is most comfortable for them at any given time. Some families will take a leadership role, choosing assessment instruments and procedures, developing IFSP goals that the rest of the team will help implement, and selecting program services that best match their child's needs. Other families, at least initially, will opt for a different level of interaction and involvement with a program, expecting the staff to take the leading role in programming decisions.

When programs and professionals provide families with the opportunity to make conscious and informed choices from an array of options, they ensure that a family's association with early intervention truly meets family needs, rather than meeting program needs, expectations, and demands. Now that Public Law 99-457 is a reality, early intervention practitioners are asking how to best make a place for families on their early intervention teams.

A more appropriate question might be posed such as how early intervention professionals can become part of the family's team, on which the family already functions as team captain and decisionmaker. Professionals can offer help in response to expressed needs and offer support that enables families to draw from their own resources to enhance the development of their children with special needs.

REFERENCES

1. Gilkerson L, Hillard AG, Schrag E, et al: *Report Accompanying the Education of the Handicapped Act Amendments (Report #99-860) and Comments on P.L. 99-457.* Washington, DC, National Maternal and Child Health Clearinghouse, 1987.
2. Fewell RR: The team approach to infant education, in Garwood SG, Fewell RR (eds): *Educating Handicapped Infants: Issues in Development and Intervention.* Rockville, Md, Aspen Publishers, 1983.
3. Woodruff G, McGonigel MJ: Early intervention team models: The transdisciplinary approach, in Gallagher JJ, Hutinger P, Jordan JB, et al (eds): *Early Childhood Special Education: Birth to Three.* Reston, Va, Council for Exceptional Children, in press.
4. Woodruff G, McGonigel MJ, Garland CW, et al: *Planning Programs for Infants,* TADS State Series Paper No. 2. Chapel Hill, NC, University of North Carolina at Chapel Hill, 1985.
5. Holm VA, McCartin RE: Interdisciplinary child development team: Team issues and training in interdisciplinariness, in Allen KE, Holm VA, Schiefelbusch RL (eds): *Early Intervention—A Team Approach.* Baltimore, Md, University Park Press, 1978.
6. Dyer WG: *Team Building: Issues and Alternatives.* Reading, Mass, Addison-Wesley, 1977.
7. Bennett FC: The pediatrician and the interdisciplinary process. *Except Child* 1982;48:306-314.
8. Linder T: *Early Childhood Special Education: Program Development and Administration.* Baltimore, Md, Brookes, 1983.
9. Peterson N: *Early Intervention for Handicapped and At-Risk Children: An Introduction to Early Childhood Special Education.* Denver, Colo, Love, 1987.
10. Bailey DB: A triaxial model of the interdisciplinary team and group process. *Except Child* 1984;51:17-25.
11. Healy A, Keesee PD, Smith BS: *Early Services for Children With Special Needs: Transactions for Family Support.* Iowa City, Iowa, University of Iowa, 1985.
12. Howard J: The role of the pediatrician with young exceptional children and their families. *Except Child* 1982;48:316-322.
13. Haynes U: The National Collaborative Infant Project, in Tjossem TD (ed): *Intervention Strategies for High Risk Infants and Young Children.* Baltimore, Md, University Park Press, 1976.
14. United Cerebral Palsy National Collaborative Infant Project: *Staff Development Handbook: A Resource for the Transdisciplinary Process.* New York, United Cerebral Palsy Associations of America, 1976.
15. Woolery M, Dyk L: Arena assessment: Description and preliminary social validity data. *J Assoc Persons Severe Handicaps* 1984;9:231-235.
16. Turnbull AP, Summers JA: From family involvement to family support: Evolution to revolution. Presented at the Down's Syndrome State-of-the-Art Conference, Boston, Mass, April 24, 1985.
17. Turnbull AP, Turnbull HR: *Parents Speak Out: Then and Now.* Columbus, Ohio, Charles E. Merrill, 1985.
18. Bailey DB: Collaborative goal setting with families: Resolving differences in values and priorities for services. *Top Early Child Spec Educ* 1987;7(2):59-71.
19. Dunst CJ: Emerging trends and advances in early intervention programs. *NJ J Sch Psychol* 1983;2:26-40.
20. Dunst CJ, Trivette CM: Enabling and empowering families: Conceptual and intervention issues. *Sch Psychol Rev* 1987;16:443-456.
21. Dunst CJ, Trivette CM, Deal AG: *Enabling and Empowering Families.* Cambridge, Mass, Brookline, in press.
22. Hobbs N, Dokecki PR, Hoover-Dempsey KV, et al: *Strengthening Families: Strategies for Improved Child Care and Parent Education.* San Francisco, Jossey-Bass, 1984.
23. Trivette CM, Deal A, Dunst CJ: Family needs, sources of support, and professional roles: Critical elements of family systems assessment and intervention. *Diagnostique* 1986;11:246-267.
24. Turnbull AP, Turnbull HR: *Families, Professionals, and Exceptionalities: A Special Partnership.* Columbus, Ohio, Charles E. Merrill, 1986.
25. Bronfenbrenner U: *The Ecology of Human Development: Experiments by Nature and Design.* Cambridge, Mass, Harvard University Press, 1979.
26. Foster M, Berger M, McLean M: Rethinking a good idea: A reassessment of parent involvement. *Top Early Child Spec Educ* 1981;1(3):55-65.
27. Dunst CJ, Leet HE, Trivette C: Family resources, personal well-being, and early intervention. *J Spec Educ,* in press.
28. Bailey DB, Simeonsson RJ: Assessing needs of families with handicapped infants: The Family Needs Survey. *Top Early Child Spec Educ,* in press.
29. Chandler LK, Fowler SA, Lubeck RC: Assessing family needs: The first step in providing family focused intervention. *Diagnostique* 1986;11:233-245.
30. Dunst CJ, Jenkins V, Trivette CM: The family support scale: Reliability and validity. *J Individ Fam Community Wellness* 1984;1(4):45-52.

Parent Participation by Ethnicity: A Comparison of Hispanic, Black, and Anglo Families

ELEANOR W. LYNCH
ROBERT C. STEIN

ELEANOR W. LYNCH *is Professor of Special Education, San Diego State University, California.* ROBERT C. STEIN *is Vice Principal, Pershing Junior High School, San Diego Unified School District, California.*

ABSTRACT: This article describes the results of a study of Hispanic parents' satisfaction with and participation in their child's special education program and compares their responses to those of Black and Anglo families from earlier investigations. Sixty-three parents of children receiving special education services were interviewed in Spanish in their homes by trained interviewers who were also parents of handicapped students. Results of the study indicated that Hispanic parents were generally very satisfied with their child's special education program but often unaware of the services that were being provided. They were aware of the assessment and Individualized Education Plan (IEP) processes but tended not to be active participants in either, though nearly half had visited their child's classroom to observe instruction. Work schedules, "nothing," lack of bilingual communication, and general communication problems were identified as the major barriers which caused them to be less active. To examine whether differences existed on five key variables, between Hispanic, Black, and Anglo families, data from two earlier studies were pooled, collapsed, and analyzed using chi squares. Significant differences were found on all key variables across ethnic groups.

■ Parents of students with handicaps were assured the right to participate in the assessment and program planning process for their child through Public Law 94-142, the Education for All Handicapped Children Act of 1975. For the first time, parents were to become equal partners with professionals in the decision-making process. Parents' responses to this enfranchisement and its outcomes have been studied from many perspectives over the past few years (Cone, Delawyer, & Wolfe, 1985; Lynch & Stein, 1982; Morgan, 1982; Strickland, B., 1982). However, most of the work has been directed toward Anglo-American families—families which, despite their diversity, are accustomed to a democratic society that values shared decision making, teamwork, and the right to question those in authority. Few studies have been conducted that investigate the ways in which parents of handicapped children from the nondominant culture have responded to the rights provided by P.L. 94-142.

As demographics in the United States change, students with diverse cultural and linguistic backgrounds comprise an increasingly large segment of the school-aged population. At present, Hispanic, Black, and Pan-Asian students make up the majority of the school-aged population in many areas of the United States. Predictions based on census figures and demographic trends suggest that by the turn of the century, minority groups will become the majority population in many states (Gold, 1983). For newly arrived Hispanics, Central Americans,

From *Exceptional Children,* October 1987, pp. 105-111.

and Pan-Asians, the entire educational system is different from that in their own countries, and the special education programs, services, and legislation have no parallel. Not only is the special education system new, but it is also

> highly complex and requires the same kind of recordkeeping, efficiency, and monitoring that is required in the business world. Each step in the identification, assessment, and placement of a student into a special education program or service is now a bureaucratic procedure leaving professionals less time and less flexibility for recognizing and attending to families' needs. Often the process itself is in direct conflict with the family's cultural values and beliefs. (Lynch & Lewis, 1982, p. 98)

Linguistic differences also play a major role in the ways in which parents and school personnel can communicate about the child. Language is essential in a forum where information is to be exchanged, considered, and acted upon; yet many families do not speak the language or the dialect of the dominant culture—the language in which decisions are made. Frequently, the concepts inherent in special education such as learning disability, instuctional strategies, advisory committee, and parent involvement defy translation as well as understanding (Gonzales, 1974; Marion, 1980). Gonzalez (1974) has pointed out the need to consciously deal with linguistic differences in our professional interactions, yet school personnel are hampered by limited numbers of bilingual personnel, especially in many of the Asian and Native American languages that have no written forms (Ramirez & Tippeconnic, 1979; Rueda & Prieto, 1979). These problems are further confounded by the fact that many newly arrived Americans are not literate in their primary language. The translators available speak a "textbook" language that is unknown to the families they are trying to serve.

These problems are compounded by lack of minority group personnel in special education. Despite increased efforts to raise cultural awareness and improve the skills of special educators in working with minority students and their families, there continues to be a large cultural gap in many systems (Preston, et al., 1984).

The purpose of this study was to examine the ways in which Mexican-American families participate in their children's special education programs and to compare their participation with Black and Anglo families.

METHOD

Preliminary Studies

During the 1980 and 1981 school years, two studies of parents' perceptions of and participation in their child's special education program were conducted in a large culturally and linguistically diverse metropolitan school district in southern California. The first study, sponsored by the Office of Program Evaluation and Research of the California Department of Education, investigated the perceptions and participation of 106 randomly selected, low-income families with children in special education programs (Lynch & Lewis, 1982). The study used a structured, in-home interview conducted by a Special Education Parent Facilitator (SEPF). Special Education Parent Facilitators are themselves parents of handicapped children; they have been trained by the school district to serve as liaisons between the school district and other families. They are paid by the districts as paraprofessionals and provide support, information, and training to other parents.

Following that study, the participating district extended the investigation. An additional 328 families of students receiving special education services were interviewed in their homes in their preferred language by a cadre of trained SEPFs (Lynch & Stein, 1982). These families, representing all income levels, were interviewed using a shortened form of the original interview instrument. Because of the overlap in instruments and method, data from the low-income study and the larger district study could be aggregated and/or compared.

In the analyses of both studies, it became apparent that Hispanic families of students receiving special education services were underrepresented. In the aggregated sample of 434 families, only 31 (7%) were Hispanic in a district in which 20% of the total school population is Hispanic. In order to alter this discrepancy and to gather information about Hispanic parents' perceptions of and participation in their children's special education programs, a third state-sponsored study was conducted. That study, using the same questionnaire and methodology, is reported here, with comparisons to the findings for Black and Anglo families in the two companion studies.

Subjects

A random sample of 213 families with Spanish surnames was drawn using ethnic code rosters of children receiving special education services in the district. The sample included families with children at all age levels and in all special education program and service categories. Based on experiences in the two earlier studies, over 200 families were included in the subject pool in an attempt to ensure that, with attrition, 100 families could be interviewed. Although the selection was random, allowing for families at all income levels with the full range of fluency in Spanish and/or English, all of the families interviewed were Mexican-American, with limited English proficiency. Consequently, all of the families were interviewed in Spanish.

Interviewers

Three Special Education Parent Facilitators whose primary language was Spanish were selected and trained in the interview procedures and techniques. In their role as SEPFs, each had completed extensive paraprofessional training in interpersonal and communication skills and supportive counseling techniques. SEPFs were selected because of their prior training, their effectiveness as interviewers in the two previous studies, and the rapport which they were able to establish with other parents. Native Spanish-speaking, bilingual SEPFs who were a part of the Hispanic community were used exclusively in this study to help ensure that the interviews would be conducted in a culturally sensitive manner in each family's preferred language.

Interview Instrument

The interview instrument, originally designed by the San Diego State University Teacher Corps School-Community Task Force to investigate parent involvement in regular education, had been used with over 400 families in the Teacher Corps study. It was modified to address special education issues for the low-income study, and shortened to 64 items for use in the district special education study. Each version of the questionnaire was available in both Spanish and English. The interview included both open-ended and forced choice items which could be easily marked during the interview. Parents were asked about their attitudes toward the district's special education personnel and processes, their participation in the development of the IEP, opportunities to participate in their child's education program, and the barriers that they encountered when they tried to participate in their child's special education program.

Procedure

A letter printed in both Spanish and English from the district's director of special education was mailed to each of the families explaining the study, inviting them to participate, and informing them that a Special Education Parent Facilitator might be contacting them to arrange for an interview within the next several days. Each facilitator was given an alphabetical list of 71 families and asked to call each family in random order to arrange for the interview. In the initial phone call, times and dates for the interviews were arranged; postcard reminders were mailed to confirm the interviews. Each interviewer was asked to try to conduct a minimum of 34 interviews in a 4-week period. Following the interviews, staff at San Diego State University's Social Science Research Lab coded all open-ended responses and analyzed the data.

RESULTS

Of the 213 families in the subject pool, 63 were interviewed. This low rate of participation (29.6%) was accounted for in two primary ways. Many of the families were no longer living at the address provided on school records and could not be reached by telephone; many other families declined to be interviewed. The reasons that families refused to be interviewed were not always clear, but one major variable which may have affected the outcome of the study occurred as families were being contacted for appointments. Initial phone contacts began in the same week that federal crackdowns were made at all border crossings between the United States and Mexico, resulting in the return of many undocumented workers to Mexico. These actions resulted in considerable fear in segments of the Mexican-American and Central American portions of the Hispanic community, and any contact from a public agency was viewed as threatening by some individuals. Finally, the low rate of participation is in itself a finding of the study. The results that follow make it clear that the Mexican-American parents interviewed do not participate as extensively in their children's special education programs as do parents from other cultural and linguistic backgrounds.

Attitudes Toward Personnel and Processes

Eighty percent of the Hispanic parents interviewed felt the district identified their children's needs as early as possible and 85% indicated they were satisfied with the time taken to provide services. Only 55% of the parents knew what services were listed on the Individualized Education Plan (IEP) and 50% felt their children were receiving all of those services. Twenty-nine percent of the parents did not know to what degree their children were receiving or not receiving services.

Ninety-seven percent rated the professionals who work with their children effective. Eighty-nine percent of the Hispanic parents indicated they were satisfied with their children's current special education programs and 85% said they were satisfied with the school as a place to learn. Only 29% of the parents said they had had problems dealing with school personnel, and the interview indicated that most contacts were with the classroom teacher, secretary or office staff, counselor, principal, or nurse.

Participation in IEP Development

In response to questions related to the development of and participation in the IEP process, 75% or more of the parents reported that they were contacted by the district prior to assessment; understood the assessment, their rights, the goals and objectives on their child's IEP; and signed and received a copy of the IEP. However, only 45% indicated that they were a part of the assessment process and 50% felt that they were not an active participant in the development of the IEP. Only 34% of the parents actually offered suggestions during the IEP meeting and fewer than half felt that they and the teacher could work together on the goals and objectives.

Opportunities to Participate

Selected parts of the interview were directed at determining the extent of contact the parents had with teachers and other school personnel and the reasons for these contacts.

Eighty-five percent of the Hispanic parents had heard personally from their child's teacher during the year and 84% had talked to the teachers. The major reasons identified in rank order for such contact were as follows:

- To report academic progress.
- To provide information.
- To share good things about the child.
- To report a behavior or attendance problem.

These findings paralleled the findings for Anglo families. Among Black families, the reason most frequently cited for teacher contact was to report a behavior or attendance problem.

Eighty-five percent felt welcome to observe classroom teaching and 43% had in fact observed. Sixty percent of the parents knew that their children's records were available for review; however, only 18% had actually examined the records. Sixteen percent indicated an awareness of the Community Advisory Committee for Special Education.

Barriers to Active Parent Participation

Several items provided parents the opportunity to cite reasons they were unable to participate in their child's educational program and what they felt schools could do to improve those situations. Fifty-four percent of the parents indicated that they were unable to attend the last school meeting held. The main reasons given for not being able to attend were:

- Work.
- Time conflicts.
- Transportation problems.
- Child care needs.

These findings were supported across all ethnic and income groups and appear to represent the experience of the majority of families.

Ninety-five percent of the Hispanic parents saw parent education as a need—especially in the areas of special education law, parent and student rights, discipline skills, and criteria for identifying and placing students in special education programs. Seventy-four percent of the parents preferred small group meetings (less than 10) or one-to-one situations. When asked what could be done to get parents to come to school they indicated (in rank order):

- Hold bilingual meetings.
- Select convenient times for parents.
- Provide transportation.
- Provide more advance notice of meetings.
- Provide child care.

Families in other ethnic groups ranked more convenient times as the first suggestion for increasing participation followed by:

- Subjects which pertain to their children.
- More interesting subjects or speakers.
- Personal calls and notes about meetings.
- More advance notice of meetings.

When asked to identify the one major barrier to their participation in their child's special education program, Hispanic parents stated (in rank order):

- Work.
- Nothing.
- No bilingual communication.
- General communication concerns/problems.

For Black families, general communication problems with the schools were listed as the major barrier with all of the other problems (except lack of bilingual communication) being reported across groups.

When asked what they felt the school could do to help solve that problem, 82% of the parents had no response. Those who had suggestions recommended that the school provide more communication and child care.

COMPARISON OF FINDINGS ACROSS ETHNIC GROUPS

We were interested in determining whether or not Hispanic parents' responses to the interview items were significantly different from those of Black and Anglo parents on the earlier studies. The data on key variables were pooled and collapsed in order to run 2×3 chi squares on the five key variables. Results of the chi squares are presented in Table 1.

Significant differences were found on all key variables. Once these differences were identified, 2×2 chi squares were used to determine where the differences were. Hispanics were significantly more positive than Blacks and Anglos regarding the school's identification of their child's special needs ($\chi^2 = 25.22$, $d.f. = 1$ and $\chi^2 = 5.95$, $d.f. = 1$ respectively). However,

TABLE 1
Significant Difference by Ethnicity in Pooled Data

	Yes			*No*					
Item	*Hispanic*	*Anglo*	*Black*	*Hispanic*	*Anglo*	*Black*	*x2*	*d.f.*	*p*
Felt that district identified needs as soon as possible	65	126	40	16	138	26	27.25	2	.00
Felt they were part of the assessment process	39	173	35	30	52	16	11.03	2	.00
Offered suggestions at the IEP meeting	28	159	27	59	129	41	16.52	2	.001
Knew services listed on child's IEP	44	169	24	25	46	22	15.87	2	.001

no differences between Blacks and Anglos were found on this item.

On the item which asked whether parents felt that they had been a part of the assessment process, Hispanic parent responses indicated that they felt significantly less involved than did Anglos ($\chi^2 = 9.90$, *d.f.* = 2) but not significantly less involved than Blacks.

Hispanic parents offered significantly fewer suggestions at the IEP meeting than did Anglos ($\chi^2 = 13.26$, *d.f.* = 1) but not significantly fewer than Blacks. On this item, significant differences between Anglos and Black also emerged ($\chi^2 = 4.70$, *d.f.* = 1) with Blacks offering fewer suggestions than Anglos. Similar trends occurred regarding knowledge of the services listed on their child's IEP. Black and Hispanic parents knew significantly less about what services their child was to receive than did Anglo parents in the sample ($\chi^2 = 12.40$, *d.f.* = 1, $\chi^2 = 5.37$, d.f. = 1 respectively).

In general, all parents were quite positive about the effectiveness of special education professionals, and no significant differences among groups were found in parents' attitudes about the effectiveness of the educational professionals who work with their sons or daughters at school when all three groups were considered. However, a significant difference was found between Hispanics and Blacks. Hispanics were significantly more likely to rate professionals as effective or very effective than were Blacks ($\chi^2 = 4.63$, *d.f.* = 1).

DISCUSSION

Although the study's limitations, including the low rate of participation, the impact of external events, and the voluntary nature of participation may have biased the study's outcome, several issues remain. Hispanic, in this case Mexican-American, families were satisfied with their children's special education programs, but they were less knowledgeable and less involved in them than parents of Anglo and Black students receiving special education services.

During the interviews, Hispanic parents often commented on issues related to culture. They spoke of the school and its programs respectfully and indicated that they felt that "the teacher knows best." In general, they felt that educational decision making was the school's job, and they entrusted that role to the school system and its personnel. This belief is in direct conflict with the special educational system's desire for joint decision making and for a strong home/school partnership. If the partnership, as we believe, does make a difference in student outcomes, then it is incumbent on the system to find ways of encouraging families from the nondominant culture to participate. We suggest the following as ways to begin to involve families from diverse linguistic and cultural backgrounds.

1. Conduct a study of parent involvement to determine the differences and needs within the community. Use the data gathered to build strategies for involving parents which are specific to the community and/or district.
2. Develop a concise position paper which addresses the importance of parental involvement in special education decision making. Contact leaders of various cultural groups and organizations (e.g., Chicano Federation, Black Federation, Urban League, Union of Pan-Asian Communities, Tribal Councils); share the position paper; and ask for their assistance in developing strategies. Make contacts through informal networks or use administrative staff or parents to access these groups.
3. Develop grant applications which support the hiring and training of parents from various cultural groups to become liaisons between the school system and other parents. Utilize nongrant dollars allocated to aide positions to initiate this program. Document cost savings (reduced fair hearings, increased parent participation, improved student achievement) and present data to local Board of Education to request program maintenance funds.

4. Work with other community groups and organizations to provide training about special education programs and services to individuals in the various cultural communities who have direct contact with families (e.g., religious leaders, elders, physicians or other healers).
5. Develop training packages for parents from diverse cultures about special education programs, services, and processes. Make nontechnical print materials in the appropriate language available at local churches, community centers, markets, and other business establishments frequented by families.
6. Provide inservice education to school personnel which describes cultural and linguistic differences and sensitizes all school staff to the values and beliefs of the families whom they serve. Use nearby universities and their students as resources as well as community groups.
7. Continue to recruit and hire school personnel who represent a wide range of cultural and linguistic backgrounds.

The first step in cultural understanding is a willingness to open ourselves to new perspectives, new views of the world. These suggestions can be effective in accomplishing that first step and in helping to ensure that the provisions of P.L. 94-142 apply to *all* handicapped children and their parents.

REFERENCES

Cone, J. D., DeLawyer, D. D., & Wolfe, V. V. (1985). Assessing parent participation: The parent/family involvement index. *Exceptional Children, 51*, 417-424.

Gold, N. *Demographic trends in California and their impact on higher education.* Paper presented at the Multicultural Seminar for Faculty and Students, San Diego State University College of Education, San Diego, January 1983.

Gonzalez, G. (1974). Language, culture, and exceptional children. *Exceptional Children, 40,* 565-570.

Lynch, E. W., & Lewis, R. B. (1982). Multicultural considerations in assessment and treatment of learning disabilities. *Learning Disabilities, 1*, 93-103.

Lynch, E. W., & Stein, R. (1982). Perspectives on parent participation in special education. *Exceptional Education Quarterly, 3*, 56-63.

Marion, R. L. (1980). Communicating with parents of culturally diverse exceptional children. *Exceptional Children, 46*, 616-623.

Morgan, D. P. (1982). Parent participation in the IEP process: Does it enhance appropriate education? *Exceptional Education Quarterly, 3*, 33-40.

Preston, D., Greenwood, C. R., Hughes, V., Yuen, P., Thibadeau, S., Critchlow, W., & Harris, J. (1984). Minority issues in special education: A principal-mediated inservice program for teachers. *Exceptional Children, 51*, 112-121.

Ramirez, B. A., & Tippeconnic, J. W. (1979). Preparing teachers of American Indian handicapped children. *Teacher Education and Special Education, 2*, 27-32.

Rueda, R., & Prieto, A. G. (1979). Cultural pluralism—Implications for teacher education. *Teacher Education and Special Education, 2*, 4-11.

Strickland, B. (1982). Parental participation, school accountability, and due process. *Exceptional Children Quarterly, 3*, 41-49.

Attitude Change: Integration of Handicapped and Nonhandicapped Children

Many classroom teachers trained in general education have had to become informed about the methods and materials needed for providing appropriate education for mainstreamed handicapped children, due to the least restrictive environment provision of PL 94-142. This role shift has generated training needs, support needs, and a fair share of fears, frustrations, and blows to self-esteem.

Conversely, many special educators prepared to work with special needs children have had to become more knowledgeable about the general education classroom. In addition, many have seen their roles shift from teachers of special classes to consultants to other teachers, itinerant teachers, or content specialists working with pull-out children in resource rooms. Such transitions have also created stresses related to delegation of responsibilities, record-keeping, and self-esteem.

Educators are not the only ones whose roles have changed as a result of PL 94-142. Many administrators have had to focus on the technical details of providing new and improved services to handicapped children, in compliance with the law, while also supervising and evaluating the roles of teachers in transition.

As for the children, a handicapped child has often had to be the only "different" child in a regular education classroom. These children have had to cope with the jealousies and jeers of nonhandicapped children as they get special materials or get pulled out of class for special work in a resource room. Many nonhandicapped children have been frightened by a disabled child mainstreamed into their classes. They have heard others use negative terms to refer to persons with disabilities, such as "afflicted," "burdened," "crippled," "unfortunate," "victim," or "the patient." They do not know what to expect from, or how to react to, the mainstreamed child.

Integration of handicapped and nonhandicapped children into regular education classrooms has not been easy. Yet daily contact with disabled persons can do a great deal to dispel the notion that the handicapped are burdens on society or second-class citizens. One of the many goals of mainstreaming handicapped children into regular classrooms (see unit 1 for others) is to create more positive attitudes toward persons with disabilities.

Educators and administrators have a responsibility to assure that the integration of handicapped with nonhandicapped children results in positive interactions for all persons. Each disabled child (emphasis on *abled*) brings strengths to a classroom. Students need to appreciate that their exceptional peers are more similar to, than different from, themselves. All educational staff members and students should develop an empathetic understanding of the effects of each unique child's area of disability. This should be done without engendering pity or fear.

When educators, peers, parents, and siblings challenge disabled children to do all they are capable of doing, the children will develop independence. A goal of the regular education initiative is to help handicapped children participate in and enjoy as many aspects of normal living as possible. Educational staffs must guard against pitying, overprotecting, and failing to challenge exceptional children. Not only will the disabled child come to expect pity, but he or she will also learn to manipulate this emotion to remain dependent on others. Furthermore, when educational staff members show pity, nonhandicapped children learn to do likewise. Instead, both educational staff members and students with positive attitudes should be demanding of and responsive to mainstreamed handicapped children.

The first article in this unit on changing attitudes addresses the question of special class placements: Do they serve as de facto labels? Do nonhandicapped children expect more of handicapped peers in regular classes than they do of peers in special classes? The second selection suggests that the most opportune time to foster positive attitudes toward disabled children is during the preschool and primary years. The authors point out that handicap awareness activities, incorporated into art, science, dramatic play, and stories, give children a head start in successful mainstreamed public school education. They include an annotated list of several good resource materials for use in preschool. The third selection suggests that high schools can use peer tutors to help provide special education services to disabled students. This not only fosters positive attitude change but also improves grades. The last article presents several strategies for use by regular classroom teachers to successfully integrate handicapped students, promote positive interactions with nonhandicapped peers, and maximize the educational benefits of all students.

Looking Ahead: Challenge Questions

Can educators separate the effects of labeling from the

Unit 2

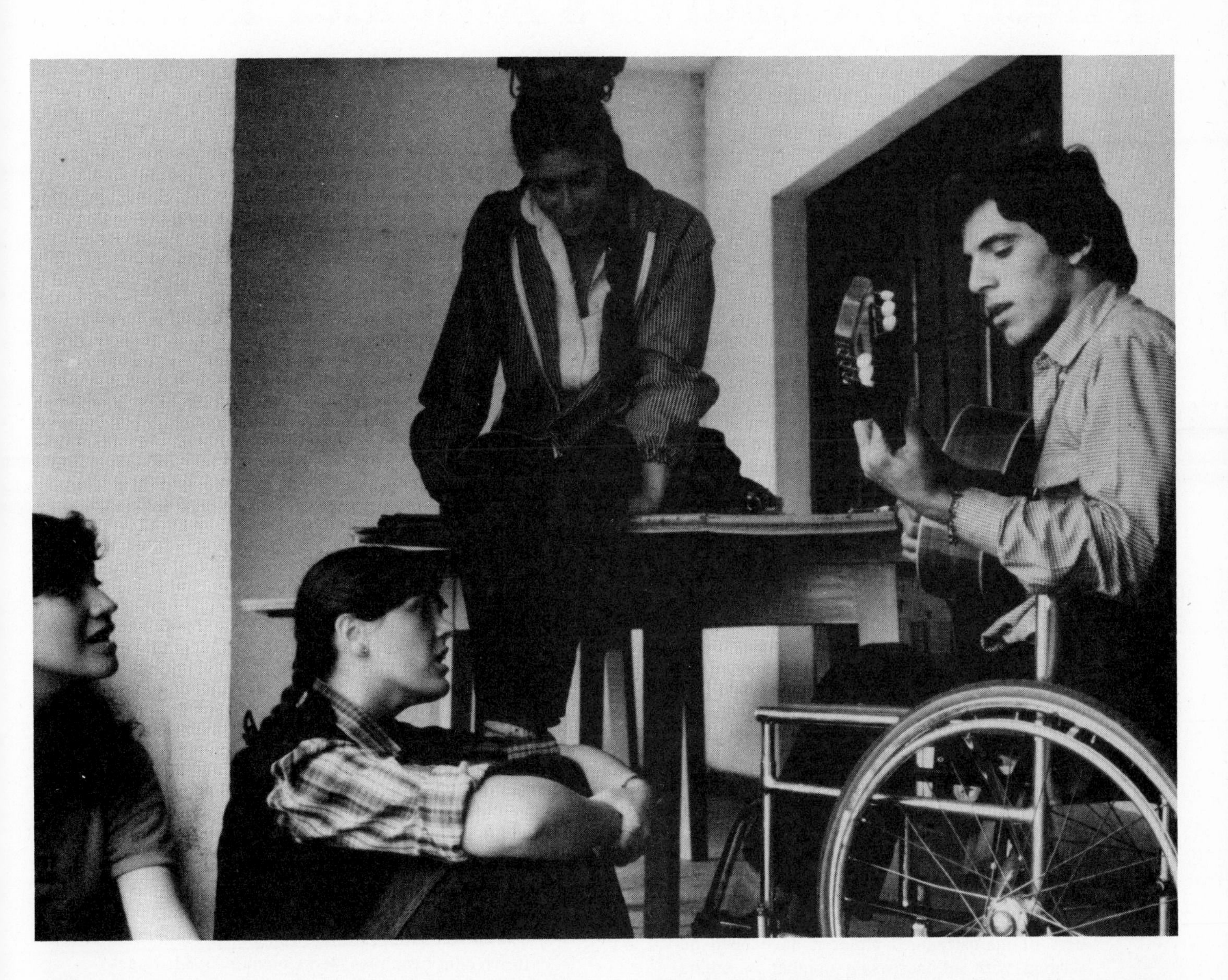

effects of special class placements, since the two are usually intertwined? Will integrated programs without labels significantly improve children's attitudes toward disabled peers?

Can more positive attitudes toward handicapped children be instilled in nonhandicapped peers by starting handicap awareness programs at the preschool level?

Mainstreamed students in high schools often have both academic and social difficulties. Will nonhandicapped peers agree to tutor them? Will this change their attitudes toward disabled peers in a more positive or in a more negative direction?

What types of strategies work best to integrate students with severe disabilities into regular education classes?

Special Class Placements as Labels: Effects on Children's Attitudes Toward Learning Handicapped Peers

JOHN J. BAK
EDITH M. COOPER
KATHRYN M. DOBROTH
GARY N. SIPERSTEIN

When the work on this study was completed, JOHN J. BAK *was Project Director,* EDITH M. COOPER *and* KATHRYN M. DOBROTH *were Research Assistants, and* GARY N. SIPERSTEIN *was Center Director at the Center for the Study of Social Acceptance, University of Massachusetts/Boston.*

ABSTRACT: This study determined whether different types of special education placements affected children's attitudes toward learning handicapped peers in a school where no clinical labels were used. Traditionally these peers would have been labeled "learning disabled" and "educable mentally retarded." Seventy-seven fourth- through sixth-graders judged the capabilities of peers depicted in written vignettes as attending one of two types of placement: a resource room or a special classroom. These placements were identical to those found in the children's school. Children saw resource room targets as significantly more capable than special class targets. This indicated that educational placements alone could act as de facto labels. Older children were found to have higher expectations of peers regardless of placement. Implications for teachers and researchers were discussed.

■ Since the passage of Public Law 94-142, the Education for All Handicapped Children Act, children with disabilities have been integrated in mainstream classrooms in increasingly large numbers. At the same time, the movement to eliminate the use of clinical labels such as "mentally retarded" has gained strength. As a result, throughout the country increasing numbers of mainstreamed children have been described with an increasing number of euphemisms.

The central thesis of the delabeling movement (here oversimplified) is that labels are harmful and therefore should not be used. In a careful review of the literature, MacMillan, Jones, and Aloia (1974) showed how the harmful effects of the label "mentally retarded" had not been clearly established by research findings. They discussed how the effects of labels on mentally retarded children appeared to be the result of complex interactions involving not only the label, but the characteristics of the mentally retarded children, their peers, their teachers, and the school environment. Subsequent research has supported and refined this assertion (for recent examples, see Coleman, 1983; Fogel & Nelson, 1983; Siperstein, Budoff, & Bak, 1980; Sutherland, Algozzine, Ysseldyke, & Freeman, 1983). However, certain questions still remain.

As noted by MacMillan et al. (1974), a major problem in trying to understand the effects of labels in the classroom concerns separating the effects of the label from the effects of special class placements. The two are usually intertwined; thus, negative effects ascribed to a label could as easily be ascribed to a special class placement alone. The placements themselves may act as de facto labels.

PURPOSE

In this study, we attempted to determine whether different placements alone could act as de facto labels and differentially affect children's attitudes toward peers who are not formally labeled but who attend two different types of remedial classrooms: the resource room (for children with mild learning handicaps) and the special classroom (for children with more severe learning handicaps). To conduct this research, we found a school which had two characteristics: it did not use labels, and it contained regular classrooms with mainstreamed children of two ability levels (traditionally they would have been labeled "learning disabled" and "educable mentally retarded").

Finding such a school was not overly difficult, for the research was conducted in Massachusetts, one of two states to have legally abolished educational placement labels. The school where the research was conducted had a strong commitment to mainstreaming severely learning handicapped (mentally retarded) children and it adhered closely to the state's ban on labeling.

In this school, we were able to seek answers to two questions: (1) In an environment where labels are not a factor, are children sensitive to the meaning of different special class placements? (2) Is that sensitivity reflected in how they evaluate their special class peers' capabilities? MacMillan et al. (1974) discussed how the effects of labels could be assessed from teacher's attitudes as reflected in their expectancies for labeled children. Much past research (see, for example, Algozzine & Stoller, 1981; Aloia & MacMillan, 1983; Shotel, Iano & McGettigan, 1972) has shown how such expectancies are affected (usually negatively) by labels.

Only recently have investigators begun examining children's expectancies. Gibbons & Kassin (1982) found junior high students to have pessimistic expectations for peers labeled mentally retarded; even so, they were found to be not as negative in some ways as college students (Gibbons, Sawin, & Gibbons, 1979). Because of these findings, we used children's expectations of their special class peers' capabilities as our measure of the extent to which children's attitudes would or would not be affected by two different types of special class placement. Furthermore, as we looked across grades, we wished to determine whether as children got older, they became more pessimistic concerning the capabilities of their peers in resource rooms and special classes. This was the general trend noted by Gibbons and his colleagues in their studies with older students.

METHOD

Subjects

Seventy-seven fourth- through sixth-graders (36 male, 41 female) from five classrooms in a suburban elementary school participated in the study. None had a disability. However, in each of the five classrooms there were children identified as having special needs (Massachusetts' generic term for handicapped children). These children attended either one of two placement settings: a resource room for 20 to 25% of the day, or a special classroom for 75 to 80% of the day.

Children in resource room placements had close to average cognitive abilities (IQ range 85 to 100) and received help only in specific academic areas in the resource room. Children in special class placements had lesser cognitive abilities (IQ range 50 to 70) and were taught most of their academic subjects in the special class. They were part of the regular class for homeroom, unified arts, library, gym, lunch, and occasional science and social studies projects.

Procedure

Children were assigned randomly to one of two conditions. Each condition was defined by a description of two fictitious target children (Jim and Sally) in an administrative placement serving handicapped children. In the resource room condition, children were presented with a vignette about targets in a resource room placement. These targets were described as being in the same grade as the subject children, spending most of their day in their homeroom class, and leaving the class for an hour a day to get special help in the resource room.

Children in the special class condition read a vignette about targets in a special class placement. These targets were described as being in the same grade as the subject children, beginning each day in homeroom with everyone else, but spending most of the day in a classroom for children with special needs, only going to gym, music, and art with their homeroom class. The two vignettes reflected types of educational placements identical to those in the children's school. In each class, half the children read the resource room vignette and half read the special class vignette. Types of vignettes were distributed equally within sex.

Instrument

Children were administered a 22-item expectancy questionnaire which consisted of a set of statements regarding the academic and nonacademic capabilities of the targets described in the vignettes. Children responded to each statement by circling "yes" or "no," depending on whether or not they thought the children could perform the activity listed. Scores could range from 0 to 22.

Items on the questionnaire were adapted from the Vineland Social Maturity Scale (Doll, 1965) and from the Prognostication About Mental Retardation Scale (Wolraich & Siperstein, 1983). The questionnaire was designed to investigate different aspects of children's experiences in school, with an emphasis on academic functioning. Fourteen items concerned academic capabilities (e.g., read, do addition). The eight nonacademic items included both social functioning (make friends) and independent functioning capabilities (brush teeth).

RESULTS

Children's expectations of the capabilities of the target children (one in a resource room, one in a special class) were assessed using a Placement (2) × Grade (2) × Sex (2) ANOVA in which placement, grade, and sex were between-subjects factors. The analysis indicated a significant main effect for placement ($F\,(1, 76) = 3.9$, $p < .05$), which showed that children responded more positively to the resource room target than to the target in the special class. Specifically, children held higher expectations for the capabilities of the target in the resource room than for those of the target in the special class. There was also a significant main effect for grade ($F\,(1, 76) = 4.8$, $p < .05$), which showed that for both targets, fifth and sixth graders responded more positively than did fourth graders. In other words, fifth and sixth graders perceived both targets as more capable than did fourth graders. (See Table 1 for means).

To analyze further the differences in children's expectations of the target's capabilities, we rank ordered the capability statements on the basis of the percentage of children who responded positively to the statements within each condition. We then compared the percentages across conditions. The results of this analysis helped to clarify the main effect for placement.

While approximately the same percentage of children responded affirmatively to the less complex capabilities, there was a difference by condition in the responses to the more complex capabilities. These included reading newspapers, behaving like other children, and reading books and spelling words that children in the same grade could read or spell. The percent differences for each of these capabilities ranged from 18.3 to 32.4; this reflected the number of children who believed that resource room peers had these capabilities while special class peers did not. Thus, the differences in expectations of capabilities as a function of administrative placement were attributable mostly to expected differences in abilities to do complex academic tasks.

TABLE 1
Mean Scores for Children's Expectations of Peers in Different Special Classes

Grade	*Resource Room*	*Special Class*	*Row Total Mean*
Grade 4	15.60	12.94	14.22 $n = 31$
Grades 5 & 6	16.92	15.71	16.37 $n = 46$
Column Total Mean	16.43 $n = 40$	14.51 $n = 37$	15.51 $n = 77$

DISCUSSION

The results of this study clearly show that children are sensitive to the differences between peers who attend different educational placements from their regular classrooms. Children responded to the de facto labels of the resource room and special classroom—they saw resource room targets as significantly more capable than special class targets. The fact that traditional educational labels that have clearly demarcated children's ability levels in the past (e.g., mentally retarded) had not been used within the participating school for a decade did not prevent children from seeing the real ability levels of children in different placements.

Although children responded less positively toward the special class targets, we cannot assume that the same targets would necessarily be treated less favorably. Previous studies (reviewed by Siperstein & Bak, 1985) have shown how children's attitudes have different dimensions reflecting cognitive responses, affective feelings, and behavioral intentions. In this study, we measured the cognitive aspect of attitudes. It is possible, given past research, that children would still have favorable affective feelings or behavioral intentions toward the group they evaluated as having lesser capabilities.

It is important to remember that most of the items which clearly differentiated the two groups concerned academic tasks. The differentiation did not generalize to nonacademic tasks or social activity, with the exception of classroom behavior. Thus, in fairness to those who would remove labels, we must say that it is still possible that removing the label has had a beneficial effect, if the label's absence is in part responsible for the failure of negative academic expectations to generalize to other areas. However, it is clear that the absence of formal labels did not prevent children from forming negative (although realistically pessimistic) expectations based on their experiences with special class children's academic limitations.

Children's responses as a function of their age did not turn out as we had hypothesized. Older children were more optimistic than younger children about the abilities of targets in both placements. The difference between the actual and the hypothesized direction of this grade effect may be explained in part by two different conceptualizations of ability. Ability may be conceptualized in terms of either specific skills or a general intellectual capacity. Depending on which sense of the term is invoked, it is possible that different developmental trends would result. The older children in this study may have been able to see more specific skills in their special class peers than did younger children, yet these same students may also have been more likely to think less of special class peers' intellectual capacity. This latter occurrence would be expected because younger children do not tend to view ability as a capacity (Nicholls, 1978).

In this study, we presented ability in terms of specific skills, not intellectual capacity; because of this, the older children may have responded more positively than the younger children. If we had made target children's intellectual capacity more salient, the older children might have responded more in line with our original hypothesis. In any event, this finding shows that age can be a critical factor to consider, particularly as researchers evaluate children's expectancies for learning handicapped peers.

This study has implications for both regular and special educators. Chief among these is that teachers should be aware of the fact that children are sensitive to differences between peers in different placements. In fact, special class placements themselves can act as de facto labels. Educational programs designed to improve children's attitudes toward special class peers should take this into account. Similarly, teachers in schools where integration is occurring may wish to be more sensitive to the effects of using special class placements as descriptive labels when speaking with children in regular classrooms.

REFERENCES

Algozzine, B., & Stroller, L. (1981). Effects of labels and competence on teachers' attributions for a student. *Journal of Experimental Education, 49,* 132-136.

Aloia, G. E., & MacMillan, D. L. (1983). Influence of the EMR label on initial expectations of regular-classroom teachers. *American Journal of Mental Deficiency, 88,* 255-262.

Coleman, J. M. (1983). Handicapped labels and instructional segregation: Influence on children's self-concepts versus the perceptions of others. *Learning Disability Quarterly, 6,* 3-11.

Doll, E. A. (1965). *Vineland Social Maturity Scale.* Circle Pines, MN: American Guidance Service, Inc.

Fogel, L. S., & Nelson, R. O. (1983). The effects of special education labels on teachers' behavioral observations, checklist scores, and grading of academic work. *Journal of School Psychology, 21,* 241-251.

Gibbons, F. X., & Kassin, S. M. (1982). Behavioral expectations of retarded and nonretarded children. *Journal of Applied Developmental Psychology, 3,* 85-104.

Gibbons, F. X., Sawin, L. G., & Gibbons, B. N. (1979). Evaluations of mentally retarded persons: "Sympathy" or patronization? *American Journal of Mental Deficiency, 84,* 124-131.

MacMillan, D. L., Jones, R. L, & Aloia, G. F. (1974). The mentally retarded label: A theoretical analysis and review of the research. *American Journal of Mental Deficiency, 79,* 241-261.

Nicholls, J. G. (1978). The development of the concepts of effort and ability, perception of academic attainment, and the understanding that difficult tasks require more ability. *Child Development, 49,* 800-814.

Shotel, J. R., Iano, R. P., & McGettigan, J. F. (1972). Teacher attitudes associated with the integration of handicapped children. *Exceptional Children, 38,* 677-683.

Siperstein, G. N., & Bak, J. J. (1985). Attitudinal responses of the nonretarded to their mentally retarded peers. In C. Julius Meisel (Ed.), *Mainstreaming handicapped children: Outcomes, controversies, and new discoveries.* Hillsdale, N.J.: Lawrence Erlbaum Associates.

Siperstein, G. N., Budoff, M., & Bak, J. J. (1980). Effects of the labels "mentally retarded" and "retard" on the social acceptability of mentally retarded children. *American Journal of Mental Deficiency, 84,* 596-601.

Sutherland, J. H., Algozzine, B., Ysseldyke, J. E., & Freeman, S. F. (1983). Changing peer perceptions: Effects of labels and assigned attributes. *Journal of Learning Disabilities, 16,* 217-220.

Wolraich, M. L., & Siperstein, G. N. (1983). Assessing professional's prognostic impressions of mental retardation. *Mental Retardation, 21,* 8-12.

This research was supported by a grant from the National Institute of Child Health and Human Development (HD 14772-03). The authors wish to thank the staff and students of the Public Schools of Brookline, Massachusetts, for their cooperation; S. Jay Kuder and Paul O'Keefe for their contributions to this project; and Christine B. Parsons for her help in preparing the manuscript.

Requests for reprints should be directed to the first author at the Center for the Study of Social Acceptance, Downtown Campus, University of Massachusetts/Boston, Boston, MA 02125.

Promoting Handicap Awareness in Preschool Children

Dale Baum
Carol Wells

Dale D. Baum *is Professor of Special Education at Iowa State University, Ames, Iowa.* **Carol Wells** *is a teacher of preschool children for the Fonda Community School District, Fonda, Iowa.*

■ With the impetus of Public Law 94-142, mainstreaming has become a reality in American education. The mainstreaming alternative to isolated and/or segregated educational programming is based on the belief that mildly handicapped students, particularly, are more similar to their nonhandicapped peers than they are different from them. Mainstreaming provides for the physical integration of handicapped and nonhandicapped students in regular classroom settings. It does not, however, assure that handicapped students will be accepted socially by their nonhandicapped peers. On the contrary, there is an abundance of research (Donaldson, 1980) indicating that handicapped individuals are likely to encounter negative and stereotypic attitudes from various population groups as they grow and mature.

RESEARCH FINDINGS

History is replete with vivid portrayals of handicapped persons who have been relegated to inferior social and economic positions (Baum, 1982). The devaluing of human differences appears to be acculturized in children as they grow and develop. Although the phenomenon of learning to devalue persons with handicaps is not well understood, Goodman (1964) has reported that children become aware of racial differences as early as 4 years of age. It is presumed that most children below age 4 are unable to differentiate subtle differences among people and therefore show little tendency to devalue individuals on the basis of their differences. Weinberg's (1978) research concerning children's attitudes toward physically handicapped individuals has also suggested that awareness begins at about age 4 and that children prefer able-bodied persons to disabled individuals. Both Wylie (1976) and Hagino (1980) have observed that younger children show more acceptance of their handicapped peers than older children do. Their awareness of handicapping conditions at about age 4 is followed by beginning negativism by about 5 years of age.

In a study of third- through sixth-grade students' attitudes toward mentally retarded people, Gottleib and Switzky (1982) reported a decrease in general negative evaluations as a function of the ages of the subjects. The decrease in negative evaluations was not countered with an increase in positive evaluations, however, even though the opportunity to do so was available to the subjects. The authors suggested that perhaps middle-class children learn as they grow older not to express negative attitudes about others less fortunate than themselves. This tendency should not, however, be interpreted to mean that more positive attitudes have replaced the negative attitudes expressed at earlier age levels.

It is becoming increasingly clear (Goodman, Gottlieb & Harrison, 1982; MacMillan, 1971; Sheare, 1978; Simpson, Parrish, & Cook, 1976) that mainstreaming programs can be successful only to the extent that they are able to create educational environments in which handicapped students can grow and develop effectively. Edwin Martin (1974), former Deputy Commissioner for the Education of the Handicapped, cautioned that unless strategies are developed for creating an attitude of acceptance within students in regular education toward the handicapped ". . . we will be painfully naive, and I fear we will subject many children to a painful and frustrating educational experience in the name of progress" (p. 150).

This brief review of research suggests that the most opportune time to initiate planned instruction concerning handicapping conditions—particularly those that are more highly visible—is during the preschool and primary years. Young children should be introduced to both the cognitive and affective aspects of blindness, physical handicaps, deafness, and mental retardation in order to develop an empathic understanding of handicapped persons. The remainder of this article provides a representative sampling of learning activities and resource materials that may be used successfully with young children.

PRESCHOOL PROGRAMMING

Curiosity, exploration, manipulation, expression, sharing, and active involvement reflect the natural abilities of healthy young children as they interact with their environment. Preschool programs are typically designed to encourage these natural abilities and tendencies while recognizing that children mature at varying rates during their years of enhanced growth and development. The range of "normalcy" expected in preschools is, therefore, much broader than that found in elementary classrooms, and teachers tend to focus on the processes of learning more than on the products of learning. The varied learning center activities and teacher-guided activities that exemplify preschool programs provide a wealth of sensory opportunities for children to learn about their world.

Both the nature of preschool children and the design of preschool curricula are amenable to teaching about handicapping conditions. The children are probably more accepting of individual differences than at any other time in their lives, and the curricula are more flexible than any others the children are likely to encounter in their school careers. With a minimum of teacher preparation time, information about handicapping conditions can be infused or integrated into ongoing activities throughout the school day.

Story Time

This special segment of the school day is an excellent time to introduce children to concepts dealing with handicapping conditions by reading all or a part of one of the books listed at the end of this article. Time should be allowed for questions and discussion as each story unfolds. Picture books should be shared with the children, with the teacher explaining any aspect of the pictures that are unclear to the children.

A well-chosen filmstrip may also be shown during this time to acquaint the children with various handicaps. Perhaps a few days after a story has been read, a filmstrip could be shown to reinforce the previous learning.

Art

Art activities can provide children with a number of opportunities to experiment with their knowledge of handicaps. When asked, children can suggest and even emulate strategies that handicapped persons might use to do the very same art projects the children are doing. For example:

"How can a person without arms paint?"
"Hold the brush in your teeth."

"How can a person without arms cut paper?"
"Somebody would have to do it."

"How can a person without legs color?"
"If he has arms, he can do it like me."

"How can a blind person paint?"
"I'd have to move his hand for him."

By experimenting with various methods of compensation the children have an opportunity to experience some of the same frustrations that are experienced by handicapped persons. They may also learn that certain handicaps cause restrictions in some activities but not in all activities. These experiences foster their understanding of handicaps as differences—differences that occur just as blue eyes or brown eyes, red hair or blond hair, tall children or short children occur.

Science

Learning about the world through sensory experiences provides children with opportunities to emulate sensory handicaps. Blind persons develop their sense of touch more highly than most sighted people do. Children can experience this by having them identify common objects placed in a "feeling box." This type of activity can also be extended to the sense of smell. Selected foods may be used to allow children to identify them by smell alone.

Discussion questions may also be asked to increase awareness, for example:

"How would a blind person know if there were a fire in his house?"
"Smell the smoke, feel the heat, hear it crackle."

"How can a blind person find his favorite toy?"
"He can feel for it."

"How can a deaf person know what you are saying?"
"He can watch my face and I'll talk louder. Maybe I can point or show him."

Dramatic Play

The value of play in fostering cognitive development, motor skills and happy, healthy personalities is generally accepted in early childhood education. Healthy children enjoy play and will normally engage in play activities spontaneously with or without adult direction. Dramatic or "guided play" activities are excellent for helping children to better understand what it is like to be handicapped. During dramatic play activities, young children can experience handicapping conditions with much more realism and sincerity than older students and adults who engage in handicap simulation activities.

Sightless activities are relatively easy to plan for children. Two or three children can be blindfolded and asked to walk forward a few steps to a table, select a chair, and sit down. Without removing the blindfolds the teacher can lead a discussion with all the children concerning how it feels to do simple things without sight. The discussion and activities can be guided to many other activities available in the classroom, from locating the restroom to riding a tricycle while blindfolded.

Providing activities that will allow children to explore orthopedic handicaps will require some advance planning to borrow such equipment as a wheelchair, crutches, leg braces, prosthetic devices (artificial limbs), canes, and walkers. Local resources to contact for equipment include hospitals, rehabilitation centers, the Easter Seal Society, the local chapter of the Association for Retarded Citizens, the local Muscular Dystrophy Association, the local Cerebral Palsy Association, and stores that sell the equipment. Once these items have been obtained they should be placed inconspicuously in a corner of the room so the children can become accustomed to seeing them. At first the teacher should discourage the children from experimenting with the equipment by explaining that they will learn about it in a few days.

The children could be introduced to the uses of the various pieces of equipment during story time. An illustrated story about a child with an orthopedic handicap provides a good introduction, as does a well-chosen filmstrip. As the teacher answers questions about the story and guides the discussion, an aide could bring the device being discussed into the area and select a willing child to try it out. As the children become more familiar with the devices, they should be encouraged to explore the limitations such devices impose and suggest how games and other activities can be altered for children who *must* use the devices.

Language

Time devoted to language development provides a good opportunity to teach children about alternative language systems. One way to illustrate speechreading (lipreading) is for the teacher to ask the children to watch his or her lips to see if they can understand what is being said. The teacher may then mouth a simple sentence such as, "I am Miss Smith." If the children do not understand the first time, they are asked to watch again. The second time, the teacher may whisper the sentence so that all can hear it. The activity is continued with one or two more sentences, but children should not be expected to become expert at this activity. Speechreading is very difficult to learn, and it can quickly become a frustrating experience for hearing children.

If a deaf person is available to visit the class, this person could be invited to show the children how deaf people communicate. Although most deaf adults communicate with sign language, some do not. These are usually people who lost their hearing later in life. Some have learned to speechread very efficiently and to speak fluently. Others rely upon sign language primarily, and it is difficult for them to communicate with hearing people who do not understand signs. Many deaf adults, however, can communicate with hearing persons by writing notes, and they are delighted to introduce children to sign language.

If a resource person is not available to the class, the teacher can easily learn some signs to teach the children with the aid of *The Signed English Dictionary for Preschool and Elementary Levels* (Bornstein, Hamilton, & Saulnier, 1975). This text is simple to use, and the picture illustrations are excellent. The teacher can prepare for the lesson by first constructing short sentences such as:

My name is (fingerspell first letter)

I see a fish
dog
cat
rabbit
etc.

Next, each of the words can be located in the dictionary and the sign of each noted. Then the teacher should practice saying each sentence while making the correct sign for each word. With this minimal preparation the teacher can introduce signing to the children, who normally enjoy learning the signs and teaching them to their parents and friends.

One phrase that children particularly enjoy learning and sharing is "I love you." It is done with the right hand held about chest high, palm open and facing forward, with the two middle fingers turned down.

Snack Time

Some teachers may want to extend handicap awareness activities into snack time. However, since most preschoolers are still developing their own table skills, particularly with beverages, it is better to approach the various handicapping conditions through problem-solving or brainstorming activities. This is done by posing questions, for example:

"How could you drink your milk if you did not have hands?"

"How could you find your cookie if you could not see?"

"How could you sit at the table with the other children if you were in a wheelchair?"

It may be necessary to discourage some children from attempting to act out certain handicaps, but with guidance they will learn to think of solutions and state them verbally.

CONCLUSION

It seems clear that the most opportune time to introduce tomorrow's public school students to the concept of handicapping conditions is during their preschool and early primary years. It is during those years that children are most accepting of human differences. Through play and exploration activities, children have the opportunity not only to develop an empathic understanding of the limitations posed by the various handicaps, but also to learn of the similarities handicapped persons share with them.

Library and community resources as well as the programming aids discussed in this article make early awareness training a viable curriculum addition for virtually all preschool and primary level programs. The relatively small effort required to implement such a program has the potential for an enormous return for both handicapped and nonhandicapped children.

RESOURCE MATERIALS

Children's Books About Handicaps

Brightman, A. (1976). *Like me.* Waltham MA: Little Brown. 48 pp.

This is a color photo story of a retarded child who is aware that he learns slower than other children but wants very much to be accepted.

Fassler, J. (1975). *Howie helps himself.* Niles IL: Albert Whitman. 32 pp.

Howie has cerebral palsy, but he is like any boy his age, except for certain physical limitations. This book has delightful illustrations.

Fassler, J. (1969). *One little girl.* New York: Human Sciences Press. 24 pp.

Laurie can do many things but is considered a slow child in school. After a psychologist says that she is slow at some things, fast at others, but quite happy with herself, everyone begins emphasizing her strengths rather than worrying about her weaknesses.

Heide, F. (1970). *Sound of sunshine, sound of rain.* New York: Parents' Magazine Press. 35 pp.

This is a sensitive story about a blind Black boy who finds life a joy. It is marvelous to read aloud.

Hirsch, K. (1977). *My sister.* Minneapolis MN: Crolrhoda Books. 45 pp.

Karen Hirsch has captured the life and feelings of a boy whose older sister is profoundly retarded. His emotions are mixed. He is sometimes jealous of all the attention she receives from parents, sometimes embarrassed by her actions, sometimes angry because of outsiders' attitudes. However, he usually expresses love and understanding. This book helps children understand the mentally retarded and their siblings.

Klein, G. (1974). *The blue rose.* Westport CT: Lawrence Hill. 64 pp.

This photo story about a mentally retarded girl tells of her happiness as well as her problems, such as the cruelty of children toward her.

Lasker, J. (1974). *He's my brother.* Niles IL: Albert Whitman. 44 pp.

The story of a slow learner is told through the eyes of his older brother. The book has action-filled illustrations.

Levine, E. (1974). *Lisa and her soundless world.* New York: Human Sciences Press. 34 pp.

A fictional character, Lisa teaches the reader about children with impaired hearing.

Litchfield, A. (1976). *A button in her ear.* New York: Concept Books. 32 pp.

A young girl who does not hear well gets a hearing aid.

Mack, N. (1976). *Tracy.* Chicago: Childrens Press. 31 pp.

Written in the first person, this wonderful story depicts a whole family cooperating and loving Tracy, a child born with cerebral palsy.

Ominsky, E. (1977). *Jon O, a special boy.* Englewood Cliffs NJ: Prentice-Hall. 26 pp.

This book discusses the early development of a mentally retarded boy who has Down's Syndrome. It also describes the initial reaction of the parents to the handicap.

Stein, S. (1974). *About handicaps.* New York: Walker. 47 pp.

The relationship between a boy with cerebral palsy and a nonhandicapped boy is described.

Vance, M. (1966). *Windows for Rosemary.* New York: E. P. Dutton. 61 pp.

Nine-year-old Rosemary was born blind but leads a full, happy life. She "sees" the world with her ears, nose, fingers, lips, and tongue and is able to participate in the activities that are part of every child's day.

Wolf, B. (1974). *Don't feel sorry for Paul.* New York: Lippincott. 94 pp.

This nonfiction book has excellent photos of a 7-year-old who wears prostheses on his right arm and both legs. It can help mitigate misconceptions of the use of prostheses.

Wolf, B. (1977). *Anna's silent world.* New York: Lippincott. 48 pp.

This tells the story of a 6-year-old, born deaf, learning to read lips and use a hearing aid in a regular school situation.

Wosmek, F. (1976). *A bowl of sun.* Chicago: Childrens Press. 48 pp.

Motherless Megan, born blind, is devoted to her father. She is terrified of losing their relationship when she moves to the big city to learn Braille.

Filmstrips/Cassettes/Activities

Accepting individual differences. Developmental Learning Materials, 7440 Natchez Avenue, Niles IL 60648

This kit contains four large flip books, an audiocassette, and four booklets. It provides a curriculum for teaching young children about mental retardation, learning disability, visual impairment, hearing impairment, and physical impairment.

The kids on the block. The Kids on the Block, Inc., Suite 510, Washington Building, Washington DC 20005

This kit is comprised of six hand and rod puppets, scripts and cassette tapes, and a program guide. Young children are introduced through puppetry to cerebral palsy, blindness, deafness, epilepsy, and mental retardation. The kit also features a nonhandicapped puppet.

Kids come in special flavors. The Kids Come in Special Flavors Co., P.O. Box 562, Dayton OH 45405

This kit contains a book of simulation activities, a cassette, and materials for simulation activities. The children are introduced to learning disability, hearing impairment, mental retardation, visual impairment, cerebral palsy, and spina bifida.

My new friend series. Eye Gate Media, Jamaica NY 11435

This kit features four filmstrips with audio cassettes to introduce young children to hearing impairment, visual impairment, mental retardation, and physical impairment.

Special friends. Listen and Learn Company, 13366 Pescadero Road, La Honda CA 94020

This kit contains eight lessons of approximately 15 minutes each. Featuring filmstrips, cassettes, and a teaching guide, it teaches young children about physical handicaps, visual and hearing impairments, learning disability, emotional disturbance, and mental retardation.

REFERENCES

Baum, D. (1982). *The human side of exceptionality.* Baltimore: University Park Press.

Bornstein, H., Hamilton, L., and Saulnier, K. (Eds.). (1975). *The signed English dictionary for preschool and elementary levels.* Washington DC: Gallaudet College Press.

Donaldson, J. (1980). Changing attitudes toward handicapped persons: A review and analysis of research. *Exceptional Children, 46,* 504–512.

Goodman, H., Gottlieb, J., and Harrison, P. (1982). Social acceptance of EMR's integrated into a non-graded elementary school. *American Journal of Mental Deficiency, 76,* 412–417.

Goodman, M. (1964). *Race awareness in young children.* New York: Collier Books.

Gottlieb, J., and Switsky, H. (1982). Development of school-age children's stereotypic attitudes toward mentally retarded children. *American Journal of Mental Deficiency, 86,* 596–600.

Hagino, J. (1980). Educating children about handicaps. *Childhood Education, 7,* 97–100.

MacMillan, D. (1971). Special education for the mildly retarded: Servant or savant. *Focus on Exceptional Children, 2,* 1–11.

Martin, E. (1974). Some thoughts on mainstreaming. *Exceptional Children, 41,* 150–153.

Sheare, J. (1978). The impact of resource programs upon the self-concept and peer acceptance of learning disabled children. *Psychology in the Schools, 15,* 406–412.

Simpson, R., Parrish, N., and Cook, J. (1976). Modification of attitudes of regular class children towards the handicapped for the purpose of achieving integration. *Contemporary Educational Psychology, 1,* 46–51.

Weinberg, N. (1978). Preschool children's perceptions of orthopedic disability. *Rehabilitation Counseling Bulletin, 21,* 183–189.

Wylie, R. (1976). Attitudes of children toward their handicapped peers. *Childhood Education, 8,* 171–173.

Classwide Peer Tutoring With Mildly Handicapped High School Students

LARRY MAHEADY
M. KATHERINE SACCA
GREGORY F. HARPER

LARRY MAHEADY *is Assistant Professor, Department of Counseling, Educational Psychology, and Special Education, Michigan State University, East Lansing.* M. KATHERINE SACCA *is Director, Pupil Personnel Services, Lewiston-Porter School District, Youngstown, New York.* GREGORY F. HARPER *is Associate Professor, Department of Education, State University of New York, College at Fredonia.*

ABSTRACT: Effects of classwide peer tutoring (CWPT) on the academic performance of 14 mildly handicapped and 36 nondisabled students enrolled in three 10th-grade social studies classrooms were examined. Effects were analyzed using a multiple baseline design across settings with a withdrawal of treatment in two classrooms. Analysis of results indicated that the implementation of CWPT produced an average increase of 21 points on weekly tests. With CWPT 60% of all students earned "A" grades, failing grades were virtually eliminated, and no mildly handicapped students received grades below "C". Anecdotal student and teacher comments were positive. Implications for secondary, mainstreamed students and teachers were discussed.

☐ The academic and social difficulties of secondary mildly handicapped (i.e., learning disabled, behavior disordered, and educable mentally retarded) students are well documented (see, e.g., Deshler, Schumaker, Alley, Warner, & Clark, 1982; Gregory, Shanahan, & Walberg, 1985). Significant among these problems are the following:

1. Severe deficits in basic academic skills such as reading, spelling, and math (Deshler, Schumaker, & Lenz, 1984).
2. Generalized failure and below average performance in content area courses such as science, social studies, and health (Donahoe & Zigmond, 1986; Gregory et al., 1985; Zigmond & Kerr, 1985).
3. Deficient work-related skills, such as listening well in class, note taking, study and test-taking skills (Carlson & Alley, 1981; Schumaker, Sheldon-Wilgren, & Sherman, 1980).
4. Passive academic involvement and a pervasive lack of motivation (see Deshler, 1978; Henker, Whalen, & Hinshaw, 1980; Torgeson, 1982; Zigmond, Kerr, & Schaeffer, 1986).
5. Poor interpersonal relationships (Gregory et al., 1985).

These studies portray students who possess neither the basic academic skills to succeed in content area courses nor the requisite work-related habits to compensate for their academic skill deficits.

Student deficiencies alone, however, cannot account for the chronic, inferior academic performance of mildly handicapped (MH) adolescents. As observational studies (Schumaker, Sheldon-Wilgren, & Sherman, 1980; Zigmond, Kerr, & Shaeffer, 1986) have indicated, the instructional environments to which many of these students are exposed may also be less than satisfactory. For example, Schumaker et al. (1980) found that mainstream teachers made infrequent use of explicit instructional directives and advance organizers while teaching. Essentially, students were expected to "know how" to listen attentively, take good notes, and follow textbook instructions. Similarly, Zigmond et al. (1986) found that regular classroom teachers made few demands on mainstreamed MH students. On average, these pupils were asked to do something (i.e., procedural requests) about twice per period. Academic-related requests occurred approximately eight times per period, but almost every one of these requests was allowed to go unanswered.

In light of these findings, it is not surprising that so many secondary mildly handicapped students possess such dismal academic records in regular classrooms. For example, Donahoe and Zigmond (1986) reported that almost 80% of all 9th-grade learning disabled students in nine urban high schools studied received grades of "D" or below in social studies. Approximately 70% earned a "D" or below

From *Exceptional Children,* September 1988, pp. 52-59.

in science, and 63% earned comparable grades in health. If the goal of regular class integration extends beyond simply increasing MH students' opportunity for socialization with nondisabled peers and encompasses learning something valuable about science and social studies, then the current state of affairs is unacceptable.

The questions facing teachers and educational researchers alike, are as follows: How do we get low-achieving students actively involved with academic tasks? How do we ensure academic success when many of these students have such pervasive deficiencies? We believe that one possible solution lies in the development of a systematic, peer-mediated, instructional intervention such as classwide peer tutoring (CWPT) (see Delquadri, Greenwood, Whorton, Carta, & Hall, 1986, for a more complete discussion). The CWPT system was developed at the Juniper Gardens Children's project. It was designed to improve the basic skills performance of low-achieving minority, disadvantaged, or mildly handicapped students (Delquadri et al., 1986).

The effectiveness of CWPT has been examined extensively by the Juniper Gardens staff, as well as by independent evaluators (Cook, Heron, & Heward, 1983; Maheady & Harper, 1987; Nielson, Buechin, Slaughter, & Westling, 1984). Data from these investigations have consistently demonstrated the powerful effects of CWPT on (a) mildly handicapped (MH) students' reading performance (Whorton et al., in press); (b) Chapter I students' performance in math, spelling and vocabulary (Delquardi, Greenwood, Stretton, & Hall, 1983; Greenwood et al., 1984); and (c) low-achieving, minority students' weekly spelling test grades (Maheady & Harper, 1987). Additional evidence suggests that CWPT is a socially acceptable classroom intervention for both teachers and students (Greenwood et al., 1987; Maheady & Harper, 1987).

Given this impressive record of success with low-achieving, elementary-aged youngsters, we decided to see if CWPT would be equally effective with older, perhaps more academically deficient learners. The purpose of this study, therefore, was to "extend" the CWPT program to the secondary level, and to evaluate its effectiveness in improving the academic performance of mildly handicapped students mainstreamed into regular social studies classrooms.

METHOD

Subjects and Setting

Fifty students (27 males and 23 females) enrolled in three 10th-grade social studies classrooms in a large urban high school in Buffalo, New York, served as subjects. All students were enrolled in a special districtwide program entitled Project PASS (Pupils Achieving Scholastic Success). Project PASS was an experimental program in which regular "content area" teachers were given relatively smaller class sizes (15-20 students) and consultative services from special educators while accepting 3 to 6 mildly handicapped students in their classrooms. The participating teachers (one regular and one resource room) were recruited following a 3-hour inservice training session on peer-tutoring instructional procedures. Neither teacher had previous experience with classwide peer tutoring programs nor extensive training in applied behavior analysis. The 10th-grade social studies instructor had been teaching for 35 years, and the special educator for 9 years. The study was carried out in mainstream classrooms during regularly scheduled instructional sessions. Both teachers participated in implementation.

The 50 student participants ranged in age from 15 years to 17 years, 11 months ($\bar{X}$ = 16-1). Date of birth information was available for only 37 of the 50 student participants in this study. Twenty-six students (52%) were Caucasian, twenty-two (44%) were Black, while the remaining two students were Native American. Fourteen students (7 males, 7 females) were identified previously as mildly handicapped (learning disabled or behavior disordered) according to New York State Special Education eligibility standards. The MH students ranged in age from 15-0 to 17-4 with a mean chronological age of 16-9. Mildly handicapped students were recommended for Project PASS by their previous self-contained classroom teacher, whereas nondisabled participants were randomly assigned from the general 10th-grade population. The most recent achievement test results (Woodcock Reading Mastery Test, Form B; Key Math administered in March 1986) on MH students indicated the following:

1. Total Reading (Grade Equivalent $\bar{X}$ = 6.13; range 5.0 to 7.7).
2. Mathematics (GE $\bar{X}$ = 7.62; range: 6.8 to 10.5).

No recent standardized achievement data were available on nondisabled students.

Materials

A key concept in CWPT is the selection of functional academic targets. This implies that selected academic behaviors should be those that teachers deem to be important. For this reason, the classroom teachers in this study became the curriculum "experts" identifying critical social studies content and developing weekly study guides and quizzes.

Weekly study guides. Each week, the regular and special education teachers collaboratively developed 30-item study guides, consisting of a series of questions—typically fact and detail with corresponding solutions—taken from 1 week's content in the existing social studies text (*Men and Nations: A World History,* by Mazour & Peoples; 1975). Topics covered included: (a) Egyptians, beginnings of civilization, (b) Greek and Roman civilizations, (c) Middle Ages, (d) the American and French Revolutions, and (e) World War I.

Weekly study guides were developed using a three-stage process. First, teachers examined the assigned weekly content during 40-minute consultation sessions and then generated lists of important instructional objectives. Second, the teachers developed a series of questions assessing comprehension of these objectives and provided correct/appropriate answers. Finally, study guides were reviewed by an independent rater (remedial reading specialist) for both accuracy and clarity.

To assist in material development, five 4-hour training sessions were held before the study began. Teachers were presented with "sample" practice sheets that had been developed and field tested previously by the staff at the Center for Social Organization of Schools, Johns Hopkins University (Slavin, 1982; 1983). Teachers were instructed to use these materials as guides in developing their own curriculum-specific practice sheets. Approximately 6 weeks of material was prepared before implementation of the study.

Weekly quizzes. Once the weekly practice sheets were developed, 20-item quizzes assessing students' knowledge of this content were constructed. Occasionally, items on the quizzes were the same as those on the practice sheet, e.g., "What does imperialism mean?" In other instances, the items differed, but similar skills and concepts were being assessed (e.g., concept: *governmental structure* of Communist Party; *item:* Name and compare the major branches of the Yugoslavian and Soviet Union governments).

Experimental Design and Procedure

The effects of CWPT on students' weekly social studies quiz performance were assessed via a multiple baseline design across settings (Tawney & Gast, 1984). The mean test scores for both mildly handicapped and nondisabled students were the primary units of analysis. In two classrooms (Classrooms 1 and 3), CWPT was withdrawn for 1 week, resulting in an ABAB design.

Baseline. The study began by having the social studies teacher instruct his class using his "traditional" classroom routine. This typically included teacher-led lecture and discussion, media presentation, and daily homework review. Two changes in normal routine were instituted. First, following 2 days of instruction, the teacher distributed practice sheets/study guides to each student, telling them that these sheets could be used in school or at home "to help prepare" for the weekly quiz.

The second instructional modification involved the use of weekly tests. Each Friday students took 20-item quizzes individually. Students were required to read each item and write the correct response. If they were unable to read test questions, the classroom teacher provided the necessary assistance. The teacher graded the student quizzes for accuracy and reported the scores during the next class period. The teacher recorded student scores in his grade book and on experimenter-provided data collection forms. The special education teacher conducted independent reliability on 25% of the administered exams. No points were deducted for student spelling errors.

Intervention. Classwide peer tutoring was introduced sequentially into each classroom. New classroom material was introduced each week via 1 to 2 days of teacher lecture/discussion followed by assigned readings and homework. For the next 2 or 3 days, CWPT was implemented for 30 minutes per day. With the exception of 2 weeks, tutoring sessions occurred twice per week for 30 minutes per day. When CWPT sessions were conducted for 3 days per week, tutoring lasted only 20 minutes per day.

The program operated as follows. The classroom was divided into two teams by having students draw colored squares (red or blue) from a covered box. Team membership (Red team vs. Blue team) stayed the same for 2 weeks. These teams competed for the highest point totals in social studies. Following the selection of teams, the teacher randomly paired students within each team to make up tutoring dyads. Throughout the next 2 weeks, these pairs worked together on designated days, using the previously described 30-item study guides.

In order to implement the tutoring procedure, the students and teachers were trained by the second investigator through two 30-minute role-play sessions. Initial, in-class supervision was also provided during the early stages of this study. After training, the ongoing tutoring procedures were initiated by the social studies teacher setting a timer for 15 minutes.

During tutoring, the tutor dictated study guide questions to the respective tutee, who was then required to write and say the correct answer. Tutors were instructed to say "that's right" or "correct," and provide 3 points for each accurate response. However, if tutees responded incorrectly, tutors said "that's wrong" and provided them with the correct answer. Tutees were then required to write the correct response three times. Two points were then awarded by the tutor for correcting the answer. Students were instructed to continue through their 30-question list as many times as possible before the 15-minute time period elapsed. At the end of the first 15-minute session, tutoring pairs reversed roles and followed the same tutoring procedures for the next 15 mintues.

Bonus points were awarded to tutors on a daily basis contingent upon their display of "good tutoring" behaviors. During tutoring sessions, teachers moved about the classroom and awarded points, up to 10 points per student, to tutors displaying the following behaviors: (a) clear and accurate dictation of questions, (b) appropriate use of the error correction procedure, (c) contingent and accurate delivery of points, and (d) use of praise and support statements.

At the end of each 30-minute CWPT session, students totaled the number of points they had earned, including bonus points, and recorded the number at the top of the paper. Student scores were then posted on a laminated chart in front of the class, and daily team totals were calculated. Peer-tutoring procedures were in effect for at least 2 days prior to the weekly

FIGURE 1
Mean Percentage Correct on Weekly Social Studies Tests Across Three 10th-grade Classrooms

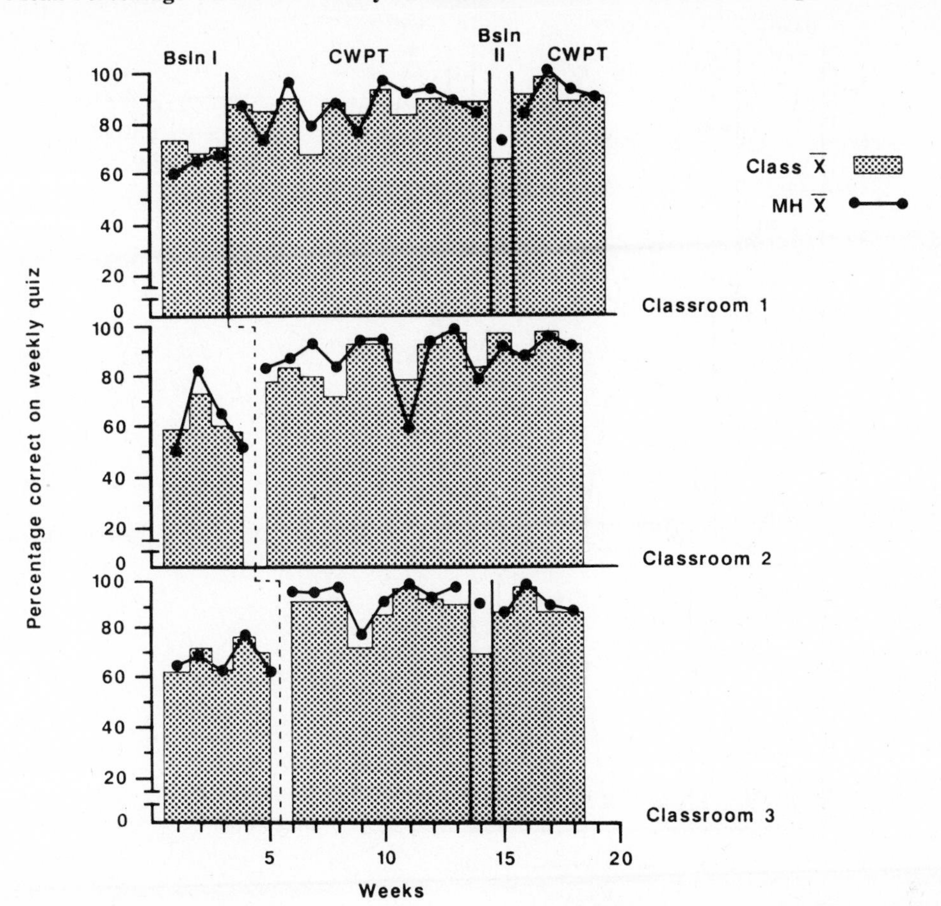

quiz. Quizzes were then administered using the standard format, i.e., students read questions silently and wrote their answers. However, students were informed that they could earn 5 points for their team for each correct answer.

Following the weekly quiz, team totals were calculated and the winning team was announced. Weekly results, as well as outstanding individual efforts, were then printed in the school's weekly bulletin. On occasion, the teacher also awarded bonus points to an individual's cumulative average or provided students with "outstanding performance certificates." Every 2 weeks, new competing teams were formed.

RESULTS

The primary dependent variable in this study was the percentage correct on weekly social studies quizzes. Means were calculated for both the entire class and the mildly handicapped students enrolled within each section. These data are presented in Figure 1.

During baseline, the mean percentage correct for each class ranged from 55 to 70, with an average of 65.96%. Classroom 2 students earned the lowest weekly scores ($\bar{X}$ = 61.33%), and student means in Classrooms 1 and 3 approached 70% (68.22% and 68.76%, respectively). It is interesting to note that the weekly mean test scores of mildly handicapped students did not differ much from the total class average. In fact, in two instances, MH students' performance exceeded that of their nondisabled peers.

The implementation of CWPT resulted in an immediate and dramatic increase in the weekly test scores of both mildly handicapped and nondisabled students. These gains ranged from 19 to 27 percentage points for the total class and averaged 21.66 percentage points over the course of the investigation. Mildly handicapped students' gains were slightly higher ($\bar{X}$ = 23.15 points), and their weekly scores frequently exceeded those of their nondisabled peers. To demonstrate further experimental control, the teacher was asked to withdraw CWPT for 1 week in two sections (teacher's choice), and to return to baseline conditions. The return to baseline resulted in a substantial drop in student performance (approximately 22 percentage points in Classroom 1 and 20 percentage points in Classroom 3). Because of ethical concerns and student complaints, CWPT was reintroduced the following week. Again, test scores rose dramatically and exceeded baseline performance in all instances.

To examine the practical significance of our findings and to determine the effects of CWPT on individual student performance, the percentage of students earning "A" and "E" grades was calculated. These data are shown in Figure 2.

FIGURE 2
Mean Percentage of Students Earning "A" and "E" Grades Across Experimental Conditions

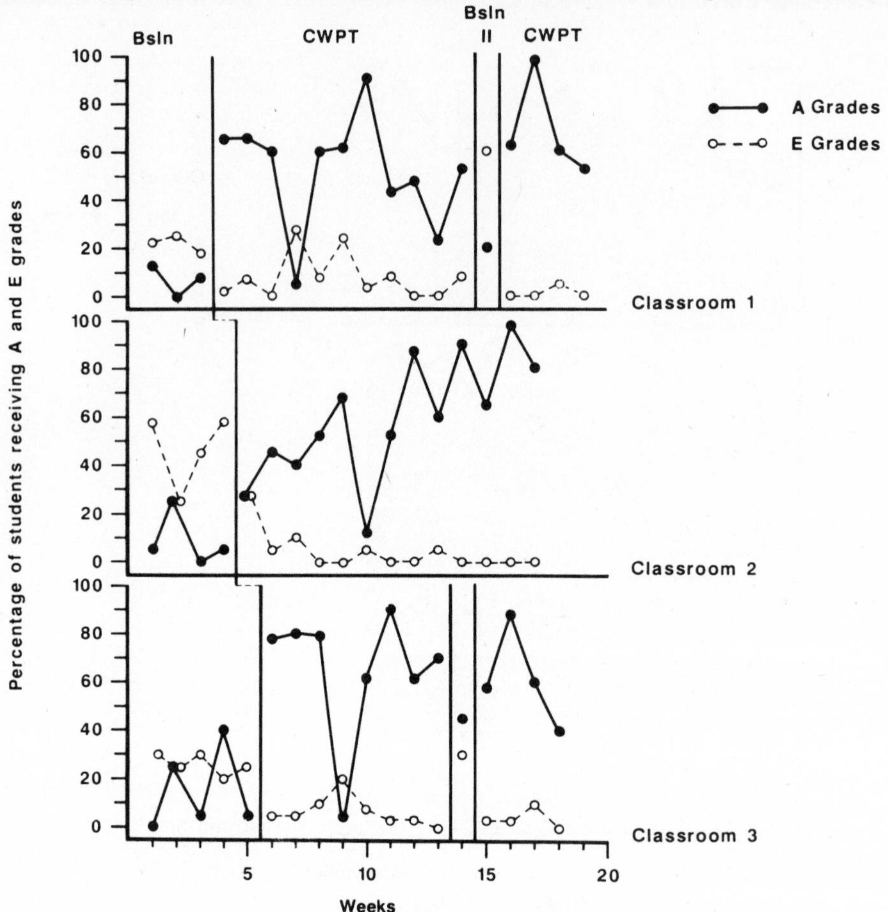

During baseline conditions, very few students earned grades above 90% correct ("A"). Approximately 13% of all students (1 to 2 students per section) received "As", whereas the average failure rate (below 60%) was about 33%. In all but three instances, the percentage of students failing weekly quizzes exceeded those earning "A" grades. When CWPT was implemented, the percentage of "A" grades rose dramatically, and "Es" were virtually eliminated. The percentage of students earning test scores of 90% and above was approximately 58%. On five occasions, over 90% of an entire class earned an "A". Failing grades, on the other hand, diminished substantially. During 16 of 33 quiz administrations, no one taking the quiz received a failing grade. In only two instances during intervention did failing grades exceed the number of "As". A withdrawal of treatment in two classrooms resulted in substantially higher failure rates, and fewer "A" grades. This trend was reversed again when CWPT was reinstituted in each section.

An analysis of individual student performance revealed that only five students in the entire population (10%) failed more than one quiz while the intervention was in effect. None of these students were mildly handicapped. An analysis of MH students' final report cards revealed that no students earned grades below "C" in social studies, and that their social studies grades were consistently the highest on their report cards. Finally, informal interviews with the classroom teachers indicated high degrees of satisfaction (both teacher and student) with the tutoring procedures and outcomes.

DISCUSSION

Results of the present investigation clearly indicate that: (a) CWPT procedures resulted in immediate and systematic increases in the weekly social studies test performance of mildly handicapped and nondisabled 10th graders, and (b) the intervention increased substantially the percentage of students earning "A" grades, while simultaneously decreasing the number of failing grades. Anecdotal student and teacher comments suggested further that the tutoring procedures and outcomes were both acceptable and beneficial.

The present results essentially replicate earlier findings attesting to the powerful effects of classwide peer tutoring (see Delquadri et al., 1986 for complete review). The present study, however, extended these effects to a new population (mildly handicapped adolescents) and to a different content area (social studies). Furthermore, this intervention was applied within a demanding instructional environment (regular classroom) in a subject area that has traditionally posed substantial difficulties for MH learners.

Data obtained from this investigation are significant in a number of other respects. First, they were obtained using a 35-year teaching veteran as the primary implementor. This individual had no prior training in the proposed methodology and did not regard himself as a major innovation implementor. The present findings are also significant in that they required neither major content modifications nor individualization of instruction. The procedure used existing classroom materials. Many MH students performed well even though materials were not "individualized"; thus, the necessity of an adequate student-materials match may be less crucial in the context of an instructional procedure that provides frequent opportunities to respond and systematic feedback procedures.

The present findings are also significant in that CWPT was equally effective for both mildly handicapped and nondisabled students. This suggests that increments in the performance of low-achieving students need not occur at the expense of their nondisabled peers. Finally, the current findings are significant because they impacted on important ecological measures, that is, weekly test scores and report card grades. Weekly test scores rose by approximately 20 points. This translated into an increase of two grade levels, for example, "D" to "B". No mildly handicapped students received a grade below "C". These changes were readily apparent to both teachers and students on a weekly basis, and the appearance of above-average social studies grades on final transcripts provided a socially valid measure of this study's impact.

Conceptual Questions

Though the present study was successful in extending the effectiveness of CWPT procedures, it also raised a number of interesting questions that warrant further empirical pursuit. Such questions appear to be both conceptual and procedural. Conceptually, one may ask under what conditions does the "opportunity to respond" construct hold true. To date, empirical evidence indicates that student performance can be enhanced significantly in basic skills, such as reading, spelling, and math, as well as in the acquisition of "fact and detail" social studies content. Whether similar findings would occur with so-called higher order cognitive skills, such as analysis and synthesis of instructional content, must still be examined.

A second conceptual issue is concerned with the efficacy of "normal" classroom instruction and the need for differentiated teaching procedures for handicapped learners. The present study found that following 4 days of traditional teacher instruction, student quiz scores were barely passing (65%). No substantial differences existed between the performance of MH and nondisabled students. Almost everyone performed equally poorly. Though the present findings are restricted to one teacher and three classrooms, similar results have been reported elsewhere (Maheady, Sacca, & Harper, 1986; Zigmond et al., 1986). The implication of these findings is that improving the overall effectiveness of regular class instruction may take precedence over the development of procedures to help MH learners compensate for the lack of quality instruction in the first place.

Procedural Questions

Procedurally, a number of issues and avenues for future empirical inquiry exist. First, additional replications of the present investigation are clearly warranted. Such analyses should include additional mildly handicapped populations, larger class sizes, and other curricular areas. Second, a more careful examination of the CWPT process must be undertaken. Questions concerning the relative contributions of specific tutoring procedures (e.g., use of points, public posting of scores, error correction procedures, etc.) to overall program effectiveness must still be addressed.

Although CWPT seemed to "work," we are unable to explain which facets of the intervention were critical to this success. Direct observations of CWPT are also essential to examine the fidelity (accuracy) with which the program was implemented. Previous research has indicated that elementary-aged students use CWPT with a high degree of accuracy over time (see, e.g., Greenwood et al., 1987; Maheady & Harper, 1987). Whether secondary students follow prescribed procedures as well must still be determined.

Problems with Implementation

The routine implementation of CWPT also possesses some potential difficulties that warrant discussion. First, the material-development demands inherent in the construction of weekly study guides and quizzes were quite substantial. In attempting to replicate this study, it is recommended that a number of practice sheets and quizzes be developed *before* the investigation begins.

A second potential problem in the CWPT system involves the accuracy of student point totaling. The social studies teacher reported that occasionally students would miscalculate their point totals, usually erring in their own favor. This problem was handled efficiently by having the teacher randomly schedule "surprise days," when he would check student papers and award 10 bonus points for each team member correctly totaling the points. One final concern involved occasional student complaints about having to rewrite corrections three times and having to take weekly exams. Some students also complained about team members. Typically, these complaints were ignored. Instead, the classroom teacher informed students that they must learn to work out their problems themselves. The teacher also intervened directly by assigning bonus points to team members *not* engaging in these behaviors.

In summary, the present investigation described a 30- to 40-minute classwide peer tutoring program that systematically increased the social studies test performance of 10th-grade, mildly handicapped and nondisabled students. The intervention proved to be not only academically beneficial, but socially acceptable as well. As such, CWPT appears to be a viable instructional alternative for secondary classroom teachers attempting to meet the needs of a diversity of students within the confines of regular, content-area classrooms.

REFERENCES

Carlson, S. A., & Alley, G. R. (1981). *Performance and competence of learning disabled and high achieving high school students on essential cognitive skills* (Research Report No. 53). Lawrence, KS: University of Kansas Institute for Research in Learning Disabilities.

Cook, N. L., Heron, T. E., & Heward, W. L. (1983). *Peer tutoring: Implementing classwide programs in primary grades.* Columbus, OH: Special Press.

Delquadri, J., Greenwood, C. R., Stretton, K., & Hall, R. V. (1983). The peer tutoring game: A classroom procedure for increasing opportunity to respond and spelling performance. *Education and Treatment of Children, 6,* 225-239.

Delquadri, J., Greenwood, C. R., Whorton, D., Carta, J. J., & Hall, R. V. (1986). Classwide peer tutoring. *Exceptional Children, 52,* 535-542.

Deshler, D. D. (1978). Issues related to the education of learning disabled adolescents. *Learning Disability Quarterly, 1*(4), 2-10.

Deshler, D. D., Schumaker, J. B., Alley, G. B., Warner, M. M., & Clark, F. L. (1982). Learning disabilities in adolescent and young adult populations: Research implications. *Focus on Exceptional Children, 15*(1), 1-12.

Deshler, D., Schumaker, J. B., & Lenz, B. (1984). Academic and cognitive interventions for LD adolescents: Part I. *Journal of Learning Disabilities, 17,* 108-117.

Donahoe, K., & Zigmond, N. (1986). *High school grades of urban LD students and low achieving peers.* Unpublished manuscript, Program in Special Education, University of Pittsburgh.

Greenwood, C. R., Dinwiddie, G., Bailey, V., Carta, J. J. , Dorsey, D., Kohler, F., Nelson, C., Rothholz, D., & Schulte, D. (1987). Field replication of classwide peer tutoring. *Jnl. of Applied Behavior Analysis, 20,* 151-159.

Greenwood, C. R., Dinwiddie, G., Terry, B., Wade, L., Stanley, S. O., Thibadeau, S., & Delquadri, J. (1984). Teacher versus peer-mediated instruction: An ecobehavioral analysis of achievement outcomes. *Journal of Applied Behavior Analysis, 17,* 521-538.

Gregory, J. F., Shanahan, T., & Walberg, H. (1985). Learning disabled 10th graders in mainstreamed settings: A descriptive analysis. *Remedial and Special Education, 6*(4), 25-33.

Henker, B., Whalen, C. K., & Hinshaw, S. P. (1980). The attributional contexts of cognitive intervention strategies. *Exceptional Educational Quarterly, 1,* 17-30.

Maheady, L., & Harper, G. F. (1987). A class-wide peer tutoring program to improve the spelling test performance of low income, third- and fourth-grade students. *Education and Treatment of Children, 10,* 120-133.

Maheady, L., Sacca, M. K., & Harper, G. F. (1986). *The effects of classwide student tutoring teams on the math test performance of secondary mildly handicapped and non-disabled students.* Unpublished manuscript.

Mazour, A. G., & Peoples, J. M. (1975). *Men and nations: A world history* (3rd ed.). New York: Harcourt, Brace & Jovanovich.

Nielson, C., Buechin, N., Slaughter, R., & Westling, K. (1984, May). *The successful use of behavioral learning packages with school and parents served by a special education cooperative (LADSE): Factors which achieve use and adoption.* Paper presented at the Tenth Annual Applied Behavior Analysis Convention, Nashville, TN.

Schumaker, J. B., Sheldon-Wilgren, J., & Sherman, J. A. (1980). *An observational study of the academic and social skills of learning disabled adolescents in the regular classroom* (Research Report No. 22). Lawrence, KS: University of Kansas Institute for Research in Learning Disabilities.

Slavin, R. E. (1985). An introduction to cooperative learning research. In R. Slavin, S. Sharon, S. Kagan, R. H. Lagarowitz, C. Webb, & R. Schmuck (Eds.), *Learning to cooperate: Cooperating to learn* (pp. 5-15). New York: Plenum Press.

Slavin, R. E. (1982). *Cooperative learning.* Washington, DC: National Education Association.

Slavin, R. E. (1983). *Student learning teams.* Washington, DC: National Education Association.

Tawney, J. W., & Gast, D. L. (1984). *Single subject research in special education.* Columbus, OH: Charles E. Merrill.

Torgeson, J. K. (1982). The learning disabled child as an inactive learner: Education implications. *Topics in Learning and Learning Disabilities, 2,* 45-52.

Whorton, D., Sasso, G., Elliot, M., Hughes, V., Critchlow, W., Terry, B., Stanley, S. O., Greenwood, C. R., & Delquadri, J. (in press). Teaching formats that maximize the opportunity to learn: Parent and peer tutoring programs. *Education and Treatment of Children.*

Zigmond, N., & Kerr, M. M. (1985, April). *Managing the mainstream: A contrast of behaviors of learning disabled students who pass their assigned mainstream courses and those who fail.* Paper presented at American Educational Research Association, Chicago, IL.

Zigmond, N., Kerr, M. M., & Schaeffer, A. (1986). *Behavioral patterns of LD, ED, and non-handicapped adolescents in high school academic classes.* Unpublished manuscript, Program in Special Education, University of Pittsburgh.

The authors gratefully acknowledge the assistance of the administration and faculty of the Buffalo Public Schools. In particular, we wish to thank Richard Quinn, Assistant Superintendent for Special Education, Rosalie Covial, Director of Special Education, and the following teachers, Frank Bucella, Sherman Connelly, Judi DiTallo, and Helen Mills for their help in the implementation of this study.

Educating Students With Severe Disabilities

Susan Stainback
William Stainback

Susan Stainback *and* **William Stainback** *(CEC Chapter #88) are Matthew J. Guglielmo Endowed Chair Professors, California State University, Los Angeles.*

Shawntell is 15 years old and has been classified as severely and multiply handicapped. She rides the regular school bus, attends regular ninth grade classes, and on weekends goes to rock concerts, parties, and horseback riding with many of her school and neighborhood peers. Shawntell's parents have found that friendships and a quality education can be achieved in regular neighborhood schools and classes.

Kathy was born with Down syndrome. While it was recommended that she be institutionalized, Kathy lived at home, attended regular classes in her neighborhood school and graduated from high school in 1987. She made many friends along the way and, according to her mother, lives an active and full life in her home community. Kathy is currently in charge of the salad bar at a well-known hotel restaurant.

Stephanie is an 8-year-old student in a wheelchair who is classified as having profound mental and physical disabilities. Stephanie's teacher in the regular classroom recently stated: "Teachers need to see that it's no big deal. They need to see videos of integration in action—to see the real Stephanie on the floor with the other kids who are doing math work, for example, while I'm telling Stephanie to sit up for body control."

■Inspired by such examples, educators throughout the nation are experimenting with ways to integrate students with severe disabilities into regular education classes. Because of these efforts, a number of integration strategies are beginning to emerge. Some of these strategies are reviewed in this article.

The strategies are based on (a) information gleaned from participating with, observing, and interviewing school personnel in several schools where students with severe disabilities were being integrated into regular classes; (b) conversations about the topic with school personnel from several locations in the United States and Canada where integration into regular classes has occurred; and (c) a review of the professional literature (e.g., Forest, 1987; Gartner & Lipsky, 1987; Strully, 1987; Stainback & Stainback, 1985; Stainback & Stainback, 1987).

Strategies for Integration

Promote Support

A strong commitment by school personnel and parents to the goal of educating all students in regular classes is critical to achieving that goal. Once a commitment has been made by people in a school community, they can help others understand the advantages. This can occur in a number of different ways. For example, in one case, a parent gained the support of a teacher, and then together they approached the principal and other school personnel. In another situation, a principal presented the idea to his faculty, and from that a task force and integration plan developed. In still another setting, a university instructor enlisted the support of a colleague in a local school, then several teachers, the school principal, and eventually the entire school faculty. Whatever the chain of events, success is unlikely unless an understanding is gained of the advantages that can result for all students participating in the educational mainstream and key school personnel and parents accept, support, and make a commitment to achieving integration.

Not everyone in a school or school district has to be committed. If only a few people in one school are committed, a small pilot or demonstration project can be started while work continues to promote wider understanding, acceptance, and support. In fact, a small, successful demonstration project that encourages school personnel and parents to visit can be very

From *Teaching Exceptional Children*, Fall 1988, pp. 16-19. Copyright 1988 by The Council for Exceptional Children. Reprinted with permission of The Council for Exceptional Children.

helpful in promoting widespread acceptance and support.

Designate a Support Facilitator

A number of schools have begun to designate a person to serve as a support facilitator. A support facilitator is a person who can either assist regular classroom teachers with suggestions or provide an extra pair of hands to help adapt and individualize instruction to meet the needs of *all* class members. In addition, the support facilitator can offer students direct support or instruction for such things as understanding and communicating with peers and teachers, completing assignments, developing positive social behaviors, learning bus schedules and routines, understanding and dealing with individual differences, and learning to support and assist others. As students who need assistance adjust to the school environment and the school environment is adjusted to meet their needs, the support provided by the support facilitator is gradually faded.

One source of support facilitators is special educators. When support facilitators were first used in the schools, they were employed to work only with students classified as having severe disabilities. They often followed or shadowed these students around in regular class settings, which tended to draw attention to the students and set them apart from their peers. This interfered with the development of natural networks of support and friendship. In recent years, support facilitators have served a broader role. As noted earlier, they often help regular class teachers adapt instruction to meet the needs of a variety of different students and/or directly assist any students, disabled or not, who are having difficulty in educational tasks and/or in gaining peer acceptance. They also are sensitive about when to help any particular student and when to allow natural peer support and friendships and opportunities to develop.

Develop Networks of Support

Because of the diversity in student needs in integrated classes and schools, it is sometimes necessary to develop networks of support. One way to provide a network of support is through a circle of friends. Support facilitators can work side by side with regular class teachers to organize buddy systems, tutors, and special friends for new students being integrated into regular classes. The regular class students can help new students feel welcomed, learn classroom routines and rules, and become an integral part of the classroom activities and programs. It should be stressed that the new student is encouraged to be a friend and help other students, whenever possible. This avoids the new student always being the recipient of assistance.

Teacher and student assistance teams (TSATs) are another way to provide support for students and teachers in regular education classes. Such teams also can be conceptualized as a circle of friends. TSATs come together to brainstorm; problem solve; and exchange ideas, methods, techniques, and activities to assist a teacher or student requiring help. A team might include two or more students, administrators, parents, classroom teachers, aides, school psychologists, and specialists.

Generally, the regular classroom teacher or the student who needs assistance is the leader or center of the TSAT: The responsibility of the TSAT is to provide ideas and support when the teacher or student is unsure of what to do. The team makes as many helpful suggestions as possible and, in some cases, becomes involved in assisting in the implementation of the suggestions.

Provide Instruction Naturally

One approach that has been successful in fostering the integration of all students into regular education is the use of natural opportunities that occur in regular education activities to develop such skills as functional community-referenced skills, braille, mobility, and the like. There is no reason why these skills have to be taught in special education classes. Specialists can work with regular educators to teach such skills in the regular education setting. Lunch and snack times can be used to develop eating and dining skills: bus riding skills can be taught when students travel back and forth to school; braille can be taught and practiced during reading classes; and mobility can be taught when students are called upon to maneuver around the playground. When skills are taught in the natural setting, peers can be exposed to ways they can assist in and promote the practice, generalization, and maintenance of the desired skills during times when the specialist may not be available.

A word of caution should be noted here. In integrated schools it is important for special education and other specialists to blend into and become an integral part of regular education. Many school personnel have found that in some cases students with disabilities are embarrassed to have specialists work with them in front of their peers, especially if the specialists are known as special teachers of the "retarded," "disordered," or "disturbed." For this reason it is better for a specialist to be viewed as just another regular education teacher who works with any student (disabled or not) who happens to need his or her expertise.

In addition to learning community-referenced and similar skills, it also is possible for severely disabled students to participate in a meaningful way in regular science, math, geography, and other academic classes in regular education. In the regular classes and schools we have worked in or visited, we have observed students with diverse abilities participating in meaningful ways in age-appropriate regular education classes. For instance, during a map reading activity, one student may be called upon to discuss the economic system of the country, another may be requested to identify a color, while another may simply be requested to grasp and hold a corner of the map. During oral reading activities, one student may be requested to read out loud, and another to listen to a story and answer questions, another to pick out a picture that describes the story, and another to pass out reading materials to classmates. In integrated, heterogeneous classrooms, what any student is requested to do to participate in a group or individualized class activity is based on what that student needs to learn and is capable of doing. When appropriately organized, regular education classes can provide a wide variety of appropriate learning opportunities and challenges for students with a wide range of learning needs, interests, and capabilities.

Finally, it should be noted that the regular class curriculum agenda and activities may not always have to be modified to accommodate students with severe disabilities. An illustration of how one student, classified as having autism and severe mental retardation, participated in a meaningful way in the usual activities of a regular sixth grade class follows.

> When we observed Ryan he was 12 years old. He was ambulatory and 80% to 90% toilet trained. He spoke mostly in single words, but did occasionally utter phrases or partial sentences that could be understood by most people.
>
> When Ryan was first integrated, he often did not participate in the regular class activities and programs. For example, during the first 15 minutes each morning the teacher asked the class to report on a news story they had seen on television or read in the newspaper. During this time, Ryan usually walked around the classroom, turned the water on and off in the sink at the back of the room, and played with the light switch.
>
> To help Ryan become more involved in the class, a TSAT recommended that his mother have him watch a television news story each night and coach him so that he could share it with the class. In this way, when the teacher asked who in the class wanted to report on a news story, Ryan would have something to say. Prompting from the teacher, classmates, and support facilitator was often necessary, but gradually Ryan did participate in the class.

One logical question this example raises is whether or not what Ryan did and learned was functional. It was functional, in our opinion, in that Ryan learned something that allowed him to participate with other students his age, which opened up opportunities for socialization and potential friendships. It also provided him an opportunity to become more aware of his environment (news stories); increase his vocabulary; learn skills in taking turns and interacting with his peers; and practice remembering, listening, and sharing ideas. Such skills are not only functional but essential to promoting an integrated society in which students learn to live, understand, and have things in common with their fellow community members.

Promote Respect

To enhance the chances of everyone being respected, accepted, and treated kindly in integrated regular classrooms, many educators attempt to foster a basic understanding of and respect for individual differences and similarities among all students. The support facilitator can take an active role in this. It is usually accomplished by infusing information about individual differences and similarities into existing reading materials; health or social studies classes; and extracurricular activities such as assembly programs, plays, school projects, service activities, and clubs.

School personnel also can encourage respect for individual differences by showing respect themselves and encouraging and reinforcing it when it occurs. This can be done during natural, daily interactions in regular class and extracurricular settings.

In some cases just having a severely disabled student in a classroom can foster greater respect and understanding about individual differences among all class members. As one classmate of a teenager with multiple handicaps stated, "I think we learned that it's important to treat other people better. The kids don't pick on him, so they don't pick on each other" (Scoglrotti, 1987 as cited in Thousand & Villa, in press).

Integrate Students, Personnel, and Resources

Finally, where integration has been most successful, personnel and resources from special education as well as the students have been integrated into regular classes and regular education (Stainback, Stainback, & Forest, in press). Even when an initial small demonstration project is organized in which only a few students are integrated into regular education, it is still important to integrate personnel and resources from special education into regular education to assist in handling the extra work required. If this is not done, the quality of services students receive in regular education could be jeopardized.

Regular educators need the resources now placed in special education to help them individualize and adapt instruction to diverse student needs in regular education classes.

It is important to avoid concentrating large numbers of former special education students into one or several regular education classes. It is better to integrate only one student into any single class, whenever possible, to avoid the potential for developing segregated clusters or pockets of former special education students within regular education classrooms, which would negate many of the advantages of integration.

Conclusion

In a growing number of schools throughout the nation, school personnel are moving beyond debating or doing research on the relative advantages of special or regular education for students with disabilities. Instead, they are integrating the best personnel and procedures from both regular and special education to provide all students, disabled and nondisabled, the best possible education in integrated classrooms and schools.

References

Forest, M. (1987). *More education integration.* Downsview, Ontario: G. Allan Roeher Institute.

Gartner, A., & Lipsky, D. (1987). Beyond special education: Toward one quality system for all students. *Harvard Educ. Review, 57,* 367-395.

Stainback, S., Stainback, W., & Forest, M. (Eds.) (in press).*Educating all students in the mainstream of regular education.* Baltimore: Paul Brookes.

Stainback, S., & Stainback, W. (1985). *Integration of students with severe handicaps into regular schools.* Reston, VA: The Council for Exceptional Children.

Stainback, S., & Stainback, W. (1987). Educating all students in regular education. *TASH Newsletter, 13*(4), 1 & 7.

Strully, J. (1987 October). *What's really important in life anyway? Parents sharing the vision.* Paper presented at the 14th Annual TASH Conference, Chicago.

Sylvester, D. (1987, October). *A parent's perspective.* Paper presented at the VT Least Restrictive Environment Conference, Burlington.

Thousand, J. S., & Villa, R. A. (In press). Enhancing success in heterogeneous classrooms. In S. Stainback, W. Stainback, & M. Forest (Eds.) *Educating all students in the mainstream of regular education.* Baltimore: Paul Brooks.

Teaching the Learning Disabled Child

The Education for All Handicapped Children Act, PL 94-142, defines children with specific learning disabilities as those children who have a disorder in one or more of the basic psychological processes involved in understanding or in using language, spoken or written. This disorder may manifest itself in an imperfect ability to listen, think, speak, read, write, spell, or do mathematical calculations. Such disorders include perceptual handicaps, brain injury, minimal brain dysfunction, dyslexia, and developmental aphasia. The term "learning disabled" does not refer to children who have learning problems that are primarily the result of visual, hearing, or motor handicaps, mental retardation, emotional disturbance, or environmental, cultural, or economic disadvantage.

Public schools in the United States provide more special educational services for learning disabled children than for any other area of exceptionality, due to the breadth of the definition of specific learning disabilities. Despite the prevalence of learning disabilities, many persons have very little understanding of what they are. The definition specifically excludes children who are disabled by visual, hearing, or physical impairments, even though some of these children may also have learning disabilities. These children are already qualified for free and appropriate education. It also excludes mentally retarded children who, by definition, are qualified for other reasons. It excludes borderline learners, who score just above 70 on IQ testing and pass a test assessing adaptive behavior. Children who are learning disadvantaged in school due to emotional stressors, environmental stressors, cultural differences, or economic poverty are likewise excluded from special educational services unless they manifest severe emotional disturbances and behavior disorders. Research has not identified these factors as primary causes of learning disabilities.

Children with specific learning disabilities and children who learn with difficulty due to these exclusionary reasons (borderline IQ, emotional stress, and environmental, cultural, or economic disadvantage) are not always easy to differentiate from one another. The assessment of specific learning disabilities is difficult; mislabeling is common.

Children with true specific learning disabilities also can be very different from each other. If they have a developmental learning disability (LD), they may have a problem with attention, language, memory, sensory perceptions, perceptual-motor ability, thinking, or social perceptions. They may also have more than one of these, in any combination. If they have an academic LD, they may have a problem with one or more of the following: reading, writing, spelling, written expression, or calculation. They may have a borderline, average, or high IQ, but they will have a problem in one or more areas that inhibits learning up to their ability level. They may be very motivated to learn and yet appear to resist any efforts to teach them. It is not surprising that persons faced with explaining learning disabilities, or teaching learning disabled children, are confused about what to say or do.

Some forms of LD, such as dyslexia (difficulty in learning to read) and attention deficit (often referred to as hyperactivity) are more common than others and consequently are more easily accepted by the lay public. However, because these terms are accepted, they are overused as umbrella labels for other forms of LD which are neither dyslexia nor attention deficit disorders. In order for each LD child to be given appropriate education, his or her unique area(s) of difficulty must be correctly assessed and an individualized education program (IEP) must be developed based on the genuine area(s) of disability.

The lead article in this unit discusses common types of learning disabilities and lists some symptoms which aid in the assessment of each type. It also presents current therapies and issues of the future. The next selection attempts to clear up confusion by differentiating between the many types of learning disabilities and focuses on the need for early, correct assessment and amelioration of disabilities. The third article helps the reader recognize certain behaviors which LD children manifest to hide their problems. It also lists characteristics common to LD students. The next two articles discuss the teaching of LD children. John Shields and Timothy Heron present strategies which can be used to help LD students organize contents, materials, and time in a meaningful way. Michael Ford and Marilyn Ohlhausen articulate nine specific ways to integrate LD children with a wide range of abilities into a regular classroom. The final article of this unit addresses the question of how to help LD students make the transition from school to work. It provides a guide for exploring employment options and obtaining and keeping a job. The program described has been an effective strategy for several LD students.

Looking Ahead: Challenge Questions

Why are some LD children described as lazy and

Unit 3

dumb? How can society's perception of LD students be altered to give LD students more hope for productive futures?

Why is it so difficult to define the various types of learning disabilities? How can identification be improved?

Can teachers recognize characteristics of LD? How do LD students hide their disabilities from adults, and why?

What strategies can be implemented to improve LD students' organizational and time management skills?

Special education specialists work with LD students one-on-one. How can their methods and techniques be adapted to regular education classrooms, where teachers must provide appropriate education for LD students while teaching one-on-thirty or more?

How can secondary schools help LD students assess their strengths and weaknesses and make appropriate employment choices and smooth transitions from school to work?

LEARNING DISABILITIES

A NEW HORIZON OF PERCEPTION

Understanding and helping the learning disabled may give them hope for a productive future.

EVELYN B. KELLY

Evelyn B. Kelly is vice president of the Florida chapter of the American Medical Writers' Association and a consultant on pediatric, psychological, and gerontological concerns.

"I just love my LD class. The teacher is so patient and nice. I really appreciate the special help and work very hard," said one seventh-grade student.

"LD—that stands for lazy, and dumb. That's me—and the other geeks pulled out for special class. I would rather be failing in regular class than be stuck where that teacher hassles you every minute," said another.

These words are from two students in a model learning disabilities (LD) program. And what's interesting—the program is in the same school and the students are in the same class!

The comments of these students mirror the great diversity in thinking about learning disabilities. Theories, therapies, and remedies, as well as criticisms, have proliferated as quickly as the number of students classified as "learning disabled."

When people lived on the farm in an agrarian society, they did not need a lot of verbal or processing skills. When they moved to town as part of the industrial revolution, they needed a few more. But, as John Naisbitt suggests in *Megatrends*, we are rapidly moving from an industrial to an information society, and the ability to learn and process information becomes imperative. As we place greater emphasis on learning and verbal skills, those people with the hidden handicaps that we have coined "learning disabilities" will be uncovered. In an information-laden society, understanding and helping the learning disabled may give them hope for a productive future.

The LD boom

In the 1960s the identification of a group of disorders termed learning disabilities ignited a spark of interest in the educational community. Fanned by high interest, and the enactment of the Education for All Handicapped Children Act in 1975, the number of LD children receiving special services exploded. According to the 1984 U.S. Department of Education report, the number rose in a seven-year period to over 1.7 million, a 119 percent increase. About 4.2 percent of the total school population was identified as LD.

Explanations for the boom vary. One reason for the popularity is that the label "LD" appeals to parents and teachers. By embracing the classification, parents can obtain special help for their youngsters and avoid such horrifying and stigmatizing labels as "disturbed," "retarded," "slow learner," or even "lazy" or "dumb."

Another explanation for the rapid growth of the LD classification is its lack of definition. It includes learning difficulties caused by motivation, personality, or environment—or any combination of these. Douglas Biklen of Syracuse University states that this wide definition means that possibly 80 percent of all school-age youth could be eligible for special classes. And only recently have people begun to realize that children with learning disabilities become adults with LD, further increasing the LD population. The old notion that a child will grow out of LD is no longer accepted.

Clearly, LD programs are an important component of American education; but the term "learning disability," at present, is more cosmetic than scientific—no one is sure of its exact meaning. Alan O. Ross, author of *Learning Disability: The Unrealized Potential* (McGraw Hill, 1980), concluded that the field of learning disabilities is long on theory and

From *The World & I*, August 1988, pp. 314-321. Reprinted with permission from *The World & I*, a publication of The Washington Times Corporation.

short on fact.

According to the Association for Children and Adults with Learning Disabilities (ACLD), "learning disability" means a handicap that keeps one from storing, processing, and producing information. The LD person may also be defined by a cluster of symptoms or behaviors: short attention span; poor memory; difficulty following directions; inadequate ability to discriminate between different letters, numerals, and sounds; eye-hand coordination problems; difficulties with sequencing; and numerous sensory problems. (A person is not disabled if he or she exhibits only a few of these symptoms.) LD seems to be a matter of degree.

No two people with learning disabilities are ever alike. The blanket label covers a heterogeneous group. However, some general categories can be established. (These conditions may affect both children and adults.)

Dyslexia

A dyslexic can recognize shapes but not sounds; he can't discriminate letter sounds and blends. The term "dyslexic" describes children and adults with average and above-average intelligence who, according to the ACLD, may exhibit the following symptoms:

- severe difficulty in learning and remembering the printed words or symbols;
- reversal of letters or improper sequencing. For example: "b" for "d," or "was" for "saw";
- bizarre spelling errors;
- illegible handwriting;
- poorly written composition.

One category, termed *specific developmental dyslexia*, is thought to be caused by a specific central nervous system (CNS) deficit. This neural defect is thought to be located in the angular gyrus of the dominant hemisphere of the brain. Specific developmental dyslexia affects boys more often than girls and may be hereditary. The condition does not affect innate intelligence and has no associated visual or physical disability. In preschool children of normal intelligence, the disorder usually manifests itself in immature language and delayed reading readiness skills.

Attention Deficit Deficiency

Attention deficits are the most common sort of disability and are frequently associated with other types of learning disorders.

"At age three, my Jason has been kicked out of nursery school," complained Margie. "This boy has terrorized our household for three years. He opens the refrigerator and climbs in. He hits or kicks his playmates. I will do anything to help calm him down."

Fourteen-year-old Don said, "My head is like a television with no channel selector. All the programs zoom over the screen at the same time." Don's performance in school is confusing and inconsistent. He does well one day and poorly the next. He is overactive one day and lethargic the next. He is constantly in trouble in school because he is impulsive and does not think through the risks he takes.

Jason and Don are suffering from a disorder so complex and baffling that doctors have had a hard time diagnosing, treating, or even naming it. "Hyperactivity," "hyperkinetic syndrome," "minimal brain dysfunction," "minor cerebral dysfunction," and a few other names have described this condition. The latest term, Attention Deficit Disorder (ADD), is the standard diagnostic reference of the American Psychiatric Association.

ADD has no single cause and is classified as a syndrome because of a cluster of symptoms:

- excessive motor activity;
- short attention span;
- impulsive behavior;
- the condition is manifest before the age of seven and lasts at least six months;
- absence of mental illness or mental retardation.

An important development from the current research of Paul Wender, M.D., at the University of Utah School of Medicine, is his recognition that ADD continues into the adult years. The symptoms can be very disruptive, but researchers are finding that ADD in adults, called "Residual Type," is treatable.

Organizing-sequencing LD

The director of a learning center for LD students agreed to tutor twelve-year-old Dana. Dana's mother was given the times for all the summer sessions, but the mother would bring Dana in on the wrong day or at the wrong time. She showed up a day early for Dana's evaluation. The mother, an adult with a sequencing learning disability, confessed a lifelong struggle with schedules and keeping things straight. She cannot tell time unless she has a digital clock.

Many LD children and adults are poorly grounded in time and space. This disability can paralyze a person for a lifetime.

Memory LD

Another group of people have difficulty retrieving information from memory—not all information, but certain kinds, such as historical events or scientific names. The problem becomes more noticeable as the child advances to secondary school, when rapid recall skills are required.

A whole series of problems can interfere with the coordination of fine muscular movement of the hands and fingers, and thus with handwriting. Affected students cannot remember how to form letters quickly and easily enough. The student may be bright and have excellent ideas, but there is a complete breakdown as the material gets lost in the process of writing.

Jim landed a job as a salesman in an auto parts store. He interacted with the public well and knew the location of the many parts. His problem was running the cash register and pressing the buttons to make change. His eye-hand coordination problem eventually cost him his job.

Some LD people, like Jim,

have perceptual problems—trouble taking information in through the senses and processing the information to perform a motor task. Some perceptual problems are visual and some are auditory. Occasionally people will have both.

Although these descriptions may have labels, it is important to realize that no two people with learning disabilities are alike.

Search for the magic cure

A cure for the Learning Disabled: Soak a flannel cloth in castor oil and apply to abdomen under a warm heating pad four times a week. The procedure will lubricate the lymphatics and correct hyperactivity. "Ridiculous," you say. Yet a California school district used this treatment recently—at taxpayers' expense.

Professionals in many disciplines are seeking answers for LD problems. If research supports a particular approach, the reports and data will appear in professional journals. On the other hand, an author may have a rational-sounding point of view, yet it may be founded on little or no research data. Therefore, parents may hear of new ideas or treatments before the professionals do.

Larry Silver, of the National Institute of Dyslexia, Chevy Chase, Maryland, advises parents to seek full knowledge when they hear of a new treatment. Development and testing of acceptable approaches require interdisciplinary efforts, often over years.

Several approaches have been used for many years. Results of demonstration projects, research, and follow-up studies support them as preferred treatments.

Educators, constantly searching for the best techniques, prefer "special education," with educators who have particular training in the field. (See subsection *Teaching LD Students.*)

The use of psychostimulants, although controversial, is an accepted therapy, especially for symptoms of ADD. Drugs do not treat the learning disability itself but make the person responsive to learning. (See *The Ritalin Controversy* sidebar.)

Several approaches may be needed: individual therapy, behavior therapy, group therapy, or family therapy. However, unless the child or adolescent is in the appropriate educational program, the effects of the therapy will be overcome quickly.

Controversial therapies

Therapies are usually listed as controversial when the reported results cannot be replicated by other researchers.

• *Neurological retraining:* Advocates claim that part of the nervous system can be rerouted or retrained by stimulating certain sensory inputs or exercising motor patterns. Three popular approaches include patterning as developed by Doman and Delacato, optometric visual training, and vestibular dysfunction treatment as described in the work of Ayres, Frank, and Levinson. A fourth, applied kinesiology, is practiced by some chiropractors. One California flyer claimed an astounding reversal of all dyslexic and learning disabilities after one kinesiology treatment.

● *Orthomolecular medicine:* This field includes therapy with large doses of vitamins, trace elements, or special diets.

● *Megavitamins:* The first researcher to suggest megavitamin treatment for children with learning disabilities was Dr. Allan Cott. The American Academy of Pediatrics and other researchers found no support for the validity of the concept or the treatment.

● *Trace elements:* Copper, zinc, magnesium, manganese, and chromium, as well as calcium, sodium, and iron are necessary nutrients, and some say deficiencies cause LD, but no one has published data to that end.

• *Food Additives and Preservatives:* In his 1975 book *Why Your Child Is Hyperactive*, Dr. Benjamin Feingold proposed that synthetic flavors and colors were related to hyperactivity. But two extensive research reviews (Kavale and Forness, 1983, and Mattles, 1983) reached the same conclusion—that the Feingold diet is not effective in treating hyperactivity in most children.

• *Refined Sugar:* Claims that refined sugar causes hyperactivity are not supported by clinical research. Studies found no significant effect of sugars on any behavioral patterns.

Parents should be aware of accepted and controversial therapies and should seek a second or even a third opinion before embracing a treatment.

LD issues of the future

His mother did not agree with relatives and neighbors that her boy, born with a large head, was abnormal. The child was diagnosed as mentally ill by his teacher, so the mother taught him herself. Ironically, this boy lighted the way for us to see in our information age—his name was Thomas Alva Edison.

Many eminent figures of the past, including Winston Churchill, Charles Darwin, Nelson Rockefeller, George Patton, and Woodrow Wilson, are reputed to have had learning disabilities. Albert Einstein did not speak until the age of three and bemoaned his poor verbal memory.

Observing the accomplishments of people with disabilities can lead to a growing appreciation of the complex nature of learning. Professionals will continue to seek to unravel such sticky questions as: After we define LD, how do we identify LD students? What are the best methods of education? Do problems arise from labeling? What are the best methods to help the learning disabled throughout their developmental lifespan?

Even with a definition, recognizing the learning disabled remains ambiguous. The Education for All Handicapped Children Act stated that there must be a severe discrepancy between performance and intellectual ability.

The Ritalin Controversy

Yesterday, Aldo, a fourteen-year-old seventh-grader, bit into a plastic notebook during class and chewed vigorously. Then he climbed under the science table, waved his hands violently, and looked around, acting as if banging bells were erupting in his head.

Today, Aldo sits in his chair, like any other student, and participates in a discussion of the dinoflagellates. What made the difference? Ritalin—a treatment questioned by some and abhorred by others, but commonly prescribed by some medical professionals for hyperactivity, or Attention Deficit Disorder (ADD).

Ritalin, a brand name for methylphenidate, is one of the stimulant drugs. In 1937 a researcher first described the "calming effect" of the psychostimulant Benzedrine on hyperactive children. Since that time, extensive research has been done on the clinical effectiveness of these stimulants and their mechanism of action. At this time, three medications are available: methylphenidate (Ritalin), dextroamphetamine (Dexedrine), and permoline (Cylert). Imipramine (Tofranil) may also be used.

What? Use a stimulant to calm people down? That's a paradox! True, we do not understand how stimulant drugs decrease hyperkinetic activity. Don, the hyperactive teenager mentioned in the accompanying article, described his mind as an uncontrollable television set. The psychostimulants may help increase his general alertness and his ability to focus attention. With responses to interfering stimuli decreased, Don is more receptive to positive reinforcement from parents and teachers.

Some tranquilizers and antidepressants have been shown to be somewhat helpful for hyperactive behavior, but not as effective as stimulants. The side effects of the tranquilizers may be more severe than those of stimulants.

The number of children in the 1960s and 70s receiving Ritalin escalated as private and government-funded research projects expanded. In 1970, testimony before a house subcommittee estimated that 200,000 children received stimulant drugs for hyperactivity. However, with these reports came unanswered questions about the nature of the disorder and the effects of treatment.

Pills for peace?

"I think it's terrible to put kids on drugs like Ritalin and help them become junkies."

Moral, ethical, social, and philosophical questions about Ritalin and its cousins abide. Parents whose children have terrorized their households for years and have never fit into school systems are grasping for solutions.

Many of these parents read the popular press avidly, seeking answers. Many opposed to medications find respite in controlling the foods that their kids eat.

Dr. Kenneth Kavale reviewed 135 studies of stimulant medications and found that they have been reported to facilitate attention, increase academic processes with familiar material, assist behavior management, and aid memory on some laboratory tasks.

Analytic studies of children on stimulants found that they could be expected to gain the equivalent of 15 percentile ranks in achievement. Still, educators resist admitting the positive effects of medication on academic achievement.

Generally the objections center around Ritalin's side effects and long-term consequences. Stimulant drugs do produce some negative symptoms such as insomnia, appetite loss, headaches, irritability, or stomachaches. Also, to this date, they do not seem to cure long-term social and academic adjustment.

Another area of controversy is how long a child should be on medication. Most experts suggest drug-free periods, such as during summer vacations, during which the doctor can reassess medication or readjust dosages. Reports that stimulants stunt growth are not supported by research; but as a precaution, physicians usually monitor the child's height and weight twice a year.

University of Utah College of Medicine's Dr. Paul Wender has treated ADD in adults (called "Residual Type") with stimulants. They have responded to Tofranil or Cylert. Drugs such as Ritalin and Dexedrine are very effective, but have other problems related to their use, such as nervousness and indigestion.

At present, most studies support that, when administered properly, stimulant drugs such as Ritalin can produce favorable results in 70 to 80 percent of hyperactivity cases. However, the search for causes of hyperactivity and the best methods of treatment are being undertaken by scientists at research centers and on the National Institute of Health (NIH) campus in Bethesda, Maryland. Studies comparing the effects of standard medications, such as Ritalin, to new drugs are ongoing.

The Ritalin controversy underscores the fact that there are no easy solutions to dealing with the hyperactive child. The one thing all parties do agree with: They are not satisfied with the status quo. Until there are more answers, the controversy over Ritalin and other medications will continue.

—Evelyn B. Kelly

Specific diagnostic procedures or requirements are left up to the individual states.

That's where the problems arise! A study of procedures used in the states showed great variation. According to the U.S. Department of Education report of 1984, between the school years 1982–83, the number of LD children in New York increased by 68 percent, in South Dakota by 17 percent, and Mississippi 16.3 percent.

Special education placement is one of the most carefully articulated and closely regulated processes in the history of education. Four major policies must be included: due process safeguards, protection in the evaluation process (PEP), an individualized education program (IEP), and placement in the least restrictive environment (LRE).

This alphabet soup of terms and requirements has led to confusion. In one state, four out of five students evaluated were placed in special education.

The most prevalent means of teaching the LD student is called the pull-out model. The identified student is "pulled out" of regular classes on a full- or part-time basis to attend a special class or resource room. Few studies of people who have been in pull-out models for several years are available. No doubt, some students have a very positive experience, and others do not.

However, some experts think this model is harmful and unrealistic. Some innovative proposals are slowly creeping in and will be in more schools in the near future.

Alternatives:

- *Prereferral school team:* Regular and special education teachers work as a team to develop ways to teach the LD student within the class;
- *Cooperative learning:* This is an innovation foreign to our present patterns. Heterogenous groups of students work on a given task, learning together and receiving a joint reward (or grade);
- *Consulting teachers:* A trained teacher is assigned to a classroom to assess, provide materials, tutor, or plan case management for special students;
- *Alternative learning environment/renewal classrooms:* Called the Adapted Learning Environmental Model (ALEM), a full-time integration model for the mildly handicapped becomes part of the elementary classroom. Developed at the Learning Developmental Center in Pittsburgh, this program helps classes combine exploratory learning and individualized instruction. Over a hundred schools are using this program.
- *Effective schools movement:* The basic belief is that if certain excellent teaching techniques are used with all students, no unique strategies for LD are necessary.

The learning-disabled adult has taken the foreground in recent years. The ACLD has become the National Association for Children and Adults with Learning Disabilities. The LD adult was the LD adolescent, who was the LD child.

In a study of thirty-three LD adults by researchers Buchanan and West of the University of Utah, learning-disabled adults viewed themselves as nervous, disorganized, moody, and easily discouraged, as well as having self-image problems. The adults had little understanding of their learning disabilities, how their disabilities affect their lives, and how they can be helped.

How would you like to live in a world that is never right? A world where the words on a printed page just look like shapes or where television channels are constantly changing in your head? As public awareness of the LD experience expands, most of us can identify with someone —child or adult—who struggles with learning problems. Don't assume that these children and adults cannot be helped.

If you suspect that your child has a learning disability, begin by checking with your pediatrician for a complete physical. The Education for All Handicapped Children Act guarantees your child proper evaluation and, if eligible, help for a learning disability. School systems must provide assistance or pay tuition to private teaching facilities.

If you want to go to college and are experiencing difficulty, contact the counselor designated to help the handicapped on campus. You may want to consider some of the special programs, such as the LAUNCH International Learning Center based at East Texas Baptist University, Marshall, Texas. This program, designed by Dr. John R. Moss, is an exciting new educational opportunity for students with learning disabilities.

In 1981 the Rehabilitation Service Administration (RSA) accepted specific learning disabilities as a medically recognized disability. RSA will provide eligible LD adults with job training and help with employment. Contact your local department of vocational rehabilitation for information.

While the LD are missing some of the faculties necessary to function optimally, they don't require the special measures used to help the extremely abnormal person. Thus, acknowledgement and appropriate treatment for the LD are warranted, because of the frustration and embarassment they bear is no fault of their own.■

FROM MY PERSPECTIVE

The Learning Disabled Preschool Child

Samuel A. Kirk

Samuel A. Kirk *(CEC Chapter #195) is Professor of Special Education, University of Arizona, Tucson, and Professor Emeritus, University of Illinois, Urbana-Champaign.*

Many people believe that a learning disability is a problem faced only by school-age children and adults. They hesitate to label a preschool child as "learning disabled." Others, including myself, believe that the term is appropriate for preschool children as well as for school-age children and adults.

I have discussed this difference in concept with some of my colleagues who feel that we should not apply the term *learning disabled* to preschool children. They state that if a child has a language disorder we should call it "a language disorder." If a child is disoriented in space we should label the problem "a disorder in orientation." If a child has a visual perceptual problem we should label it as a "visual perceptual problem."

I do not see the logic in such arguments. At the school-age level we see children with reading disabilities, arithmetic disabilities, spelling disabilities, and other academic disabilities. We could label them as such, but during the last decade or so we have been using the umbrella term of *learning disability* to include all of these disabilities. Similarily, we can use the term *developmental learning disabilities* with regard to preschool children if they have a perceptual problem, an orientation problem, a language disorder, or other disabilities that are associated with development.

Learning disabilities consist of two broad categories, developmental learning disabilities and academic learning disabilities (Kirk & Chalfant, 1984; Kirk & Gallagher, 1986).

Developmental learning disabilities affect the prerequisite skills that a child needs to learn the academic subjects. Learning to write, for example, requires many motor skills, eye-hand coordination, memory sequencing, and so forth. Reading requires language abilities and visual and auditory perceptual skills. In general, developmental learning disabilities include deficits or disorders in attention, visual auditory perception, memory, thinking, and language. These disorders are identified at the preschool level. If not remediated at an early age, they will contribute, singly or in combination, to disabilities in learning the academic subjects later on. *Academic learning disabilities* include deficits in reading, writing, spelling, written expression, and calculation at the school-age level.

Two Case Studies

I became cognizant of learning disabilities in preschool children when I organized a program to study the effects of preschool education on the social and mental development of young mentally retarded children. In this experiment (Kirk, 1958), we organized a class in the community and a class in an institution and established contrast groups for the experimental groups. All of the children in the experiment were diagnosed as mentally retarded by pediatricians and psychologists. After working with these preschool mentally retarded children for a while, we discovered that many of them had abilities and disabilities instead of general mental retardation. A few examples may illustrate this point.

Sally was referred to our community preschool by a pediatrician at the age of 4 years 5 months. She had been diagnosed as mentally retarded as a result of rubella in the mother during the first trimester of pregnancy. She also had been diagnosed as blind by an ophthalmologist.

We admitted Sally into the experimental preschool and began to study her abilities and disabilities. At the time of this experiment, we did not have the wide number of tests we now have for preschool children and had to make our diagnosis informally. Our clinical judgment was that Sally's IQ of below 50, as reported by the clinic, was an underestimation of her verbal intelligence. In language ability, she was observed as functioning at a level higher than a mental age of 2. However, she had a severe visual handicap. In spite of the diagnosis of blindness, she did have some functional vision and a marked condition of nystagmus (a continuous and jerky movement of the eyes). In trying to determine how much usable vision this child had, we used informal methods and found that she could learn to identify pictures of common objects if given sufficient time. Because of her nystagmus, she could recognize a picture only after many movements of the eye. Our diagnosis of this child was that because of her nystagmus and slow response to pictures, she had a deficit in *speed of perception*, a term used by Thurstone in his tests of primary mental abilities.

To correct this deficit, we organized

a program to increase her ability in speed of perception. We began by flashing pictures of common objects on cards, teaching her the labels of the pictures, and then presenting them to her at a faster and faster speed. A little later we used a tachistoscope to allow her to respond at her own speed. The speed of presentation was then increased gradually. After 4 months of such training, Sally was responding to pictures on the tachistoscope in 1/25th of a second. This specific training in speed of perception on projected pictures tended to transfer to pictures in books. She now began to tell us what the pictures were all about and was able to describe the actions in them. When the ophthalmologist reexamined her, he was surprised to note that she could identify pictures even though both her visual acuity and her nystagmus remained the same. He told us that we must have trained her "central process."

Sally made rather rapid progress in the preschool and began to respond to visual objects in a way similar to her peers in spite of her nystagmus. When she was 6½ years old, the family moved to a military base in Georgia and enrolled her in the regular first grade. She learned to read and adjusted well in the regular class.

When she was 10 years old, we had the opportunity to reexamine her. Her IQ on the Stanford Binet Intelligence Scale was now close to 90, and on educational tests she scored at the third grade level in reading and arithmetic.

Sally was a child with a developmental learning disability, identified as a deficit in speed of perception resulting from a severe nystagmus. Early identification of the deficit led to remedial education designed to improve her speed of perception. Her case demonstrated that intensive early intervention can help ameliorate developmental learning disabilities resulting from neurological deficits.

Another child, Martha, in the same school was unable to talk when she was admitted to the preschool at age 5. She had been diagnosed as mentally retarded and aphasic. The psychological clinics reported that her IQ was 37. The audiologists stated that her hearing had a decibel loss of 70 on one examination and 30 on a later test. For Martha, we prepared a program of training that emphasized auditory discrimination, understanding language, and oral expression. By the age of 7 she had made great improvement in receptive and expressive language, entered school, and progressed at a rate close to that of her nonhandicapped peers. Her IQ when tested at age 7 was close to average.

Sally and her schoolmate are examples of children who had what we now call *developmental learning disabilities*. The remediation of the deficits of these two children, both of whom were diagnosed as mentally retarded, required intervention procedures that were totally different: one intensive visual training, the other intensive auditory training.

Identification

At the preschool-age level a developmental learning disability can be identified in children who have developed unevenly. A major indication of a developmental learning disability is a discrepancy among language abilities, cognitive abilities, and visual-motor performance areas. Figure 1 is an example of discrepancies in developmental abilities of two children of preschool age. This figure shows profiles of two preschool children enrolled in a class for trainable mentally retarded children. It should be noted that Harry has a relatively even profile ranging between ages 2 and 3 through 6, which represents a child whose ability level is substantially below his chronological age of 5. John, on the other hand, has wide discrepancies among abilities. He tested markedly below his chronological age of 4 on the auditory-vocal tests and substantially above his chronological age on visual-motor tests. Note that on auditory reception he tested at age 2 years 5 months, while on visual reception he tested at age 6, a discrepancy of 3½ years. The other tests showed similar discrepancies. This child is not mentally retarded, rather, he has a developmental learning disability in language.

The National Joint Committee on Learning Disabilities, on February 10, 1985, presented a position paper on *Learning Disabilities in the Preschool Child*. They stated that preschool children demonstrate specific developmental delays or deficit patterns that are early manifestations of learning disabilities. These include atypical patterns of development in communication, perceptual-motor abilities, cognitive abilities, and/or social and personal behaviors that adversely affect later academic learning.

The developmental learning disabilities in young children are attention, memory, perceptual and perceptual-motor, thinking, and language disorders. They are defined as follows:

- *Attention disorders* include hyperactivity, hypoactivity, fixation of attention, distractibility, and impulsivity.
- *Language disorders* include deficits in receptive, integrative, and expressive language as well as delays in development of adequate semantics, phonology, morphology, syntax, and pragmatics.
- *Memory disorders* include deficits in visual, auditory, and haptic memory, as well as short- and long-term memory.
- *Perceptual and perceptual-motor disorders* include deficits in auditory and visual figure-ground and haptic discrimination; visual and auditory closure; visual-motor integration; perceptual speed; visual, auditory, or haptic perceptual modality preferences; and perseveration.
- *Thinking disorders* include deficits in problem solving ability, concept formation, and other related cognitive functions.
- *Social perception disorders* are reflected in an inability to recognize the meaning of the behavior of others (body language, verbal communication, distance, clothing, make-up).

(For a more detailed discussion of these developmental learning disabilities, see Kirk & Chalfant, 1984.)

Remedial Intervention

Some of the many and diverse developmental disabilities found in young children are quite unique. Many of these aberrations in development are ascribed to genetics and neurological or biochemical abnormalities. A biological defect occurring at an early age may cause the child to withdraw or avoid activities that are uncomfortable and not rewarding, thus perpetuating

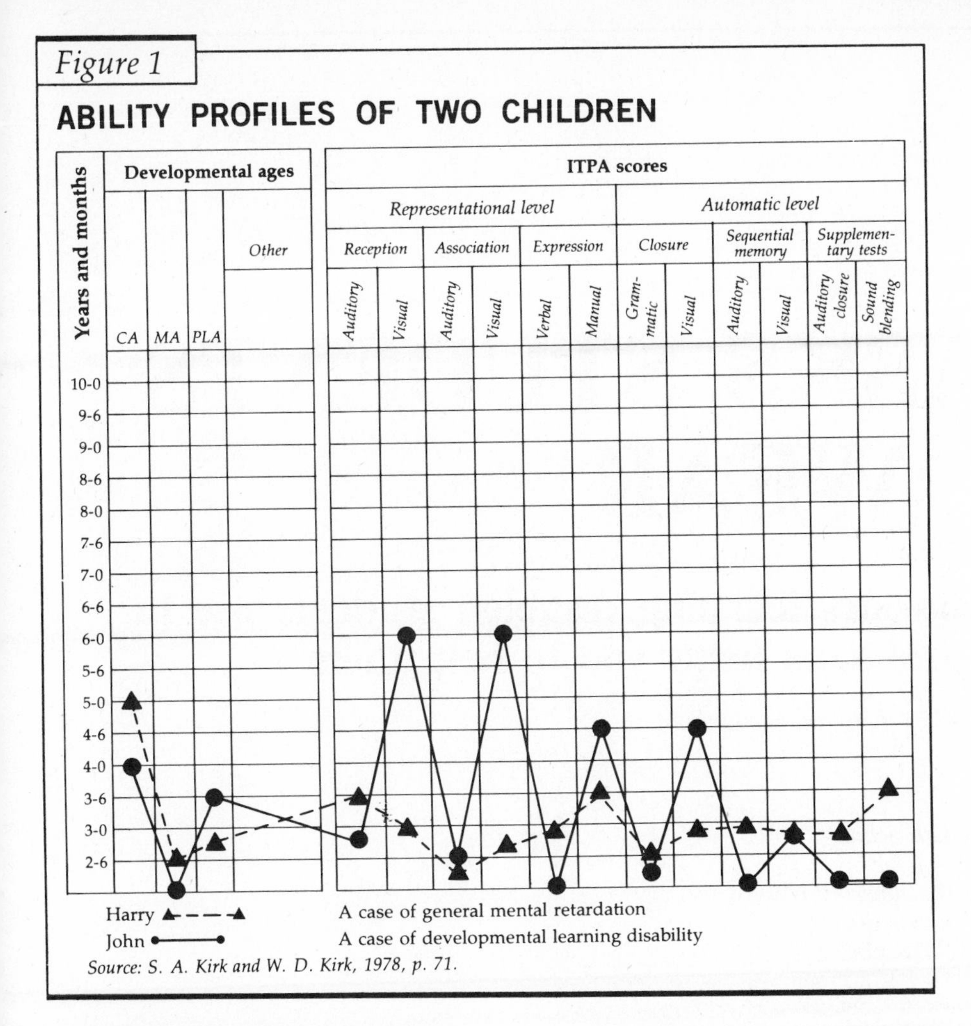

Figure 1

ABILITY PROFILES OF TWO CHILDREN

Source: S. A. Kirk and W. D. Kirk, 1978, p. 71.

the disability. A neurologically handicapped child with a visual-motor problem will tend to avoid tasks that require visual-motor activities. The child may compensate by verbalizing a great deal, giving excuses for why he or she cannot tie shoes or dress properly or play with certain toys. Parents also avoid asking the child to do things that the child resists. They show off things the child can do and avoid activities the child cannot perform. Thus, the child grows and the discrepancy between verbal abilities and visual motor abilities becomes wider.

Remediation at an early age does not alter the genes and probably does not regenerate brain cells. What it does is to fill in the functions from which the child has withdrawn. Sally, the child described earlier who had a speed of perception problem, avoided visual activities because her nystagmus made them uncomfortable, but she coped with her problems by using verbal abilities. Remediation by specific training filled in what could have been developed earlier if the parents had given her practice in speed of perception. The second child, who did not talk, was aggressive with her hands. Instead of telling a child to move away, she pushed the child away. When she was taught how to use language, her manual aggression toward other children markedly decreased. Thus, many developmental disabilities, although initially caused by a biological problem, are prolonged or exacerbated by the environment that allows the affected children to withdraw or avoid uncomfortable activities. Remedial intervention in these cases provides an alteration of the environment to give children practice in the areas previously avoided.

Both our experience with preschool children and results of the research that has been carried out with children who have developmental learning disabilities are very encouraging. The research demonstrates that if we start with children at a young age we can partially or totally overcome these disabilities by the time they enter school. By correcting and ameliorating these disabilities we can help prevent children from becoming learning disabled when they enter elementary school.

References

Kirk, S. A. (1958). *Early education of the mentally retarded.* Champaign, IL: University of Illinois Press.

Kirk, S. A., & Gallagher, J. J. (1986). *Educating exceptional children.* Boston: Houghton Mifflin.

Kirk, S. A., & Chalfant, J. C. (1984). *Academic and developmental learning disabilities.* Denver: Love Publishing.

Kirk, S. A., & Kirk, W. D. (1978). Uses and abuses of the ITPA. *Journal of Speech and Hearing, 43,* 58-75.

National Joint Committee on Learning Disabilities. (1985). *Learning Disabilities and the Preschool Child: A Position Paper of the National Joint Committee on Learning Disabilities.* Baltimore, MD: Orton Dyslexia Society. (ERIC Document Reproduction Service No. ED 260 544)

THE MASKS STUDENTS WEAR

Recognizing the behaviors learning disabled students use to hide their problems helps you to help them

Sally L. Smith

Sally L. Smith is the founder/director of The Lab School of Washington, a full professor and director of the graduate program in learning disabilities at The American University in Washington, D.C. and the author of the book, No Easy Answers: The Learning Disabled Child at Home and at School.

Learning disabled adults are telling educators what learning disabled children can't. What we learn from these adults can improve the teaching of children and the training of teachers.

There are many types of learning disabilities including auditory, vision and language disabilities. And students can have combinations of different learning disabilities.

One of the most important messages learning disabled adults are giving is that the greatest challenge learning disabled children face is the battle for self-esteem. These adults say they felt stupid and were treated in school as though they were. They felt defeated, worthless and "dumb." Over the years, these adults learned to mask their hurts.

"I learned to act a certain way so I couldn't be teased. I would appear bored, tired, eager to be of help, all-knowing or funny, depending upon what was going on. In other words, I would do anything but let them know I couldn't read the material," confesses one learning disabled adult.

"I faked my way all through school," says another. "I had the gift of gab and an excellent memory."

Unfortunately, many dyslexic and learning disabled adults started to develop masks in first or second grade when they could not read what others could. Few ever received special education. They were not identified as learning disabled or dyslexic. Instead, their teachers often labeled them "lazy," "willful," "poorly disciplined" and "spoiled" when actually they were trying their hardest.

These students were called "retarded" if they had any speech and language problems and "disturbed" if they were hyperactive, impulsive or had any of the behavioral manifestations of a learning disabled child. Often these children were gifted, above average in intelligence, and unable to bear their inability to accomplish the simplest academic task.

Think of the energy many learning disabled students spend hiding their disabilities and masking the feeling of being stupid. The masks are an elaborate subterfuge that make students feel worse about themselves. The masks protect the students from being thought of as "stupid," but isolate them from others. Often the masks interfere with students' ability to learn.

Recognizing the masks learning disabled students sometimes wear to hide their inabilities will help you take action to have the problem treated. Masking behavior comes in many variations. The following types are among the most common masks students wear.

The mask of super competence

"Easy!" "Oh, sure! Everyone knows that!"

With a great deal of bravado, this student tries to make everything look simple. He knows he can talk his way

Characteristics of a learning disabled child

- Looks typical but doesn't learn typically.
- Is intelligent, often gifted.
- Has reading, spelling, writing and/or math achievements that are significantly below child's capability level.
- Has a short attention span.
- Is easily distracted.
- Has poor listening skills.
- Has trouble following directions.
- Doesn't seem to be trying, acts lazy or is defiant.
- Sometimes uses immature speech and language.
- Confuses left and right.
- Sometimes uses immature movements, is awkward, clumsy. Shows poor motor coordination (i.e., reaches one hand out and the other hand follows).
- Exhibits immature behavior.
- Displays general disorganization, poor organization of time and space.
- Often has difficulty with tasks employing paper and pencil.
- Produces many reversals (i.e., "b" instead of "d") and rotations (i.e., "b" instead of "q") in written work.
- Is inconsistent in behavior and work.
- Frequently displays exceptional ability in the arts, sports, science and verbalization.

Steps you can take if you suspect a student is learning disabled

1. List the child's personal and academic strengths and areas of weakness. Back up the list with anecdotal records after a week of careful observation and listening.
2. Check student's recent eye and hearing test records as well as general physical health records to rule out physical problems.
3. Confer with parents to discuss the list; ask them if they see similar strengths and weaknesses at home.
4. Recommend an evaluation by a school psychologist. In some schools, initial referral is to the pupil personnel worker; in others it is to the interdisciplinary team or principal.
5. Inform parents about Public Law 94–142, the *Education for All Handicapped Children Act*. Specify parents' rights to have their child evaluated, and if not satisfied with the evaluation results to seek a second evaluation.

If a child is diagnosed as being learning disabled, the child is entitled by law to appropriate services. These range from support in the classroom to resource assistance to placement in self-contained classrooms. These services may or may not include speech and language therapy, occupational therapy and adaptive physical education.

Resources

Organizations

Association for Children with Learning Disabilities (ACLD)
This grassroots organization serves parents, teachers and other professionals. It provides needed support and information to help follow the latest educational and medical research and supports legislation for special education classes and teachers in the field. To find the organization nearest you, write the National ACLD, 4156 Library Road, Pittsburgh, PA 15234, or call (412) 341-1515.

Council for Exceptional Children (CEC)
This organization for professionals publishes books, media, journals, periodicals and research findings. Low-cost informational flyers are available. For a catalog or more information, write to CEC, 1920 Association Drive, Reston, VA 22091, or call (703) 620-3660.

Foundation for Children with Learning Disabilities (FCLD)
This organization for parents and professionals is a source of information for publications concerning the learning disabled child. It also provides grants. For more information, write to FCLD, 99 Park Ave., New York, NY 10016, or call (212) 687-7211.

The Orton Society
This organization for professionals is also open to parents. It studies preventive measures and treatment for children with specific language disabilities, sponsors research, and shares its findings. For more information, write to The Orton Society, 724 York Road, Baltimore, MD 21204, or call (301) 296-0232.

Books

Smith, Sally L. *No Easy Answers: The Learning Disabled Child at Home and at School*, Bantam Books, New York, 1981.

Stevens, Suzanne. *Classroom Success for the Learning Disabled*, John Blair Publisher, 1984.

through anything. His logic is impeccable. He's good with people, numbers, problem solving and trouble shooting.

Gen. George S. Patton, a dyslexic, assured his daughter that Napoleon couldn't spell, either, and quoted Jefferson Davis as saying, "A man must have a pretty poor mind not to be able to think of several ways to spell a word."

The mask of helplessness

"I don't know." "I don't understand." "I can't do anything."

Through pity, this person gets everyone around to help her do her work and assume responsibilities so she never fails. She refuses to risk failure, but feels even worse because she knows she didn't do any of the work.

The mask of invisibility

"I would hide in my shell, hold my neck in like a turtle, almost pleading with the teacher not to call upon me."

By looking frightened, whispering to teachers and acting terrified with peers, this person gets everyone else to do his work for him.

The student realizes he can get through school by not talking, just repeating when necessary, taking a low profile, and making no waves. With his head down and sitting quietly for a long time, nobody bothers him. He has the talent of melting into the crowd. Teachers and supervisors later realize they never got to know this student or acknowledge he was there.

The mask of the clown

"Isn't that a riot!" "Ha, ha, ha." "What a joke!"

Everything is funny when this student is around. Laughter, however, hides the real issue—a learning disability.

Cher, the Academy Award-winning actress/singer, admits she was the "class clown" to divert attention from her inability to read, write or do arithmetic in school. Despite her problems, she was exceedingly verbal and outstanding in the arts. A teacher proclaimed that she was not working hard enough. Feeling stupid, she dropped out of school at 16 and wasn't tested for learning disabilities until after she was 30.

The mask of the victim

"It's not fair." "Everyone picks on me." "There's no justice anywhere."

Injustice is a basic theme with this person. Often called a "jailhouse lawyer" because he has an argument for everything, this student feels victimized and takes on a "poor me" attitude. He assumes no responsibility for anything. He angers others around him.

The mask of not caring

"I don't care." "Nothing matters." With this mask, the student is never vulnerable, and risks no failure. If she tries to succeed and fails, she says she never tried and it doesn't matter. The mask is a way of keeping others at a distance, making her feel woefully inadequate. If nothing matters, it's very difficult to change or motivate this person.

The mask of boredom

"This is boring!" *Yawn.* "What time is it now?" *Yawn.*

With big yawns, loud sighs, tapping fingers and toes, this person lets the teacher know how bored he is. This behavior puts the teacher on the defensive. Usually this person is not bored, but frustrated, and can't do what he's been asked to do.

Thomas Edison was kicked out of schools for not following instructions. He probably did not understand the instructions due to his auditory problems. Severe learning disabilities prevented him from being able to write what he was told.

The mask of activity

"Gotta run." "Sorry, I'm in a hurry, I can't talk." "I'm busy now, I'll do whatever you want later."

This student is always on the move. Standing still may bring her close to others, and she precludes any intimacy. Constant activity wards away others and keeps her from having to perform.

The mask of outrageousness

"I'm way out." "I don't like being a conformist." "I believe in individualism to the extreme." Through wild clothing, hair style and color, wigs, extraordinary glasses, stockings, boots, and so on, this student projects eccentricity and hides his problems.

Robert Rauschenberg, a famous artist who had extreme difficulty with math and spelling, did outrageous, unheard of things in school and in his career. Many artists feel he expanded the definition of art for a generation of Americans by daring to innovate.

The mask of the Good Samaritan

"Let me help you." "What can I do for you?"

This student wants to please at any cost. Frequently, she is too nice and too accommodating. She will echo what you say, work longer hours than necessary and be overly helpful to get out of doing what she can't do.

The mask of contempt

"They don't know how to teach." "This whole place sucks."

Negativity encompasses this mask. This joyless student has a negative word for everything. If it's sunny out, it could be sunnier. He wears out the people around him because nothing is ever good enough. He takes no pleasure in small successes. He's angry at the world for making him feel stupid and believes the world owes him something. He puts everyone around him on the defensive.

The mask of the strong silent type

"I'm Joe Cool." "Nobody comes too close to me, but they follow me everywhere." "Get out of my face. Nobody moves on me." "Every sport is for me. I live for sports."

Personified by a sleek body and prowess in sports, this student is revered by many and endowed, in her own mind, with every fine feature.

Bruce Jenner, Olympic decathlon champion who is dyslexic, says sports gave him his self-esteem. Jenner says reading aloud in the classroom was much harder and more frightening for him than competing in the decathlon.

The mask of perfection

"If they don't recognize my talents, that's their problem." "Good artists don't have to read really well, anyhow."

Proclaiming loudly that there are machines to spell and write, secretaries to take dictation and lawyers to read for him, this student presents himself as perfection. He tolerates no mistakes in himself or others. He often carries an impressive book or magazine he can't read and saunters into a room looking completely pleased with life. He makes everyone around him miserable.

The mask of illness, frail health and vulnerability

"My head." "My stomach." "My side." "My bladder." "My migraine."

To receive extra attention and get out of the work she can't do, this student calls in sick, leaves sick, constantly pretends to be sick and talks about her frailties.

Given something to read, she uses her illnesses and frailties as an excuse or cries if necessary. Expecting special attention, special privileges, while avoiding what she can't do, this student confuses everyone around her and usually gets by with this behavior.

The mask of seduction

"Hey, woman, write this down for me. Men don't write." The "macho man" often gets a female to do for him what he can't do. He hides behind his macho mask, making himself appear sexy.

"Math is men's work, girls can't do it." The "helpless female" asks a "macho man" to do what she can't do and hides behind her female mask to make it appear sexy.

The mask of being bad

"Don't mess with me. You'll be sorry." "I threw the book at him, so what?" "I'd rather be thought of as bad than dumb."

Losers at school often become winners on the street. This student feels stupid, powerless and useless at school and often directs his frustration and anger towards his teachers. His peers enjoy his bad behavior and encourage more of it.

Billionaire Dallas real estate manager Rick Strauss changed schools several times, always suffering the humiliation of not learning to read or write due to his severe dyslexia. He compounded his problems by cutting up. Doing so diverted his teachers' attention away from his poor work. It wasn't until he was a high school senior that he learned that his inability to read and write resulted from his learning disabilities.

The mask of fantasy

"I'm going to be a millionaire by the time I'm 30!" "The world will understand me soon." "I'll have a Ph.D. once I learn to read."

Characterized by a fertile imagination and a great deal of creativity, this student tends to live more in her hopes and fantasies than in reality, which is filled with daily frustrations.

Hans Christian Andersen didn't learn to read and write, even with the help of 10 royal tutors of the Danish Court. He dictated his wonderful fairy tales to a scribe. His mask of fantasy protected him from the pain of facing reality, even though glimpses of his suffering appear in some of his stories, such as "The Ugly Duckling."

Removing the masks

The masks can be removed when students reach a certain comfort level. This usually happens when a student realizes he is not stupid, but suffers from a learning disability. The student experiences enormous relief when he discovers why he has been having difficulties learning.

What learning disabled adults have to say about the masks they wore in school alerts educators to the need to reach children in their early years, identify those children who have trouble learning before they begin to wear the masks, and teach them in ways that will help them succeed.

Teaching Organizational Skills to Students with Learning Disabilities

John M. Shields
Timothy E. Heron

John M. Shields *(CEC Chapter #652) is a doctoral student, The California School of Professional Psychology, Berkeley-Alameda.* **Timothy E. Heron** *(CEC Chapter #652) is Professor, Department of Educational Services and Research, Ohio State University, Columbus.*

The competence of students with learning disabilities to understand, manipulate, make decisions about, and complete assigned tasks successfully is not related solely to their academic skill. It also depends on their proficiency to *organize* content, material, and time in a meaningful way.

Alley and Deshler (1979) have described some of the problems that students with learning disabilities have in organizing their materials as follows:

- Difficulty perceiving organization in a set of materials such as notes, texts, and assignments.
- Lack of appreciation of the importance of organizing information.
- Failure to realize that information or materials can be rearranged to produce organized structure.
- Trouble dealing with an isolated task in an organized fashion.
- Trouble dealing with multiple tasks (such as assignments) in an organized fashion.

According to Heron and Harris (1987), students with learning disabilities generally have not mastered a strategy for allocating time among tasks or designating enough time to complete tasks. Specifically, a student may "forget" homework assignments, claim a lack of time to obtain them from the teacher, or remember only at the last minute that four chapters must be reviewed for a test the next day.

This article describes several strategies that can be used to improve the organizational and time management skills of students with learning disabilities. They are divided into two categories: antecedent strategies, which set the occasion for the students with learning disabilities to become more organized, and consequence strategies, which reinforce demonstrated organizational skill.

Antecedent Strategies

The five antecedent strategies that follow—assignment logs and charts, work stations, color coding materials, timers, and guided notes—have been shown to be useful for improving organizational skills either by themselves or in combination (Heron, 1987).

Logs and Charts

Providing students with a visual representation of the content that must be learned, the tasks that need to be accomplished, or the time frame within which the tasks must be accomplished is a central component of the log and

Figure 1

PERT NETWORK FOR DELIVERING A SPEECH

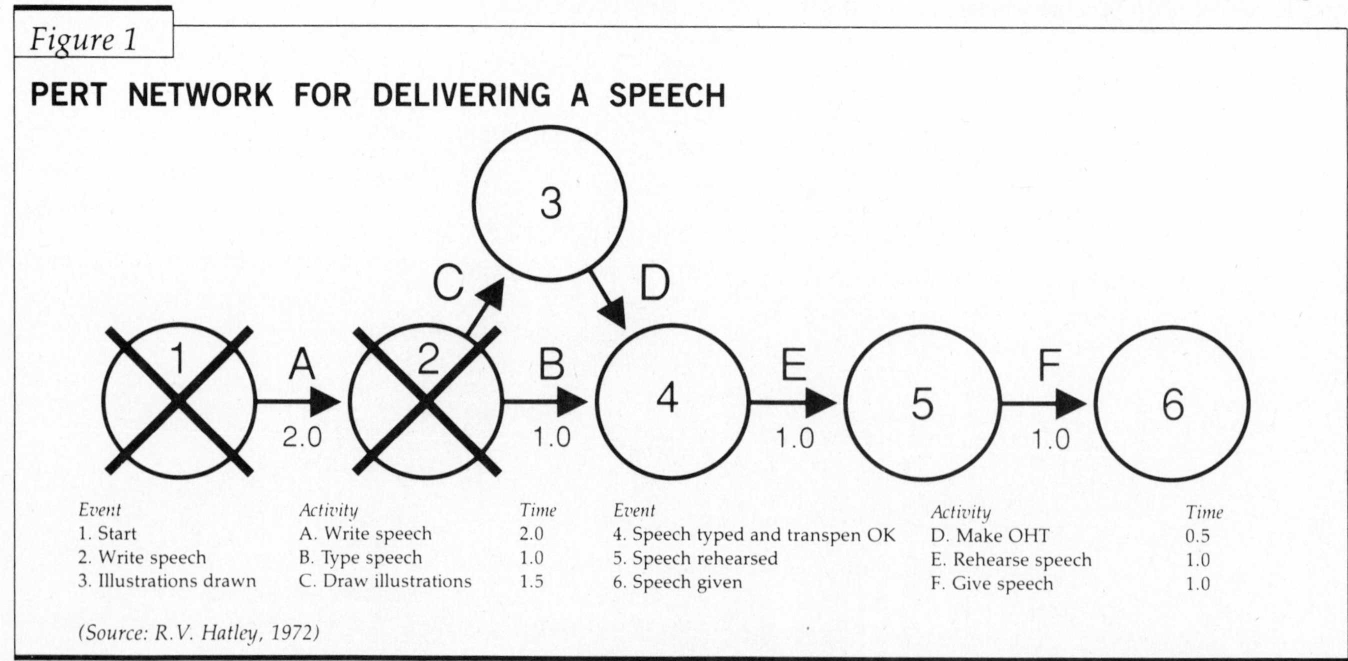

Event	Activity	Time	Event	Activity	Time
1. Start	A. Write speech	2.0	4. Speech typed and transpen OK	D. Make OHT	0.5
2. Write speech	B. Type speech	1.0	5. Speech rehearsed	E. Rehearse speech	1.0
3. Illustrations drawn	C. Draw illustrations	1.5	6. Speech given	F. Give speech	1.0

(Source: R.V. Hatley, 1972)

chart format. These systems also provide a built-in way for teachers, students, and parents to recognize when a particular step in a sequence of assignments has been completed. Logs allow students to monitor performance and record progress in completing homework assignments.

Assignment log. An assignment log allows students to keep assignments arranged with the necessary papers and instructions in one place. The log is made out of a standard two-pocket folder with built-in brads in the center for securing notebook paper. Each log contains an assignment sheet on which the following categories have been written across the top: date; assignment; due; homework; parent; turned in. Vertical lines are drawn between categories to form a matrix for recording the information.

Upon receiving an assignment, the student fills in the next available line on the assignment sheet, listing the date the assignment was given, the book and page number of the assignment (or in the case of worksheets, the title of the worksheet), and the due date of the assignment. In the front of the log there should be a "To Be Completed" pocket. Papers to be completed are placed in this front pocket of the folder. At the end of the class session, the teacher or an assigned peer inspects the assignment log notebook, making sure that all assignments are listed accurately, all papers are in the "To Be Completed" pocket, and all books needed for homework assignments have been marked with stick-ons. The inspector then initials the homework column.

The back pocket of the folder is labeled "Completed Work." After finishing an assignment at home, the student must show it to a parent for review. If the work is satisfactory, the parent initials the assignment sheet. The completed assignment is then placed into the back pocket, where it remains until the teacher initials it as well at the next class meeting.

PERT charts. PERT charts are helpful for students with learning disabilities insofar as they provide the overall scope and sequence for projects and serve as a practical means for students to gauge the amount of time needed for each task (Hatley, 1972). Figure 1 shows a PERT chart for delivering a speech. The chart contains six behaviors or events with their associated activities and time estimates. The arrows show the direction that should be followed to complete the project. (Note: PERT charts are not always linear; they can be designed to show associated tasks necessary to complete the overall project.)

Once a given step in the process has been completed, an X can be written at that point. Each X might produce an interim reinforcer, sustaining the effort of the student until all of the steps have been completed.

The Uncalendar. The Uncalendar (People Systems, 1977) is a management tool that allows students to see how their time is spent on a daily and/or weekly basis. For instance, the Uncalendar can show school tasks to be completed as well as jobs to be performed inside or outside the home (see Figure 2). A "Comments" section allows students to note any special assistance that might be needed. Initially, students with learning disabilities would likely need the help of teachers and parents to plan the calendar, along with encouragement and support for completing the jobs shown.

Work Stations

A work station is an area set aside in the classroom that is specifically designed to set the occasion for responding. A work station can be any of the following:

- A desk that can be partitioned from potentially distracting stimuli.
- A table.
- A carrel or study booth (Haubrich & Shores, 1976; Hewett & Taylor, 1980).
- Undesignated floor space.

When a student comes to the work station, only academic responding is expected to occur. As such, the work station signals academic engagement to the student.

Similarly, at home, parents should try to arrange as quiet a location as possible for homework completion. All of the materials necessary for the tasks should be on hand, eliminating the need for excessive meanderings to get organized.

Color Coding

Color coding can be used for two purposes. First, it can alert the student to the assignments that should be completed initially in a sequence. For example, "red" assignments might signal tasks that have an immediate deadline, whereas "green" assignments might not be due for a week.

Second, the color code might signal to the student which assignments are to be completed independently and which are to be completed only after discussion with the teacher. Attending a resource room program and using color codes can help students with learning disabilities organize their folders or worksheets, and set the occasion for them to complete assignments systematically.

Timers

A kitchen timer used to signal the beginning and end of each activity segment can be an excellent tool for helping students manage time. According to Alley and Deshler (1979), this technique also ensures that the students apply themselves to their maximum ability, thereby increasing productivity. By applying rate measures to student tasks regularly, parents and teachers can determine proficiency with organizational skill development.

Guided Notes

Guided notes are a type of advanced organizer that provide the means for organizing new material. Specifically, they are a note-taking strategy in which the teacher provides the student with a structured outline of a class lecture or topic. As the teacher presents the material, the student follows along with the outline, filling in missing words or documenting important points. According to Kline (1986), guided notes aid in retention, can be used repeatedly across a variety of subject areas, serve to signal the main points of the chapter or topic to the student, and can increase the student's opportunities to respond.

An example of guided notes for a lecture on air pollution might contain the following:

- A list of key terms such as *air pollution, acid rain, toxic, carbon dioxide, greenhouse effects,* and *heavy industry.*
- Two short paragraphs that define the terms and summarize the major concepts.

- Several comprehension questions such as the following that the student is asked to answer after reading the notes: "Define air pollution." "What is acid rain and how is it harmful to trees?" "Name two effects of air pollution." "Name one phenomenon that might happen if the earth's atmosphere warmed up too much."

Consequence Strategies

Reinforcement

Organizational skills can be acquired through example, practice, and reinforcement. Schedules of reinforcement are needed to increase the likelihood that organizational skills will be demonstrated. These can vary from student to student, but in all cases they must be implemented consistently so that organized behaviors can be maintained and generalized to other settings.

Cooper, Heron, and Heward (1987) have outlined a number of reinforcement schedules and programs that can be used at the elementary and secondary levels to facilitate the development of organizational skills in students. A continuous schedule of reinforcement is best used to strengthen behavior during the *initial* stages of acquisition. For example, when a student's materials are placed properly in the assignment log notebook or in the correct color-coded folder, or when a PERT chart is developed properly, the student can be issued a reinforcer (e.g., posting the student's name on the bulletin board). Such programs are most effective when students identify their own reinforcers and are confident that they are supported by the teacher.

Once students have demonstrated the desired organizational skills, an intermittent schedule of reinforcement can be used to maintain the desired behavior. Eventually the schedule can be modified so that many more instances of a demonstrated organizational skill are required for reinforcement. It helps if students are informed through written rules, directions, and signs what must be accomplished to receive reinforcement.

Feedback

Performance feedback is specific information provided to a student subsequent to a reponse that provides specific data on the response. Feedback can be oral, or written, and it can serve either as a reinforcer for a previous response or as a discriminative stimulus to prompt or cue a response (Van Houten, 1980). To increase student performance, feedback should be precise, specific, and positive. Not only will such feedback give students information about how they are performing, but also it can encourage them to improve their performance.

One powerful technique that can motivate students and maximize the effect of performance feedback is public posting. This means that a student's work record is displayed in clear view so that other students and classroom visitors have access to it (Van Houten, 1980).

An example of a publicly posted feedback on a chart can relate to organizational skill development. Here, public posting can be used for the number of assignments turned in on time, the number of times in a day that students had their materials arranged correctly on their workspace, and the number of consecutive days that all homework assignments were submitted on time. To reinforce the use of the assignment logs described earlier, posting can include the number of days that students remembered to obtain their parents' signatures or had all of their completed assignments in the proper pockets of their folders when they entered the classroom. Finally, feedback charts can be adapted to show each student's best score for the day or week, maximizing the quality and quantity of information the student receives relative to performance.

Home-School Communication

Home-school communication includes a broad range of oral or written messages between parents and teachers for the purpose of exchanging information and providing training to the parents (Heron & Harris, 1987). Communication of this nature has been used to increase parents' knowledge of school-related activities or as a method of developing home-based instruction (Heron & Heward, 1982, Weiss et al., 1982). Communication between teachers and parents can also be used to help students develop organizational skills, with the parents acting as agents of the school to provide students with feedback about their organizational skills.

Teachers can prepare short tapes for parents to hear on a telephone answering machine that describe homework assignments to be completed. Parents can be given recording forms to initial after they have reviewed daily assignments with their children, and

Figure 2

TIME MANAGEMENT CALENDAR, THE UNCALENDAR

WHAT NEEDS TO BE DONE THIS WEEK?

SCHOOL TASK	DUE	TIME TO DO IT
Bookreport	Friday	6 hrs.
Math Homework	Monday + Wednesday	2 hrs.
Social Studies	Tuesday + Thursday	2 hrs.

HOME

TASK	Due	Time
Clean Car	Sat.	1 hr.

WORK

TASK	TIME
McDonald's	4-8 M-F

WEEK-END	MONDAY DATE	TUESDAY DATE	WEDNESDAY DATE	THURSDAY DATE	FRIDAY DATE
SCHEDULE:	SCHEDULE:	SCHEDULE:	SCHEDULE:	SCHEDULE:	SCHEDULE:
	7-8am bus ride (Home work) 8-3pm School 4-8pm Work 8:30-10:00 Homework	→	→	→	→
Tasks: Time:	Tasks: Time:	Tasks: Time:	Tasks: Time:	Tasks: Time:	Tasks: Time:
Book Report 2 hrs.	Math 1 hr. Book Report (w/Patty) 1 hr.	Soc. St. 1 hr. Book Report 1 hr.	Math 1 hr. Book Report (w/patty) 1 hr.	Soc. St. 1 hr. Book Report 1 hr.	Clean Car 1 hr.
Comments:	Comments:	Comments:	Comments:	Comments:	Comments:
Need help outlining Book Report - See Patty		Have Patty proofread bookreport			

(From: People Systems, 1977)

teachers can follow up with periodic phone calls to reinforce and encourage parent participation.

Another possibility for establishing communication outside the classroom is to use a "buddy system," which promotes communication among peers. After obtaining parental consent, each student is given the telephone number of a classroom peer. Each night at a designated time, peers make phone calls to their chosen "buddies" to ensure that their assignment logs are accurate and that the assignments have been completed, checked by parents, and placed in the proper pocket for the following day.

Self-Management Programs

Cooper and his colleagues (1987) define self-management as the personal and systematic application of behavior change strategies that results in the desired modification of one's own behavior. Self-management programs used in the classroom can help students to develop independent, self-directed skills without the supervision of others.

To develop self-management ability, students must learn a series of skills including self-selection and definition of the target behavior; self-observation and recording of the target behavior; specification of behavior-change procedures; implementation of those procedures; and evaluation of the self-management program (Heward, 1979). If students can master self-management skills as a way to organize content, material, or time, they will have an effective means for dealing with situations in which there is little, if any, external control.

The assignment log notebook lends itself to use in a self-management system as well as a teacher- and parent-monitored system. In a self-management program, the columns for the teacher's and parent's initials can be replaced with a student initial column. Here the student monitors personal behavior by making certain that materials are organized in a way that ensures that all assignments will be completed and turned in on time.

Other examples of self-management include students' using library stamps with changeable dates to stamp due-dates on their papers, or placing small paper "stick-ons" on the bindings of books that need to be taken home. Stick-ons also can have assignments written directly on them. Students can place charts and graphs in the backs of their assignment logs to record the number of days on which the program is used efficiently. Completed charts that meet a criterion designated by the student and the teacher can then be submitted for a mutually agreed upon reinforcer.

To maximize the effectiveness of self-monitoring and to ensure generality of behavior change, the program should be implemented in more than one setting. Middle schools or high schools provide opportunities for generalization in that students are likely to attend more than one classroom with more than one teacher. If the program is implemented consistently across all classrooms, not only it is likely that organizational skills will develop more quickly, but also more efficiently.

References

Alley, G., & Deshler, D. (1979). *Teaching the learning disabled adolescent: Strategies and methods*. Denver: Love Publishing.

Cooper, J. O., Heron, T. E., & Heward, W. L. (1987). *Applied behavior analysis*. Columbus, OH: Merrill.

Hatley, R. V. (1972, August). *Flowcharting, program evaluation and review technique, and critical path method*. Paper presented at the Educational Research and Development Training Program, University of Kansas, Lawrence.

Haubrich, P. A., & Shores, R. (1976). Attending behavior and academic performance of emotionally disturbed children. *Exceptional Children, 42*, 337-339.

Heron, T. E. (1987, March). *Developing organizational skills for LD students with attention deficit disorder*. Paper presented to the Ohio Council for Learning Disabilities Mid-Winter Conference, Columbus.

Heron, T. E., & Harris, K. C. (1987). *The educational consultant: Helping professionals, parents, and mainstreamed students* (2nd ed.). Austin, TX: PRO ED.

Heron, T. E., & Heward, W. L. (1982). Ecological assessment: Implications for teachers of LD students. *Learning Disability Quarterly, 5*, 117-125.

Heward, W. L. (1979). Teaching students to control their own behavior. *Exceptional Teacher, 1*, 3-5, 11.

Hewett, F. M., & Taylor, F. D. (1980). *The emotionally disturbed child in the classroom: The orchestration of success*. Boston: Allyn & Bacon.

Kline, C. S. (1986). *Effect of guided notes on academic achievement of learning disabled high school students*. Unpublished master's thesis: The Ohio State University, Columbus.

People Systems, Inc. (1977). *The uncalendar*. Scotsdale, AZ: Author.

Van Houten, R. (1980). *Learning through feedback: A systematic approach for improving academic performance*. New York: Human Sciences Press.

Weiss, A. B., Cooke, N. L., Grossman, M. A., Ryno-Vrabel, M., Hassett, M. E., Heward, W. L., & Heron, T. E. (1982). *Home-school communication*. Columbus, OH: Special Press.

Nine Ways to Cope with Varying Abilities

Helping Disabled Readers in the Regular Classroom

Michael P. Ford
and Marilyn M. Ohlhausen

Michael P. Ford is Assistant Professor, Reading Education, University of Wisconsin-Oshkosh. Marilyn M. Ohlhausen is Assistant Professor, University of Nevada-Las Vegas.

From *The Reading Teacher*

IT'S no wonder teachers are skeptical of recommendations from clinical personnel who have worked one-on-one or in small groups with reading-disabled children now placed in their classrooms. Many of the techniques and methods are clearly not as workable in the regular classroom as in a clinic.

As staff members of a university summer reading program, our setting is quite different from the regular classroom. The program provides instruction that involves participating in a reading classroom with other disabled readers for three hours every morning and attending a tutoring session with a clinician every afternoon. After the program, we make recommendations to help the children as they return to their regular classrooms. Each report suggests techniques that were successful during the summer. Many are especially appropriate for the child's resource room or remedial reading teacher, whose programs are similar to the clinic. It is not as easy to make recommendations for the regular classroom teacher, but we'd like to share nine that teachers have found helpful.

1. **Focus on real, meaningful learning through the use of themes, without regard for reading-ability and age differences.** With a theme approach, a range of reading/writing activities may be incorporated, even when reading ability and ages differ drastically. It seems perfectly normal for one child to be an expert in a certain area while another may know more about a different topic.

Our clinic has focused on themes like the Olympics, magic, the Statue of Liberty, and mysteries. With the mystery theme, students wrote and performed mystery plays, and met and interviewed a mystery writer to learn how mystery books are written. A visit to the police station to discover how real detectives solve crimes became the basis for language-experience stories. By focusing on a theme, teachers can incorporate many activities for which all readers can make a significant contribution.

2. **Maximize participation of disabled readers by using whole-language activities which capitalize on oral skills.** Students in special reading programs often demonstrate strong oral skills. Classroom activities which allow them to utilize this strength help to minimize differences that separate them from other students. Whole-language activities may be among the best for this goal.

Brainstorming was a technique that we used frequently. When the mystery theme was introduced, teachers asked the group to think about everything they knew about mysteries. As the class contributed ideas orally, teachers transcribed their ideas on a large semantic map. All students were able to participate because the contributions were primarily expressed orally and transcribed by the teacher. Results from the brainstorming were on display all summer. Students could refer to

From *The Education Digest*, January 1989, pp. 48-51. Condensed from *The Reading Teacher*, October 1988, pp. 18-22.

the chart to assist them in comprehending and composing text in the following weeks.

In a regular classroom, similar techniques could be used to involve disabled readers in content-area learning. This would help to make text that is normally inaccessible to them readily available for a variety of content-related activities.

3. **Implement whole-room activities which have built-in individualization.** Two of the best activities that are inherently individualized are sustained silent reading (SSR) and journal writing. In SSR, self-selection allows students to find materials that suit their abilities and interests. With quality high-interest, low-vocabulary materials and some guidance in selecting suitable reading, even disabled readers benefit from an SSR program with better readers. Modifications, such as allowing oral as well as silent reading, and permitting children to read in pairs, may be appropriate for disabled readers.

Journal writing also allows students to record their own thoughts about self-selected topics in a way that suits their abilities. Those with limited writing skills may dictate their thoughts or use nonverbal methods, such as pictures, to express them. The teacher can adjust the quantity and quality of vocabulary used in responding to students' journals based on their reading abilities.

Activities which utilize students' oral skills can minimize ability differences.

4. **Use open-ended projects which allow students to contribute at various levels with various skills.** Using classwide projects that require many different contributions can ensure that the strengths of all will be utilized. Two good examples are a class newspaper and production of a drama.

In both cases, more than language skills are needed. When students in the clinic published their newspaper, they realized that it required a wide range of talents, including oral interviewing, cartooning, and layout design. When they wrote and performed mystery plays, all were able to contribute, whether performing, designing sets, or creating sound effects. Using such activities in the regular classroom incorporates the talents of all students.

5. **Plan writing activities which allow individuals to respond at their own levels.** Using patterned stories and poetry to foster reading and writing skills helps to bridge the gap in students' abilities. The natural, predictable language patterns of these genres are easily accessed by readers of all abilities after only a few repetitions. Students with a wide range of writing skills can compose new passages based on the patterns. Such activities can be performed individually or in groups, according to needs and interests. We've found that even the most reluctant writers become involved when they realize it's O.K. to "borrow" another author's pattern.

Relaxation training is one way to help children deal with individual differences.

Patterned Stories

In keeping with the mystery theme, summer teachers read several spooky or mysterious stories from a series. Students discussed the story patterns and brainstormed ways to change the stories to construct their own. Next, they broke into small groups to write or dictate stories; in some cases, individuals composed their own. The stories were typed, and the students illustrated and bound them into their own published books. Similar activities can be used in regular classrooms where all students can respond at their own levels.

6. **Use group incentives and internal competition in order to motivate disabled readers.** In our clinic, an independent recreational reading program encouraged students to spend the summer reading for "Olympic Medals." Earning a bronze medal for 800 minutes of reading was within reach of all readers. A silver medal was awarded for 900 minutes, and a gold for 1,000 minutes. Students were asked to count minutes of reading, not pages or books. In this way, effort was rewarded, and disabled readers were not penalized for reading at a slower rate.

Group Goals

Perhaps the best way of avoiding the negative consequences of competition between students of differing abilities in the regular classroom is to establish group goals to which all children make a contribution. For example, medals could be earned for each student after the whole class had read for 25,000 minutes. Another way of avoiding unfair competition is to focus on individuals competing against their own goals. This helps students monitor their own progress but avoids asking poor readers to compete against good readers.

Students can set their own goals, decide how to graph and chart their progress, and keep records of their improvement. A variety of skills—for example, counting the number of sight words read in one minute—can be structured this way. This shifts the focus to beating individual records, not bettering a classmate's performance.

7. **Implement a cross-grade arrangement with a group of younger students.** In an exchange with a classroom of younger students, less-skilled readers have a reason to practice reading books which may be appropriate for their reading levels but not socially acceptable by peers. This stigma may be reduced if the reader can justify reading the book to share it with younger children.

The same may be true for writing projects. Work which may not be appreciated by peers may find a very receptive audience with younger children. Writing for this audience may lead to experimentation with topics and forms that otherwise might not be perceived as socially acceptable. Providing appropriately matched disabled readers with the opportunity to assist younger students as they read and write is destined to improve their self-concepts.

8. **Obtain the help of school psychologists to implement relaxation techniques.** Many learning-disabled children also suffer from attention-deficit disorders or exhibit other behaviors which cause them to stand out in the regular classroom. In addition, because of their learning disability, many children feel frustrated

and highly anxious. Relaxation training is one way to help children deal with individual differences.

A number of taped programs teach children techniques for dealing with stress. Students can learn to monitor their own levels of stress and then instigate deep breathing, muscle relaxation, etc. Such programs can be appropriate for all students. The school psychologist is often an excellent resource for helping to implement stress reduction in the regular classroom.

9. **Organize and participate in a support group with other teachers who work with disabled readers.** Clinicians in our clinic have two advantages over many regular classroom teachers. First, they attend daily techniques classes in which they share and discuss methods with other professionals, thus refining and enhancing their own teaching. Second, they are coached as they work with their students. Supervisors provide daily feedback about teaching techniques and behaviors. Regular classroom teachers could certainly benefit from regular interaction with colleagues who have similar concerns.

The most obvious way that many special programs attempt to cope with varying abilities is to completely individualize the instructional program. However, there are a number of well-structured, large- and small-group activities that help teachers cope with the wide range of reading abilities found in almost any classroom. These tips may even assist classroom teachers to go beyond merely coping with disabled readers to capitalizing on the individual strengths that make them unique.

Learning Disabled Students Make the Transition

Debra A. Neubert
Jennifer Foster

Debra A. Neubert *(CEC Chapter #0504) is Assistant Professor, Department of Special Education, University of Maryland, College Park.* **Jennifer Foster** *is Transition Support Teacher, Montgomery County Public Schools, Maryland.*

■Career exploration, planning and decision making are critical components of the process of transition from school to work or postsecondary education for learning disabled students. Secondary special education teachers often must assume a primary role in guiding and planning realistic career, vocational and transitional goals for these students as they near graduation. Recent evidence suggests that learning disabled students may leave school without adequate job-seeking and job-keeping skills, and they may have difficulty negotiating job changes and advancement in the world of work (Neubert & Tilson, 1987). This article outlines a guide to help special educators, parents, and adult service providers assist learning disabled individuals in exploring employment and postsecondary options and enhance the transition planning process.

Community-Based Exploration Guide

The Community-Based Exploration Guide (CBEG) was developed to meet several needs of learning disabled individuals who participated in a postsecondary transition program. When these individuals entered the transition program, they lacked an employability profile capsulizing their vocational strengths, weaknesses, and experiences. Many of them had unrealistic career goals that had not been explored in a systematic manner. Similarly, parents were often confused about their sons' and daughters' vocational skills and the types of vocational and educational options available at the postsecondary level.

In general, the students lacked the self-confidence to contact community personnel and assume responsibility for career decision making. Several other problem areas noted through systematic observation and formal testing included the following:

- Limited awareness of personal strengths and weaknesses.
- Unrealistic expectations regarding attainment of higher education degrees.
- Lack of knowledge of support services offered at postsecondary institutions.
- Lack of knowledge regarding education and training options other than college.
- Limited awareness of local employment opportunities.

The CBGE was developed over a 2-year period, and in its final form it proved to be an effective transition planning strategy for over 30 learning disabled individuals. First, the students learned a specific strategy to use in exploring employment and training options. Second, since students observed work environments, talked with prospective employers, and investigated actual job and training requirements, they were able to formulate more realistic career goals.

The five steps of the CBGE are described in the following sections. The CBGE takes approximately 4 weeks to complete. It can be used on more than one occasion (e.g., as an individual changes jobs or graduates from a vocational or postsecondary program).

Step 1: Develop an Employability Profile

Assessment data are available on each

From *Teaching Exceptional Children*, Spring 1988, pp. 42-44.

student from a variety of sources such as psychological reports, medical reports, vocational evaluation and assessment reports, informal teacher observations, and observations from work experience and vocational training. Once a student leaves the school system, it is often difficult to obtain this type of information. Therefore, when students leave school they should have an employability profile that consists of information on the following:

- Reading level
- Math level
- Tested vocational interests
- Dexterity: Fine finger and Gross motor
- Work habits
- Learning style
- Work environment preference
- Recommendations from Vocational Evaluation Report
- Overall strengths
- Overall weaknesses

This profile serves as the starting point for exploration activities in the CBGE and is later used to match individual strengths and weaknesses with specific job/school/training requirements.

The teacher is responsible for compiling the assessment data needed to develop the employability profile. The profile can be incorporated easily as part of each student's individualized transition plan (ITP).

Step 2: Identify Areas to Explore

Based on the assessment data, the student and teacher begin the exploration process by identifying and discussing several occupational areas or postsecondary education options. First, occupations are identified using the following activities:

1. Students select a specific occupational area to explore.
2. Using the *Dictionary of Occupational Titles* and the *Worker Trait Group Guide*, students identify information about the occupational area chosen.

Next, postsecondary options are identified using the following activities:

1. Students select a specific postsecondary site to explore: Community college, University, Apprenticeship, Transition program, Vocational training program, or other.
2. Students identify a major area of study.

The purpose of this step is twofold: (1) to gather information on occupational areas and specific jobs and (2) to identify a postsecondary institution of interest (e.g., community college, university, apprenticeship program, or vocational training program), along with a tentative area of study. For example, one student using the CBGE decided to explore two specific areas of interest, jewelry repair and chauffering. Since the student had taken 2 years of drafting at the high school level, he also decided to explore entry-level graphic arts positions and course offerings related to drafting at a community college and a private postsecondary institution.

Teachers can encourage students to explore additional occupational areas that they may be unfamiliar with. For example, if a student is interested in the food service sector, the teacher can discuss options such as catering or bakery and restaurant management, in addition to the traditional fast food options the students may be familiar with. During this step, it is important not to discourage students from exploring options that may appear unrealistic. As the students investigate jobs or postsecondary program requirements, they will begin to determine appropriate goals as specific requirements are matched with individual strengths, skills, and limitations (outlined in Step 1).

Step 3: Conduct Community-Based Exploration Activities

Based on areas of interest identified in Steps 1 and 2, the teacher helps students locate potential employment or postsecondary sites in the community by using a variety of references such as telephone books, information from employment agencies, and community resource guides, or by referring the students to friends, parents, and guidance counselors for ideas and leads. For example, a teacher assisting the student who is interested in jewelry repair might use the Yellow Pages to locate the names of three companies involved in this activity.

The student would then be responsible for contacting these sites to conduct a telephone information interview or arrange for a personal information interview (Bolles, 1980). An information interview is a process of collecting information about an employment site or postsecondary institution without the pressure of applying for a job or a specific program. If a student is interested in attending a community college or university, the teacher and student can either request catalogs from nearby schools or use library resources to review college catalogs for specific areas of study and support services. In Step 3 the teacher delineates the type of information the student should collect during the information interview. The teacher can help by developing a worksheet with these guidelines for the student to use at each information interview. For students exploring occupational areas the following activities are useful:

1. Identify job site locations by using the telephone books; talking to friends, parents, and guidance counselors; and looking up references from employment agencies.
2. Arrange and conduct information interviews at the identified job sites. Collect information on such aspects as types of jobs available, job duties, salary/benefits/hours, work environment, opportunity for advancement, and process for applying for job.

For students exploring postsecondary options, the following activities can be used:

1. Identify postsecondary site locations.
2. Arrange and conduct information interviews at the identified sites. Collect information on such things as contact person and phone number, entrance requirements, cost and financial aid, course requirements, procedure for application, and process for obtaining brochures and catalogs.

The community-based exploration activities are designed to encourage students to take responsibility for the exploration process, collect information that they will be able to use in making realistic transition plans, and develop the skills and self-confidence needed to contact employers. If a student is too timid to make community contacts, the teacher can assist the student in making the first contact or role-play exactly what to say when calling an employer or representative from a postsecondary program.

Step 4: Summarize

At the completion of the exploration activities, the teacher and student set aside a time to discuss how the requirements of a specific job or postsecondary program actually match the student's strengths, weaknesses, and interests as outlined in the employability profile drawn up in Step 1. The teacher encourages the student to discuss what he or she liked and disliked about a job or program (e.g., work environment, hours, salary, advancement opportunities) and to begin formulating realistic transition goals. If a match is evident between the requirements of a job or program and the student's abilities and interests, a tentative employment or postsecondary goal is identified. If the match is incongruent, the exploration process can be continued by returning to Step 2 to identify alternative employment and postsecondary opportunities.

In summarizing the occupation exploration, the following items are asked about the job site:

1. What jobs did you observe?
2. What did you like about the job site?
3. What did you dislike about the job site?
4. Do the requirements of this job match your interests and abilities?
5. Are there any prerequisite skills you need to obtain this type of job?
6. Is this a realistic employment goal for you? If yes, identify tentative job goal.—Now go to Step 5. If no, repeat Steps 2 and 3. Explore another area of interest.

In summarizing postsecondary exploration, the following items are asked about the site and program:

1. What did you like about the site?
2. What did you dislike about the site?
3. Do the requirements of the program match you interests and abilities? Why or why not?
4. Is this a realistic postsecondary option for you? If yes, identify program of interest.—Now go to Step 5. If no, repeat Steps 2 and 3. Explore another program of interest.

Step 5: Next Steps

Once realistic transition goals have been identified and discussed with parents, strategies for obtaining these goals can be incorporated into the student's IEP or ITP. During this step, the teacher may need to explore program options at both the secondary and postsecondary levels to assist the student and parents in deciding on the best plan of action. The teacher may need to call on other support personnel to facilitate appropriate planning.

Since the transition planning process is individualized, the teacher and student may consider the following guidelines in determining a plan of action:

- Contact the vocational instructors in the local school system to determine whether or not there is a vocational program that will assist the student in developing related skills in an area of interest.
- Contact the work experience coordinator to determine whether or not the student could work part time in an area of employment interest before he or she leaves the school system.
- Contact postsecondary personnel to determine prerequisite skills or courses the student will need to enter a community college, apprenticeship program, or postsecondary vocational program.
- Based on the requirements of the job and the student's current level of performance, determine whether or not the student will need to develop related academic skills, social skills, or independent living skills before successfully making the transition into competitive employment.
- With the assistance of the parents and IEP team, determine the type of assistance or support the student will need to make the transition from school to an identified area of employment or a postsecondary education site.

Step 5 involves seeking the information the student needs to achieve his or her goals for employment or postsecondary education. This information can either be collected by the teacher, parent, or student. The information must be incorporated into the student's IEP or ITP to facilitate a smooth transition process from school to work or postsecondary education. Students pursuing tentative employment goals and postsecondary goals would develop a strategy plan for obtaining employment in this area.

To develop a strategy plan, the following items are answered:

1. How do I go about attaining my goal?
2. Who is responsible? List any assistance needed.
3. What is the timeline?

Conclusion

It is important for learning disabled students to engage in a focused community-based exploration process before leaving the school system. This process should be based on synthesizing and making use of assessment data to match individual abilities and interests with realistic employment and postsecondary options. The CBGE is one method of encouraging students to understand their strengths and weaknesses, gather career-related information through community exploration, and assume greater responsibility for decision making in transition planning. This process also promotes independence and self-confidence by providing new experiences in the community. Finally, the CBGE provides a structured format for special education teachers to engage students in ongoing transition planning with input from vocational teachers, adult service providers, employers, and parents.

To obtain a copy of the Community-Based Exploration Guide, contact: Dr. Juliana Taymans, Center for Disabilities Studies, Suite 524, Funger Hall, The George Washington University, Washington, DC 20052.

References

Bolles, R. (1980). *What color is your parachute?* Berkeley: Ten Speed Press.

Neubert, D., & Tilson, G. (1987, Fall). The critical stage of transition: A challenge and an opportunity. *The Journal for Vocational Special Needs Education, 10*(1), 3-7.

Teaching the Mentally Retarded Child

Mentally retarded children differ widely from one another. Some mildly retarded students, called educable mentally retarded (EMR), can read, write, and eventually hold semi-skilled jobs. Even within the EMR category, there are wide variations of abilities, however. Some EMR students finish high school; others lag many grades behind their peers, quit school, speak poorly, and have difficulty working even at an unskilled level. Some moderately retarded children, called trainable mentally retarded (TMR), can learn sufficient self-care and social skills to eventually live in group homes or sheltered workshops and participate in supervised employment. TMR students also vary widely in their accomplishments. The severely, or profoundly, mentally retarded need custodial care for life; even within this category there are wide variations in self-care skills.

What causes these problems in learning? The majority of retarded individuals cannot have the origins of their mental retardation clearly established. Numerous circumstances and conditions, singly or in combination, may be responsible for mental retardation. These include underdevelopment of neurons due to drugs, viruses, radiation, genetic messages, or extra chromosomal material during the prenatal period; anoxia, prematurity, low birth weight, or infections during birth and the neonatal period; and head injuries, malnutrition, neglect, or serious illnesses during infancy or early childhood. Other causes may also be implicated; this is not an inclusive list of etiological factors. It is difficult to classify MR persons when so many levels of ability and so many causative factors are involved.

Classification of MR individuals can only be done after thorough assessment involving, at the very least, some analysis of intelligence and a test of adaptive abilities. It is desirable to make other assessments as well. Many people feel that IQ tests to determine degree of intelligence (or degree of mental retardation) are inaccurate, unreliable, invalid, and detrimental. A 1979 court case in California, *Larry P. v. Riles*, concluded that the IQ tests used in California to assess mental retardation for the purpose of placing students in special classes were racially and culturally biased. Grossly disproportionate numbers of minority children were wrongly placed and maintained in EMR classes through IQ testing, in violation of PL 94-142, the Civil Rights Act, and the Rehabilitation Act. The judge ruled that every minority child in an EMR class in California must be reevaluated without the use of a standardized IQ test. Diagnostic tests designed to reveal specific learning needs, adaptive behavior observations, developmental histories, and health histories were to be used instead. Any future IQ tests, ruled the judge of *Larry P. v. Riles*, were to be submitted to the court for approval before use. California's ban on IQ tests has had enormous repercussions in regard to the assessment of mental retardation throughout the country. While most states still use standardized IQ tests, they also emphasize cognitive processes and problem-solving strategies in the assessment of intelligence, and place more weight on measures of adaptive abilities. Increasingly, EMR children are being mainstreamed in regular classrooms. Each has an individualized education plan and is provided with an appropriate education in keeping with a thorough assessment of his or her unique skills and abilities.

In the first article of this unit, Polloway and Smith discuss implications of the *Larry P. v. Riles* case and other class action law suits which have wrought changes in the education of the EMR population. Current programs reflect the changing perspectives about mentally retarded individuals. The next article describes the characteristics of Down's syndrome. The author argues that not all children with the syndrome are profoundly retarded. Many can be educated to relatively advanced levels and benefit from mainstreaming. Surgery can change the appearance of children to reduce the obviously recognizable physical anomalies. The third article describes the characteristics of autism. The author argues that not all autistic children are alike. The movie *Rain Man* portrayed an autistic savant with good language skills. This article discusses the wide range of linguistic and behavioral symptoms of autism, to inform readers that all autistic individuals are not similar to the *Rain Man*. It is a positive article, emphasizing educational progress. The last three selections of this unit focus on specific educational programs. Lee and Glen Dunlap suggest ways to motivate retarded students through task variation in the classroom. Suzanne Wiggins and Michael Behrmann describe a community program which uses such locations as banks, grocery stores, restaurants, and drugstores as extended classrooms to teach MR students skills they need to maximize their independence. Finally, Sandra McClennen points out the need to provide sex education for MR students. She outlines specific areas in which instruction should be provided, and suggests several resource materials to use in such lessons.

Unit 4

Looking Ahead: Challenge Questions

How have PL 94-142 and recent class action lawsuits changed the way educable mentally retarded students are provided with appropriate education in the least restrictive environments?

What is Down's syndrome? What can be expected of a Down's syndrome student in an educational setting?

What is autism? What can be expected of an autistic student in an educational setting?

Can task variation facilitate learning and heighten motivation among MR students inside the classroom? How is it accomplished?

Can community settings be used as extended classrooms for MR students? How would such a program be structured?

Do MR students have the same range of sexual needs and desires as nonretarded students? Should they be given sex education? How should it be structured?

Changes in Mild Mental Retardation: Population, Programs, and Perspectives

EDWARD A. POLLOWAY
J. DAVID SMITH

EDWARD A. POLLOWAY *is Associate Professor of Special Education, Lynchburg College, and* J. DAVID SMITH *is Professor of Special Education, Lynchburg College, Lynchburg, Virginia.*

Abstract: Recent developments in special education have begun to produce a significant change in the population being served under the label of mild retardation. The specific factors influencing this change and the effects of the overall functional levels of students enrolled in EMR programs are examined. Data on decreasing prevalence within programs are presented. Implications are drawn for emerging group characteristics, placement and curricular decisions, and labeling relative to such programs and for concerns about noncategorical grouping. An apparent shift in the conceptualization of mild retardation underscores the discussion of each of these issues.

■ Much of the initial work in the field of special education in this century, and the initial involvement of many professionals, can be traced back to a focus on individuals served under the label educable mental retardation (EMR) or mild retardation. Despite this fact, there has been an accelerating trend away from professional interest in this group. As Bartlett (1979) noted, much of the attraction of the mild retardation field seems to have diminished in recent years. Certainly the formulation of learning disabilities as a separate field and the recognition of severely handicapped as a distinct area have been major factors in this apparent decline.

A significant change in the population served under the EMR label and, in a sense, a redefinition of the term mild retardation has coincided with decreasing interest in this field. The interplay between trends toward reduced professional involvement and enthusiasm and toward changes in population has resulted in a rather dramatic lack of attention to demographic, programmatic, and research concerns for this population as compared to its relative status in special education a decade ago. The purpose of this article is to analyze the concept of mild retardation as it relates to the current and future state of affairs in the delivery of educational services. The article will address four subtopics: factors influencing change in the EMR population, transformations in the characteristics of the population, implications for programming, and the implications of these program modifications for the overall field of special education.

FACTORS INFLUENCING POPULATION CHANGE

An arbitrary distinction could be made in the traditional EMR class between those students identified by Dunn (1973) as "adaptive" and those identified as "nonadaptive" in the sense that the former were more likely to demonstrate the skills associated both with a higher degree of success in part-time mainstream programs and with greater success in terms of postschool adjustment. In considering changes in the EMR constituency, we must recognize the possibility that this adaptive, higher-functioning group will now often fail to meet eligibility criteria as required on national, state, and local levels; that is, they no longer "qualify" as being mentally retarded. At the same time, the efficacy of early intervention programs has prevented some cases of mild retardation. There is also the increasing phenomenon of the "promotion" to EMR placements of individuals previously stereotypically viewed as moderately retarded and placed in trainable classes (e.g., Down's syndrome children).

In considering the first general factor resulting in population transformations, the EMR declassification of adaptive students, an obvious beginning point is the American Association on Mental Deficiency's (AAMD) definition (Grossman, 1973, 1977) that, compared to the previous Heber definition (1959, 1961), resulted in two significant changes. In terms of measured intelligence, the definition, in effect, acknowledged professional reluctance to accept an IQ score of 85 and lowered the ceiling score by an additional standard deviation to 70. However, despite the fact that the AAMD intended that this ceiling score be viewed as a guideline to be subjected to clinical judgment rather than being seen as an absolute requirement (Begab, 1981), in practice the EMR category has been increasingly reserved for those with an IQ of 65 or lower (Gottlieb, 1981). The importance of considering the ceiling IQ of 70 as an approximation subject to clinical judgment has been reaffirmed in the AAMD's most recent definitional revision (Grossman, 1983).

The more significant result of the wide acceptance of Grossman's definition has been increased attention to adaptive behavior (AB). By complementing IQ with this second dimension, the definition clearly decreased the potential number of individuals who could accurately be identified as retarded. Although this shift in public policy has had a direct effect on school procedures, it is surprising to note that a review of research showed no evidence that this change in policy is reflected in any increased use of AB in subject selection and description (Smith & Polloway, 1979).

Litigation has also played a major role in the shift within the EMR population, particularly by calling into question the placement of minority group children. The two most important cases, *Diana* v. *State Board of Education* (1970) and *Larry P.* v. *Riles* (1972), were concerned with the educational rights of Mexican-American and Black children, respectively, in the California public school system. The basic assumption in both cases was that the placement of these children in such classes was based on discriminatory procedures and that the outcomes of such placement had a negative effect on their educational progress. Clearly discrimination was the major factor in the court's deliberations. As Reschly (1982) has pointed out, in *Larry P.* and related cases the key issue should have been the effectiveness of the programs, but the focus instead was limited primarily to criteria for placement.

Regardless of focus, the results of the litigation, at least in California, have been clear. MacMillan and colleagues (MacMillan, 1982; MacMillan, Meyers, & Morrison, 1980) summarized the direct implications of these cases for EMR programming. They noted that in the intervening years significant decreases of 11,000 to 14,000 individuals had occurred in the state EMR enrollment largely reflective of the declassifying of minority children in response to the court's mandate. Similar, though less dramatic, results have been noted elsewhere, although substantial variance in prevalence figures between states continues to be the rule (Patrick & Reschly, 1982).

The direct consequences of these cases have been a rethinking of identification procedures and, thus, a reconsideration of the concept of mental retardation. The work of Jane Mercer (e.g., 1970, 1973) and others has stressed a sociological perspective on retardation, which encourages a limited view of retardation as a comprehensive impairment involving permanent incompetence—quite contradictory to the typical picture of persons who have been classified as EMR and to the Grossman (1983, p. 15) manual's specification that retardation is a current life status, which "carries no connotation of chronicity or irreversibility." In lieu of the traditional use of IQ scores, Mercer and Lewis (1977) have offered the System of Multicultural Pluralistic Assessment (SOMPA) toward the goal of unbiased assessment.

The adoption of the SOMPA itself or the acceptance of its rationale even without the use of the tool would have several key effects on identification procedures in EMR programs. By offering a method for the adjustment of IQ scores based on sociocultural status, the instrument yields an Estimated Learning Potential that increases scores for many children. Second, the SOMPA focuses on adaptive behavior *outside* school and, therefore, downplays the real difficulties experienced within school that may have led initially to referral. Assuming that students are referred primarily by teachers for academic and behavioral performance deficits, it should be safe to suggest that IQ tests are not being used by psychologists to ". . . attempt to catch unwitting victims in their psychometric nets" (Reschly, 1982, p. 23). Thus, a change in identification procedures, though decreasing the number of students *eligible* for services, will clearly not decrease the number who are in *need* of services.

The consequences of such a decrease in population is evident. Reschly (1981) estimated that the use of the measures and criteria built into SOMPA would result in a prevalence figure of less than .5% for mild mental retardation and clearly would have a major effect on children who would no longer be eligible for services. His brief review of research on those found ineligible is not encouraging; of those declassified from EMR programs, one-half were eligible for other special education services, but the others were not despite their continuing intellectual limitations and academic deficiencies. Similar consequences stemming from changes in identification criteria have been reported by Childs (1982) and Mascari and Forgnone (1982). Thus, although a restrictive concept of mild retardation, requiring, for example, an out-of-school focus for adaptive behavior deficits, may reduce the prevalence of identified EMR students, the question remains as to whether this is in their best interest.

Table 1 summarizes federal data on the number of retarded children served on a state-by-state basis between 1976–77 and 1980–81. Although the data does not make a differentiation according to levels of retardation, it can be assumed that the changes are reflective primarily of mild retardation since this group represents the large majority of the overall MR population. Given the fact that these years followed the passage of P.L. 94-142, it is significant to note that *all but eight* states and territories showed a decrease in the number of children served during this five-year period and that six of the eight did show a drop-off between 1979–80 and 1980–81. These changes came in spite of an apparent federal mandate for an increase in the identification of handicapped children. As noted in Table 1, the overall percentage decrease for the nation was 12.9%. Although none of the specific factors discussed earlier can be pinpointed as the critical agent in such a dramatic change, it is reasonable to assume that all were influential to some extent in producing this trend.

A second general factor potentially influencing population change stems from early intervention efforts with poverty level children and their parents. The prevention of mild retardation from psychosocial sources has been well-documented and is fully discussed in volumes edited by Begab, Haywood, and Garber (1981). Clearly the evidence supporting such programs points to the alterability of intellectual levels for children deemed to be at high risk for mild retardation and related learning difficulties in school (e.g., Garber & Heber, 1981; Ramey & Haskins, 1981). The most impressive results have been limited to specific projects, but the evidence suggests that the application of these principles and procedures to poor families in general would reduce the prevalence of EMR students in school programs.

Although recent practices in education have begun to reduce the prevalence of higher functioning, adaptive children identified as EMR in special education programs, there has been an increase in EMR class enrollment of those children traditionally served in programs created for a lower functioning population. As MacMillan, Meyers, and Morrison (1980) accurately pointed out, the openings in such classes due to the reduced prevalence of EMR students have often been filled by children with more serious handicaps who previously would have been placed in trainable classes and labeled moderately retarded.

The most encouraging reason for this change has been the success of early intervention programs with handicapped preschool children. The work of Rynders, Spiker, and Horrobin (1978) is most important in alerting professionals to one aspect in the shift in population in groups from TMR to EMR. After reviewing data on Down's syndrome children who have participated in early intervention programs, they indicated a "temptation" to predict a 30–55% chance that a Down's child would subsequently function in the EMR range. Their review of 29 studies of Down's syndrome children indicated that for all three karyotypes (trisomy 21, translocation, and mosaicism), IQ ranges superseded the current ceiling on IQ scores for MR placement. Similar results have also been reported by other researchers involved in related efforts (e.g., Connolly, 1978).

EMERGING CHARACTERISTICS

Given these shifts in population, the characteristics of students who are labeled EMR are undergoing a metamorphosis that should alter our traditional view of the group. An interesting basis for comparison comes from the list of general characteristics provided by Dunn (1973) as an elaboration on Rothstein (1971). He identified twelve generalizations that were considered to be more accurate for students classified as EMR than for students within the general school population. Mildly retarded students were more likely:

TABLE 1
Number and Change in Number of Mentally Retarded Children Ages 3–21 Years Served Under P.L. 89–313 and P.L. 94–142 Annually Since School Year 1976–1977

State	*1976–77*	*1977–78*	*1978–79*	*1979–80*	*1980–81*	*1980–81 – 1976–77*	*% Change 1980–81 – 1976–77*
Alabama	31,203	31,990	33,923	35,127	34,840	3,638	+11.7
Alaska	1,277	1,294	1,051	906	734	– 543	–42.5
Arizona	8,608	7,879	7,238	6,879	6,592	–2,016	–23.4
Arkansas	14,674	16,489	17,703	17,433	17,449	2,775	+18.9
California	42,916	40,768	41,023	39,810	38,947	–3,969	–09.2
Colorado	10,077	8,235	8,259	6,808	6,423	–3,654	–36.3
Connecticut	10,132	10,330	8,954	8,212	7,940	–2,192	–21.6
Delaware	3,199	3,264	2,839	2,629	2,405	– 794	–24.8
District of Columbia	2,918	1,695	1,882	1,309	1,318	–1,600	–54.8
Florida	34,311	33,844	31,990	29,973	27,978	–6,333	–18.5
Georgia	31,744	30,478	31,214	30,274	30,021	–1,723	–05.4
Hawaii	2,434	2,478	2,465	2,120	1,807	– 627	–25.8
Idaho	3,567	3,642	3,721	3,021	2,759	– 808	–22.7
Illinois	48,974	50,022	46,977	50,770	46,058	–2,916	–06.0
Indiana	27,784	28,086	28,269	27,165	26,666	–1,118	–04.0
Iowa	12,663	12,825	12,786	12,955	12,643	– 20	–00.2
Kansas	8,665	9,141	7,946	7,780	7,413	–1,252	–14.4
Kentucky	22,872	23,138	23,060	23,321	23,193	322	+01.4
Louisiana	24,547	24,537	22,661	20,713	19,164	–5,383	–22.0
Maine	5,664	5,311	5,467	5,293	5,200	– 464	–08.2
Maryland	17,523	15,311	12,134	11,870	11,060	–6,463	–36.9
Massachusetts	34,972	31,380	26,671	26,822	26,834	–8,138	–23.3
Michigan	34,715	34,064	32,921	31,188	29,882	–4,833	–14.0
Minnesota	15,140	15,812	14,973	14,894	14,098	–1,042	–06.9
Mississippi	15,487	16,365	18,330	18,720	18,593	3,106	+20.1
Missouri	25,304	23,539	24,717	23,192	22,076	–3,228	–12.8
Montana	2,114	2,167	2,126	1,780	1,615	– 499	–23.6
Nebraska	7,557	7,837	7,887	7,015	6,610	– 947	–12.5
Nevada	1,586	1,595	1,780	1,365	1,217	– 369	–23.3
New Hampshire	2,720	2,859	2,360	2,453	1,787	– 933	–34.3
New Jersey	22,394	21,612	21,386	18,489	16,537	–5,857	–26.2
New Mexico	4,519	4,231	3,930	3,439	3,139	–1,380	–30.5
New York	55,582	51,782	48,566	47,960	41,675	–13,907	–25.0
North Carolina	46,334	44,662	45,557	43,507	39,986	–6,348	–13.7
North Dakota	1,974	2,168	2,050	2,083	1,809	– 165	–08.4
Ohio	67,626	67,567	66,411	64,422	62,682	–4,944	–07.3
Oklahoma	12,753	13,126	14,025	13,781	13,372	620	+04.9
Oregon	7,697	7,008	6,195	5,991	5,518	–2,179	–28.3
Pennsylvania	56,461	53,221	51,340	49,276	49,202	–7,259	–12.9
Puerto Rico	8,132	9,290	13,510	10,539	13,062	4,931	+60.6
Rhode Island	2,483	2,200	2,243	1,989	1,974	– 509	–20.5
South Carolina	29,944	27,260	27,276	26,090	24,941	–5,003	–16.7
South Dakota	1,787	2,291	1,374	1,245	1,260	– 527	–29.5
Tennessee	23,019	26,319	26,510	23,302	21,945	–1,074	–04.7
Texas	47,580	42,154	36,259	31,033	28,591	–18,989	–40.0
Utah	5,117	5,281	3,532	3,327	3,194	–1,923	–37.6
Vermont	2,133	2,069	2,593	3,363	3,095	962	+45.1
Virginia	22,359	21,344	19,468	18,950	18,425	–3,934	–17.6
Washington	11,684	12,311	11,374	11,063	10,799	– 885	–07.6
West Virginia	11,963	11,559	11,181	11,552	11,508	– 455	–03.8
Wisconsin	19,187	17,714	15,792	15,004	14,668	–4,519	–23.6
Wyoming	1,197	1,046	1,081	1,044	1,050	– 147	–12.3
American Samoa	71	94	84	65	69	– 2	–02.8
Guam	739	907	1,457	921	919	181	+24.5
Northern Marianas	-	4	13	9	11	-	-
Trust Territories	526	109	42	19	23	– 503	–95.6
Virgin Islands	954	619	586	732	792	– 162	–17.0
Bur. of Indian Affairs	-	672	718	821	612	-	-
U.S. & Territories	969,547	944,980	917,880	882,173	1,844,180	–125,367	–12.9

Source: U.S. Department of Education, Office of Special Education, Data Analysis System, November 6, 1981.

> (1) to have met defeat, frustration, and rejection in the regular grades where they were first placed; (2) to have exhibited substantial behavior disorders in general education; (3) to be from racial or ethnic minority groups; (4) to have parents who place little value on education; (5) to have inadequate health and nutritional provisions; (6) to be unclean and unkempt; (7) to live in poverty and deprivation; (8) to be boys rather than girls; (9) to come from broken or disorganized homes; (10) to be seriously retarded in school achievement; (11) to have restricted oral language skills in standard English; (12) to have obtained IQ scores ranging between 65 and 78 on individualized tests of verbal intelligence administered in standard English. (p. 131)

Dunn's prediction that dramatic changes would occur in the subsequent decade has been realized and certainly has implications for a number of these characteristics. Although the number of children from poverty backgrounds remains high in EMR classes, the "cultural-familial" stereotype fostered by a number of the listed characteristics (e.g., 3, 4, 5, 6, 7, and 9), faulty as an initial conception, will soon result in an even greater misconception of this population. The designation of mildly retarded children collectively as cultural-familial, indicative of an interplay of genetic and environmental factors in the absence of specific pathological causes (Heber, 1961), is less accurate as the population of children served in EMR classes is increasingly affected by additional etiological agents (e.g., chromosomal anomaly).

The first characteristic listed must be revisited due to the fact that a larger number of EMR children are likely to come into such programs directly from TMR or preschool programs for the handicapped or to have been referred earlier in their school careers. Such a change requires a review of the data on outer-directedness and failure set (e.g., Zigler, 1966), which have been cornerstones in an understanding of the learning styles of mildly retarded children.

The reference to substantial behavior disorders was a reflection of the fact that, given intellectual and academic functioning levels that are roughly consistent with traditional EMR guidelines, the referral of a given child was more likely to have been made when he or she had experienced difficulty with conformity to rules in the regular classroom (Polloway & Patton, 1981). The advent and growth of programs for disturbed or disordered children has likely decreased the prevalence of such behavioral problems in EMR classes, although it is reasonable to assume that concomitant behavioral disorders will continue to increase chances for referral and thus continue to bias identification and the make-up of the population.

The tenth generalization focuses on deficits in school achievement. Given a move to a more handicapped population, this assumption should be of greater concern. The discrepancy between chronological age and achievement level would be expected to be greater, thus presenting a challenge to teachers concerning the possibilities of having students identified as EMR reach at least a level of partial literacy.

In terms of oral language development, the shifting nature of the population should result in more evidence of language delay in this group, as would be common, for example, with Down's syndrome children even after successful early intervention (e.g., Hayden & Dmitriev, 1975; Rynders & Horrobin, 1975) rather than just the dialectical and linguistic differences. Considerations of the interaction between delay and difference will be critical in the educational assessment of the population (Polloway & Smith, 1982).

Clearly the greatest change from Dunn's 1973 list is in intellectual level. The range of IQ scores within EMR programs has been limited significantly by the more widespread adoption of the cut-off established by Grossman. Although in practice this figure has not been universally adopted in eligibility guidelines on a state-by-state basis (Huberty, Koller, & Ten Brink, 1980), the fact remains that cut-offs of 75 or 80 are rarely employed today.

The apparent changes in characteristics as discussed in the foregoing leave the programs serving what MacMillan and Borthwick (1980) termed "a more patently disabled group" (p. 155). This requires a rethinking of EMR programs particularly as related to service delivery and curriculum.

PROGRAMMING IMPLICATIONS

Discussions of the appropriate *placement* for students classified as EMR have been a legacy of special education with efficacy research reviews (e.g., Cegelka & Tyler, 1970; Dunn, 1968; Johnson, 1962). Subsequent to the enactment of P.L. 94-142 much of the "conventional wisdom" was subjugated to the increasing trend toward mainstreaming in the public schools, the Zeitgeist of the times (Meyen & Altman, 1975). Although mainstreaming as the wholesale return of all children to regular classes was not the intent of the legislation, clearly the effects were significant in terms of the placement of many students identified as EMR.

The question that arises at this time is what effect population change will have on the appropriateness of the regular class as the least restrictive environment. Though all placements must be made on an individual basis, some group considerations need to be addressed.

The key issue is that although school practice of the late 1970's featured an increasing emphasis on regular-class-based programs for students classified as EMR, the change operated in a paradoxical fashion. MacMillan and Borthwick (1980) reported that in California very limited integration of EMR students was being achieved and that when this occurred, it was most often in nonacademic areas. They saw this as indicative of the limited potential of this group for success in the regular classroom.

The data generated through efficacy studies, though typically weakened by design limitations, failed to demonstrate significant differences between regular and special classes in achievement. However, as Gottlieb (1982) noted, since the population of students who continue to be classified as EMR occupies the lower-ability levels of the traditional EMR category, past research efforts that analyzed the effectiveness of mainstreaming efforts have limited relevance to the current situation.

In summary, it appears that, where significant population changes have occurred or are occurring, the mainstreaming debate as originally enjoined is now moot. Those students for whom Dunn (1968) urged alternative programming are in many cases simply no longer placed in EMR programs—the original problem has been solved although other problems now must be addressed.

Curriculum is a second major programmatic concern that must be evaluated in light of population change. Despite the general discrediting of the concept of the "watered-down" curriculum, mainstreaming in effect encouraged a dominant emphasis on academic skills in the regular-class curriculum. Simultaneously, the criticism focused on classes for students identified as EMR in the 1970's (e.g., "there's only two things wrong with special education: it's not special and it's not education") began to erode the vigor of the early days of the field of retardation. Bartlett (1979) concluded that a primary outcome of this shift from the efforts of the 1950's and 1960's was a greater emphasis on a purely academic curricular orientation, which he deemed questionable at that time; at the present time it seems even less warranted.

Two factors now dominate curricular concerns. Within special-class settings, a greater degree of "curricular freedom" should accompany the increased recognition of problems in academically integrating the more handicapped EMR population. Such an opportunity should encourage what Kolstoe and Frey (1965) two decades ago referred to as the study of "persistent life problems" and what more recently has been termed as instruction in functional daily living skills and career preparation.

Such an orientation is inconsistent with the cry in regular education for "back-to-the-basics." Smith and Dexter (1980) evaluated this movement for its potential effects on curriculum for the mentally retarded and concluded that such an emphasis could result in over-attention to the three R's and, thus, possible exclusion of the broad-based curriculum needed for most EMR students.

The question of appropriateness of curriculum is most critical for adolescents and is compounded by the requirement in many states of minimum competency tests (MCT). Whereas secondary programs can be most effective by focusing on vocational and practical considerations, an emphasis on tests with unproven relevance for adult success are likely to have a negative impact on EMR programs by encouraging a more restrictive curriculum (Cohen, Safran, & Polloway, 1980).

The second consideration deals with curricular emphasis as related to part-time regular-class placement. Given the fact that mainstreaming efforts are likely to occur during nonacademic periods (MacMillan & Borthwick, 1980), an increased emphasis on social skills definitely appears warranted (Gottlieb, 1982). Gresham (1982) addressed this particular area of concern in a recent review. He pointed to the past failures of mainstreaming to achieve increased social interaction, social acceptance, and behavioral modeling of nonhandicapped by handicapped students. He concluded that systematic efforts at social-skills training are requisite to student success in these areas.

DISCUSSION

The changes in population, and thus characteristics, and the resultant need for reconsideration of curriculum represent major departures from the former status of EMR programs in public schools. The scope of these trends is such that implications can be drawn for several concerns within special education.

Concept of mild retardation. The most direct implication of these changes is the possible reconceptualization of mild retardation. As the emphasis has shifted toward a more seriously disabled group, the schools have begun the search for the "truly retarded," that is, those demonstrating low competence across all social roles (Reschly, 1981). By thus effecting the removal of those previously misdiagnosed, a positive step toward the elimination of the major discriminatory effects of special education has been achieved. However, continued efforts to eliminate pupils who demonstrate primarily school-based problems ignores the reality of why they were initially referred for services. As Reschly (1981) aptly stated, ". . . the interest of declassification stems from concerns for social equity. The consequences of the methods required in order to achieve this social equity may extend far beyond what was anticipated" (p. 18).

Any radical change in the concept of mild retardation must be carefully evaluated. Although courts or legislatures can encourage such a shift, "...learning problems cannot be mandated or legislated away" (MacMillan, 1982, p. 316). Clearly the population no longer found eligible for EMR programs has a continuing need for assistance beyond regular-class instruction. Any further shift emphasizing the evaluation of adaptive behavior entirely outside the school will accentuate this need.

Noncategorical programming. The rationale for noncategorical efforts in special education in terms of pupil placement must be reevaluated in light of the changes within the EMR group. Areas of categorical overlap that have been noted (e.g., Hallahan & Kauffman, 1977), are based on suppositions that should now be subject to renewed scrutiny. For example, Becker (1978) reported on data from five learning tasks administered to students in California, the state experiencing the most significant changes in population. He questioned the assumed overlap between the mildly handicapped categories and the implications for noncategorical educational programming and teacher training.

The need for a reevaluation of the trend toward noncategorical placement stems directly from the central assumption on which it is based. As Hallahan and Kauffman (1977, p. 147) stated "...grouping according to behavioral characteristics is more advisable than grouping according to traditional categories." The merits of such an orientation are apparent; now, however, we must consider whether behavioral characteristics are more often discrepant across categories than hypothesized previously and, thus, whether there is an increased level of characteristic differences between categorical groupings.

The significant increase in the number of children being served under the LD label (as noted in DOE/OSE figures, 1981) most certainly includes many children previously identified as EMR. Thus many students to whom the noncategorical movement applied have already been subsumed within the LD category. However, there is concern over whether special education services will continue to be available for those who will be declassified in the future. Implicit in much recent work in learning disabilities (e.g., Hammill, Leigh, McNutt, & Larsen, 1981; Poplin, 1981) is an effort to focus that field on the specifically learning disabled and away from the generalized slow learner.

The implication for noncategorical teacher-training programs has more to do with program content than with affiliation with specific as opposed to generic labels. Effective teaching methods selected according to task requirements and individual student responses certainly cut across categories. Curriculum, however, presents the most significant concern. Noncategorical training programs, such as those identified for the mildly handicapped, must reject a narrow focus on academic and remedial concerns in favor of a broader base inclusive of instruction in such areas as personal, social, and vocational development.

Labeling. The continuing concern that underlies trends away from EMR placement is the assumed stigmatizing effects of labeling. Despite the lack of clear-cut support for such an effect (MacMillan, Jones, & Aloia, 1974), this supposition is indeed a powerful one among parents and professionals. In fact, as Lovitt (1982) posited, labels are frequently more upsetting to adults than to the children to whom they are given.

A current investigation into the labeling issue was reported by Reschly and Lamprecht (1979) who questioned the assumptions underlying hypotheses of labels as stigmatizing. They reported that teachers did not retain the initial expectancy if they were presented with an opportunity to observe specific behavioral events that were inconsistent with a given label. They concluded that labels had significant effects only in the absence of other information about an individual child.

Given the acquired power of the label "mentally retarded" and yet mindful of the mixed research data on its effects, an attractive option would be to consider the labeling of services instead of children, in the way that was initially proposed in the field of learning disabilities (Lilly, 1982). Providing programs under a designation such as *academic and adaptive-skills training* would provide a beginning point in serving those students who no longer meet the more stringent EMR identification criteria and yet also fail to qualify as learning disabled. This system of service delivery would facilitate a more intensive instructional arrangement than is typically available, for example, in Title 1 programs. Recognition by federal and state agencies that this approach is an appropriate one for children who have experienced educational retardation would certainly be preferable to the two alternatives: requiring that the label mentally retarded be inappropriately affixed as a condition for eligibility or failing to provide programs.

For those students who remain in EMR programs or who are likely to be destaffed primarily because of professional and parent fear of the label, consideration of a new term may be in order. Consistent with Zigler and Balla's (1981, p. 198) call for "...some term in the area of intelligence that is analogous to the term 'short' when referring to height," we suggest the term *educationally delayed*. It encourages a comprehensive view of the deficits of the population while refraining from the powerful statement that has come to be associated with "mentally retarded."

Research cogent to the topics discussed in this paper is clearly limited at this time. Thus, while calling for public scrutiny of policies tied to the various issues addressed herein, we are calling for empirical study as well. Some of the specific areas of significant need are: comparison of the cognitive and functional levels of the "new" EMR student with "traditional" EMR students; the effectiveness of mainstream procedures with this population; the result of destaffing procedures on former EMR students with attention to where they are placed and how they fare; analysis of changes in the frequency of clinical types (e.g., Down's syndrome) of retardation within EMR classes; and, finally, an analysis of the relative benefits and potential effects of the focus on out-of-school versus in-school adaptive behavior.

After years of abuse and neglect by policymakers and professional educators, special classes for students classified as EMR have often become, either intentionally or inadvertently, the "whipping boys" of education. However, to permit court decisions to convince us that such programs are educational anachronisms and "dead-end" classes (as in *Larry P.*, 1972) essentially allows us to be convinced that we are unable to regulate our own profession. There remains a sizable population of school-age children who, without appropriate special education services, will fail to reach their academic and personal potential. Educational concerns demand educational solutions.

REFERENCES

Bartlett, R. H. Mental retardation—Where does the future lie? *Education and Training of the Mentally Retarded*, 1979, *14*, 3–4.

Becker, L. D. Learning characteristics of educationally handicapped and retarded children. *Exceptional Children*, 1978, *44*, 502–511.

Begab, M. J. Issues in the prevention of psychosocial retardation. In M. J. Begab, H. C. Haywood, and H. L. Garber (Eds.), *Psychosocial influences in retarded performance: Issues and theories in development* (Vol. 1). Baltimore: University Park Press, 1981.

Begab, M. J., Haywood, H. C., & Garber, H. L. (Eds.), *Psychosocial influences in retarded performance: Issues and theories in development* (Vols. 1 & 2). Baltimore: University Park Press, 1981.

Cegelka, W. M., & Tyler, J. L. The efficacy of special class placement for the mentally retarded in proper perspective. *Training School Bulletin*, 1970, *67*(1), 33–37.

Childs, R.E. A study of the adaptive behavior of retarded children and the resultant effects of this use in the diagnosis of mental retardation. *Education and Training of the Mentally Retarded*, 1982, *17*, 109 - 113.

Cohen, S. B., Safran, J., & Polloway, E. A. Minimum competency testing and its implications for retarded students. *Education and Training of the Mentally Retarded*, 1980, *15*, 250–255.

Connolly, A. Intelligence levels in Down's syndrome children. *American Journal of Mental Deficiency*, 1978, *83*, 193–196.

Diana v. State Board of Education. C-70-37 (RFP, District Court for Northern California), 1970.

Dunn, L. M. Children with mild general learning disabilities. In L. M. Dunn (Ed.), *Exceptional children in the schools*. New York: Holt, Rinehart, and Winston, 1973.

Dunn, L. M. Special education for the mildly retarded: Is much of it justifiable? *Exceptional Children*, 1968, *35*, 5–22.

Garber, H. L., & Heber, R. The efficacy of early intervention with family rehabilitation. In M. J. Begab, H. C. Haywood, and H. L. Garber (Eds.), *Psychosocial influences in retarded performance: Strategies for improving competence* (Vol. 2). Baltimore: University Park Press, 1981.

Gottlieb, J. Mainstreaming. *Education and Training of the Mentally Retarded*, 1982, *17*, 79–82.

Gottlieb, J. Mainstreaming: Fulfilling the promise? *American Journal of Mental Deficiency*, 1981, *86*, 115–126.

Gresham, F. M. Misguided mainstreaming: The case for social skills training with handicapped children. *Exceptional Children*, 1982, *48*, 422–433.

Grossman, H. J. *Classification in mental retardation*. Washington DC: American Association on Mental Deficiency, 1983.

Grossman, H. J. *Manual on terminology and classification in mental retardation*. Washington DC: American Association on Mental Deficiency, Special Publication (No. 2), 1973, 1977.

Hallahan, D. P., & Kauffman, J. M. Labels, categories, behaviors: ED, LD, and EMR reconsidered. *Journal of Special Education*, 1977, *11*, 139–149.

Hammill, D. D., Leigh, J. E., McNutt, G., & Larsen, S. C. A new definition of learning disabilities. *Learning Disabilities Quarterly*, 1981, *4*, 336–342.

Hayden, A. H., & Dmitriev, V. The multi-disciplinary program for Down's syndrome at the University of Washington preschool center. In B. Z. Friedlander, G. M., Sterritt, G. E. Kirk (Eds.), *Exceptional infant: Assessment and intervention* (Vol. 3). New York: Brunner/Mazel, 1975.

Heber, R. A manual on terminology and classification in mental retardation. *American Journal of Mental Deficiency*, 1959, 1961. (Monograph supplement)

Huberty, T. J., Koller, J. R., & Ten Brink, T. D. Adaptive behavior in the definition of the mentally retarded. *Exeptional Children*, 1980, *46*, 256–261.

Johnson, G. O. Special education for the mentally handicapped—A paradox. *Exceptional Children*, 1962, *29*, 62–69.

Kolstoe, O. P., & Frey, R. M. *A high school work-study program for mentally subnormal children*. Carbondale IL: Southern Illinois Press, 1965.

Larry P. v. Riles. C-71-2270 (RFP District Court for Northern California), 1972.

Lilly, M. S. *Divestiture in special education: A personal point of view*. Paper presented at the 60th International CEC Convention, Houston TX, April, 1982.

Lovitt, T. *Because of my persistence, I've learned from children*. Columbus OH: Charles E. Merrill Publishing Co., 1982.

MacMillan, D. L. *Mental retardation in school and society* (2nd ed.). Boston: Little, Brown, & Co., 1982.

MacMillan, D. L., & Borthwick, S. The new educable mentally retarded population: Can they be mainstreamed? *Mental Retardation*, 1980, *18*, 155–158.

MacMillan, D. L., Jones, R. L., & Aloia, G. F. The mentally retarded label: A theoretical analysis and review of research. *American Journal of Mental Deficiency*, 1974, *79*, 241–261.

MacMillan, D. L., Jones, R. L., & Meyers, E. C. Mainstreaming the mildly retarded. *Mental Retardation*, 1976, *14*, 3–10.

MacMillan, D. L., Meyers, C. E., & Morrison, G. M. System-identification of mildly mentally retarded children: Implications for interpreting and conducting research. *American Journal of Mental Deficiency*, 1980, *85*, 108–115.

Mascari, B. G., & Forgnone, C. A follow-up study of EMR students four years after dismissal from the program. *Education and Training of the Mentally Retarded*, 1982, *17*, 288 – 292.

Mercer, J. R. Sociological aspects of mild mental retardation. In H. C. Haywood (Ed.), *Socio-cultural aspects of mental retardation*. New York: Appleton-Century-Crofts, 1970.

Mercer, J. R. *Labeling the mentally retarded*. Berkeley: University of California Press, 1973.

Mercer, J. R., & Lewis, J. P. *System of multicultural pluralistic assessment: Parent interview manual*. New York: Psychological Corporation, 1977.

Meyen, E. L., & Altman, R. Research implications. *Education and Training of the Mentally Retarded*, 1975, *45*, 526–530.

Patrick, J. L., & Reschly, D. J. Relationship of state educational criteria and demographic variables to school-system prevalence of mental retardation. *American Journal of Mental Deficiency*, 1982, *86*, 351 – 360.

Polloway, E. A., & Patton, J. R. Biological causes. In J. S. Payne & J. R. Patton, *Mental retardation*. Columbus OH: Charles E. Merrill Publishing Co., 1981.

Polloway, E. A., & Smith, J. E. *Teaching language skills to exceptional learners*. Denver: Love Publishing, 1982.

Poplin, M. S. The severely learning disabled: Neglected or forgotten? *Learning Disability Quarterly*, 1981, *4*, 330–335.

Ramey, C. T., & Haskins, R. The causes and treatment of school failures: Insights from the Carolina Abecedarian project. In M. J. Begab, H. C. Haywood, and H. L. Garber (Eds.), *Psychosocial influences in retarded performance: Strategies for improving competence* (Vol. II). Baltimore: University Park Press, 1981.

Reschly, D. J. Evaluation of the effects of SOMPA measures on classification of students as mildly mentally retarded. *American Journal of Mental Deficiency*, 1981, *86*, 16 – 20.

Reschly, D. J. Assessing mild retardation: The influence of adaptive behavior, sociocultural status, and prospects for non-biased assessment. In C. R. Reynolds and T. B. Gutkin (Eds.), *A handbook for school psychology*. New York: John Wiley, 1982.

Reschly, D. J., & Lamprecht, M. M. Expectancy effects of labels: Fact or artifact? *Exceptional Children*, 1979, *46*, 55–58.

Rothstein, J. H. (Ed.) *Mental retardation: Readings and resources* (2nd ed.). New York: Holt, Rinehart, & Winston, 1971.

Rynders, J. E., & Horrobin, J. M. Project EDGE: The University of Minnesota's communication stimulation program for Down's syndrome infants. In Friedlander, B. Z., Sterritt, G. M., & Kirk, G. E. (Eds.), *Exceptional infant: Assessment and intervention* (Vol. 3). New York: Brunner/Mazel, 1975.

Rynders, J. E., Spiker, D., & Horrobin, J. M. Underestimating the educability of Down's Syndrome children: Examination of methodological problems in recent literature. *American Journal of Mental Deficiency*, 1978, *82*, 440–558.

Smith, J. D., & Dexter, B. L. The basics movement: What does it mean for the education of mentally retarded students? *Education and Training of the Mentally Retarded*, 1980, *15*, 72–79.

Smith, J. D., & Polloway, E. A. The dimension of adaptive behavior in mental retardation research: An analysis of recent practices. *American Journal of Mental Deficiency*, 1979, *84*, 203–206.

U.S. Department of Education, Office of Special Education, Data Analysis System. Numbers and change in number of children ages 3–21 years served under P.L. 89-313 and P.L. 94-142 annually since school year 1976–1977. November 6, 1981.

Zigler, E. Research on personality structure in the retarded. In N. R. Ellis (Ed.), *International Review of Research in Mental Retardation* (Vol. 1). New York: Academic Press, 1966.

Zigler, E., & Balla, D. Issues in personality and motivation in mentally retarded persons. In M. J. Begab, H. C. Haywood, & H. L. Garber (Eds.), *Psychosocial influences in retarded performance: Issues and theories of development* (Vol. 1). Baltimore: University Park Press, 1981.

Special Talents

FOR YEARS DOWN SYNDROME WAS ANOTHER NAME FOR PROFOUND MENTAL RETARDATION AND A ONE-WAY TICKET TO AN INSTITUTION. NOT ANYMORE.

CAROL TURKINGTON

Carol Turkington is a freelance writer who specializes in the behavioral sciences.

When Mindie was born, physicians said she would always be hopelessly retarded, that she would never sit up, never walk, never speak. "She will never know you're her mother," they told 25-year-old Diane Crutcher. "Tell relatives your baby is dead."

Today, the child who would never sit up is a lively seventh-grader. The child who would never walk is the star of dance recitals. The child who would never talk or know her own mother told a symposium of physicians she was "glad Mom and Dad gave me a chance."

Yet the experts were right about one thing: Mindie does have Down syndrome, a genetic disorder that occurs when a third chromosome slips into chromosome pair 21. One of the most common birth defects and the leading physical cause of mental retardation, the syndrome occurs in North America in about 1 out of every 1,000 births. The chance of a woman giving birth to a Down child is about 1 in 1,500 when the mother is between 20 and 24, about 1 in 100 when she reaches age 40.

In addition to being retarded, children with Down syndrome often have heart defects, anomalies of the digestive system and problems with vision, muscle tone, hearing and breathing. Some experts believe that the more of these characteristics a child has, the lower the child's intellectual and social potential. But others disagree, and even if there is a correlation, most experts now believe that it is a mistake to tell a parent, "Your child has X number of characteristics, so she will never learn to read."

Indeed, experts have become increasingly wary of making any predictions about what these children can and cannot do. It used to be believed that most such children would be severely retarded and that they were doomed to life in an institution. "Normal people have the feeling that the world is open to them," explains Crutcher, now executive director of the National Down Syndrome Congress. "They know that they have the chance to grow, to become something. That feeling was denied to children with Down syndrome, and it crushed the hopes of their parents."

But recent research has shown that Down children are not all alike, that many can do very well outside of institutions, that most are only mildly retarded and a few can even reach normal levels of intelligence. This has led to a new definition of what having Down syndrome means.

Researchers now believe that one reason they and others failed to appreciate the potential of many Down children was their characteristic facial features: the slanting eyes, flattened nose and protruding tongue that give them away. Because of their appearance, these children have always felt the keen blade of discrimination (see "Changing the Look of Mental Retardation," this article).

Although physician J. Langdon Down, who described the syndrome in 1866, believed these children could learn, others through the years have dismissed them in terms ranging from "orangutans" (1924) to "nonpersons" (1968) to "uneducable" (1975) and locked them away. Until the 1970s, half of the patients in large state mental institutions had Down syndrome. Because Down children look very much alike, it was easy to believe that they were very much alike in intellectual ability. Now experts believe that these children vary widely in potential and that in many instances their retardation is as much the product of low expectations, understimulation and lack of education as it is the product of a genetic defect.

The first clues came in 1975 with

passage of the Education for All Handicapped Children Act, which required that all handicapped children be given an education, and that the education be provided in the least restrictive environment possible. This meant that thousands of institutionalized children had to be given instruction, whenever practical in regular classrooms.

The surprise to educators was that many Down syndrome children proved to be adept students. Some, like Paige Barton, now 35 years old, have a rare form of Down syndrome called mosaicism. Such children sometimes have normal potential, yet Barton had been placed in an institution because, prior to 1975, that was simply what one did with Down children. Following passage of the new law, Barton began academic training, and in 1980 she emerged from the hospital that had been her home with the equivalent of a high school diploma and a dream: She

THESE CHILDREN HAVE BEEN DISMISSED IN TERMS RANGING FROM ORANGUTAN TO NONPERSON.

wanted to teach young children. Last May, she received a two-year associate's degree in early-childhood education from the University of Maine, and she hopes to begin work on a four-year degree in special education. "Someone just told me that a person with Down syndrome couldn't graduate from college," Barton said ruefully. "I think that society should never underestimate us, and I don't feel they should put a label on us, either. Because once we've got that label, it's on us for the rest of our lives."

With pressure to educate Down children came research on how to teach them, and that research has shown that early-intervention programs, often beginning soon after birth, may be the key to unlocking the potential of these children. A study by researcher James MacDonald and his colleagues at Ohio State University showed that parents of Down syndrome children could be trained to help them learn language skills. The children used more words and more complex grammar than did children whose parents had not had training.

In a 1975 study by psychologist Reetta Bidder of the Welsh National School of Medicine and colleagues, mothers of children with Down syndrome were taught to use behavior-modification techniques to increase their children's verbal skills, self-care and motor coordination. Although the six-month program had no effect on the children's coordination, their verbal skills did improve and they became more independent.

Intensive parent-child educational training can improve the language ability of many Down syndrome children, according to a recent study by psychologist John Rynders and his colleagues at the University of Minnesota. Their five-year study, called EDGE (for Expanding Developmental Growth through Education), tried to improve communication skills through positive parent-child play lessons beginning at age 30 months. When the 35 children in the project were given an IQ test at age 5, 11 of the 17 who had had the special lessons scored in the educable range, meaning among other things that they could learn basic academic and social skills and live outside of an institution. Of the 18 children who had not received the special lessons, only 9 scored as high, and 3 were unable even to take the test. Today, Project EDGE children have been in public schools as long as 10 years after the end of their experimental early education. In 1984, a follow-up study of 13 EDGE children found that 11 were reading with comprehension at or above the second-grade level, which Rynders believes is "an acid test" for the argument of educability. Seven of the 13 children are currently in educable classes or a combination of regular and educable classes.

Based on a review of the research literature, Rynders has concluded that it is fairly common for people with Down syndrome to have IQ's in the educable range. His project suggests to him that at least half of children with Down syndrome who are reared at home in middle- or upper-middle class families can be expected to be educable when they enter school. Further, he thinks that children given some kind of early intervention can be expected to read at or above the second-grade level during the middle elementary years. "Nearly 75 percent of the EDGE children [who received special training] are reading with comprehension at that level already," he says. "They have several years of education remaining in which to achieve at much higher levels."

Early-intervention programs involving parents are helpful, but development of the full potential of Down children depends as well upon the quality of formal education they receive. One of the biggest problems for parents with Down syndrome children, however, is that when their children are ready for school, they find the school is not ready for them. Many school districts are reluctant to include these children in regular classes (a practice called mainstreaming), according to Rynders and other experts. The mainstreaming movement is only about 10 years old, and while professionals may have succeeded in convincing people that children with Down syndrome are not orangutans, they have not yet managed to convince all school districts they can benefit from schooling.

"We keep getting calls from parents who feel that their kid is ready to go into a much more rigorous program, but there isn't one available," said Donna Rosenthal, executive director of the National Down Syndrome Society. As a result, the society and the New York Board of Education have developed a program to mainstream 6- and 7-year-olds into regular classrooms for basic education. The society hopes the program, which pairs regular and special-education teachers in four city schools, will serve as a mainstreaming model.

One of the main objections to providing more than minimal education to Down children is the belief that these children soon reach an intellectual plateau beyond which they cannot advance. The belief is based on the fact that test scores level off—and may even decline—after the first few years of education. Because of this, some people argue that further education is pointless. But others disagree. They point out that the test scores compare the Down children not with their earlier performance but with the perfor-

CHANGING THE LOOK OF MENTAL RETARDATION

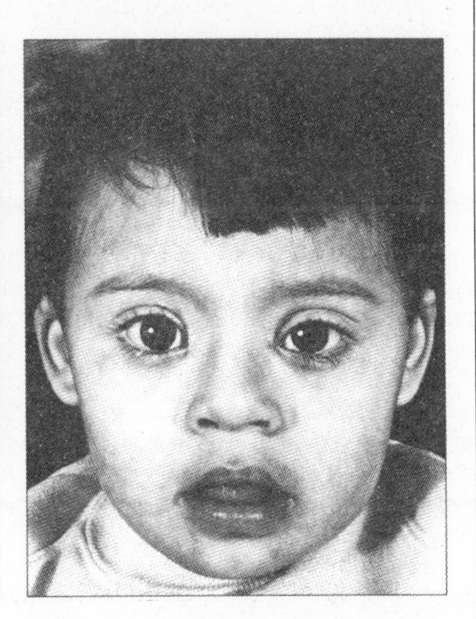

Before and after: Advocates of surgery say it reduces the stigma often associated with Down syndrome. Critics say it sends the message that the children are unacceptable in appearance as they are.

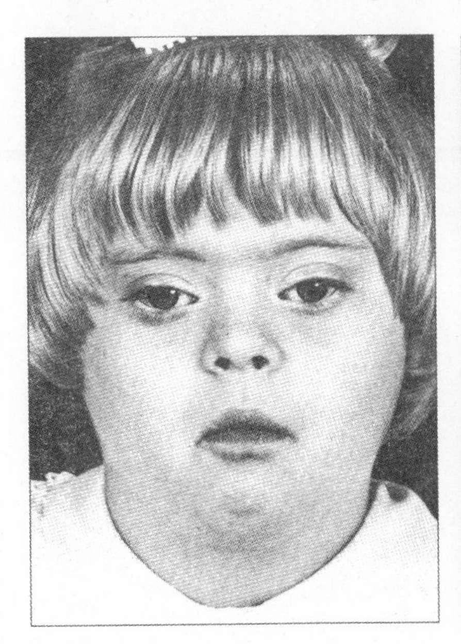

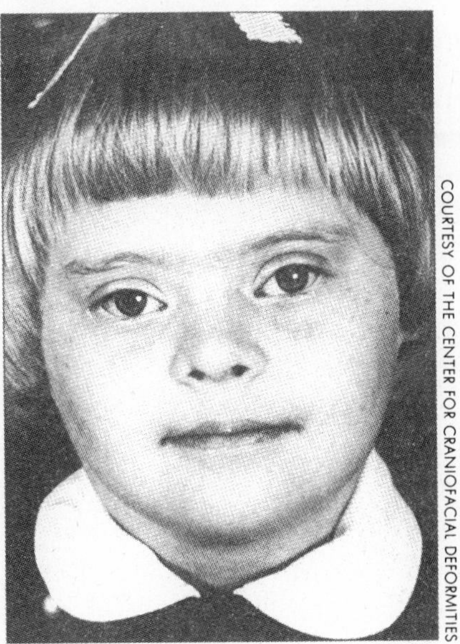

COURTESY OF THE CENTER FOR CRANIOFACIAL DEFORMITIES

Plastic surgeons can straighten the slanted eyes, build up the cheekbones and minimize the protruding tongue commonly found in children with Down syndrome. But should they? Plastic surgery remains the most controversial treatment offered Down syndrome children.

The 1½- to 2½-hour operation is fairly straightforward. Surgeons can build up the bridge of the nose, cheekbone and chin with bone grafts or synthetics, change the slant of the eyes and cut fat from the lower eyelids. There are usually no facial scars because the work is done through the mouth or by cutting skin flaps behind the hairline. The tongue, which appears too large and protrudes from an unusually small oral cavity, is reduced by about one-fifth.

Advocates of surgery believe that children with Down syndrome are rejected partly because of their physical features, and that improving their appearance may result in greater social acceptance. Critics respond that there is little hard evidence that the surgery has these effects. In fact, it has to be admitted that even the most gifted plastic surgeons can't make a child with Down syndrome look entirely normal. After surgery, the gait, neck and body proportions are still unusual. Even the face remains clearly different. "I've yet to see a child after the operation," says Diane Crutcher of the National Down Syndrome Congress, "who doesn't look like a child with Down syndrome." Moreover, say some critics, the surgery is itself a kind of rejection, a message that the children are not acceptable as themselves. It is society's preoccupation with "good looks" that should change, these critics argue, not the faces of Down children.

Even those who advocate the operation admit that not every child with Down syndrome is a good candidate for surgery, and both parents and child must go through an intensive screening process before their surgeon lifts a scalpel. "The surgery should only be performed in children whose quality of life can be improved by the procedures," cautions Garry S. Brody, clinical professor of plastic surgery at the University of Southern California. Surgery is immediately ruled out if the child is profoundly retarded or has life-threatening physical problems. In addition, parents must be realistic about what the surgery will and won't do. "If you think the child is going to roll out of the operating room with 20 more IQ points," says Crutcher, "you're going to be disappointed."

While controversial, plastic surgery remains an option for those willing to try every avenue. The American Society of Plastic and Reconstructive Surgeons operates a toll-free number (800/635-0635) for information on reconstructive and cosmetic surgery for Down syndrome and offers a referral list of board-certified plastic surgeons qualified to perform the operation.

mance of normal children. Those children advance more quickly than children with Down syndrome, so that the Down children appear to make no progress or even to slide backward. In fact, however, they are advancing, albeit more slowly than their nonhandicapped classmates. Rynders adds that "even if the plateau were real, that wouldn't mean we should stop educating them. They can continue to learn. In fact, we have evidence that they continue to develop their academic skills well into adolescence."

With an increasing number of studies, plus real-life examples such as Mindie Crutcher and Paige Barton, the National Down Syndrome Congress is pushing for progress in early intervention, recreation, secondary school programs, vocational opportunities and parent training. "We are seeing a raising of consciousness," says Diane Crutcher, "but attitudes change slowly. We all have a battle to wage to convince people to raise their sights where Down children are concerned." She notes that, despite the evidence that many Down children can benefit from schooling, resistance is strong. "This is a serious problem for parents," Crutcher says. "I can work with the local school district and overcome resistance because I have a lot of knowledge. But what about the thousands of parents who aren't so well informed? I think many of them, and their children, fall victim to the system."

Nevertheless, the situation is improving. More and more parents are arming themselves with facts and beginning to speak out. More importantly, perhaps, people with Down syndrome are beginning to speak out. A 21-year-old woman with Down syndrome testified before a Wisconsin legislative subcommittee in 1982. She spoke eloquently on behalf of those with Down syndrome when she reminded the legislators that people are better judged by what they can do than by what they cannot do:

"There are a lot of things I can do. I can swim. I can read. I can make friends. I can listen to my records. I can watch television. I can make my own lunch. I can go to see a movie. I can take the bus by myself to Chicago and to work. I can count money. I can sing like a bird. I can brush my teeth. I can do latch hook rugs. I can cook dinner. I can think. I can pray. I can square dance. I can play drums. I know what is right. I know what is wrong."

FOR MORE INFORMATION

Free information on Down Syndrome can be obtained from:

National Down Syndrome Society
141 Fifth Avenue
New York, New York 10010
(800) 221-4602

National Down Syndrome Congress
1800 Dempster Street
Park Ridge, Illinois 60068-1146
(800) 232-NDSC

AUTISM: THE CHILD WITHIN

He does not reach up for his mother's outstretched arms.
He does not return his father's smile.
He is a child tuned out, living in a wordless solitude where
other human beings appear and disappear
like irrelevant shadows.
He does not care to speak to them.

Mary B. Jones

Autism is the name we have given to this child's withdrawal from our world. Fortunately, it is rare; it is also frightening, for it is so lonely and so incomprehensible. It chills us in its rejection of the warm, gregarious pull toward one another that is the very lifeblood of our humanity.

It is natural to want to turn away.

But a few people will not do this. They are the parents and grandparents, the brothers and sisters of the autistic; and they are the teachers, researchers, and therapists who believe, in the face of heavy odds, that it is possible to break through the isolation cells that imprison these children.

Bit by bit, their amazing, hopeful determination is doing just that.

One of the most determined and most unfailingly hopeful of the professionals who have made this their lifework is Sandra Harris, a Rutgers University professor of psychology. She simply "got hooked" 17 years ago, she explains, with her warm, ready smile. Her department asked her to establish an on-campus center where psychology students could get practical experience working with autistic children; she did, and the center, with Harris in charge, has been changing the world for small groups of these children ever since.

Perhaps the most painful misconception about autism—until recent research removed its dreadful accusation—was that the parents, by the way they treated their child, somehow caused the condition. Up through the 1960s, this was the predominant view.

"We still don't know what causes autism, but the evidence is increasingly convincing that it's biologically based," Dr. Harris says. "There may be a hereditary component in some families, or there may be damage to a chromosome from exposure to a chemical or something like that. But there's just no evidence that child-rearing patterns can precipitate autism."

Nor is it unique to Western societies, Harris adds. Autism was not identified in this country until the 1940s, but what research has been done elsewhere suggests that it is a universal disorder. And, though it is rare—from 4 or 5 to 15 in 10,000 children, depending on the rigor of one's definition—there are hints that it has been around a long time: the so-called feral children, said to be raised by wolves and therefore lacking in speech, may actually have been children abandoned in the woods because they were autistic.

What autism *is* has become clearer through the studies of the last two decades. Harris cites what are recognized as the chief distinguishing features: lack of response to other people, lack of normal language development, early onset, and various forms of bizarre behavior.

"Some parents say their child seemed normal until a particular age," she says, "but many others say that, in retrospect, from as early as they can remember they think there was something wrong. The earliest clues are a lack of responsiveness—not making eye contact, not cuddling, not seeming particularly interested in being with the parents. But these things can be relatively subtle; the parents will say, 'This child was almost too good.'

"Then when the child doesn't start talking, certainly by age two, the problem becomes apparent. And when language does appear—many autistic

Reprinted from *Rutger's Magazine*, January/February 1988, pp. 10-14, by permission.

children, especially with help, do develop *some* language—it's often very peculiar in quality. The child may echo other people's speech: if you ask, 'Do you want an apple?' the child's response may be 'Do you want an apple?' Or the speech may be odd in its tonal qualities."

Between ages two and a half and five, Harris continues, various unusual or disruptive behaviors emerge. Some autistic children develop odd physical gestures, flicking their fingers in front of their faces or rocking back and forth. Sometimes, though less commonly, they will hurt themselves—biting themselves, banging their heads against a wall.

How much can be done to help an autistic child depends in large part on a separate issue: whether and how severely the child is retarded. (Admittedly, IQ tests of the autistic are difficult, Harris notes, but a good tester can make a fairly accurate evaluation.)

"Something like 70 percent of autistic children have IQs of 70 or lower, so they're cognitively very impaired," she says. "Some are of normal intelligence or even very bright, and one young man I've been working with has an IQ that must be in the genius range. But typically, autistic children are also retarded, and that has a lot to do with the prognosis, because the child that has more resources to begin with can usually make more progress."

The center Harris directs—the Douglass Developmental Disabilities Center on the Douglass campus—takes all kinds of autistic children, the high-functioning ones as well as those who are not so lucky, and offers a comprehensive educational program from preschool through adolescence. Because early treatment is very important, generally only children up through age six are accepted for entry, though there are occasional openings for older children. The center has an enrollment of about 40. Advanced undergraduates serve as individual tutors; they are supervised by experienced teachers and doctoral students in psychology.

Children at the center progress from one-to-one interactions to group work. The youngest often need individual help; the intermediate class of seven to nine year olds usually work in twos or threes; older youngsters may be able to enter the general community or may need to stay in the adolescent class.

Given the teenagers' disabilities, a typical day's activities for their class at the center are as impressive as they are revealing. The morning begins with greetings and a discussion of the weather—"We want to teach them what to wear," Dr. Harris explains—followed by concrete, functional academics.

"We're trying to teach them practical things, to read a menu or a sign that says 'Men's Room,' to use a typewriter, to put their social security number in the right place on a form," she says.

"About 11:30 they start meal preparations. They make fairly elaborate meals for themselves—spaghetti sauce, soup from scratch. One day a week they work at the Douglass College Student Center, where they portion out meat for hamburgers, fix raw vegetables for the salad bar, and clean up. On Fridays, they prepare lunch for the staff, which we buy; they use that money to go out to lunch on Wednesdays—with staff accompanying them, of course—at a regular local restaurant."

The afternoon is spent in learning manual skills that may lead to a job.

"They might practice putting the cap on a ballpoint pen, putting a group of 10 pens in a package, and stapling it shut," Dr. Harris says. "They might have to practice that for 200 to 300 days before they master it—it's a real challenge for some of these youngsters to get the

An Unusual Success Story

To show what sometimes *can* be done—with luck and patience and skillful early treatment—for a bright autistic child, Dr. Harris gives the case history of a child—here called Barbara—who came to the center as a two and a half year old:

"She was one of the brighter children, with a real stubborn streak in her. She had no speech and limited responsiveness, but she was less profoundly withdrawn than some of the children.

"One of the first things we had to do was to teach her to follow our instructions, because she was so stubbornly unyielding about doing everything her own way. So we tried to create a very reinforcing, very rewarding interaction, but where the rewards were contingent on her compliance.

"Predictably, she kicked up a fuss We might ask her to make eye contact, saying 'Barbara, look at me.' And she would tantrum and resist and holler and scream. We just kind of waited through all that and continued our demands.

"And when she would comply, then we would be lavishly rewarding, with attention and affection and food. We don't want the children to remain hooked on food—we want interpersonal exchanges to become rewarding—so we always pair the food with praise: 'Good girl, I like the way you did that,' and we might stroke her arm or her cheek or pat her tummy.

"Some children like physical contact, but they like it kind of indiscriminately. A complete stranger can walk over to one little girl in our school, pick her up and toss her in the air, and she will laugh with delight—where a normal five year old would freak out if a stranger did that. So it's not pleasure in the exchange, it's just pleasure in the sensation. But other children may not want to be touched, and we have to teach them to tolerate touch. What we're trying to do is to teach them to value touch from specific people, in a personal way.

"So with Barbara, our initial thrust was to teach her to value us, and also her family, as sources of rewards, and to insist that she comply with adult requests. Once she was complying reasonably reliably and her tantrums had diminished, we began to ease off on the demands and we could move her into a much more normal preschool.

"Her language has emerged, and she's able to greet people appropriately and talk about her experiences. And she smiles all the time now. She's a very reinforcing child for the staff to work with—she's really quite a cheerful little girl. Meanwhile, her family has been trained in our techniques, and they've been magnificent in their follow-through.

"If she continues to receive the right kind of support, there's good reason to think she may make it into a regular kindergarten. So she's an example of what can be done with a very high-functioning child."

cap on the right end, get all the pens lined up the same way, count out 10, staple the package, . . ."

The last 20 minutes or so is reward time, during which the teenagers may have a chance to watch rock video, ride the exercise bike, or be taken out jogging. The teachers are very creative in devising activities with teenage appeal, Harris says, but the young people have to earn the privilege by good behavior.

For preschoolers, the center last fall began an integrated program in which higher-functioning autistic children—whose behavior is manageable—attend classes with normal peers. Recent research has shown that this kind of contact helps autistic children make better progress, Harris says, and the center has been fortunate in finding parents understanding enough to enroll their normal preschoolers.

"The normal kids are called 'pals.' One is the daughter of a graduate student, another is the daughter of a staff member, one is the brother of an autistic kid, and the others are children whose parents responded to an ad we ran."

The class, she says, operates much like a normal preschool, and a casual observer might not realize which children were autistic and which were not. What would seem remarkable is the intense effort of the special education teachers, who perform nonstop for five hours, drawing the maximum from each child.

Harris's own research and much of her effort has centered on the parents of the autistic children who come to the center. Studies have shown that consistent follow-up is essential for making permanent changes in the children's speech and behavior, so Harris has been teaching parents to use the behavior modification techniques that the school has found effective.

"The idea is to make the teaching very systematic, break things down into small steps, and make sure it's rewarding for the child—make sure there's a maximum opportunity to be rewarded and a minimum of failure," Harris says. "If we want to teach a child to say *ball,* for instance, we might first just reward the child with bits of ice cream for making *b* sounds, then the other sounds, and then combining them all—step by step.

"We've shown that within 10 weeks, parents can become skillful in using these techniques, and that the children respond to the changes in their parents."

Harris believes it is misleading, and even cruel, to claim that even a parent's best efforts can procure a completely normal life for most autistic children. The brighter ones, treated intensively and early, may indeed be able to enter a regular public school. But for most, the realistic hope is that—instead of winding up on the back wards of an institution, as they once would have—they may, as adults, be able to live in group homes, perhaps holding simple jobs in the community.

And if they do? Will they really be happier?

"It depends on what you mean by happiness," Harris says. "I don't get the sense that most of these children are subjectively suffering. Given kind physical care and a supportive environment, I don't know that autistic people are any less happy than the rest of us.

"What they would be denied, and what it is possible for a well-educated autistic person to achieve, is some sense of self, some feeling of accomplishment.

"When I see our young people at the salad bar, they're looking around at other people who are also cutting up vegetables, and they sort of stand up straighter—they don't pose behavior problems there—it's almost as if they're saying to themselves, 'I'm a person among people,' and there's an awareness of that, there's a pride in themselves, whether they can ever articulate it or not.

"That's a kind of happiness that goes beyond physical contentment. That's the humanity, that's the sense of oneself as a self.

"I take a lot of pleasure in the brighter little ones, who will be going on to regular schools. But these teenagers who have had to work so hard to overcome their handicap, and they're doing it—to me that's *really* satisfying."

A Question of Ethics

An encounter with Sandra Harris can hardly help leaving an interviewer with an impression of extraordinary warmth, good humor, and commitment to an often thankless task. And—naggingly—a question comes too: in the scheme of things, is this the best use of such dedicated talent?

"It's an important social question—the extent to which we are morally justified in investing our resources in treating such a small population," Harris agrees. "It's a question I pose to my students regularly. If we had a school on campus for kids from inner cities, for example, and gave them a leg up by providing the same kinds of intensive educational experiences, might not that benefit society more?—because those are kids of normal intelligence, and many of them might go on to accomplish very impressive things in their lives.

"Clearly, since I've chosen to put my effort into working with this autistic population, I feel it's justified."

For society as a whole, she explains, there's the prospect of learning where social relatedness comes from.

"Unlike retarded children, who are often very responsive, autistic children have this very specific deficit. Is there something in the brain that predisposes us to be interpersonally responsive? Can we find that place in the brain? Does it carry implications for other people who have trouble with relatedness?

"And it's the same with language—why is language in these autistic children so much more impaired than the language of retarded children with a similar IQ? Does the lack of language impair social relatedness, or does the social lack diminish the incentive to learn language?"

Persuasive arguments indeed for continuing research—but Harris pauses here, for these are not, after all, the central issue to her. Or not the whole of it.

"Just on a philosophical level," she says, "I feel that *every* child has rights. Every child deserves the opportunity to become as much as he or she can. And as we begin to document that there's a chance of normalcy for at least some autistic children, that point becomes all the more persuasive.

"It also seems to me that we diminish our society if we regard only the rights of the well and strong or the many. If we push aside the autistic and the retarded, we deny our own humanity; we could never become as human as we can be, ourselves."

USING Task Variation TO Motivate Handicapped Students

Lee Kern Dunlap
Glen Dunlap

Lee Kern Dunlap *is a special education teacher in the Cabell County Public Schools, and* **Glen Dunlap** *is Director of Training and Research at the Autism Training Center, Marshall University, Huntington, West Virginia.*

■ Teachers of handicapped and nonhandicapped students share the goal of increasing their students' motivation to learn new skills. This goal is particularly important to teachers working with students who have slow learning rates and histories of frustration and failure. Careful consideration of variables and implementation of procedures that affect learning rate and motivation is essential. This article focuses on a procedure known as *task variation*, which recent research has found to influence the motivation of students with a broad variety of handicapping conditions.

When attempting to increase motivation and learning rate, teachers most commonly consider consequences. For example, reward systems, including the delivery of tokens or free time, often are implemented to encourage and reinforce successful task completion. While these techniques are valuable, studies have shown that antecedent variables also play an important role in increasing student learning rate and motivation (Dunlap & Egel, 1982; Mulligan, et al., 1980). In particular, task variation, which involves the selection and scheduling of tasks within a teaching lesson, has been shown to affect the motivation and learning of many handicapped students in a positive way.

Much of the research on task variation has been conducted with mentally retarded or autistic students. These studies have demonstrated that task variation can facilitate learning (Cuvo, et al., 1980; Dunlap, 1984; Neef, Iwata,

The first step in programming task variation is to select the new task to be taught.

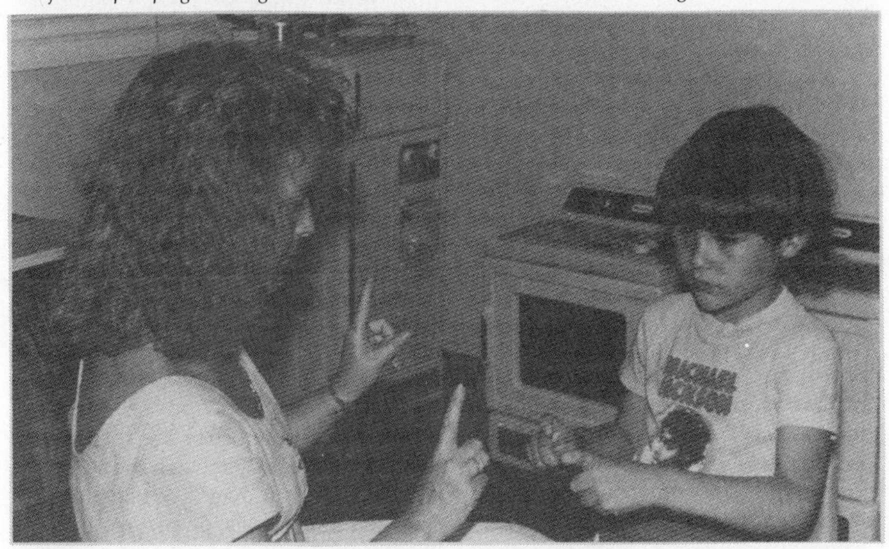

Next the teacher chooses task(s) that the student has already mastered.

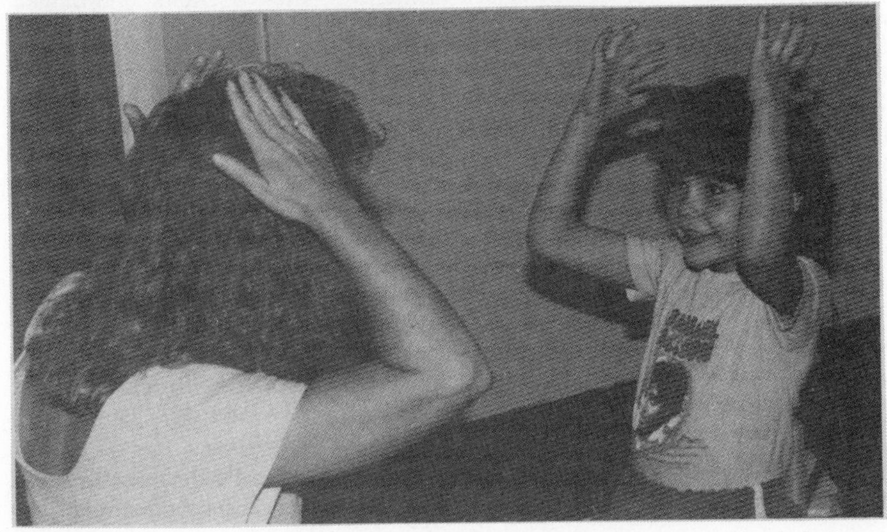

By use of task variation, the student's enthusiasm is obvious.

& Page, 1980) and produce heightened levels of motivation (Dunlap & Egel, 1982). Other investigations have shown that task variation is effective with students who have aphasia or learning disabilities (Dunlap, Koegel, Koegel, & Dunlap, 1985; Koegel & Koegel, 1986, in press). The procedure also can reduce levels of off-task and disruptive behaviors (Winterling, Dunlap, & O'Neill, in press). Finally, observers have noted that when students are taught using a task variation approach, they appear to be happier, more enthusiastic, and more interested in the instructional activities (Dunlap, 1984; Dunlap & Koegel, 1980).

What Is Task Variation?

Task variation is the process of presenting both mastered and unmastered tasks intermittently during a teaching session. Previously-learned tasks are interspersed among new tasks to be taught in the student's curriculum. Related methods of varying task sequences have been described as "interspersal" or "distributed trial" procedures. However, the term *task variation* is used here to indicate specifically that the procedure involves frequent variation of the instructional request and frequent presentation of tasks at which the student is already proficient.

Task variation is contrary to the commonly used constant task (or massed trials) approach, in which a new task is presented repeatedly throughout a teaching session. For example, when teaching multiplication facts, teachers often present flashcards with only the facts the students have yet to learn, drilling them on these facts until a certain criterion level is reached. Similarly, with autistic or other severely handicapped students, teachers have ordinarily focused on only one skill, such as picture labeling, throughout a 10- to 20-minute session. However, when the new skill is relatively difficult for a particular student, studies have shown that such constant task strategies often result in declining levels of motivation and performance and increases in off-task behaviors (Winterling, et al., in press). In contrast, the use of task variation has been successful in maintaining relatively high levels of motivation and learning for extended periods of time (Dunlap & Koegel, 1980).

Because task variation requires frequent presentation of previously mastered or "review" tasks during an instructional session, teachers may be concerned about the most efficient use of their limited *instructional time*. But, research has shown that, at least for relatively difficult tasks, task variation produces more rapid and more efficient learning than constant task sequences (Dunlap, 1984). In addition, task variation provides for review of previously learned material and produces more desirable behavior and heightened levels of student enthusiasm (Dunlap & Koegel, 1980).

Steps in Programming Task Variation

The first step in programming task variation is to select the new task or tasks to be taught. The new task(s) should be selected from the student's curriculum and should be appropriate to his or her learning rate and level of performance. The optimal number of new tasks to be presented during a session will vary depending upon the difficulty of the tasks and the motivation of the student. The number should be limited to ensure a high level of success.

After selection of the new task(s), the next step is to choose a set of tasks that the student has already mastered. These previously mastered tasks will interspersed regularly and frequently among the new task(s) that are being taught. These mastered tasks must be tasks that the student can perform easily and successfully, and they should be convenient to the setting in which the new task is being taught. For example, if the new task requires sitting at a desk reading words from flashcards, mastered tasks should be chosen that can be performed in a sitting position inside the classroom. Likewise, if the student is learning a new task outdoors—a new exercise, for example—the mastered tasks should also be outdoor tasks, perhaps including other gross motor skills.

During the teaching session, presentation of the new task should be randomly alternated with requests to perform the mastered tasks. A one-to-one ratio of new and mastered task presentations is suggested, but this ratio will vary depending on the individual student's motivation and learning rate. The student should be rewarded for each successful performance of the already mastered task as well as success with the new task being taught. Corrective feedback, prompting, and other procedures should be provided when the student does not perform the new task successfully.

Examples of Task Variation Sessions

During Individual Instruction

Example 1. Herb is enrolled in a self-contained junior high school classroom for students with mild to moderate mental retardation. He is reading on approximately a second grade level and can read some sight words as well as simple phonetic words. His teacher is now teaching him to read emergency and "survival" words and phrases including "Danger," "Exit," "High Voltage," "Wet Paint," and "No Admittance." The teacher also makes a list of words Herb has already mastered, including "and," "for," "cat," "top," and "sit." She writes each of these words on a flashcard.

During the teaching session, Herb is asked to read the first card, "Danger." When he says he does not know it, the teacher tells him the word is "Danger." The teacher then presents the next flashcard, which is printed with the word "and." Herb reads the word correctly and is given a point (to be spent at the end of the day) for his success. The next card, which has the word "Exit" printed on it, is then presented. This procedure is repeated until each word has been presented three times, and then the session is terminated. These sessions continue each day until the mastery criterion is reached. Herb's teacher has decided that his mastery level should be correct reading of a new word three consecutive times on three consecutive days. Herb reaches mastery level on the word "Danger" within a week. Another new word, "Flammable," replaces "Danger" on the new words list, and "Danger" is then used as a mastered word to reinforce his newly acquired skill.

Example 2. Sally is a 7-year-old who has been diagnosed as autistic and severely mentally retarded. She is nonverbal, has poor attending skill, and exhibits many repetitive, stereotyped behaviors such as body rocking and hand flapping. During previous attempts to teach her simple signs, Sally would get upset after a few minutes of instruction and her behavior would quickly deteriorate to the point that continued instruction appeared to be futile. Acquisition of expressive signs (beginning with "drink," "eat," "hug," etc.) is a high priority objective, but the lessons have been difficult and frustrating for Sally. Her teacher, Mr. Moore, decides to try task variation.

Mr. Moore first decides that the new tasks will be the signs for "drink" and "hug," both of which refer to activities that Sally enjoys. He then identifies skills that Sally has mastered previously. These include clapping hands upon instruction, pointing to a magazine picture of ice cream, pointing to herself when asked "Who is Sally?", and imitating a variety of gestures when asked to "Do this." During task variation sessions, Mr. Moore never presents trials on the new tasks more than three times in a row. He frequently intersperses trials on the previously mastered activities. Sally's behavior improves immediately. She works cooperatively throughout 15-minute sessions, and within three sessions she has learned to sign for "drink." A new sign, "eat," is then included, and "drink" becomes a mastered task.

During Small Group Instruction

Ms. Grant teaches learning disabled students in an elementary school resource room. Her goal is to teach her group of four students to identify adjectives in simple sentences. The students have previously mastered the identification of nouns and verbs in simple sentences. After describing and demonstrating what an adjective is, Ms. Grant gives each of her students a worksheet containing 10 sentences. The students are then asked to read the first sentence and identify the noun by writing the letter N above it. Ms. Grant glances at each of the student's papers, sees that they have all identified the noun correctly, and praises them for doing a fine job. They are then asked to identify the adjective in the sentence by placing an A over it. While glancing at their papers, Ms. Grant see that two of her students have not identified the adjective correctly. She then explains why the students' choices were incorrect, identifies the adjective, and describes why that word is an adjective. Then the students are asked to identify the verb by writing a V over the word. Again, all are successful and are praised. They are then asked to identify the adjective in the next sentence. This procedure continues until the students must return to their regular classroom and the lesson can be resumed the next day.

In Settings Outside the Classroom

Miles is a 10-year-old boy with traumatic aphasia caused by a stroke. He attends a classroom for learning handicapped students in an elementary school. Each day the classroom aide takes Miles for a walk, during which time she works on his ability to identify objects in his environment. Miles's aide has decided to work on three new vocabulary words each day. She knows he is able to identify the objects "tree," "school," and "car." The aide points to a car and asks Miles to name it. He correctly names it and receives a token. She then picks up a rock and asks Miles to identify it. When he is unable to do so, she teaches him that this object is a "rock." Next, she points to a tree and asks him what it is. He correctly identifies it and receives another token. She then picks up the rock again and asks him to name it. This interspersal of known and unknown items continues until Miles has correctly named each of the three new items at least one time.

The teacher presenting new skills to the students.

The teacher presenting skills that have already been mastered to the students.

Summary

Task variation is an instructional procedure that increases the motivation and learning of students with handicaps. There are two key components to the procedure. First, teachers should incorporate variety in their lessons by presenting different types of instructions rather than the same task repeatedly. Second, teachers should ensure a level of student competence by presenting tasks that have been mastered previously.

Many research studies have shown that task variation can facilitate instruction with students who have a broad diversity of handicapping conditions. Task variation is not difficult to use, and it can have a favorable influence on motivation, learning, and overall student behavior.

References

Cuvo, A. J., Klevans, L., Borakove, S., Borakove, L. S., Van Lunduyt, J., & Lutzker, J. R. (1980). A comparison of three strategies for teaching object names. *Journal of Applied Behavior Analysis, 13,* 249-258.

Dunlap, G. (1984). The influence of task variation and maintenance tasks on the learning and affect of autistic children. *Journal of Experimental Child Psychology,* 37, 41- 64.

Dunlap, G., & Egel, A. L. (1982). Motivational techniques. In R. L. Koegel, A. Rincover, & A. L. Egel (Eds.), *Educating and understanding autistic children* (pp. 106-126). San Diego: College-Hill Press.

Dunlap, G., & Koegel, R. L. (1980). Motivating autistic children through stimulus variation. *Journal of Applied Behavior Analysis, 13,* 619-628.

Dunlap, L. K., Koegel, L. K., Koegel, R. L., & Dunlap, G. (1985, May). *Instructional variation: Effects on the academic performance of learning handicapped students.* Paper presented at the eleventh annual convention of the Association for Behavior Analysis, Columbus, OH.

Koegel, L. K., & Koegel, R. L. (1986, in press). The effects of interspersed maintenance tasks on academic performance and motivation in a severe childhood stroke victim. *Journal of Applied Behavior Analysis.*

Mulligan, M., Guess, D., Holvoet, J., & Brown, F. (1980). The individualized curriculum sequencing model (I): Implications from research on massed, distributed, or spaced trial training. *Journal of the Association for the Severely Handicapped, 5,* 325- 336.

Neef, N. A., Iwata, B. A., & Page, T. J. (1980). The effects of interpersonal training versus high density reinforcement on spelling acquisition and retention. *Journal of Applied Behavior Analysis, 13,* 153-158.

Winterling, V., Dunlap, G., & O'Neill, R. E. (in press). The influence of task variation on the aberrant behavior of autistic students. *Educ. and Treatment of Children.*

Increasing INDEPENDENCE *through* COMMUNITY LEARNING

SUZANNE B. WIGGINS
MICHAEL M. BEHRMANN

Suzanne B. Wiggins *(CEC Chapter #158) is the Community Living Instructor, Key Center, Fairfax County Public Schools, and* **Michael M. Behrmann** *(CEC Chapter #45) is Associate Professor and Coordinator, Severely/Profoundly Handicapped Teacher Preparation Program, George Mason University, Fairfax, Virginia.*

■Public school curricula for moderately and severely handicapped adolescents and young adults are changing. Recent trends have been away from specification of curricular goals on the basis of developmental age and toward instruction in chronologically age-appropriate skills students need to meet the demands of their community environments (Gaule, Nietupski, & Certo, 1985; Peters, Templeman, & Brostrom, 1987). Deficits in student performance during the school years and beyond suggest that this skill instruction must be conducted in real-world settings in the presence of nonhandicapped people and using naturally occurring materials and situations (Hamre-Nietupski, Nietupski, Bates, & Maurer, 1982).

Many professionals have suggested that handicapped students' own communities become expanded school environments (Aveno, Renzaglia, & Lively, 1987; Brown, Nietupski, & Hamre-Nietupski, 1976). This theory is based on the premise that moderately and severely handicapped individuals have difficulty generalizing skills from an artificially structured environment to the natural environment. To remedy this, skills are taught in their naturally occurring environment, with the classroom used as a resource for teaching prerequisite skills and providing remediation.

Recent literature on community living programs for moderately and severely handicapped individuals focuses on two main areas. The first involves programs for adolescents age 15 and above who are actually living in the community, in group homes, for example (Landesman-Dwyer, 1981; Welch, Nietupski, & Hamre-Nietupski, 1985). The second area of focus involves school-based programs that teach a variety of community living skills by simulating the natural setting in the classroom. A mastery criterion must be met in the classroom as a prerequisite for performance of the skill in its naturally occurring environment (Van Den Pol, Iwata, Ivancic, Page, Neef, & Whitley, 1981).

Because moderately and severely handicapped students have difficulty transferring skills they learn in the classroom to natural environments such as stores, restaurants, and public transportation, they require instruction beyond that simulated in the classroom. The Fairfax County public schools system, in Fairfax, Virginia, offers a program beginning at an early age with a structured program that teaches skills in the actual environment in which they will be used. Classroom simulation is not required as a prerequisite; each skill is introduced initially in the community. This approach, termed *community learning,* is an extension of the community integration program that all moderately and severely handicapped students participate in. The community learning program begins at age 10 and emphasizes a more intensified instructional schedule to prepare students for the home and work environments they may encounter by the time they complete the school program.

In this program, the extended classroom incorporates areas such as restaurants, grocery stores, banks, and drugstores. Student need, parental preference, and future employment opportunities are considered when selecting the areas in which each student needs to maximize independence.

Program Structure

During the last 2 school years, 45 children have participated in the community integration program on a weekly basis. An additional 50 children from other classes have rotated into the program on the buddy system. The four-stage instructional sequence begins in September with street crossing, then progresses to using public transportation by November and on to the remaining environments from December to June. The amount of time spent on each instructional area depends on the goals for each student and the degree of competence

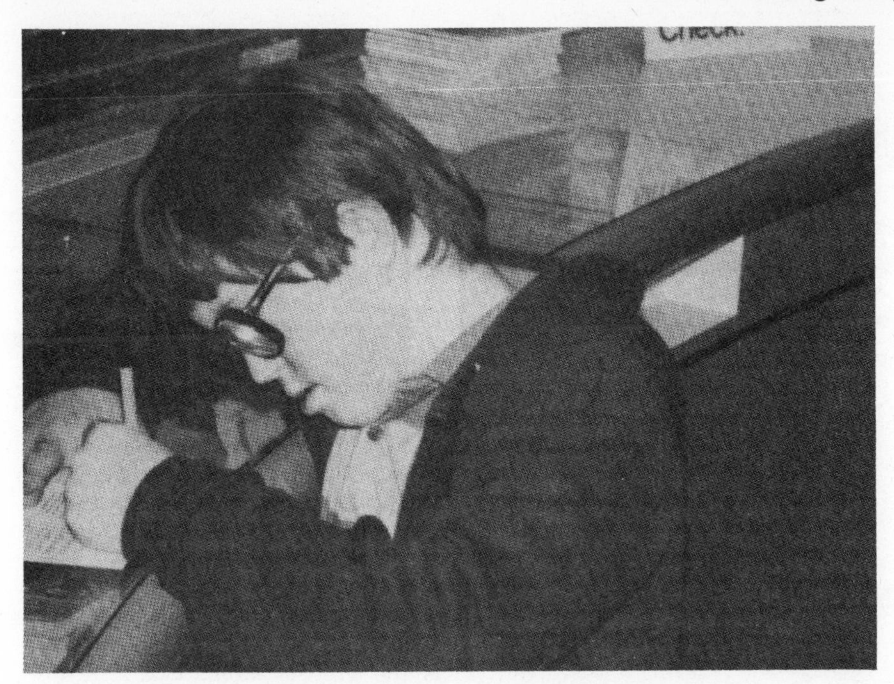

Skill instruction is taught in naturally occurring environments with the classroom used as a resource for teaching prerequisite skills and providing remediation.

the instructor feels is adequate before moving on to another area. At the conclusion of instruction in each of the four areas, the students are tested on attainment of their individually determined goals and objectives by going to different shopping malls, grocery stores, and restaurants to see whether or not the skills are carried over. Parents are encouraged to go along on community trips so they see their children performing the community living skills and can encourage repetition of those skills on family outings.

Team teaching, using two or more teachers, allows one teacher to assume the role of community integration instructor, taking small groups of students into the community every day. The other teachers continue classroom instruction, with students changing classes on a bell schedule or staying in a self-contained setting. With a different group of students going into the community daily, at the end of each week all students have received 1 day of community instruction. A minimal amount of time is spent in the classroom, and skills are taught as they relate to the community program. For example, students receive instruction in money identification and usage as they select their fare to ride the public bus. After initial introduction to the community environment and the discussion of the goals for that day's trip, the students prepare to go out. They comb their hair, check their appearance, and may try using cologne or perfume. Awareness of personal appearance becomes increasingly important as students mature; therefore, grooming skills are emphasized prior to each community integration experience. With skill reinforcement at this early age at school and follow-up at home, these skills have a better chance of becoming habit.

Preparation

The students prepare for community-based instruction by acquiring two identification cards. First is the Metro ID, which allows them to ride the public bus and subway systems at a reduced rate. The students go to the Metro bus center to have their IDs made, or in some cases Metro transportation staff will come to the school if a large number of handicapped students need IDs. Next, students are taken to the Division of Motor Vehicles, where they obtain IDs for nondrivers. Many skills are taught through this process, for example, signing the application, waiting in line, getting money from their wallets, and responding to verbal cues from the person behind the counter. The students take pride in having their own IDs made and are careful not to lose them.

Traffic and Public Transportation Instruction

Following preparation, classroom discussion, and a personal appearance check, the students are ready to begin the first community instruction area, traffic and public transportation. This area is broken into two sections. The first, street crossing, has two goals: to develop awareness of potential danger and to initiate safe crossing. An adult is present at all instructional sessions. The second section is riding public transportation, with goals of: increasing independence in selecting bus fare, boarding public buses, and exhibiting age-appropriate behavior while riding buses. Each step of instruction is task-analyzed, and data sheets accompany the student so that skill progress may be charted and sent home to parents following the community trip. Instruction in street crossing is initiated on the sidewalk rather than in the classroom, so students can see immediately the relationship between the lesson and where it will be used in the community.

Parent volunteers are an essential part of street crossing instruction. Acting as volunteer drivers, they assist in creating traffic situations, enabling the students to practice in controlled, yet realistic, environments.

The importance of looking both ways is emphasized as vehicles driven by two parent volunteers come from opposite directions. Checklists of students' individualized goals and objectives are used to record progress and are sent home to parents each week. A student who has attained his or her individual degree of competence for crossing the street is awarded a certificate. This is an important part of the program, serving as immediate feedback as well as being something to take home.

The next step in public transportation instruction is learning to ride public buses. Walking to the bus stop reinforces the previously learned street-crossing skills. Organizing and sequencing skills are taught as the students arrive at the bus stop, take out their wallets, select the correct bus fare, and get out their Metro ID cards.

Remembering the sequential steps poses various challenges to students at different levels of functioning. Some students may have the objective of selecting the correct bus fare from a wallet containing bus fare and lunch money, while the objective of others may be simply to hold all the items (purse, wallet, money, gloves, Metro ID) without dropping them.

Safety Instruction

Goals of safety instruction are to (1) learn to discriminate between friends and strangers and (2) learn what to do if lost in a public place. A busy shopping mall is a good place to begin safety instruction because it requires the student to concentrate despite many distractions. This skill is one of the most critical components of community instruction, because skills are learned that will apply to all community environments. Initially, the students learn the difference between a friend and stranger. Instruction is initiated in the shopping mall rather than in the classroom, because the concept of a "stranger" is easier to grasp when a stranger is actually pointed out.

Students begin to identify a "friend" or "helper" as either someone behind a counter in a store or someone wearing a name tag. Many employees do not wear name tags, so students are initially taught that the counter is the safest place to go. Once a student has the idea of who and who not to approach when lost, a structured set of steps is taught. When lost, students are instructed to go into a store, walk to the counter, and stand in front of it. They are taught not to talk to anyone who does not have a name tag or is not behind the counter. At the counter, students should say "Excuse me" to gain attention, and take out their wallets containing their identification cards and communication cards, which have a preprinted message they can point to (see Figure 1). While pointing to the words and pictures on their communication cards, students should attempt to speak as clearly as possible. The communication cards aid students in clarifying their messages, since salespeople, who are unfamiliar listeners, may have much more difficulty understanding their speech than those who work with them on a daily basis. Another reason for using communication cards is that students who are usually intelligible may become frightened if lost and forget what to say.

Using a shopping list is one goal for students.

After learning the sequence of what to do if lost, the students practice in several stores and in different shopping malls to ensure that the skill will carry over to other environments should they actually get lost.

Grocery Store Instruction

The third community instruction area is the grocery store. Goals include using a shopping list, communicating the need for assistance to a salesperson, locating aisles, locating food items, and checking out. Functional academic skills such as counting and number recognition; money recognition and usage; sight word recognition; and auditory, visual, and tactile skills are also incorporated in grocery shopping instruction, based on the student's level of functioning. In preparation for instruction in the grocery store, students develop a shopping list at home with their parents (see Figure

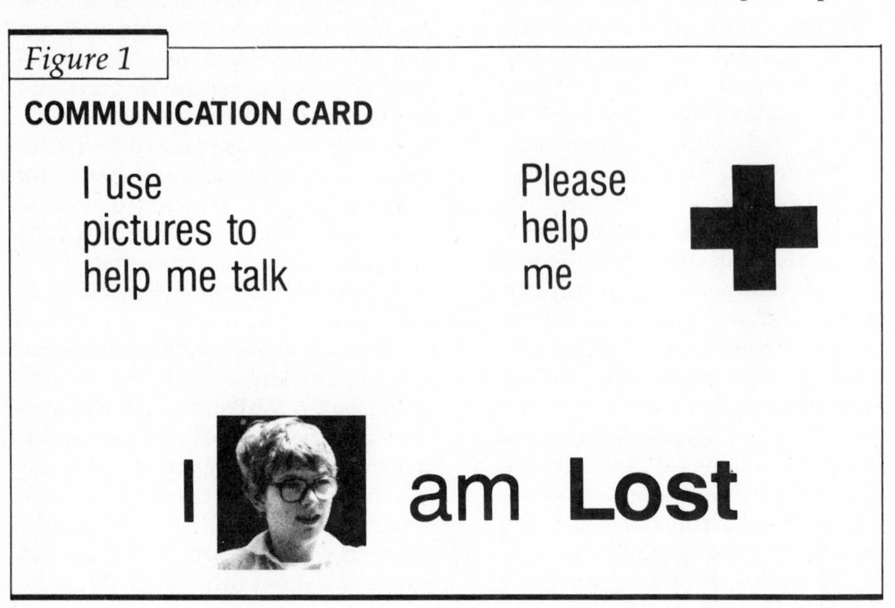

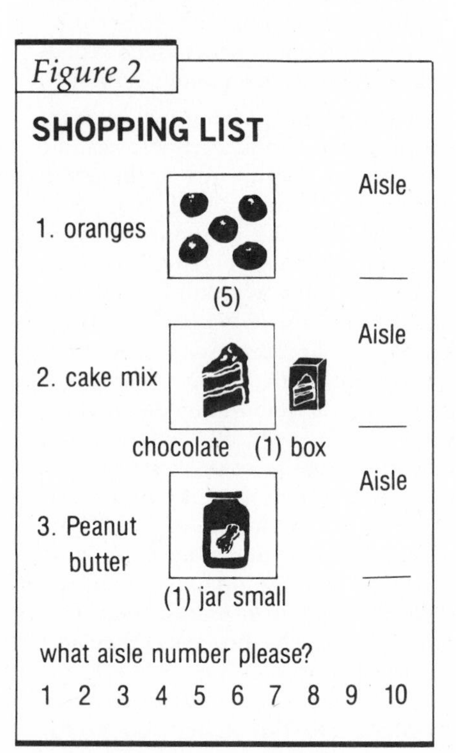

2). At school, the nonreaders add pictures to the words, so that students at all levels can participate.

When they arrive at the grocery store, the students' first challenge is to enter the building. Learning the words "in" and "out" can be more meaningful in this natural setting than when they are seen on flashcards in the classroom. If they are unsure of where to locate a particular item, the students' safety skill instruction has taught them how to identify a friend who can assist them. Communication skills are again stressed as the students express their needs and store personnel assist them with directions for locating items on their shopping lists. For students who have difficulty remembering the number the grocery clerk tells them, the aisle number is circled on a list of numbers at the bottom of the shopping list. The students can then match the marked number with the large number hanging from the ceiling over the aisle.

The buddy system can be beneficial to students at different functioning levels. Students with varying ability levels can be paired, with each student having his or her own objective, but at the same time learning from the other. For example, one student's objective might be to locate a food item and take it from the shelf, while another's might be to hold the item for a few seconds or make eye contact with the item. Three students of different functioning levels can also work together nicely. One student's objective might be to hold on to the cart and walk with the others; the second student's objective might be to match the aisle number to a written number and locate a food item in that aisle, while the objective of the third student might be to add up the prices of the items on a calculator.

Money skills are reinforced as the students pay for their purchases. Money values are more relevant in a grocery store because students are rewarded with tangible items to take home, rather than just pretending to buy groceries in a simulated store at school. The final highlight of the grocery store trip is the chance to take the food home to share with families. This makes the entire shopping sequence cohesive for the students, from initially making the shopping list at home with their parents to actually coming home with the food items.

Students order from menus to practice communication skills.

Restaurant Instruction

The fourth area of community-based instruction is the restaurant. Goals in this area include developing good table manners, ordering skills (communication), eating skills, utensil usage, and behavior in a public restaurant. Instruction begins at a sit-down, rather than fast-food, restaurant because of the calmer atmosphere. In this setting the students have the opportunity to order from a menu, a very common community activity. The menus can be adapted by adding pictures so that all students, even nonreaders, can participate (see Fig. 3).

A speech and language clinician may accompany the group, instructing them in proper speech and language as it occurs naturally, as well as assisting students who use electronic speaking devices such as the Minspeak and Handi-voice, which produce voice-synthesized words and phrases when the student presses picture-coded buttons.

Home living skills such as cutting food and using proper utensils and table manners are incorporated. Proper table manners and behaviors are reinforced strongly, since they are more likely to be displayed in small groups and around nonhandicapped customers than in a noisy school cafeteria. At the end of the meal, the students must pay for their food; thus, functional money-handling and counting skills are again reinforced in this natural setting. High school volunteers often accompany the students into the community to assist with instruction as

Figure 3

MENU ADAPTATION

well as providing peer companionship.

Program Evaluation

Children have benefited from the program in a variety of ways including changing of inappropriate behaviors, improved academic functioning, and improved therapeutic functioning. Individual student performance data on functional and academic skill areas and behavior were collected in each setting. All 45 students participating on a weekly basis showed improvement in at least one skill area and in behavior. The need to communicate with people in community environments resulted in increased social and communication skills in most children.

The program has been successful in either diminishing or extinguishing many inappropriate behaviors, which is attributed to the more normalized settings and the models of behavior in a "real-world" environment. Functional academics also have improved, with better acquisition and retention related to number recognition, money skills, and sight word recognition. Improved therapeutic outcomes include better communication and age-appropriate social skills and more independent mobility and assertiveness.

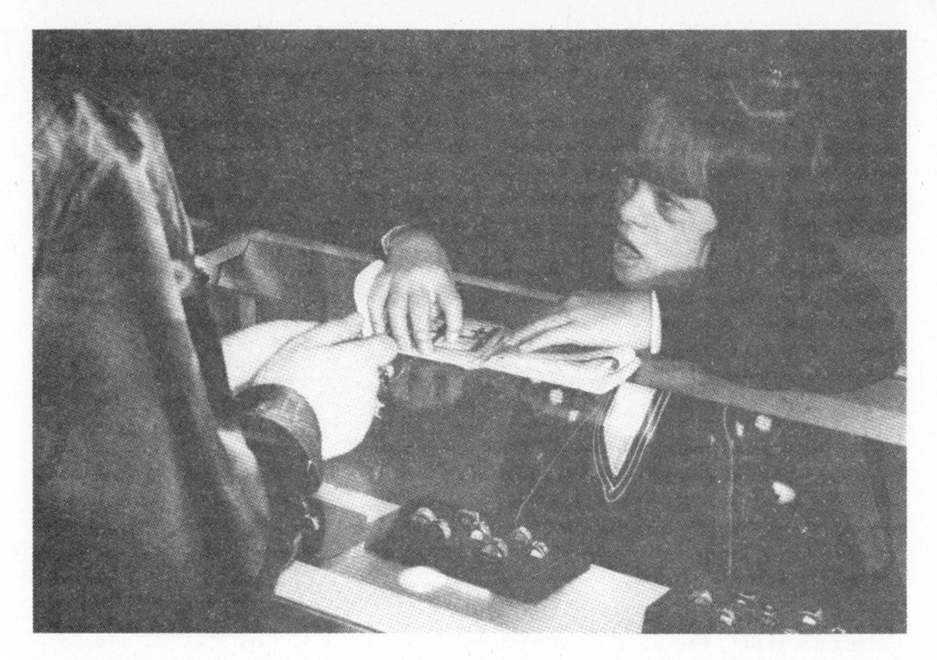

Students learn to discriminate between friends and strangers in the event they need assistance.

Conclusion

Starting with the building principal, who encouraged a pilot program, Fairfax County public school administrators have endorsed the cost-benefits and the academic, behavioral, and social gains that such a program provides. They have extended support for the program through their regular instructional programming budgets. They have provided the flexibility of teacher scheduling and class roles that allow a teacher, aides, and therapists to work in community settings. They have also provided the additional transportation necessary for trips into the community, as well as summer employment for the teachers who developed the program to write and produce a curriculum that can be used in other settings. The county has also produced a videotape of the community integration program that can be shown to parents and teachers.

The community learning approach is beneficial for all school-age handicapped students. The earlier the program is introduced, the more opportunities the students have for interaction with nonhandicapped individuals, and the better prepared they are for independent living. By going into the community once a week for the entire school year, the students have ample opportunity to learn skills that will help them for the rest of their lives, as well as the self-assurance to use them.

References

Aveno, A., Renzaglia, A., & Lively, C. (1987). Surveying community training sites to insure that instructional decisions accommodate the site as well as the trainees. *Education and Training in Mental Retardation, 22* (3), 167-175.

Brown, L., Nietupski, J., & Hamre-Nietupski, S. (1976). The criterion of ultimate functioning. In M. A. Thomas (Ed.) *Hey, don't forget about me! Education's investment in severely/profound, and multiply handicapped,* (pp. 2-15). Reston, VA: The Council for Exceptional Children.

Gaule, K., Nietupski, J., & Certo, N. (1985). Teaching supermarket skills using an adaptive shopping list. *Education and Training of the Mentally Retarded,* 53(1), 53-59.

Hamre-Nietupski, S., Nietupski, J., Bates, P., & Maurer, S. (1982). Implementing a community-based educational model for moderately/severely handicapped students: Common problems and suggested solutions. *Journal of the Assoc. for the Severely Handicapped, 7,* 38-42.

Landesman-Dwyer, S. (1981). Living in the community. *American Journal of Mental Deficiency, 86* (3), 223-234.

Peters, J., Templeman, T., & Brostrom, G. (1987). The school and community partnership: Planning transition for students with severe handicaps. *Exceptional Children, 53,* 531-536.

Van Den Pol, R., Iwata, B., Ivancic, M., Page, T., Neef, N., & Whitley, P. (1981). Teaching the handicapped to eat in public places: Acquisition, generalization and maintenance of restaurant skills. *Journal of Applied Behavior Analysis, 14,* 61-69.

Welch, J. Nietupski, J., & Hamre-Nietupski, S. (1985). Teaching public transportation problem solving skills to young adults with moderate handicaps. *Education and Training of the Mentally Retarded, (12),* 287-295.

Sexuality and Students with Mental Retardation

Sandra McClennen

Sandra McClennen *(CEC Chapter #223) is Professor of Special Education, Eastern Michigan University, Ypsilanti, Michigan.*

Sexuality, which in its broader context includes affection and the pleasure of being close to people one cares for, is an area of risk for people with mental retardation. To be "at risk" is to be, through the accident of one's attributes or environment, subject to a higher than average likelihood that events leading to negative consequences will occur. Students with severe mental retardation can be "at risk" for learning inappropriate sexual behaviors.

Mentally retarded people have the same range of sexual needs or drives as nonretarded people. They are neither asexual nor sexually deranged. If physical development is normal, sexual development follows chronological rather than cognitive development. For example, retarded infants need holding and stroking; most retarded children derive pleasurable sensations from touching their genitals; and adolescence brings a strong interest in the opposite sex. As with nonhandicapped people, some retarded people seem to have little need for physical contact and some express more need than usual, while the majority fall into the middle range.

Need for Appropriate Education

Students with mental retardation are placed at risk for developing unacceptable sexual behaviors when we do not educate them in this area or when we "teach" them the opposite of the behaviors we want. When retarded people display sexual behavior far from the norm, it is almost always the result of the way they have been treated rather than the fact that they are retarded. Retarded children depend on others for help with many basic functions. How this help is given has a major impct on their understanding of public and private behavior, modest and immodest behavior, and ownership of their own bodies. This article looks at some of the strategies teachers can use to be certain that they teach their moderately and severely retarded students the behaviors they want them to learn.

Showing Respect for Privacy

To teach about privacy and modesty, teachers must always practice it with their students. When a student is being taken to the toilet or having clothes changed, the teacher should emphasize privacy. ("Let's close the door. This is *private*.") Even students who do not understand exactly what the teacher is saying will learn that closing the door is an important step in the activity.

Asking Permission

Teachers should imagine someone walking up to them, wiping their faces with wet washcloths, and walking on without a word. If being treated this way happens frequently to a student, that student may learn that his or her body belongs to anyone who wants to touch it. Whenever possible, teachers should ask for permission before performing tasks that involve touching children's bodies.

Teaching Appropriate Social Interaction

Sexuality must be considered in a social context. By allowing inappropriate behavior, teachers communicate that such behavior is acceptable. By teaching appropriate behavior—always with kindness—they can help students present themselves socially so that they can experience the joy of loving closeness. Students with moderate and severe retardation should be taught behaviors such as practicing good hygiene, engaging only in appropriate physical interaction, and respecting personal space. For example, Tom, a 19-year-old man with an IQ in the 45 to 55 range, stood so close when talking to people that it made them uncomfortable. Tom's teacher placed two pieces of tape parallel to each other at a distance comfortable for talking. She told Tom, "I like to talk with you. I don't like to stand so close. You stand there and I'll stand here and we'll talk." The next time he came too close, she said, "Let's go to the talking tapes." After some practice, he learned to stand at a comfortable distance.

Providing Sex Education

People with mental retardation have genital sexual feelings whether or not anyone tells them about such feelings. Those with moderate mental retardation (generally, IQ range of 30-35 to 50-55 depending on test and circumstances) need sex education programs that include instruction in the following areas:

1. *Learning about their bodies and how they work.* Teaching programs are available that focus on this group of students and include slides and scripts (Figure 1).

2. *Sharing in a safe environment their thoughts, wishes, and feelings and finding that many are universally shared.* Individuals, whether retarded or not, often think that they are the only ones to have sexual thoughts and feelings and may be ashamed or confused by them. A group discussion, led by a teacher with specific training in sex education, can offer adolescents or adults the opportunity to find how common sexual thoughts and feelings are. Then they must learn to differentiate thoughts from actions. All thoughts are acceptable. However, some behaviors are not acceptable or are only acceptable in certain circumstances.

3. *Learning what is public and private, appropriate and inappropriate behavior.* Drawings or photographs of people dressed in day clothes or bedclothes, performing a variety of hygienic activities, interacting in affectionate ways with another person, and interacting sexually with another person facilitate decisions and discussions about where, when, and under what conditions each activity is acceptable.

4. *Learning a variety of ways to express affection.* Teachers can have their students practice identifying whether different people are family, friends, acquaintances, or strangers and deciding on appropriate ways to greet each. They can play a game in which each person has to think of a different way to greet friends or co-workers. Each person can be asked to think of ways to tell someone you like him or her. Most people are much more concerned about friendship and nonsexual but caring relationships than they are about sexual intercourse.

5. *Learning what constitutes sexual intercourse and the possible consequences of that behavior.* Such consequences include pregnancy, disease, and making the people on whom one depends very unhappy. Teaching programs are available that explain about sexual intercourse and its possible consequences of pregnancy and disease. In class discussions, each student should be asked to identify relatives and friends who would be very unhappy about pregnancy or illness. Personalizing reactions may help students remember how they want to behave.

6. *Learning alternative ways to deal with genital sexual feelings.* Some people deal with genital sexual feelings by ignoring them. However, this is not a realistic solution for the majority. Students need to learn about masturbation. Most will have already discovered it and need reassurance that it is acceptable behavior when it is done privately and does not interfere with other responsibilities. People with severe mental retardation sometimes appear to masturbate more than the norm because they have not been taught that this is a private behavior. They need to be taught where and under what conditions it is appropriate to

Figure 1

SAMPLE LIST OF PROGRAMS

Circles, A 2-part sound/slide series. James Stanfield Publishing Co., P.O. Box 1983-C, Santa Monica, CA 90406. (S, B, I)

Being Me: *Teacher's Guidebook,* Sex education slides; Assessment Scale and Photo Cards; *Sara & Allen: The Right to Choose,* Ednick Communications, P.O. Box 3612, Portland, OR 97208. (S, B, I)

Life Horizons I (B, I) and Life Horizons II (S, I), slides and teacher's curriculum guide for both by Winifred Kempton. James Stanfield Publishing Co., P.O. Box 1983-TT, Santa Monica, CA 90406.

An Easy Guide to Loving Carefully, by L. McKee, W. Kempton, and L. Stiggall, Planned Parenthood-Contra Costa, Inc., 1291 Oakland Blvd., Walnut Creek, CA 94596 (B, I).

Human Sexuality Portfolio for the Mentally Retarded, illustrations on 11" x 17" plate cards. Planned Parenthood of Seattle-King County, 2211 E. Madison, Seattle, WA 98112 . (B, I)

Personal Development and Sexuality: A Curriculum Guide for the Developmentally Disabled. Planned Parenthood, 312 Broadway Terrace Bldg., Tacoma, WA 98402. (S)

*Life-Sized Instructional Charts,*to teach male and female anatomy. Planned Parenthood of Minnesota, Inc., 1965 Ford Parkway, St. Paul, MN 55116. (B)

A Teacher's Guide: Sex Education for Persons with Disabilities that Hinder Learning, by Winifred Kempton. Planned Parenthood of S.E. Pennsylvania, 1220 Sansom St., Philadelphia, PA 19050. (S)

*(**Code:** S=social-sexual materials and curriculum; B=about bodies and how they work; I=about sexual intercourse, pregnancy, and disease.)*

masturbate. (Also, teachers should check—privately, of course—to find out whether what looks like masturbation is actually coping with underwear and other clothing that is too small or ill-fitting.

Sometimes, students who are pursuing opportunities for sexual intercourse, especially when their interest is not shared, do not know about masturbation as an alternative. They need to be taught about it by teachers with special training.

7. *Learning that one's body belongs to oneself and that individuals must decide for themselves what behaviors to engage in.* Class discussions of this subject can begin with obvious examples. For instance, a teacher can ask, "If someone said to you, 'Let's rob the bank,' what would you say?" Students then can practice responding: "I don't want to rob the bank. That's wrong." "No. We might have to go to jail." Then the teacher can use more subtle examples: "Your boyfriend (girlfriend) wants to kiss you on the bus. What could you say?" "We have to kiss in private, not public." "We're not supposed to kiss on the bus." After students have practiced how to say "no," the teacher can present situations in which either a yes or no decision is appropriate. The choice is a matter of preference. "You and your friend are alone, talking. Your friend wants to kiss you and says it's OK because no one is around. You like your friend but you don't want to kiss him (her). What could you say?" "I like you but I don't want to kiss you." "You're my friend, not my family." Through these activities students learn that each of us has the right and the responsibility to say "no" when we want to.

Students also need to learn how to avoid stangers' advances and how to report sexual abuse by family members or acquaintances.

Conclusion

When people with mental retardation are treated with dignity, are provided with privacy and taught when to seek it, receive age-appropriate and situation-appropriate expressions of affection, and are taught to say "no" to advances they do not want, they can begin to take responsibility for their sexuality. Like all of us, people with mental retardation want to like and be liked, love and be loved, and be considered acceptable and pleasant to be with.

Teaching the Gifted and Talented Child

The Education of All Handicapped Children Act of 1975 does not mandate free and appropriate public education for gifted children in the United States because they are not considered handicapped. Congress, in its Omnibus Education Bill of 1987, provided modest aid to gifted children to support research, development of special projects, and preparation of staff to educate the gifted. Some state education departments or local school boards will provide education for gifted and talented students. Most will not.

Gifted and talented students are defined as those capable of high performance in (1) a specific academic area, (2) creative or productive thinking, (3) visual and performing arts, or (4) leadership. In addition, a child may be defined as gifted by virtue of placing at the top of a ranking of his or her peers in general intellectual ability as defined by an IQ test. Despite problems with the validity of judging intelligence with an IQ test, this last criterion is the one most frequently used to define giftedness. Untold numbers of students with exceptional talents remain unrecognized and underserved. They do have special needs.

Many myths exist about gifted children. These myths hamper efforts to obtain money for appropriate education for the gifted. One of the most prevalent is that they come from affluent families who can afford to buy them whatever kinds of special enrichment materials, services, or experiences that they require. In fact, there are gifted children at every economic level of society, from every ethnic or racial group, from every country, from every religion, and from both sexes. Many of them are, concurrently, handicapped in some other way (e.g., blind like Stevie Wonder, deaf like Helen Keller, physically impaired like Franklin Roosevelt, learning disabled like Thomas Edison). Due to problems with assessment, many students are not selected for the gifted programs that exist. Examples of students who are frequently overlooked are bilingual children, minority children, females, very young children, underachievers, poor children, children with emotional or behavioral disorders, and children with learning disabilities or other handicapping conditions.

Why should our society be concerned about special education for the gifted? Another prevalent myth is that too much of a good thing is bad. Many people would prefer to coerce the gifted to decrease their performance toward the mean rather than to help them excel to reach new levels of creativity.

Another myth abut the gifted is that they are all overachievers who have pushy parents and who will crack under the strains of perfectionism. In fact, a majority of gifted and talented students hide many of their abilities in order to be more socially acceptable.

A similar myth is that all gifted students have psychological problems and demonstrate abnormal behaviors. On the contrary, gifted students' emotions are not different from those of their less talented peers. Like everyone else, they become upset when they are treated with suspicion, faced with unrealistic expectations, bored, teased, or berated for accomplishments which differ from "acceptable" norms. Special educational services could alleviate these problems to a large extent.

A fifth myth exists: letting all gifted students skip grades is the best way to provide them with appropriate education. Gifted children are all different. A few may benefit from academic acceleration, but many are harmed by the practice. Each unique gifted or talented student should be individually assessed and provided with a truly appropriate, annually updated, written individualized education plan (IEP).

The first article in this unit addresses the current status of education (or lack of it) for gifted children, or, as the author refers to them, "Our Most Neglected Natural Resource." In the next selection, Ann and Elizabeth

Unit 5

Lupkowski argue for much earlier identification of the young gifted. Enrichment strategies can be employed through preschool programs to meet their special needs as early as age 3 or 4. Today most people would agree that Thomas Edison, Albert Einstein, Woodrow Wilson, Virginia Woolf, George Patton, Nelson Rockefeller, Charles Darwin, and August Rodin were all gifted. They were all learning disabled as well. Marcia Weill stresses the importance of assessing the "buried treasure" of gifted but learning disabled children to assure that future Einsteins are not overlooked in our contemporary schools. Silvia Rimm discusses creative underachievers in the next article. Many gifted and talented students have problems with self-image and/or motivation and have poor school grades. They can be helped to achieve up to their superior potential. The final selection in this unit addresses the assessment of children with special gifts and talents from low income and minority cultural backgrounds. They, too, should be recognized and responded to appropriately.

Looking Ahead: Challenge Questions

Why are gifted children neglected by our educational system?

Can gifted children be identified in early childhood before they begin public school? Are preschool programs beneficial for the young gifted?

Is it possible that learning disabled students can also be gifted and talented?

Why are an alarming number of highly creative children doing mediocre to poor work in typical classrooms?

What measures can be taken to identify and appropriately educate gifted children with disabilities or from low-income or minority cultural backgrounds?

Our Most Neglected Natural Resource

Harold C. Lyon, Jr.

Director, Office for the Gifted and Talented, U.S. Department of Education; Author of Learning to Feel—Feeling to Learn, It's Me and I'm Here, *and* Tenderness Is Strength; *Coauthor of* On Becoming a Teacher.

In recent years, the American educational system has recognized cultural, physical, and social differences among students. Indeed, the average student—once the focal point of American education—is fast becoming an endangered species. And rightfully so. The ideal of an average student was at best a myth and at worst a destroyer of human potential. Yet, despite this newfound sensitivity to individual needs, many schools still ignore the unique qualities and characteristics of many students. One group, the gifted and talented, suffers—ironically—the neglect of a system and a society that could reap inestimable benefits from the development of its potential.

The gifted and talented is a minority distinguished not by race, socioeconomic background, ethnic origin, or impaired powers, but by its exceptional ability. Its members come from all levels of society, from all races and nationalities, and from both sexes in about equal numbers.

The children in this group have an unusual endowment of talent—analytical or creative in an intellectual, artistic, or social way or even in some ways that neither schools nor society yet understands. Whatever their special talent, their ranks will produce that small percentage of humans whose work will greatly affect the disciplines they specialize in, the societies they live in, and perhaps all humankind. They are the future Albert Einsteins, Ludwig von Beethovens, Pablo Picassos, and Martin Luther Kings.

The gifted and talented constitute approximately 5 percent of the school-age population or about 2.5 million children. These statistics may appear low to those who, in an effort to remove the stigma of elitism from education for the gifted, would label as many as 15 percent of the school-age population gifted. Bloating the estimate in this way might make gifted education more palatable politically, and it is compatible with my belief that schools need to search for the gifts in every child. I believe, however, that as arbitrary as the 5 percent figure may be, we need to begin with a population that is noticeably different from the majority in order to establish public acceptance of gifted education.

In spite of the significant number and vast potential of gifted children, our government and our society have taken only occasional interest in them. The federal government began its wavering commitment to the gifted in 1957, when it was faced with what it perceived to be a national crisis, the launching of Sputnik. This event triggered some hysteria over the Soviet Union's superiority in space technology and in science education. The uproar produced the National Defense Education Act (NDEA) of 1958, a massive aid-to-education program originally designed to help the schools improve instruction in chemistry, physics, mathematics, biology, and economics for the most academically able students.

During the 1960's, as we matched and later exceeded the Soviets in quality of space exploration, the national panic about the caliber of our best schools ebbed. Other concerns—most notably, civil rights—moved into the educational spotlight. American educational priorities shifted from the most able students to the least fortunate, and interest in educating the gifted waned. Promising programs vanished, and the number of articles on the subject in educational journals dropped sharply.

It was not until 1969, 12 years after Sputnik, that the gifted again came under federal scrutiny. In that year, Congress mandated a study of gifted education—the so-called Marland Report—that produced a startling and disturbing portrait of neglect. This landmark document revealed that—

"Our Most Neglected Natural Resource," by Harold Lyon, *Today's Education,* February/March 1981. Reprinted by permission.

• The schools were adequately serving fewer than 4 percent of the 2.5 million gifted and talented population.

• Only 10 states had full-time directors of gifted education, despite a high correlation between full-time effort at the state level and excellence in programming.

• Only 10 universities had graduate-level programs specializing in gifted education.

• Fifty-seven percent of school administrators were unaware of any special needs of the gifted and talented population.

• A high percentage of dropouts were actually gifted children who left school because of boredom with a lockstep system geared to the average child.

The report concluded its analysis by asserting that gifted and talented children reached their potential not because of our schools, but in spite of them.

The education community responded to the Marland Report with shock and dismay. In line with many of the Report's recommendations, the federal government established, in early 1972, the Office for the Gifted and Talented (OGT) within the U.S. Office of Education.

Today, 10 years after the Marland Report and despite public apathy, bureaucratic obstacles, and severe budget restraints, a recent Office for Civil Rights survey of school districts indicates that our schools are serving approximately 35 percent of the gifted population. In addition, 40 states have full-time directors of gifted education; the remaining states and territories maintain at least part-time consultants. The number of universities with graduate-level programs specifically in gifted education has expanded to approximately 26. Perhaps most important, many educators and parents are now aware of the special needs of gifted children.

Indeed, gifted education has never before stood on such firm ground. Currently, 17 states have laws mandating appropriate education for all gifted children. Another 33 states have established guidelines for gifted programs.

Moreover, state funding has increased sevenfold in less than 10 years. When the Marland Report came out, total state expenditures for gifted education stood at approximately $15 million. Today, that figure has grown to about $117 million.

As we begin a new decade, the future of gifted education appears promising. But we must always temper our optimism with the knowledge of past regressions and frustrations. Many fundamental challenges and issues remain unsolved, and we cannot count the current moratorium on public apathy as permanent.

In a policy paper presented to the U.S. Congress, James Gallagher, author of *Teaching the Gifted Child,* points out that federal expenditures for the handicapped are 200 times greater than for the gifted:

> Are these the appropriate expenditure proportions for exceptional children in our society? Probably not. The situation does reflect the political realities that attend our present system of crisis decision making in government. Gifted children suffer because they are a "cool," or long-range problem. Budget and legislative decisions are made not on the basis of what might be of ultimate benefit to society but on what is the greatest immediate crisis. Gifted children may be our best long-range investment in education, but they do not create problems of immediate significance; nor have they had a vocal constituency capable of extracting attention and dollars from public policymakers.

Other, specific obstacles to gifted education exist. These include the powerful myths—which must be destroyed—surrounding gifted children and programs for the gifted.

• Myth 1: "The gifted and talented will do fine on their own. They do not need special help."

Unfortunately, this statement is far from true. Just as children of less-than-average mental ability frequently have trouble keeping up with their classmates, so children of above-average ability have trouble staying behind with their classmates. Prevented from moving ahead by the rigidity of normal school procedures and assigned to classes with others of the same age but not necessarily of the same ability, gifted youngsters typically take one of three tacks: They drift into a state of lethargy and apathy; they conceal their ability, anxious not to embarrass others or to draw their ridicule; or they become discipline problems.

• Myth 2: "Teachers love gifted children. These children already receive all the extra attention they need."

In addition to identifying widespread teacher indifference to gifted and talented children, the Marland Report identified some teacher and administrator hostility toward them. Some educators resent the gifted for quite human reasons, including impatience with any unusual child and an assumption that the gifted are a favored elite who deserve less than normal consideration.

• Myth 3: "Gifted education is an elitist and racist concept and is inappropriate in our egalitarian society."

In the past, minority and ethnically different groups did not fare well in selection procedures for admission to programs for the gifted. This situation is changing for the better. Federal programs for the gifted have consistently sought to eliminate bias. Most gifted education programs now use a variety of criteria to identify the gifted. Many have reduced their reliance on culturally slanted IQ tests and increased their reliance on more subjective criteria. Peer, parent, and teacher evaluations are becoming as important as IQ tests in identifying the gifted and talented. The commitment to minority participation in gifted programs is strong and will remain so.

• Myth 4: "A massive federal program is the answer to our problems in educating the gifted and talented."

Constitutionally, in the United States the education system is characterized by federal concern, state responsibility, and local control. Accordingly, the real future of gifted education rests primarily with the states, individual school systems, and the teachers who deal directly with gifted children.

Once a school system has identified and assessed its gifted population, it can pursue any of a host of strategies. Following are categories of gifted and talented students and some of the programs available to them.

The academically gifted. These students may possess high IQ's and generally high achievement levels in all areas, or they may be "single shot" achievers with outstanding ability in a single academic field. Most often schools provide advanced placement courses, enrichment, independent study, or mentorships for these students. Mentorships make use of community resources, pairing students with individuals who are willing to share their expertise in a particular field. (As part of the 1968 White House Task Force on the Gifted, I participated in interviews with some of this country's most brilliant people to find out what had made the biggest difference in their development. Almost all pointed to a mentor as the single most important factor for success.)

Creative and productive thinkers. These children may benefit from being in classes where they have opportunities to explore, to ask questions, to express themselves, to experiment, to react to different stimuli, and to use a variety of materials. Affective education and development of skills in problem solving are important to these students.

The artistically talented. While some schools offer courses in art and music, children talented in the arts have traditionally had to find their instruction outside the school system. This pattern is slowly being changed, however, with some states (New York, North Carolina, Texas, Louisiana, and others) offering high school programs for those talented in the

OGT Works for the Gifted

The Department of Education's Office for the Gifted and Talented (OGT) addresses four primary objectives:

• Strengthening the capacity of state education agencies (SEA's) to deliver services to gifted and talented children through local education agencies (LEA's) and by other indirect modes.

• Strengthening the capacity of LEA's to deliver direct services to gifted and talented children.

• Strengthening leadership through professional development and training programs (only 1 of every 6 teachers of the gifted has had any formal training for this special work).

• Finding through research and distributing widely some answers to key questions concerning education for the gifted and talented.

Under legislation (PL 95-561) enacted in 1978, OGT initiated the State-Administered Grant Program. This program allows states to apply for two types of federal funds: a basic minimum grant award open to all states and additional grant awards distributed to about half the states on a competitive basis. This seed money, 75 percent of OGT's meager but highly leveraged $6.28* million budget for fiscal year 1980, is designed to stimulate the investment of approximately 20 state dollars and 80 local dollars for every federal dollar invested. A full 90 percent of these state awards must flow through to local schools that compete successfully in a statewide competition. Fifty percent of these projects must have a component for the gifted who are economically disadvantaged.

The remaining 25 percent of OGT's budget is for discretionary grant awards, including national model projects, professional development and leadership training in gifted education, statewide activities grants for further assistance to less developed SEA's, and research and information products.

States may also obtain funds for gifted education from a variety of other sources in the federal government, including the Office of Indian Education, the Office of Bilingual Education, Title IV C, Title I, and the National Institute of Education.

Despite the slowly increasing federal commitment to gifted education, the responsibility for providing adequate programming rests primarily with SEA's. In addition to running their own programs, SEA's support and stimulate LEA's.

Perhaps the most significant result of the growing state leadership role is a new three-way relationship of cooperation and understanding among the federal government, the SEA's, and the LEA's. Only a few years ago, this relationship hardly existed. State and local agencies operated independently of one another without coordination. From time to time the federal government gave them assistance. Today, many state and local agencies are beginning to work in harmony, and the federal government supplies them with timely information, funds, and technical assistance. Perhaps more than any other single factor, this new relationship accounts for the remarkable progress in gifted education that has been made in such a short time.

*In fiscal year 1981, the federal government authorized $35 million for the level of funding for gifted and talented education; in fiscal year 1982, $40 million; in fiscal year 1983, $50 million. In the 1981 budget year, however, the federal government provided only $6.28 million—only 18 percent of the authorized level of funding.

arts. Some of these schools offer a full-day program in academics in addition to special instruction in dance and other art forms.

Leaders. Some students demonstrate leadership ability by winning offices; others are still "emerging" leaders. Schools should provide special programs for these categories of students as well as for those who show leadership ability in negative ways—the gang leaders and con artists. The development of leadership skills could take place in any class where students engage in discussion or debate or practice group-process skills. Schools may also set up separate classes to develop leadership abilities. For example, in 1979-80 OGT funded the Leadership/Social Giftedness/ Decision-Making Project in North Chelmsford, Massachusetts, which has attempted to teach potential leaders to base future decisions on sound moral and ethical values. In this program, the teacher would introduce an issue or problem, and students would discuss it and evaluate the lesson.

Beyond these practical teaching strategies, we are now on the verge of some incredible breakthroughs in scientific discovery and levels of awareness and consciousness about the gifted and talented.

Carl R. Rogers has done significant research in the last couple of decades in determining traits of the successful therapist. Over the last 14 years, Rogers' colleagues David Aspy and Flora Roebuck have conducted empirical studies that apply Rogers' findings to teachers. Rogers found three traits present in the successful therapist, and Aspy and Roebuck corroborated that the very same traits exist in the successful teacher. The first one is *genuineness:* the ability to be a human being with strengths and weaknesses, to be genuine with students. The second trait is *empathic understanding:* the ability of the teacher to put herself or himself in a student's shoes. The third trait is *prizing:* the opposite of apathy. It's caring enough about the uniqueness of an individual to celebrate that uniqueness. Aspy and Roebuck found that the governing trait of these three is empathic understanding. Teachers with high empathy tend to have the other traits as well.

Aspy and Roebuck studied the high-empathy teachers and found that their students had significantly higher achievement scores than students whose teachers were not highly empathetic. High-empathy teachers also smiled 200 percent more than low-empathy ones—and so did their students. High-empathy teachers tended to have greater influence on students the earlier the students were exposed to them.

In a forthcoming book, *On Becoming a Teacher,* Dr. Rogers and I give a more detailed analysis of the Aspy and Roebuck study.

For every gifted child who is not allowed to reach his or her potential, there is a lost opportunity. That child might have eventually composed a concerto, found the cure for a hitherto terminal disease, or developed a formula for world peace. Wasting the potential of a gifted mind is reckless for a society in desperate need of creativity and inventiveness.

Meeting the Needs of Gifted Preschoolers

Three-year-old Chris takes a book from the shelf and begins reading aloud. Four-year-old Michelle has been working several days building an intricate block-machine she says can be used to make "spaghetti ice cream." Daniel is playing a tune on the piano as he sings along. Susie has organized other children on the block to construct a "time machine."

Ann E. Lupkowski and Elizabeth A. Lupkowski

Ann E. Lupkowski is a doctoral student in educational psychology at Texas A & M University, College Station. Elizabeth A. Lupkowski is a teacher with the Bradford/Tioga Head Start Program, Mansfield, Pa.

Children like these may be part of the three to five percent of the population that can be classified as "gifted" or "talented." It is likely that Head Start and other preschool teachers will have at least one of these gifted children in their classrooms during their careers. In order to adequately meet their needs, it is necessary for teachers to be aware of characteristics of gifted children and to develop strategies for meeting their needs.

Generally, a child is characterized as "gifted" if he or she shows above-average ability or potential in one or more of the following areas: 1) general intellectual ability, 2) specific academic aptitude, 3) leadership ability, 4) creative or productive thinking, 5) visual and performing arts, or 6) psychomotor ability.

Identification

Gifted children, who come from all socioeconomic backgrounds, can be identified by using traditional intelligence tests and parent reports or through observation of behaviors exhibited in the classroom and at home.

Gifted children can be identified at a young age. The Seattle Project at the University of Washington, which was one of the few programs in the country established to serve gifted young children (and is no longer in operation), identified young children through age five who demonstrated intellectual superiority.[1] Project researchers identified young children who were able to perform extraordinary intellectual feats but did not necessarily score at the highest ranges on general intelligence tests. Children were selected on the basis of intelligence, spatial reasoning, reading and mathematics skills and memory.

Gifted young children may show "peaks" of extraordinarily high performance in some areas—but not necessarily in all cognitive ability areas—when they are tested using standardized intelligence tests.[2] A child may not do well on parts of an intelligence test because of a short attention span, discomfort with unfamiliar people or strange surroundings, or because the child plays games with the test materials. Because many intelligence tests require verbal responses to items, children who have difficulty expressing themselves verbally may not score as high as they could on a non-verbal test.

Standardized intelligence tests have been fairly unsuccessful in the identification of young gifted children since IQ tests are only partially reliable before the child reaches the age of five or six.[3] Data from the Seattle Project suggest that scores in the areas of best performance may be the best indicators of a child's capabilities. Those concerned should look at what the child can do instead of what he or she cannot do. A profile of the child—composed of a variety of test scores and teacher and parent reports—could be compiled. Those involved with identification of gifted children could then examine the profiles and focus on the areas of highest performance as possible indicators of giftedness.

Since even the most complete battery of tests may not provide a good estimate of children's abilities, it is necessary to include parent reports detailing children's capabilities.

Parent Reports

Parents can be used as an immediate

From *Children Today*, March/April 1985, pp. 10-14. Reprinted by permission of the authors and Children Today.

screening device in the identification of preschool gifted children. Parents do know their own children: There is evidence from previous research that parents are reasonably accurate when it comes to estimating their own child's intellectual abilities.[4] Questionnaire and interview formats can be used to elicit information. Information from parents is especially useful if they provide examples of the children's behavior rather than simply estimating their ability level. Trained judges can then rate the parents' information to assess the extent of the child's intellectual precocity.

Parents may tend to over-estimate their children's abilities. However, the Seattle Project collected several years of evidence demonstrating that parental ratings compare positively with a child's later test performance. Researchers found several children who earned average test scores at age two but had extraordinary test scores two years later. Parent reports obtained when these children were two years old did predict their later extraordinary performance.

Observations

If they participate in the screening process, parents and preschool teachers must be aware of the characteristics of young gifted children. It is important to remember that the gifted child may show peaks of high performance in some areas, but not necessarily in all cognitive areas. However, isolated incidents cannot confirm a child's giftedness; it is necessary to look for trends and patterns in the child's development. Following are some of the behaviors, which we and others have observed, that may be displayed by young gifted children.

- **Long attention span.** The attention span of gifted children is often longer than that of their peers. For example, when asked to count the elephants on a book cover, 3-year-old Chris persisted until she had counted all 103 elephants. Michelle, also 3, would continue "projects" from one day to the next. Some young gifted children are able to work on projects for blocks of time as long as 45 minutes to 2½ hours.
- **Creativity and imagination.** Gifted children may have unique and innovative ideas for the use of common materials or unique names for possessions. Young Joey for instance, named his toy car "Tweety Stem." These children may also design unusual dramatic play situations, such as astronauts landing on the moon, and they often have imaginary friends or companions.
- **Social relationships.** All children have varied social skills, and gifted children are no exception. They may be leaders of other children, with advanced social skills for their age, or they may prefer to be alone to work on their own interests. For example, other children seemed to recognize that Judy had good ideas and were enthusiastic in following her lead. Some gifted children may find innovative ways to settle disputes. Also, young gifted children may prefer to interact with older children and adults rather than with their same-age peers.
- **Number concepts.** Some gifted children seem to be fascinated with numbers before they begin formal schooling. Peter could tell time at a young age and often calculated the minutes left until a specific time (such as snack time). He also showed the ability to use numbers in adding, subtracting, multiplying and dividing before he entered kindergarten.
- **Verbal skills.** Gifted preschoolers may recognize letters early and show an early interest in printed matter. They may be interested in foreign languages and also exhibit correct pronunciation and sentence structure in their native language. Young gifted children may show an advanced vocabulary and may begin reading before they start school, although the significance of early reading as an indicator of giftedness has not been established.[5]
- **Memory.** Gifted children may show exceptional memories—2-year-old Bobby would sit at the window for long periods of time and recite the makes of cars as they drove past.
- **Specific interests.** The young gifted child may show an in-depth interest in one or more areas and spend a great deal of time developing a collection of a class of objects, such as rocks or plastic animals.
- **Attention to detail.** Gifted children often notice "insignificant" details in pictures and situations. They also enjoy making things more complex—elaborating on rules for games, for example.
- **High energy level.** Some gifted children have been called hyperactive because of the high level of energy they show. These children also seem to need little sleep.
- **Reasoning ability.** The ability to form analogies at a young age and to justify those responses may be another indicator of giftedness. In one study, 4- and 5-year-olds were given colored blocks—a yellow triangle, a red triangle and a yellow circle—and asked to choose the fourth block (a red circle) to complete the analogy.[6] The children were also asked to justify their responses. Perhaps the ability to successfully complete and justify this type of task is an indicator of advanced cognitive development.
- **Insight ability.** Exceptional insight ability has been postulated as another characteristic of the intellectually gifted.[7] They may be superior in insight ability because of the ability to sift out relevant information, blend those pieces of information and add new information to appropriate information acquired in the past. These children have the ability to find solutions to complex problems.

Programs

Early identification of preschool gifted children creates the opportunity for early intervention. Gifted programs with an early childhood focus should challenge the children's strengths and counteract weak areas.

Individualization should be the rule for preschool curricula for the gifted. While this does not have to mean a constant one-to-one ratio for teacher and student, the curriculum content is closely linked to the quality of the relationship between the child and adult.

An ideal preschool gifted program would help children develop independence in learning to prepare them for the expectations teachers will have for them as they grow older. Its format would combine the informal style of kindergarten with advanced content matched to the child's advanced intellectual and academic skills. Appropriate acceleration in subject matter would be made without expecting equally accelerated skills in other areas. The program should emphasize discovery learning, open-endedness, group process and interaction, and encourage independence and self-direction.

"Systematic nurturance" is a technique that was used in the Seattle Project to match learning experiences with children's competence levels in each subject area and allow the children to progress at their own rate. Since preschool children—including those who are gifted—have a shorter attention span than older children, advanced materials can be adapted to shorter time periods of presentation. The development of large and small motor skills and social skills are also emphasized.

Preschool classrooms often use the unit approach, studying a topic such as animals or the seasons for a week or more. This practice is easily adapted to education for the gifted preschooler because the amount of instruction planned at each level depends on individual needs and interests. Programs for gifted children should be developed for the child's actual level, not just by age level.

Identifying the gifted younger child can be difficult; consultations with the parent and teacher are the more dependable and effective means of identification. When a child is diagnosed as gifted it is important to develop programs that emphasize individualization and foster independence in learning.

The Ideal Teacher

An important person in a young child's life is the preschool teacher. Ideally, teachers of young gifted children should accept all children and appreciate each child's uniqueness. They should demonstrate flexibility and a willingness to change lesson plans to accommodate special interests and abilities. The ideal teacher values initiative and inquiry on the part of the children and avoids initial detailed structuring of assignments to encourage creativity. We recommend that teachers also have a background in child development and the ability to recognize when a child performs above or below norms.

Teachers must create a comfortable learning environment for all children in the classroom. They should answer children's questions and give them individual attention but also allow them time alone. Teachers should communicate the understanding that it is OK to be different. They should also hold frequent parent conferences to tell parents what the child is doing in school and to learn about what is happening at home.

An important thing to remember when dealing with gifted children is that they are first of all children, with the same social, physical and emotional needs as all children. Thus, curricula should be designed to meet the needs of the whole child.

Curriculum

Not only should basic skills development be included in the educational plan for gifted children, but as much enrichment as possible should be provided by the teacher. In class, teachers can respond to gifted preschoolers (and other children) by structuring, modeling and using positive reinforcement to sustain prosocial behaviors already present. Discussion, creative movement, field trips, role play, collections, drawings, music and stories can all be used effectively by teachers.

Such resource people as a father who speaks French or a mother who demonstrates the uses of a calculator may visit the classroom. A piano with color-coded keys and color-coded music may be used with all children, is especially appropriate for use with gifted preschoolers. These children, however may want to go into more detail than the rest of the class. In a unit on transportation, for example, the gifted children may be interested in hydroplanes and balloons as forms of transportation, and the teacher could have them look through magazines for pictures and words about different types of transportation. A unit on likenesses and differences in people could be expanded to include people in different geographic areas as well as those of different races.

In addition to field trips to usual places such as the fire station, the children might visit art museums and interesting buildings to study architecture. After the trips, children may want to make "experience charts."

The unit approach, which can be provided for children who show an interest in music. Children also enjoy dramatic play and science experiments.

Conclusions

While traditional standardized intelligence tests may be useful in identifying gifted children, these tests have been fairly unsuccessful in the identification of *young* gifted children. The option of using parent and teacher observations of the children is a more dependable and effective means of identification. Characteristics associated with the "ideal" teacher of young gifted children—such as flexibility and acceptance—play a crucial role in the development of the gifted child. Finally, programs for young gifted children should emphasize individualization and foster independence in learning.

Resources

National Association for Gifted Children (NAGC)
5100 N. Edgewood Dr.
St. Paul, Minn. 55112

The Association for the Gifted (TAG)
Council for Exceptional Children
1920 Association Dr.
Reston, Va. 22091

World Council for Gifted and Talented Children
HMS 414
University of South Florida
Tampa, Fla. 33620

---

[1]H.B. Robinson, W.C. Roedell, and N.E. Jackson, "Early Identification and Intervention," in W.B. Barbe and J.S. Renzulli (Eds.), *The Psychology and Education of the Gifted*, (3rd. ed.), New York, Irvington Publishers, Inc., 1981.

[2]W.C. Roedell, *The Development of Giftedness in Young Children*, paper presented at the 1982 Annual Meeting of the American Educational Research Association, New York.

[3]A. Roeper, "The Young Gifted Child," *Gifted Child Quarterly, 21*, 1977.

[4]T.E. Ciha, R. Harris, C. Hoffman and M. Potter, "Parents As Identifiers of Giftedness, Ignored But Accurate," *Gifted Child Quarterly, 18*, 1974.

[5]S.C. Perino and J. Perino, *Parenting the Gifted*, New York, R.R. Bowker Co., 1981 and Robinson, Roedell and Jackson, op. cit.

[6]C.S. White, P.A. Alexander and J.D. Fuqua, "Reasoning Ability in Young Children," in M.T. Riley, J. Tucker and R. Swearengen (Eds.), *Research in Action III: Conference Proceedings* (in press).

[7]J.E. Davidson and R.J. Sternberg, "The Role of Insight in Intellectual Giftedness," *Roeper Review, 28*, 1984.

Training for Staff, Parents, and Volunteers Working With Gifted Young Children, Especially Those With Disabilities and From Low-Income Homes

Merle B. Karnes and Lawrence J. Johnson

Merle B. Karnes, *Ed.D., is Professor of Education at the University of Illinois. She has researched, written about, and directed projects serving young, low-income, and disabled gifted children.*

Lawrence J. Johnson, *Ph.D., is Associate Professor and Chairperson of Early Childhood Education of the Handicapped at The University of Alabama. He has served as evaluator or director of several projects focusing on young exceptional children.*

Young gifted children with disabilities and/or from low-income homes are often not spotted and responded to appropriately.

In general there has been a paucity of programs and research focusing on preschool gifted/talented children (see Karnes, 1983; Neisworth, 1986; and Whitmore, 1986 for collections of recent research on young gifted/talented children). To our knowledge only four demonstration/research projects focusing on young gifted children have been reported in the literature. One is the Astor Program for Gifted Children developed at Teachers College, Columbia University, formerly directed by Virginia Ehrlich (1978). Other projects are at the University of Washington as part of the Child Development Research Group, currently directed by Nancy Robinson (Robinson, Jackson, & Roedell, 1978), New Mexico State University's Preschool for the Gifted (Kitano & Kirby, 1986), and the program directed by Merle B. Karnes (Karnes & Johnson, 1987b) at the University of Illinois in the College of Education.

This lack of research and supportive data is particularly serious when one considers children from culturally different and low-income backgrounds. Although there has been an increased emphasis on educational opportunities for children from low-income and minority cultural backgrounds, most of this effort has been directed toward children at risk for educational difficulty and not at the top 10% to 20% of these children who are potentially or functionally gifted (Karnes & Johnson, 1987a). Several factors contribute to the underserving of this population, including: an attitude that giftedness does not exist among children from low-income backgrounds (Clark, 1983; Frasier, 1987; Kitano & Kirby, 1986); definitions of giftedness that reflect the majority culture's values (Frasier, 1987; Maker, 1983); use of identification procedures that are un-

Author Note: *The authors wish to thank Tsivia Cohen and Jane Amundsen, co-coordinators of this project, for their dedication and hard work in the implementation of project BOHST. We would also like to thank Mary Alice Buchannon, Director of the Champaign and Vermillion County Head Start Program, and her staff for their exemplary cooperation in fieldtest efforts. Project BOHST was partially funded by the Department of Health and Human Services, Office of Development Services, Office of Program Development, Coordinated Discretionary Funds Program.*

From *Young Children,* Vol. 44, No. 3 (March 1989), pp. 49-56. © 1989 by the National Association for the Education of Young Children, 1834 Connecticut Avenue, N.W., Washington, D.C. 20009.

favorable to minority and low-income students (Davis & Rimm, 1985; Frasier, 1987; Kitano & Kirby, 1986); and few environmental opportunities that could enhance intellectual achievement (Gallagher, 1985; Frasier, 1987; Kitano & Kirby, 1986; Maker, 1983). Underserving the gifted among the low-income population is a critical problem because clearly there are gifted children in every ethnic and racial group at all socioeconomic levels (Clark, 1983; Davis & Rimm, 1985; Frasier, 1987; Gallagher, 1985; Kitano & Kirby, 1986).

Bringing Out Head Start Talents project

Allowing the abilities of gifted/talented children from low-income households to go unnoticed and unnurtured is a tremendous waste of potential resources and is intolerable. Clearly, we must provide opportunities so that these children can actualize their potential. In recognition of the needs of this group of children, the Department of Health and Human Services provided funds to the University of Illinois to develop a model to better serve this segment of the Head Start population. The project is entitled Bringing Out Head Start Talents (BOHST).

It's easier to spot gifted children from advantaged homes than from low-income homes.

The main purpose of BOHST was to modify existing materials and procedures to train Head Start personnel, parents, and volunteers to identify and more appropriately program for children who would develop their potential more fully if nurtured. For 10 years, the Office of Special Education Programs has funded the University of Illinois's Project to develop and disseminate a model entitled Retrieval and Acceleration of Promising Young Handicapped and Talented (RAPYHT, pronounced *rapid*) for identifying and more appropriately programming for all gifted/talented/handicapped children (Karnes & Bertschi, 1978; Karnes & Johnson, 1986; Karnes & Johnson, 1987a; Karnes & Shwedel, 1987; Karnes, Shwedel, & Kemp, 1985; Karnes, Shwedel, & Lewis, 1983a, 1983b; Karnes, Shwedel, & Steinberg, 1984).

Using RAPYHT materials with the handicapped in Head Start programs led to the conclusion that they needed to be adapted to be appropriate for Head Start. The language was clarified and examples were added to reinforce concepts. Teacher training was made competency-based and geared to an individualized interpersonal approach. Project staff structured lessons to provide support and guidance to Head Start teachers with limited formal professional training. However, teachers were provided with suggestions and strategies to modify lessons to meet the specific needs of their children. Teachers were encouraged to be flexible in the use of materials and expand on concepts or pursue the children's current interests. Parent programming and materials were adapted for flexible use in meeting the needs of each family.

The final organization of the BOHST project consisted of five components:

- general programming,
- identification,
- talent programming,
- parent programming, and
- transition to public schools.

Each of these components and data regarding the effectiveness of the program are discussed in greater detail in the sections that follow.

General programming

General programming focuses on enriching thinking skills of all children by giving teachers the opportunity to observe their children in new ways and to enhance the higher level thinking skills of all the children in the class. Typically, the procedure for identifying gifted/talented children has been to provide teachers with some guidelines for observing children to determine whether they are gifted/talented and to rely on their observations. However, this procedure has been found ineffective because young children from low-income homes and even from more affluent homes have often not been provided with a sufficiently stimulating environment to enable their gifts/talents to emerge. Recognizing this fact, we felt it imperative to provide children with a stimulating curriculum that promoted higher level thinking and encouraged expression of talent before asking teachers to identify gifted/talented children in their classes.

Using methods based on Guilford's Structure of the Intellect model (Guilford, 1956), our classes teach children three types of thinking—convergent productive thinking, divergent productive thinking, and evaluative thinking. These three kinds of thinking are introduced through three animal mascots: Delores Detective, Ivan the Inventor, and Julius the Judge. Mascots provide teachers, parents, and children with cues easily associated with each type of thinking and at the same time motivating to children. Teachers read provided stories about the mascots to the children. These stories describe the methods each mascot uses in her or his profession and the characteris-

It's easier to spot gifted children who have no obvious disabilities than those who do.

tics they have that make them good at their kind of thinking.

Delores Detective is a clever and tenacious fox dressed in a trench coat who helps the children learn about convergent productive thinking. In her story, she turns up her trench coat collar, pins on her detective badge, and takes on a mystery that she then solves. Detective lessons involve solving mysteries by paying attention to clues. The children are given a general clue first, followed by more specific clues. Through these lessons teachers learn ways to stimulate convergent thinking in children.

Ivan the Inventor is a free-thinking pig dressed in a white lab coat who helps the children learn about divergent productive thinking. He is very good at coming up with new ways of viewing things and solving problems. In his story, Ivan invents a new use for a bottle that he has found in his laboratory. The story emphasizes that Ivan always looks for more ideas until he finds one that is really creative. Through these lessons teachers learn methods to help children become more fluent, flexible, and original.

The third character is Julius the Judge, a lion in a long robe who teaches the children about evaluative thinking. Julius is good at making decisions by carefully considering all the options. Children learn to weigh ideas and pick the best one based on available information. In his story, Julius rules on a court case involving two sisters who had trouble deciding on a gift they were going to buy.

Identification

The second component of the model focuses on identifying the children with potential talent in one

Table. *Talent and Skill Areas of Project BOHST*

TALENT AREA	SKILL AREA
Intellect	*problem solving*—the ability to think things out, by focusing on a problem, thinking up lots of solutions, and selecting the best one
	remembering—the ability to recall information, by developing an efficient storage and retrieval system for things experienced both during the lesson and in the past
	communicating—the ability to explain, by stating ideas in clear and interesting ways
	seeing relationships—the ability to see differences, similarities, and connections, by recognizing how things do or do not fit together
Creativity	*fluency*—the ability to produce a large number of ideas in response to a question or problem
	originality—the ability to produce new and unusual ideas
	elaboration—the ability to add great detail to an idea or product
	flexibility—the ability to take an idea in a different direction by changing one's approach or point of view
Leadership	*self-confidence*—possessing a high opinion of oneself; feeling secure about one's strengths and weaknesses
	organizing—being interested in and having the ability to plan and complete projects or involvement
	persuading—the ability to influence others, attracting others' interest and participation
	sensitivity—demonstrating a caring or concerned attitude toward others (other children, adults, animals, etc.)
Visual and performing arts	
• Art	*visual awareness*—noticing, remembering, and discriminating between details, colors, textures, designs, and sizes
	appreciating art—enjoying and evaluating artworks
	technique—using art tools and materials skillfully and in visually attractive ways
	originality—producing artwork that is unique, unusual, different, or distinctive
• Music	*listening*—being alert to sounds in music and the environment
	performing—inventing or repeating musical phrases by singing, clapping, humming, and/or playing an instrument

or more of six areas: intellectual ability; creativity; visual and performing arts; leadership; academic abilities in the areas of science, math, and reading; and psychomotor ability. Identifying talents or gifts is especially difficult at the preschool level because children have not had the experiences necessary to develop and demonstrate their talents. For this reason, information provided by both the child's teacher and his or her parents is used to assess the child's skills as accurately as possible.

The three instruments used to select children with potential talent are: the *Teacher Check List*, the *Parent Check List*, and the *Talent Identification Summary*. Both the parent and teacher check lists contain a set of four abilities or behaviors indicative of talent in each area. The teacher rates each child in the classroom on the items tested. Parents fill out a check list for their child. Ratings from both these check lists are recorded on the *Talent Identification Summary*.

At a "talent conference," the classroom teacher, aide, ancillary staff, BOHST trainer, and children's parents meet to review the information recorded on the *Talent Identification Summary* for children whose scores equaled or exceeded the cutoff of 24 in one or more talent areas. If the child passes the cutoff in more than one talent area, only the top one or two areas are reviewed. The following questions are considered at the talent conference:

1. Did the child exhibit many of the characteristics commonly attributed to children who are gifted or talented in that area?
2. Was the child significantly superior to classmates or peers in that talent area?
3. Did the ratings on the parent

Table. *Talent and Skill Areas of Project BOHST* (continued)

TALENT AREA	SKILL AREA
• Music (continued)	*appreciating music*—recognizing, enjoying, and evaluating different types of music *originality*—producing or appreciating music that sounds new, different, or unusual
Academic	
• Reading	*decoding*—the ability to see subtle differences in how things look *listening phonetically*—the ability to detect similarities and differences in how words, parts of words, and letters sound *speaking clearly*—the ability to use words in interesting and creative ways *understanding ideas*—getting meaning from spoken and written language; understanding a wide range of words; collecting facts and knowledge from observation
• Math	*knowing numbers*—the ability to remember and understand numbers, quantities, and shapes *seeing connections*—the ability to recognize, duplicate, and extend patterns; the ability to see relationships by comparing, sorting, classifying, graphing, and sequencing numbers at the concrete and abstract levels *abstraction*—the ability to identify and understand the underlying concept of a problem *using math*—the ability to apply learned processes to solve new problems
• Science	*organizing*—matching, sorting, grouping, or ordering objects and/or information *remembering*—recalling information related to an area of science *observing*—seeing and identifying attributes, differences, and similarities of objects or events *problem solving*—figuring out answers by observing, asking questions, making hypotheses, and/or experimenting
Psychomotor ability	*fitness*—having the energy and physical ability to perform physical activities for varying amounts of time; having strength and endurance *expressiveness*—producing and exploring movements in imaginative or original ways *ease and quickness*—demonstrating agility, flexibility, and grace when doing a physical activity *coordination*—having the balance, rhythm, and control to perform various physical activities; having eye-hand or eye-foot coordination

Help children zero in on the solution, or figure out many ways to solve the problem. Encourage "detective work" and originality.

check list and the teacher check list generally seem accurate?

4. Did the additional information provided by other team members seem to verify the child's talent potential?

After considering these questions, the team makes the final determination as to which children will be identified as potentially talented or gifted and thereby eligible for talent programming.

Talent programming

The talent programming component is designed to develop the identified child's potential talents by providing opportunities and experiences in the talent area. The programming is both broad in scope and individually tailored to the child. Teachers use with the children a manual consisting of 10 small-group activities for each talent area. Each activity within a talent area is organized to develop four skill areas for that particular talent, except for the talent areas of academic and visual and performing arts, which are divided into several subtalent areas with their own sets of skills. Skills related to each talent or subtalent area are the same constructs contained on the identification check lists. As a result, teachers not only identify the child's area of strength, they also have a sense of the child's ability on skills within the talent area. Talent areas and skill areas within talent areas are contained in the Table (pp. 52–53).

Each talent or subtalent area has 10 activities for the teacher to use in the classroom. These activities are presented in the same format throughout the manual and are set up so the teacher can assess the child's progress in the four skill areas while teaching the lesson. Procedures for lessons are presented in one- to two-page lesson descriptions. Each description is in a two-column format. On the right-hand side of the page are assessment questions based on the lesson objectives, and on the left side of the page are the objectives and procedures. Lessons are designed for small groups of two to five children. The groups can include both identified children and unidentified children who exhibit an interest in the area.

After completing the first three lessons, the teacher evaluates the child's progress and designs a talent education plan for each identified child. Teachers are encouraged to use materials and procedures developed in the project to meet each child's individual needs and abilities.

Parent programming

The parent programming component covers several different areas: general enrichment in the home, the identification process, home activities for children identified as gifted/talented, and volunteering and child advocacy.

Project staff introduce the general enrichment programming to the parents at a workshop to which all the parents are invited and present information about strategies that can be used in the home to encourage the child's convergent, divergent, and evaluative thinking skills. A manual, *Activities for the Home*, provides activities for each parent to use to encourage the child's creativity.

The parent's knowledge of the child is incorporated into the identification process by means of a home visit arranged by the teacher. During this interview, the teacher and the parent work together to fill out the parent check list. This part of the process includes the parents of all the children. Parents are also invited to the talent conference at which the final determination of talent identification is made. Parents of identified children then attend a second workshop where they receive information about their child's potential talents, activity booklets for the talent area, and specific strategies for developing their child's talents. In addition, parents are encouraged to volunteer in the classroom to become an active part of the educational process, to be actively involved in the transition of their child to the public school, and to become an advocate for their child.

Transition to public schools

The final component of the model is transition of the target children to the public school. The public school administrators and the child's kindergarten teacher must be aware of the child's special abilities to facilitate the continued development of each identified child's talent area. To encourage this process, the teacher completes and sends to the receiving school an end-of-the-year talent report that briefly explains the child's involvement in the BOHST project and describes the child's particular talent(s). In addition, the report includes a general description of the

Parents must be respected and involved as partners.

kinds of activities and skills provided to the child during BOHST programming and of the child's performance during this participation.

Evaluation methods

Four hundred and forty-six Head Start children, 32 teachers, and 32 teacher aides participated in field testing this project (for a more detailed discussion of methods used in and results of field testing, see Karnes & Johnson, 1987a). Participants came from the Head Start program that encompassed the Illinois counties of Champaign and Vermillion. Vermillion County Head Start sites received the standard inservice program; the staff and parents received no additional training other than that required to identify gifted/talented Head Start children. Staff and parents in Champaign County Head Start sites received BOHST training.

All children at both sites were administered the following tests on a pretest basis: *Children's Task Persistence* (Karnes, Johnson, Cohen, & Shwedel, 1985), *Thinking Creatively in Action and Movement* (TCAM; Torrance, 1980), four subtests of the *Kaufman Assessment Battery for Children* (K-ABC; Kaufman & Kaufman, 1983), and the *Self-Concept and Motivation Inventory* (SCAMIN; Milchus, Farrah, & Reitz, 1967).

Teachers and aides completed two attitude questionnaires on a pre/post basis. The *Teacher Questionnaire* focused on attitudes toward educating gifted/talented children, and the *Classroom Questionnaire* used a semantic differential approach to measure teachers' degree of positive attitude toward their classes. Although these measures were given prior to BOHST training, teachers and aides had at least one month's experience with their classes before completing the questionnaires.

Conclusion

Results from this project are encouraging and suggest that the project had a positive impact on teachers, children identified as gifted/talented, and children not identified as gifted/talented. Findings from the K-ABC and the TCAM are particularly dramatic. On the TCAM, children in the comparison group had substantial decreases on their posttest scores, while scores of both groups of children in the intervention group increased. This suggests that children in the intervention group might have become less creative had it not been for BOHST training. On the K-ABC, both children identified as gifted/talented and nonidentified children made gains over their counterparts who did not receive BOHST training. It is important to note, however, that children not identified as gifted/talented made the biggest gains on the K-ABC, indicating that exposing children to higher order thinking skills may have a beneficial impact on all children. In addition, the attitudes of teachers in the intervention group changed. The way they described their class became significantly more positive at the end of BOHST training, while the descriptions of the comparison group remained relatively stable, indicating that having teachers focus on identifying the strengths of children and then programming for these strengths may improve the teachers' attitudes toward these children (see Karnes & Johnson, 1987a, for a more detailed discussion of findings).

At this point it is important that we comment on the structured nature of the BOHST project. First, we feel that structure was important to the accurate replication of the model. Teachers need specific guidelines and written materials to support replication of a model; otherwise, key components of the project may be lost. Structure was particularly important in this project because some of the teachers who participated had limited formal professional training. Secondly, the written lesson plans to promote higher level thinking and talent development serve as tools to train teachers in using strategies suggested in these lessons. We hope the strategies they learn to use in these structured lessons will become part of their teaching repertoire. Moreover, workshops provide information to help teachers take advantage of opportunities as they occur during the day to encourage higher level thinking skills and talent development in children.

As we stated earlier, parent involvement is an important component of the program. Parents, too, are provided with specific suggestions. Again, the notion is that when parents learn new strategies for providing higher level thinking processes and talent development they can apply these strategies in a variety of everyday situations.

These data suggest that focusing on the strengths of all children, providing all children with practice in higher order thinking skills, identifying the gifted/talented children, and providing home and classroom programming for the special talents of the potentially gifted had a positive impact on the overall program. Although this project focused on children from disadvantaged backgrounds, we believe that these findings should be carefully considered by all who work with young children. This project implemented activities typically thought to be appropriate for gifted children with all children. Findings indicated that children not identified as gifted/talented made the most dramatic gains in cognitive development as measured by the K-

Help children consider options and make their own decision.

ABC. Such findings clearly underscore the importance of providing all children with stimulating and challenging activities.

Giftedness comes in many forms. Is the child an unusually creative thinker? Artistic? Musical? Mentally sharp? Good grades and giftedness are not the same thing.

References

Clark, B. (1983). *Growing up gifted* (2nd ed.). Columbus, OH: Merrill.

Davis, G., & Rimm, S. (1985). *Education of the gifted and talented.* Englewood Cliffs, NJ: Prentice-Hall

Ehrlich, V. (1978). *The Astor Program for gifted children: Pre-kindergarten through grade three.* New York: Columbia University, Teachers College and New York City Board of Education. (ERIC Document Reproduction Service No. ED 166 889)

Frasier, M. (1987). The identification of gifted Black students: Developing new perspectives. *Journal for the Education of the Gifted, 10*, 155–180.

Gallagher, J. (1985). *Teaching the gifted child* (3rd ed.). Boston: Allyn & Bacon.

Guilford, J. P. (1956). The structure of intellect. *Psychological Bulletin, 53,* 267–293.

Karnes, M. B. (1983). *The underserved: Our young gifted children.* Reston, VA: The Council for Exceptional Children.

Karnes, M. B., & Bertschi, J. (1978). Identifying and educating gifted/talented nonhandicapped and handicapped preschoolers. *Teaching Exceptional Children, 10,* 114–119.

Karnes, M. B., & Johnson, L. J. (1986). Early identification and programming for young gifted/talented handicapped. *Topics in Early Childhood Special Education, 6,* 50–61.

Karnes, M. B., & Johnson, L. J. (1987a). Bringing Out Head Start Talents: Findings from the field. *Gifted Child Quarterly, 31,* 174–179.

Karnes, M. B., & Johnson, L. J. (1987b). An imperative: Programming for the young gifted/talented. *Journal for the Education of the Gifted, 10*, 195–214.

Karnes, M., Johnson, L., Cohen, T., & Shwedel, A. (1985). Facilitating school success among mildly and moderately handicapped children by enhancing task persistence. *Journal of the Division for Early Childhood, 9*, 151–161.

Karnes, M. B., & Shwedel, A. M. (1987). Differences in attitudes and practices between fathers of young gifted and fathers of young non-gifted children: A pilot study. *Gifted Child Quarterly, 31*, 79–82.

Karnes, M. B., Shwedel, A. M., & Kemp, P. (1985). Preschool: Programming for the young gifted child. *Roeper Review, 7*, 204–209.

Karnes, M. B., Shwedel, A. M., & Lewis, G. (1983a). Long-term effects of early programming fôr the gifted/talented handicapped. *Journal for the Education of the Gifted, 6*, 266–278.

Karnes, M. B., Shwedel, A. M., & Lewis, G. (1983b). Short-term effects of early programming for the young gifted handicapped child. *Exceptional Children, 50*, 103–109.

Karnes, M. B., Shwedel, A. M., & Steinberg, D. (1984). Styles of parenting among parents of young gifted children. *Roeper Review, 6*, 232–235.

Kaufman, A. S., & Kaufman, N. L. (1983). *Kaufman assessment battery for children.* Circle Pines, MN: American Guidance Service.

Kitano, M., & Kirby, D. (1986). *Gifted education: A comprehensive view.* Boston: Little, Brown.

Maker, J. (1983). Quality education for gifted minority students. *Journal of the Education of the Gifted, 6,* 140–153.

Milchus, M. J., Farrah, G. A., & Reitz, W. (1967). *SCAMIN: Self-Concept And Motivation Inventory.* Dearborn Heights, MI: Person-O-Metrics, Inc.

Neisworth, J. T. (Ed.). (1986). Gifted preschoolers [Special issue]. *Topics in Early Childhood Special Education, 6*(1).

Robinson, H., Jackson, N., & Roedell, W. (1978). *Annual report to the Spencer Foundation: Identification and nurturance of extraordinarily precocious young children.* Seattle: University of Washington Child Development Research Group. (ERIC Document Reproduction Service No. ED 162 756)

Torrance, E. P. (1980). *Thinking creatively in action and movement.* Bensenville, IL: Scholastic Testing Service.

Whitmore, J. R. (1986). *Intellectual giftedness in young children: Recognition and development.* New York: Haworth.

Gifted/Learning Disabled Students

Their Potential May Be Buried Treasure

MARCIA PETERSON WEILL

Ms. Weill is completing her doctoral degree in educational and counseling psychology at the University of the Pacific in Stockton, California.

Many educators strive to inspire students to achieve their unique potentials. The "real world" standard of achievement, however, is performance near grade level, and those students with unique potential whose classroom performance does not vary significantly from this norm are generally not recognized. One type of student is especially vulnerable to this oversight—the gifted/learning disabled (G/LD) child. Some of these G/LD students learn to use their high intellectual abilities to compensate for their learning disabilities, permitting them to perform near grade level but preventing their needs for special educational services from being identified.

The needs of G/LD students were recognized as early as 1937 by Samuel Orton, whose research into dyslexia disclosed that in any group of nonreaders, all ranges of intelligence may be found. The Goertzels (1962) compiled biographies of four hundred eminent people, estimating that one-quarter of them were handicapped in some way. Krippner's classic studies (1968), finding that reading disabilities of the academically talented deserved as close attention as they do for average or slow learners, encouraged further research. Federal funds supported First Chance Projects in 1975 to identify gifted students who were handicapped or economically deprived (Gerken 1979). In 1977, C. June Maker's (1977) research on providing programs for the gifted handicapped was achieving professional recognition, and the term "Gifted/Handicapped" appeared as a descriptor in ERIC. Research into G/LD students since then has focused primarily on needs for effective curriculum and adequate identification procedures.

Who are these G/LD students? The current definition of "gifted" has evolved from Terman's (1926) unidimensional description of superior intellect to the Marland Report (1972), which broadened the concept of "superior child" to include creativity and other nonintellective factors. The official meaning of "learning disabilities" is found in P.L. 94-142, operationally defined as difficulty performing on an average level academically for a variety of reasons (Klein 1980). Combining these two terms, G/LD students are those who have an outstanding gift or talent and are capable of high performance but who also have a learning disorder that makes this achievement difficult (Porter 1982).

G/LD students are the fourth of Maker's (1982) categories of gifted/handicapped, gifted/sensorily handicapped, gifted/mobility impaired, gifted/socially-emotionally disturbed, and gifted/learning disabled. Among G/LD students are two categories: G/LD achieving near grade level and G/LD low achievers (Daniels 1983). Although neither group's potential is likely to be discovered, the disabilities of G/LD low achievers are often recognized and remediated. The focus of this paper will be on the G/LD students achieving near grade level whose strengths and weaknesses remain undetected due to their compensating skills.

These compensating skills represent unique ways some G/LD students attempt to circumvent their handicaps and perform near the class average. A dyslexic person whose weak visual memory prevents learning to read may use superior reasoning to cope in several ways: the student may learn to spell "by ear," as evidenced by peculiar spellings and word reversals (Thompson 1971). Some students have learned to memorize pages of a reader from hearing a teacher or classmate recite (Orton

From *The Clearing House*, Vol. 60, No. 8, April 1987, pp. 341-343. Reprinted with permission of the Helen Dwight Reid Educational Foundation. Published by Heldref Publications, 4000 Albemarle St., N.W., Washington, DC 20016.

1937). Some develop a basic sight vocabulary, using context clues and a little imagination to "fake out" their teacher. Some pick out enough clues from a reading comprehension question to answer it adequately (Rosner and Seymour 1983).

A gifted nonreader, whose substantial stores of knowledge and impressive vocabulary help in processing new information, may use these skills with cues from sentence structure, syllabication, or context in learning to read (French 1982). Some G/LD students compensate for weak skills by focusing their interest and strengths on a portion of the disability itself. Rack (1981) profiles a case history of a twenty-three-year-old dyslexic man who, although needing a week to read a simple play, was successfully writing plays on his own. This creativity is an important by-product of the G/LD student's method of maintaining homeostasis; higher creative skills seem to result from the increased practice of divergent thinking the student must use in order to accomplish daily activities. This creativity leads to skills in fluency, originality, and elaboration (Maker 1982).

If only the top two percent of the school achievers are identified as gifted, seventy percent of the most creative children will be missed.

The Goertzels' (1962) research disclosed almost every conceivable handicap being overcome by at least one of the four hundred eminent people studied. Sixty percent of these people had difficulty in school; many avoided school and learned on their own using complex compensating skills. Despite a lack of formal education, Thomas Edison coped with dyslexia and a hearing deficit by listening to his mother reading great literature, teaching himself some basic reading skills, and focusing his energies on inventing. Similarly, the artist, August Rodin, dyslexic and a failure in school, taught himself to read as an adult. George Patton compensated for poor reading skills by punctilious keeping of rules, developing an extraordinary auditory memory and oral vocabulary, which allowed him to memorize whole lectures and repeat them verbatim. Woodrow Wilson, also a poor reader and self-taught student, became a fluent speaker (Thompson 1971). These people who failed in school from not adapting to traditional methods of teaching have often been those who made big strides and changed life for others (Goertzel and Goertzel 1962). Albert Einstein's theory of relativity was a product of a completely nonverbal and visual thought process (Patten 1973). The creative power of this unusual method of thinking, unhampered by traditional verbal cues, may have allowed his ideas to soar above those of his peers. His method of compensating for a severe language disability may have actually allowed his unique potential to be realized.

If G/LD students learn enough productive coping methods to achieve near grade level and may become eminent despite their learning disabilities, then why must they be identified? The learning disability must be severe in a person of high IQ in order to be given early recognition (Maker 1977), and as children get older and learning demands increase, the compensating methods that once permitted them anonymity and average performance are no longer effective. Increased frustration may negate the compensating skills that must later protect a fragile ego, frustrated and weakened by unrewarding attempts at learning. Meisgeier (1978) tells the story of a G/LD student in early adolescence who attempted suicide rather than go back to school. Students' low self-esteem may cause them either to withdraw into a fantasy world and stop trying or to use more aggressive defensive behaviors such as negativism, fighting, or clowning to draw attention from the threatening learning situation (Tannenbaum and Baldwin 1983). In either case, these destructive behaviors distract teachers from identifying the students' real needs for challenge and remediation.

The most important reason for identifying these students and maximizing their creative potential was recognized in the Marland Report (1972):

> There is an enormous individual and social cost when talent among the Nation's children and youth goes undiscovered and undeveloped. These gifted and talented students cannot ordinarily excell without assistance. . . . Gifted and talented when deprived can suffer psychological damage and permanent impairment of their abilities to function well. . . . Services to gifted and talented can and do produce significant and measurable outcomes. (p. 115)

Despite the success of eminent persons who overcame disabilities, one must wonder what else they could have accomplished if their creative potential had been identified earlier and who else might have significantly contributed to society had their latent creative talents not languished undetected.

Caring detective work is needed to identify these children. Traditional methods of identifying students for gifted placement are inappropriate for G/LD students. Average academic performance would not single out the G/LD student either by measures of standardized tests or by teacher judgment of academic potential. If only the top two percent of the school achievers are identified as gifted, seventy percent of the most creative children will be missed (Klein 1980). Since a valid group test does not exist for identifying G/LD students, school psychologists should note the following:

1. individual IQ testing, including careful clinical observation of compensating defensive mechanisms and patterns of academic strengths and weaknesses (Rosner and Seymour 1983)

2. lower than 130 IQ points cut-off for initial screening if a unique skill is suspected (Stefanich and Schnur 1979)
3. continuous assessment over a number of years
4. varied methods of assessment (mandated by P.L. 94–142) including talent checklists, interviews, and school records
5. comparison of LD students with other similarly handicapped students in order to discover those with special abilities
6. use of nonintellective factors affecting performance, including the quality of skills used to compensate for disabilities (Maker 1977)

Implications for teachers and counselors involve recognizing characteristics of G/LD students. Daniels (1983) compiled a list of four academic characteristics of the G/LD student. This child may have a good but narrow and unsophisticated vocabulary, a tendency to ponder and react slowly, especially in language areas, an inflexible approach to problem solving, and difficulty adapting to new routines. Recognizing defense mechanisms of denial, withdrawal, attention seeking, low frustration level, and lack of self-esteem may alert the educator to the student's special needs.

Once G/LD students are identified, a counselor can help them to understand their own attitudes as well as those around them, to recognize their strengths and weaknesses, and to develop a realistic self-concept (Wolf and Gygi 1982). Teachers need special training to know when to remediate and what skills to challenge and encourage. They need to know when to stop remediating and start teaching the use of adaptive techniques, such as taping responses if the student cannot write well, teaching use of a calculator if the student cannot compute, or providing a reader if the student has good listening comprehension but cannot read.

The twentieth century definition of "gifted" in America is so culture bound that children who are not outstanding in areas society values, especially scholastic performance, are not expected to make significant contributions to society as adults. Educators must commit themselves to identifying special talents in all students, expecting to find resources of skills and creativity among average and low-achieving children. How many potential Edisons and Einsteins have already been overlooked?

REFERENCES

Daniels, P. R. 1983. *Teaching the gifted/learning disabled child*. London: Aspen Publications.

French, J. N. 1982. The gifted learning disabled child: A challenge and some suggestions. *Roeper Review*, 4(3):19–23.

Gerken, K. 1979. An unseen minority: Handicapped individuals who are gifted and talented. In *New voices in counseling the gifted*, edited by N. Colangelo and R. T. Zaffron. Dubuque, Kendall/Hunt Publishers.

Goertzel, V., and M. G. Goertzel. 1962. *Cradles of eminence*. Boston: Little, Brown and Co.

Klein, P. S. 1980. Right and left hemispheres represent two modes of learning: The overlooked or misused talents of learning disabled children. *Creative Child and Adult Quarterly*, 5(1):30–4.

Krippner, S. 1968. Etiological factors in reading disability of the academically talented in comparison to pupils of average and slow learning ability. *Journal of Educational Research*, 61(6):275–79.

Maker, C. J. 1982. *Curriculum development for the gifted*. London: Aspen Systems Corporation.

Maker, C. J. 1977. *Providing programs for the gifted handicapped*. Reston, VA: Council for Exceptional Children.

Marland, S. P. 1972. Education of the gifted and talented, Volume 1. *Report to the Congress of the United States by the U.S. Commissioner of Education*. Washington, D.C.: U.S. Government Printing Office.

Meisgeier, C. 1978. Factors compounding the handicapping of some gifted children. *Gifted Child Quarterly*, 22(3):325–31.

Orton, S. 1937. *Reading, writing and speech problems in children*. New York: W. W. Norton.

Patten, B. M. 1973. Visually mediated thinking: A report of the case of Albert Einstein. *Journal of Learning Disabilities*, 6:15–20.

Porter, R. M. 1982. The gifted handicapped: A status report. *Roeper Review*, 4(3):24–5.

Rack, L. 1981. Developmental dyslexia and literary creativity: Creativity in the area of deficit. *Journal of Learning Disability*, 14:262–63.

Rosner, S. L., and J. Seymour. 1983. The gifted with a learning disability. In *Learning-disabled/gifted children*, edited by L. Fox, L. Brody, and D. Tobin, 77–97. Baltimore: University Park Press.

Stefanich, G., and J. Schnur. 1979. Identifying the handicapped gifted child. *Science and Children*, 17:18–19.

Tannenbaum, A. J., and L. J. Baldwin. 1983. Giftedness and learning disability: A paradoxical combination. In *Learning-disabled/gifted children*, edited by L. Fox, L. Brody, and D. Tobin, 11–36. Baltimore: University Park Press.

Terman, L. M. 1926. *Genetic studies of genius: Mental and physical traits of a thousand gifted children, 1*. Stanford: Stanford University Press.

Thompson, L. J. 1971. Language disabilities in men of eminence. *Journal of Learning Disabilities*, 4:34–45.

Wolf, J., and J. Gygi. 1981. Learning disabled and gifted: Success or failure? *Journal for Education of the Gifted*, 4(3):199–206.

Creative Underachievers

Marching to the Beat of a Different Drummer

Sylvia B. Rimm

Underachieving children are not always creative. Creative children do not always perform below their abilities in school. However, there seems to be an alarming number of highly creative children who are not achieving well in typical classrooms. When parents of these highly creative children share their problems in our clinic, they frequently conclude with a certain amount of pride that "their child has always seemed to march to the beat of a different drummer." I have heard that statement so frequently that it has almost become a signal for understanding the problems ahead.

Highly creative children do have a reputation for causing some problems in school (Davis & Rimm, 1985). Why do so many of them underachieve? Are our schools not providing appropriate programs for expressing their creativity? Are parents causing the problems? Is nonconformity in school necessary for developing creativity? These are the obvious questions that plagued me as I continued to see talented, but unhappy children and their puzzled parents. I'll share some typical cases with you:

Case #1

Jack, a first grader, pushed his hand into the bottom of the newly opened paste jar, observing in delight the paste which then overflowed the jar onto the table. The gushy, cool mixture felt good on his hand and wrist. Then his fingers finally touched the cold hard glass at the bottom of the tall jar. "Neat," he thought, "that paste on the outside matches the size of my whole hand."

Mrs. Stayman's piercing voice punctured his delighted discovery.

"Jack," she shouted in exasperation, "Go and wash your hand! And then get to your seat and do your work *immediately*." Her fury and impatience, however, went far beyond that simple command. Jack's paste exploration was only one in a series of unorthodox individual scientific experiments, but it was the proverbial straw that broke the camel's back. Mrs. Stayman requested a staffing for Jack. "Surely," she concluded, "this child must be emotionally disturbed."

At the end of the staff and parent meeting that followed, Jack's mother protested that Jack was discovering the law of displacement and insisted that schools, very simply, were not creative enough for her son. The principal and teacher pointed out that although Jack's IQ score was in the very superior range and his reading was excellent, his written work was careless, sloppy, and incomplete and that he refused to complete most of his workbook material. He had few friends and often seemed immersed in an imaginary world of his own. He refused to conform to teacher-given instructions. Although he was not an aggressive or noisy child, he clearly seemed to be "marching to the beat of a different drummer."

Case #2

Bob, a sixth grader, hated school and hated his teacher. He protested on a daily basis about being bored. He loved to read and often read a book beneath his desk when he was supposed to be doing math. Although he was bright, fluent and verbal, he rarely completed assignments and almost never handed them in. Despite his dislike of school written work he took pride in a collection of adventure stories he had written, but wouldn't share with the teacher or the class.

Bob was disciplined by the teacher frequently and had earned a reputation as "bad boy" of the class. He was tormented on the playground and in fights regularly although no one was quite sure who started the battles.

When the principal asked Bob about his fighting, Bob maintained that the "other guys started it." When I asked Bob about the frequent battles, he explained it this way: "When I was younger, I was shorter than most of the kids and they teased and made fun of me. Now I'm a lot taller and I'm tired of all the taunting. If kids say anything I don't like, I take care of them and I know they won't pick on me anymore. I can take on any of the kids now when they're by themselves, but I do get into trouble when a gang of guys get together. That really gets me mad!"

Bob's parents had been engaged in a continuous struggle with the schools. They maintained that schools did not offer enough protection on the playground, that Bob wasn't sufficiently challenged, that teachers didn't like gifted kids and most of all that school wasn't creative enough for their son. Furthermore, Bob's dad admitted to his son that school had not been creative enough for him either and that he, too, "had marched to the beat of a different drummer."

Case #3

Pat, a high school junior, was often depressed. She returned from school each day, locked herself in her bedroom and slept. However, by midnight, when the rest of the family retired, Pat could be heard moving around her room. Although no one was sure of her activity, everyone knew she was awake. She made just enough noise to be disturbing and played just-slightly-too-loud music. This served to bring her parents to her locked door with reminders of consideration for family members as well as her own need for sleep.

Pat said that she was a "night

Reprinted from *The Gifted Child Today,* January/February 1987, pp. 2-6.

person" and she had to work on her writing or major homework projects when others were asleep, because she could truly concentrate only at night. The sound of footsteps to the kichen and quantities of missing food gave indications of the binging that supported Pat's creative production. However, there were also creative products. School long-term projects almost always received A+'s, but were also *always* late. The constant pushing of deadlines resulted in reducing the A+ grades to C's or D's, depending on their tardiness. Quality creative writing was submitted and published in the school literary journal, but was also always late.

Pat's style of dress was uniquely "punk." Her room was extraordinary by teen standards; bizarre by adult assessment. She prided herself on her popularity with significantly different kids and viewed herself as the pacesetter of her crowd.

Pat's parents were frequently embattled about how best to control Pat. Mainly, they argued aimlessly because although Pat said she felt her parents were far too controlling, her parents both agreed on one conclusion, no one could control Pat. They said, "She had always marched to the beat of a different drummer."

Three highly creative underachieving children? No, three composites of several hundred highly creative underachieving children who have come to our clinic during the past 5 years. What do they share in common? How do we help them? How can you, as parents and teachers make a difference for them?

Underlying Characteristics

The highly creative underachievers who come to our clinic do have some like characteristics in terms of IQ and creativity test scores, personality similarities, peer relationship styles, school performance histories, and family interaction backgrounds. Since we see many of these children, it is possible not only to describe their similarities in general, but also to describe them in their typical evolutionary development. Deliberate interventions and dramatic life changes will naturally change that course of development. But, if there is no modification of environments, these children will continue to behave in reasonably predictable patterns. Because their childhood and adolescence is likely to be stormy for parents, teachers, and the children themselves, adults in their environments would benefit by becoming sensitive to daily frustration signals. They can help these children cope with the paradox that frustrates them: how to balance their creative wishes with society's demands for reasonable (and sometimes unreasonable) conformity.

Test Scores

Intelligence test scores based on Wechsler Scales of Intelligence — Revised (1974), indicate highly creative children are more likely to be in the superior range than in the very superior range (Torrance, 1966). Our underachieving, creatively gifted children's IQ scores tend to be in the range of 118-138 and mainly in the 120s. Since IQ scores are typically adversely affected by underachievement, it is not surprising that adolescent's scores tend to be lower than those of creative children tested in elementary school.

Creativity scores as tested by GIFT (Group Inventory for Creative Talent) (Rimm, 1976, 1980) are almost always above the 75th percentile, but by early adolescence GIFFI I (Group Inventory for Finding Interest I) (Rimm & Davis, 1979) scores usually exceed the 90th percentile. By senior high, GIFFI II (Group Inventory for Finding Interest II) (Davis & Rimm, 1979) scores are typically at the 95th percentile and above. The characteristics and interests of these children appear to become more dramatically nonconforming and creative with increasing maturity.

IQ scores and creativity scores thus vary conversely as age increases, IQ scores going down as creativity scores go up.

Personality Similarities

Although *creative* children in general exhibit many similarities to each other, including fluency and originality of ideas, awareness of details and critical thinking, *underachieving, creative* children have some additional characteristics in common. They are dominant, rather than dependent (Rimm, 1986). That is, they insist on being in control of home, school, and peer activities. If things are not done their way, they are likely to withdraw completely from participation. They seem driven to be unique and are determined to attract attention to that uniqueness. In early childhood, this may not be quite so apparent, but by preadolescence both their behaviors and their dress are selected mainly for attracting attention.

Typically they will deny that their unusual style is intended for an audience, but are likely to admit that they enjoy being different. Some of the more introspective and less defensive adolescents, who may be struggling with their problems, may acknowledge their personal feelings of pressure to be different and may also admit to their sense of awareness of an audience. In one young lady's approximate words, "It always feels like everything I do is intended to make an impression on others. I wish so much I could manage to do things without thinking that there is an audience for my performance."

Family and School Developmental Patterns

Creative underachievers, as well as creative achievers, are given a message early about the importance of creativity by at least one parent. The value system is laid down in the first 5 years of life before the children ever enter school. It comes most simply by the praise given to children for their creative products and actions so they learn that when they do something unusual or if they have a funny or different idea, it brings attention. If it brings a lot of positive attention, it is likely to be internalized as a personal and positive pressure to be creative. It will not lead to underachievement if home and school environments cooperate to foster the creative process.

An early indicator of a potential problem will be in the differential valuing of that creativity by two parents. Thus, if mother values creativity more than father, or vice versa, we have the beginning of a likely problem. The child who identifies with the creative parent is likely to be creative; but if the other parent does not value that creativity, the seeds of opposition and underachievement are then planted.

At elementary school level these children may be seen as achievers, although the telltale signs of creative opposition are usually already visible. They may be voicing complaints about boring reading workbooks and teachers who don't like them. Parents may ally with them against the teacher, justifying their requests for less busy work and more opportunity for individual expression. They may also side with these children on issues such as extending time deadlines for assignments to permit their creative production or convincing principals that too strict discipline is unfair. Conversations of parents with other adults, which may often take place within children's hearing, include references to the lack of creativity in schools or the inadequacy of specific teachers. These same discussions, also within children's hearing, may comment on the invidious comparisons of routine schoolwork with the more challenging out-of-school activities in sports, drama, or music.

In Summary

The school curriculum is interpreted by these children and a one parent ally as inadequate in terms of lack of challenge, interest, and creativity. The elementary child thus early develops the power that comes with an alliance of control with one adult against a system. If the adult and child together are realistic in assessing the problem and the curriculum is adjusted and the child is then expected to conform to those modifications, the alliance may be a productive one and will not result in educational harm to the child. If the assessment of the problem is not appropriate, or even if it is appropriate and parent and child do not effectively change their attitudes, the child will respond by not conforming to the requirements of the teacher and will feel justified in that nonperformance. They will then gain too much oppositional control in that alliance with a parent against the teacher. The creative underachiever will have begun his or her pattern of determined and oppositional nonconformity. Jack in Case #1 was an example of the elementary stage of creative underachievement.

By middle school or junior high, the pattern will be exacerbated. The size of the school and the number of different teachers provides a double risk. The first problem, size, increases competition dramatically. There are fewer roles for winners and more children feel like losers. Typical peer pressure at this age promotes conformity. The creative underachiever easily feels like an academic loser as well as a failure in the preadolescent popularity contest. Since children have a number of teachers simultaneously, they will always be able to find some to complain about and blame for their problems.

These young people are faced with impossible pressures. Their internalized value system says to be creative. They translate that to mean *don't conform.* By now, parents are concerned about their underachievement and communicating to them that they should achieve. To the child, that message is interpreted as a message to conform. Peers are also demanding conformity for acceptance. Conforming to friends seems antithetical to these youths' wishes to be creative. During these preadolescent years, creative underachievers are typically at their least happy selves, usually unappreciated by parents, teachers, and peers alike. Bob in Case #2 is an example of this stage.

By senior high school, opposition is firmly entrenched and is a style of life. The opposition that began as an alliance between a parent and a teacher has expanded to become opposition against one or both parents, and any number of teachers. The manipulated ally varies. Frequently, the adolescent will be successful in getting mom on his side against dad, or vice versa. Either or both parents may share in a protest against the school. The most likely alliance group of all, however, will be an oppositional peer group, preferably one that identifies itself as "different." Our creative underachiever has finally found acceptance by friends who value nonconformity. Pat in Case #3 represents this last and most frustrating developmental stage for the creative underachiever. She defines her creative identity in an alliance with an openly nonconforming peer group determined to be as different as possible from what parents and teachers expect instead of establishing an identity based on her own productive creativity.

What Parents and Teachers Can Do to Help Creative Underachievers

Ideal home and school environments which foster both creativity and achievement include parents and teachers who value creativity within the limits of reasonable conformity. That is, children are praised and encouraged in unusual and critical thinking and production, but this difference does *not* become a device or a manipulation for avoidance of academic or home responsibility. If in any way creativity takes on a ritual position of avoiding a parent's requirements or the school's expectations, then creativity will be used as "a way out" of achievement. Although the children's creativity will be reinforced, it will be at the expense of quality performance in school and there is a high risk that the child will close educational doors for future creative careers. Here are some specific recommendations for parents and teachers for prevention and/or cure of Underachievement Syndrome for creative children:

1. *A parent should not, if at all possible, ally with a child against a teacher in the name of creativity.* This is essentially an *avoidance* alliance which gives a child too much control and encourages the child to manipulate school escapes. Parents, of course, should communicate their concerns to teachers, but that must be done carefully so that the teacher or school is not "put down" in the process and so that the child does not view this as an excuse for not fulfilling school expectations. It is better if the child is not even aware of the parent-teacher communications which reflect disagreements in curriculum.
2. *One parent should not, if at all possible, ally with a child against another parent in the name of creativity.* This becomes especially difficult in a divorce situation but even in an intact marriage, if one parent values creativity more than the other, it becomes very easy to use that child's creative needs as an excuse for not fulfilling the requests or requirements of the other parent. This will cause the child to be oppositional and rebellious while using creativity as an excuse for that rebellion.
3. *Encourage creative children to be productive in at least one area of creative expression at all times and help them to find an audience for their performance.* Children or adolescents who are happily and productively involved in creative areas are less likely to be using their high energy to fight authority. Whether their choice of creative expression is art, drama, music, or poetry, a creative outlet frees them of some of their internalized pressure to be nonconformists in other areas. Be sure, however, not to permit them to use that creative outlet as a means of evading academic assignments. Demanding music practice or impending art show deadlines may be reasons for

flexibility in academic requirements, but not an excuse for avoidance of responsibility.

4. *Find appropriate models or mentors in areas of children's creativity.* The descriptor, *appropriate*, should be emphasized. These children, particularly in adolescence, easily discover inappropriate models who are also creative underachievers. They are attracted to them because they see the similarities between themselves and these models. Appropriate models should share their creative talent area, but must also give the message of self-discipline and reasonable conformity which the underachievers have not developed. An *appropriate* model should be an achieving creative person.
5. *Find a peer environment which combines creativity and achievement so that these children may feel comfortably accepted by other achieving and creative young people.* Gifted resource and pull-out programs frequently provide a haven for creative underachievers provided the identification process has not eliminated them from participation. Schools which emphasize creative and critical thinking or the creative arts help to foster achievement in these youngsters. There are many summer opportunities for drama, music, art, photography, computers, science, math or foreign languages that provide creative outlets as well as a supportive peer group for children with special talents despite their past underachievement. These help to build their self-confidence, their motivation to achieve and their sense of peer acceptance.

Encourage intrinsic motivation while also teaching competition. Children should learn to enjoy the creative process for the joy and satisfaction of their personal involvement. They should not feel that all their work must be judged or rated in competition. However, they should not be permitted to entirely avoid the competitive arena. They may fear failure to the extent that they refuse to perform in competition or enter a contest. They should have a balance of winning and losing to build the inner sense of personal control which will encourage their continued productiveness. Although winning builds confidence, taking the risk of losing provides their entry toward real accomplishment.

Use creative strengths to build up weaknesses. Children do not have to be equally strong in all areas, but they do have to accomplish at least minimally in school required subjects so that they do not close educational doors for themselves. Artists who do not like math or creative writers who do not like memory work can use their creative strengths as means of coping with their weaknesses. Creative children will often find their own solutions to dealing with their weaknesses and some flexibility and encouragement on the part of teachers will foster this form of solution.

So for the creative writer, unique mnemonic (memory) devices will often make dull memory tasks more interesting. Artistic folders or assignment notebooks may help the nonmathematician to remember to do assignments, particularly if he is encouraged to share his artistic creations with his mathematically or scientifically oriented peers. Identifying an adolescent's kindness may help you to direct this strength toward being more sensitive and considerate toward the adults in his or her environment. Sometimes, helping an adolescent see these adults (teachers and parents) as people with their own personal needs and problems provides surprising insights to them.

8. *Avoid confrontations, particularly if you can't control the outcomes.* This is not an excuse to avoid firmness and reasonable consequences, but it is a warning to prevent overreactions, overpunishments, and the continuous power struggles and battles that often plague the creative adolescent's environment.

They are automatic battlers. They will manipulate parents and teachers into confrontations. Don't buy into their game. They choose the battles they plan to win. Each time they overpower parents and teachers they feel pressured to continue their victories. Oddly enough their power without wisdom makes them feel terribly insecure. This results in the ups and downs and the mood swings that lead to slammed doors and depressions.

Use fairness as your guide and try to keep them in a positive alliance by reminding them that you care about them at the same time that you remain firm in your expectations. Don't make a spouse or teacher into the enemy. Modeling and sharing positive work and play experiences are more effective than lectures and threats and you're much more likely to come out a winner. Speak to them horizontally, not vertically. They will appreciate your respect and return it.

9. *Help creative adolescents to plan a creative future.* Though they are underachievers at this time, it is most critical that they understand most creative careers are open to achievers. If they are not willing to compromise and conform to reasonable requirements, they are likely to close doors to future creative opportunities. On the other hand, if they are willing to recognize that preparation for a creative career demands a combination of conformity, self-discipline and creativity, they will have made the most important step toward creative achievement.

There is a fine line of balance between conformity and creativity. Creative children often feel so internally pressured to be creative that they define their personal creativity only as determined nonconformity. If they are not willing to conform at least minimally in the reasonable ways which most schools and parents have a right to expect, they risk losing the opportunities to develop their unique talent. If parents and teachers can foster their creative productiveness and can avoid facilitating escape or avoidance of responsibility in the name of creativity, these creative children can channel that important talent toward productive contributions.

References

Davis, G.A. & Rimm, S.B. (1985). *Education of the gifted & talented,* Englewood Cliffs, NJ: Prentice-Hall.

Davis, G.A. & Rimm, S.B. (1979). *GIFFI II: Group inventory for finding interests.* Watertown, WI: Educational Assessment Service.

Rimm, S.B. (1976). *GIFT: Group inventory for finding creative talent.* Watertown, WI: Educational Assessment Service.

Rimm, S.B. (1980). *GIFT: Group inventory for finding creative talent.* Watertown, WI: Educational Assessment Service.

Rimm, S.B. (1986). *Underachievement syndrome: Causes and cures.* Watertown, WI: Apple.

Rimm, S.B. & Davis, G.A. (1979). *GIFFI I: Group inventory for finding interests.* Watertown, WI: Educational Assessment Service.

Torrance, E.P. (1966). *Torrance tests of creative thinking.* Bensenville, IL: Scholastic Testing Service.

Wechsler, D. (1974). Wechsler intelligence scale for children-revised (WISC-R). New York: Psychological Corporation.

Teaching the Emotionally Disturbed and Behaviorally Disordered Child

PL 94-142 stipulates that related supportive services, such as psychological services and counseling, may be required to assist handicapped students in benefitting from a free and appropriate education. State and local education agencies do not have to bear the total cost for supportive services; numerous other public agencies can and should assist in providing and/or paying for them. If a student is assessed as seriously emotionally disturbed or behaviorally disordered, each year the parents or guardians, the teacher, a special educational supervisor, and the child (when appropriate) must meet to develop or update an individualized education program (IEP) to meet the unique needs of the disturbed child. The IEP must clearly "show cause" if the child is to be moved from a least restrictive to a more restrictive environment for educational purposes. While the law does not mandate mainstreaming of seriously emotionally disturbed children, it does suggest that, whenever possible, related supportive psychological or counseling services should be utilized to achieve the least restrictive environment possible.

In 1988, the Supreme Court heard the case of *Honig v. Doe*, involving two emotionally disturbed students who had been expelled from school for aggressive acts. It ruled that school officials cannot remove students from school because of dangerous or disruptive behaviors. The "stay put" ruling permits only brief suspensions (up to 10 school days) to allow students to make adjustments in the IEPs, find appropriate alternative placements, or provide workable solutions to decrease future discipline problems.

> *Doe (a pseudonym) in* Honig v. Doe *was a 17-year-old violent, assaultive boy with speech difficulties and poor grooming habits.*
> *Ray (a pseudonym), the other plaintiff in* Honig v. Doe, *was an 11-year-old hyperactive boy with a history of stealing, extorting money, and making lewd, sexual comments to females.*
> *Mei (a pseudonym) was a 15-year-old hapless, helpless, hopeless Asian female refugee, suffering from a series of misfortunes over which she had no control, who slashed her wrists in the high school lavatory.*
> *Fa and So (both pseudonyms) were both sexually abused. Fa, a 6-year-old boy, was a victim of his pedophiliac uncle's obsessions for over 2 years. So, a 13-year-old girl, ran away from home, was "rescued" in a bus terminal by a pornographer, and was drugged, raped, and exploited in X-rated films for 5 months before she escaped.*

These children, and thousands more with similar disturbances, are entitled to appropriate education in a least restrictive regular classroom placement, with pull-out time for counseling or other related supportive services.

The category emotionally disturbed/behaviorally disordered includes children with very diverse problems: from conduct disorders to extreme anxieties, from eating disorders to toileting accidents, from transient tics to elective mutism. While a majority of school-age children have occasional emotional upheavals, only a minority are seriously emotionally disturbed. Some exceptional children in other classifications (e.g., learning disabled, mentally retarded, gifted) develop concurrent severe emotional/behavioral disorders.

Teachers who have mainstreamed emotionally disturbed and behaviorally disordered children in their classrooms have several problems. They must provide appropriate education, allow pull-out time for related services, maintain discipline, and prevent modeling of emotional/behavioral abnormalities by their other students. They also must be ever alert to signs of frustration, anxiety, and distress in their emotionally handicapped students which could lead to disruption in the class.

The first article in this unit stresses the necessity of helping teachers develop positive attitudes and the skills necessary for managing behavior in an environment where children have very diverse needs. The next selection addresses teachers' responsibilities for students who are seriously depressed and/or at risk for suicide. It stresses both recognition and a preventive curriculum. The authors of "Meeting the Mental Health Needs of Severely Emotionally Disturbed Minority Children and Adolescents" focus on the stresses which may particularly affect children from minority cultural backgrounds, and the special needs of these children. Bilingual support, family support, and cultural advocacy groups can help improve the quality of educational services to minority children with emotional/behavioral disorders. In the next

Unit 6

article, George Singer and Larry Irvin discuss the legal aspects of disciplining, or suspending from school, students whose behaviors are dangerous or disruptive to others. Teachers should be aware of their rights and restrictions in this regard. Finally, the last article of this unit describes a comprehensive coordinated system of care for severely emotionally disturbed students.

Looking Ahead: Challenge Questions

Do teachers perceive handicapped students as having more behavior disorders than nonhandicapped students?

Can teachers recognize the symptoms of severe depression and suicide risk in children and adolescents? Can preventive measures be implemented in schools?

How can school personnel better meet the needs of disturbed students from minority cultural backgrounds?

Can teachers use intrusive disciplinary techniques with students with emotional/behavioral disorders who are dangerous or disruptive? What legal implications are involved?

What constitutes a comprehensive, coordinated system of care for students with emotional/behavioral disorders?

Educator Perceptions of Behavior Problems of Mainstreamed Students

Abstract: The behavior problems of students in mainstreamed classrooms may be due in part to the expectations of educators who have not internalized information on teaching the diversity of students found in that setting. The educators involved in this study were predominantly regular classroom teachers but also included counselors, librarians, special educators, administrators, etc. They appeared to perceive student behavior problems as more serious when displayed by nonhandicapped or physically handicapped students than when displayed by mentally handicapped students. The same educators recommended more behavioral treatments having an authoritarian orientation for nonhandicapped than for physically handicapped students. This study indicates educators need to develop attitudes and skills necessary for behavior management in the mainstreamed school environment.

N. JO CAMPBELL,

JUDITH E. DOBSON,

JANE M. BOST

N. JO CAMPBELL *is Associate Professor, and* JUDITH E. DOBSON *is Professor, Oklahoma State University, Stillwater, Oklahoma;* JANE M. BOST *is Counseling Psychologist, Southwestern University, Georgetown, Texas.*

■ As one result of the 1975 Education for All Handicapped Children Act, increased numbers of educators are directly involved with handicapped students even though regular educators have received little training in teaching special students in the mainstreamed classroom. Lakin and Reynolds (1983) reported that 70% of all students who have been identified as having some form of handicapping condition spend at least a part of each school day with a regular classroom teacher. While agreement exists among educators about the impact of the teacher's intellect and personality upon learning, little is known about the effects of students' handicapping conditions upon teachers' perceptions of students' behavior problems. Teachers' inequitable perceptions and treatments of students' behaviors in the mainstreamed classroom have the potential to produce more serious discipline problems which can limit the value of carefully planned lessons. While managing student behaviors in the mainstreamed classroom is a relatively new concern for educators, discipline in the schools has been a highly ranked concern for years. The results of the 15th Annual Gallup Poll of the Public's Attitudes Toward the Public Schools (Gallup, 1983), as in 12 out of 13 previous years, indicate that the number one concern regarding education is discipline in the schools.

There are many opinions as to the causes of student misbehaviors. Some researchers have suggested teachers may be inadvertently responsible for students' behavior problems. In a review of research on student misbehaviors, Duke (1978) reported several situations in which the biases and expectations of educators were contributory factors to student misbehavior. The results of research by Algozzine (1976) and Larsen (1975) indicate that teachers who are not special educators may have lower tolerance for certain student behaviors than teachers educated to work with exceptional students. Algozzine (1976) suggested that this lower tolerance may actually contribute to the behavior problems occurring in the classroom.

The impetus for this investigation was provided by the lack of research on how teachers interact with the diversity of students in a mainstreamed classroom. Jackson (1968) reported that some students invoke apathy or, at the other extreme, animosity in their teachers. Research that supports Jackson's assertion has demonstrated that a variety of student characteristics, both physical and intellectual, are related to differing teacher expectations. These characteristics include achievement level (Brophy & Good, 1970), racial and ethnic identity (Jackson & Cosca, 1974; Rubovitz & Maehr,

1973), diagnostic category label, i.e., emotionally disturbed and learning disabled (Algozzine & Sutherland, 1977; Foster, Schmidt, & Sabatino, 1976), and sex (Schlosser & Algozzine, 1979). Regular classroom teachers are now expected and required to teach students who 10 years ago would have been taught by teachers educated to work with handicapped students in a restricted situation, i.e., a special education class.

The purpose of this research was to compare public school educators' perceptions regarding the seriousness and recommended treatments for behavior problems of six hypothetical students who might be found in a mainstreamed classroom. The hypothetical male and female students are described as being nonhandicapped, mentally handicapped, or physically handicapped.

METHOD

Subjects

A total of 105 currently employed educators enrolled in five evening graduate courses in the College of Education of a large land-grant university were subjects in this study. A total of 70 educators indicated that they were either regular elementary (n = 39) or secondary teachers (n = 31). Of the remaining 35 educators, 7 were special education teachers, 5 were school counselors, and 23 indicated they held various other positions in the schools (i.e., librarian, media consultant, administrator, etc.). The subjects' length of employment as educators varied from 1 to 28 years with a mode of 3 years and a median of 4.8 years. Only 53% of the educators reported having taken one or more college courses focusing on handicapped children, while 62% reported having an acquaintance who was handicapped.

Instrument

For use in this study, six forms of an instrument designed to collect educators' perceptions of the seriousness and recommended treatments of specified behavior problems of students were developed. Each form contained a stimulus paragraph presenting a different hypothetical student. The six paragraphs were of the following format. Each sex was crossed with each handicap type:

> J.P. is a (male, female) student. (He, She) (has an I.Q. of 70; is crippled as a result of birth defects and confined to a wheelchair; has an I.Q. of 110). (His, Her) last year teacher describes (him, her) as (an educable mentally retarded student; having impaired fine motor skill development; an average, normal student).

To avoid confounding the results, the age of J.P. was not specified in the descriptions. Specifying a particular student age would have required educators to rate the seriousness of behavior problems at age levels with which they may have not had teaching experience.

The remainder of the instrument was consistent across forms and included adapted versions of the Behavioral Problems Inventory (BPI) (Dobson, 1966), the Behavioral Treatment Response Sheet (BTRS) (Dobson, 1966), and items requesting selected demographic data. The BPI and BTRS were selected for adaptation and use in this study because the form and content of the two instruments more closely met the requirements imposed by the research design than did other more frequently used instruments.

The original BPI consists of a list of 37 acts of behavior on which teachers are requested to indicate their perceptions of the seriousness of each act by ranking it as high, medium, or low in seriousness. Because the list of behaviors on the BPI was developed over 15 years previous to this study, the researchers asked a panel of 11 educators, 8 employed in public schools and 3 College of Education faculty members, to review the list of behaviors and to identify any which they felt were not behavior problems in the schools of the 1980s. The responses of the panel indicate that over 75% of the behaviors are considered to be the problem behaviors in today's schools. Only 2 of the behaviors, slovenly appearance and sissy or tomboy, were identified as not being current behavior problems by as many as four of the panel members. The researchers believe these results indicate the validity of classifying the behaviors on the BPI as current problem behaviors of students. These behaviors are listed in Table 1. The BPI was adapted by increasing the 3-point response scale to a 5-point scale in order to maximize the reliability of the responses (Ferguson, 1941).

The original BTRS lists 22 possible actions a teacher might adopt in responding to students' behavior problems. Of the 22 treatments listed (see Table 1), 11 are generally considered nonauthoritarian or positive methods of teaching self-discipline and 11 are more often viewed as coercive or authoritarian in nature (Dobson, 1966). The BTRS was adapted for this study by requesting educators to select 1 or 2, if 2 were considered equally effective, of the 22 treatments they felt would be most effective in responding to each of the 37 behavior problems acted out by the described hypothetical student. The original BTRS directed the respondent to select only 1 treatment for each behavior problem. The directions for complet-

TABLE 1
Behavior Problems and Treatments Listed on the BPI and BTRS

Behavior Problems		*Treatments*	
Running in the hall	Willful disobedience	Give pupil opportunity to make contribution to class[a]	Send child to principal's office[b]
Rudeness to class member	Cruelty, bullying	Pupil apologizes[b]	Role playing[a]
Cheating	Quarrelsomeness	Teacher uses simple control (a look, nod of head, etc.)[a]	Isolate the pupil[a]
Defacing property	Tattling on others	Parent-teacher conference[a]	Emphasize good qualities of child's behavior
Habitual tardiness	Stubbornness, contrariness	Teacher lowers grade[b]	Accept misbehavior as normal for child and attempt to change through a positive approach[a]
Petty thievery	Rages, temper tantrums	Detention after school[b]	Physical control of student[b]
Lying, untruthfulness	Rudeness to teachers	Pupil-teacher conference[a]	Require additional assignment[b]
Masturbation	Shyness, withdrawal	Pupil temporarily suspended from room[b]	Some action by fellow students[b]
Truancy	Acting smart	Pupil temporarily suspended from school[b]	Behavior called to attention of other class members[b]
Swearing	Unhappiness, depression	Pupil loses some privileges[a]	Assess and improve through group discussions[a]
Smoking	Daydreaming	Pupil referred to special service personnel[a]	
Obscene notes, talk	Slovenly appearance	Corporal punishment is used[b]	
Playing with genitalia	Sissy or tomboy		
Disorderliness in class	No interest in class work		
Whispering, writing notes	Sex offense		
Interrupting	Eating candy		
Does not pay attention	"Horseplay"		
Carelessness in work	Physical attack on teacher		
Physical laziness			

[a] Generally considered positive methods of teaching self-discipline.
[b] Generally considered coercive methods of teaching self-discipline.

ing the BTRS were altered to increase the probability that educators' responses were actually indicative of their true philosophical orientation, coercive or positive, toward the treatment of behavior problems of the described student. Allowing the choice of 2 responses results in the identification of educators who do not hold a clearly defined orientation regarding the treatment of a particular behavior problem and permits the omission of their responses for that behavior problem from the data analysis. This results in a more reliable and valid measure of the educators' philosophical orientations toward dealing with the described students' behaviors.

Procedures

The six forms of the instrument were randomly ordered and then delivered to the professors teaching the graduate classes involved in the study. The professors administered the instruments during regular class time. The data collection was completed within a 2-week period because one of the professors had an exam scheduled on the evening the other four professors wished to administer the instruments. Data were collected from that professor's class the following week. Educators who were enrolled in more than one of the classes involved in the study were requested by the professors not to complete the instrument more than once.

Total scores on the adapted BPI were created by summing the 37 responses of each subject. The Coefficient Alpha subprogram from the

TABLE 2
Means and Standard Deviations of Perceptions of Seriousness of 37 Behavior Problems of Different Types of Students[a]

Student Stimulus	N	*Mean*	SD
Nonhandicapped	38	119.06	14.42
Male	17	121.31	14.71
Female	21	117.24	17.45
Mentally Handicapped	33	105.32	21.77
Male	16	102.65	19.58
Female	17	107.84	23.97
Physically Handicapped	34	118.51	23.39
Male	20	121.00	24.28
Female	14	114.95	20.97

[a] Perceptions were indicated on a 5-point scale.

SPSS Update 7-9 (Hull & Nie, 1981) was used to obtain estimates of reliability (internal consistency) of the total scores on the six forms of the instrument. The six estimates of coefficient alpha vary from .88 to .95 with a mean of .92.

In scoring the adapted BTRS, 2 treatments of a nonauthoritarian nature, 2 of a coercive nature or 1 treatment recommended for any behavior problem of the hypothetical student were coded "positive" or "negative," depending on the nature of the educator's recommended treatment. If nonauthoritarian and coercive treatments were both recommended for the same behavior problem by an educator, the responses were coded as undecided and not used in the data analysis. The 105 educators coded 2 such noncongruent responses on less than 8% of the 3,885 items. The Analysis of Variance (ANOVA) and Crosstabs subprograms from the *Statistical Package for the Social Sciences* (Nie, Hull, Jenkins, Steinbrenner, & Brent, 1975) were used to analyze the data collected using the adapted BPI and BTRS, respectively.

RESULTS

The means and standard deviations of the total responses to the adapted BPI and the number of subjects responding to each student stimulus are presented in Table 2.

The results of a 2 × 3 (student sex by student handicap) analysis of variance calculated using responses to the adapted BPI as the dependent variable reveal one significant effect, type of student handicap ($F = 5.88$, $df = 2/99$, $p < .01$). Using the formula for η^2 (Linton & Gallo, 1975), it was determined that 11% of the variance in the perceived levels of seriousness of the behavior problems can be accounted for by differences in the type of student handicap. A post hoc analysis using Tukey's Honestly Significant Differences (HSD) test indicated that the various types of educators rated the behavior problems of the nonhandicapped and the physically handicapped students as being significantly ($p < .05$) more serious than the same behavior problems of the student described as mentally handicapped. The difference between the mean ratings of the seriousness of the behavior problems of the nonhandicapped student and of the physically handicapped student was nonsignificant.

The differences between frequencies of the 2 types of treatment for the behavior problems of the 6 hypothetical students recommended by the educators were investigated using a 2 × 2 (type of treatment, authoritarian versus nonauthoritarian, by sex of student) chi-square analysis and a 2 × 3 (type of treatment by student handicap) chi-square analysis. No difference in type of treatment recommended due to sex of student was found. The results of the second chi-square analysis indicated a significant difference ($\chi^2 = 6.69$, $df = 2$, $p < .05$) between the types of recommended treatments for the 3 types of students. Ryan's procedure (Linton & Gallo, 1975), used as a post hoc analysis, revealed a significant ($p < .05$) difference between the types of treatments recommended for the nonhandicapped student and the physically handicapped student. More behavioral treatments of an authoritarian nature were recommended for the nonhandicapped student than for the physically handicapped student. The frequency of authoritarian or coercive treatment recommendations was approximately 6 times greater than the frequency of nonauthoritarian treatment recommendations across all 6 groups of subjects.

DISCUSSION

The conclusions which can be made based on the results of this study do not apply only to regular classroom teachers since the subjects included a variety of types of educators. The results of this investigation indicate educators' perceptions of the seriousness of students' behavior problems do differ according to the type of student handicap. These educators perceived the behavior problems of the mentally handicapped student as being less serious than the same misbehavior of either the physically handicapped or the nonhandicapped student. It appears that the discrepancies among the educators' perceptions of the seriousness of behavior problems may be based, in part, on the judgment of whether the student has the capacity to "know better."

Another explanation for the educators judging the behavior problems of the mentally handicapped student as less serious might be that educators expect those students to exhibit more behavior problems than other students and thus do not view the expected misbehaviors as serious in nature. Finn (1972) wrote that teacher expectations are powerful forces in shaping children's behaviors and these expectations, along with other factors such as the physical environment and the curriculum, form a network which makes up an important component of each student's educational environment. This network plays a significant role in the process through which students develop their self-expectations which become determinants of their personal behaviors. One might hypothesize that inappropriate behaviors of mentally handicapped students in the mainstreamed environment is perpetuated by educators who have not internalized information for working with handicapped children.

A significant difference between the nature of treatments recommended for the behavior problems of students having different types of handicaps was also found. Educators tended to recommend more coercive types of treatments for the misbehaviors of nonhandicapped students than for the misbehaviors of physically handicapped students. It was somewhat alarming to note that a 6:1 ratio was found between the frequency of authoritarian types of recommended treatments to the frequency of nonauthoritarian types of recommended treatments. This finding is a cause for concern because research findings such as those reported by Meacham and Wiesen (1974) indicate that punishment is generally ineffective and may even lead to further behavioral problems.

The results of this study indicate that the diversity of educators who work with children in the school setting need to acquire skills relative to dealing with behavior problems of both handicapped and nonhandicapped students in an equitable and appropriate manner. Teacher training institutions must prepare educators to effectively deal with the behavior problems of handicapped and nonhandicapped students. Colleges and universities cannot continue to prepare educators as though they will encounter a homogeneous group of students. Preparing all types of educators to function effectively in mainstreamed environments necessitates providing information and opportunities for internalization of techniques in managing the behavior of all students, both those with identified special needs and the so-called "normal" students. Educators may then be able to provide a learning environment conducive to increasing student achievement and self-discipline.

REFERENCES

Algozzine, B. (1976). The disturbing child: What you see is what you get? *The Alberta Journal of Educational Research, 22*, 330–333.

Algozzine, B., & Sutherland, J. (1977). The LD Label: An experimental analysis. *Contemporary Educational Psychology, 2*, 292–297.

Brophy, J., & Good, T. (1970). Teachers' communication of differential expectations for children's classroom performance: Some behavioral data. *Journal of Educational Psychology, 61*, 365–374.

Dobson, R. L. (1966). *The perceptions and treatment by teachers of the behavioral problems of elementary school children in culturally deprived and middle-class neighborhoods.* Unpublished doctoral dissertation, University of Oklahoma.

Duke, D. L. (1978). Why don't girls misbehave more than boys in school? *Journal of Youth and Adolescence, 7*, 141–158.

Ferguson, L. W. (1941). A study of the Likert technique of attitude scale construction. *Journal of Social Psychology, 13*, 51–57.

Finn, J. D. (1972). Expectations and the educational environment. *Review of Educational Research, 42*(3), 387–410.

Foster, G., Schmidt, C., & Sabatino, D. (1976). Teacher expectations and the label "Learning Disabilities." *Journal of Learning Disabilities, 9*, 58–61.

Gallup, G. H. (1983). The 15th Annual Gallup poll of the public's attitudes toward the public schools. *Phi Delta Kappa, 65*(1), 33–51.

Hull, C. H., & Nie, N. (1981). *SPSS Update 7-9*. New York: McGraw-Hill.

Jackson, G., & Cosca, C. (1974). The inequality of educational opportunity in the southwest: An observational study of ethnically mixed classrooms. *American Educational Research Journal, 11*, 219–229.

Jackson, P. (1968). *Life in the Classroom*. New York: Holt, Rinehart, & Winston.

Lakin, K. C., & Reynolds, M. C. (1983). Curricular implications of Public Law 94–142 for teacher education. *Journal of Teacher Education, 34*(2), 13–18.

Larsen, S. C. (1975). The influence of teacher expectations on the school performance of handicapped children. *Focus on Exceptional Children, 6*(8), 2–16.

Linton, M., & Gallo, P. S., Jr. (1975). *The practical statistician: Simplified handbook of statistics.* Monterey CA: Brooks/Cole.

Meacham, M. R., & Wiesen, A. E. (1974). *Changing classroom behavior*. New York: Intext Educational Publishers.

Nie, N., Hull, C. H., Jenkins, J. G., Steinbrenner, K., & Brent, D. H. (1975). *Statistical package for the social sciences* (2nd ed.). New York: McGraw-Hill.

Rubovitz, P., & Maehr, M. (1973). Pygmalion black and white. *Journal of Personality and Social Psychology, 25*, 210–218.

Schlosser, L., & Algozzine, B. (1979). The disturbing child: Is it a he or she? *Alberta Journal of Educational Research, 25*, 30–36.

Meeting the Mental Health Needs of Severely Emotionally Disturbed Minority Children and Adolescents:

A National Perspective

Judith Katz-Leavy, Ira S. Lourie, and Roxane Kaufmann

Judith Katz-Leavy is Deputy Director, Child and Adolescent Service System Program, and Ira S. Lourie, M.D., is Director, Child and Adolescent Service System Program and Assistant Chief, Community Service Systems Branch, Division of Education and Service Systems Liaison, National Institute of Mental Health. Roxane Kaufmann is Director of Special Projects, Georgetown University Child Development Center, Washington, D.C.

The movement during the 1980s to improve the delivery of mental health services to severely emotionally disturbed children and adolescents, beginning with the publication of Jane Knitzer's *Unclaimed Children* (Children's Defense Fund, 1982), has led to the development of the Child and Adolescent Service System Program (CASSP) at the National Institute of Mental Health (NIMH). As CASSP has struggled to help states and localities change the way that services have been provided to this population, it has become evident that the needs of minority youngsters had to be approached with a special emphasis.

The major goal of CASSP is to improve the quantity and quality of services delivered to seriously emotionally disturbed children and youth. This requires two major systems changes on both state and local levels. The first is the development of an administrative focus for child mental health in the government and a related increase in the ability of the mental health system to respond to the needs of children and adolescents. The second is the development of a mechanism to link those agencies that offer education, child welfare, juvenile justice and health services to this population, along with mental health. CASSP adds an extra dimension to the task of system development by increasing the role of parents in planning and advocating for mental health services, as well as caring for their children.[1]

CASSP calls for the provision of a full continuum of service options, which should be offered in a manner that allows each child to receive the type and level of care that is most appropriate. To the extent possible, this care should be provided in the community, including the family.

Appropriateness of care carries extra meaning when applied to services for minority populations, and CASSP has moved to assure that the systems developed offer services in a culturally appropriate way to each child and adolescent. Three activities highlight the federal CASSP minority focus. First, a national workshop was held in 1986 to explore the important issues to be addressed. Second, a range of technical assistance activities, designed to meet the needs identified in the workshop, are being provided through the CASSP Technical Assistance Center at the Georgetown University Child Development Center. Third, each state receiving a CASSP grant is required to develop a minority objective; the services of the Center are available to assist states in meeting this objective.

National Workshop

The 3-day workshop, held in the winter of 1986, clarified the culturally specific needs of emotionally disturbed minority children and their families and explored how these needs could best be addressed in both the program development process and at the policy level. The workshop brought together professionals representing the four major minority population groups in the United States (blacks, Hispanics, Asians and Native Americans), who were asked to delineate the major issues. It became clear that these populations are commonly subjected to very similar—if not identical—environmental stresses that impact greatly on their mental health, including institutional racism, a sociopolitical environment that often ignores the natural helping and support systems among minority groups, lack of employment opportunities, and the stresses associated with living in a poor urban environment. The workshop also elucidated cultural and service delivery barriers shared by a number of minority populations.[2]

From *Children Today*, September/October 1987, pp. 10-14. Reprinted by permission of the author and *Children Today* magazine.

Among the cultural barriers that were identified, the most significant was the issue of assimilation into the majority culture. There are both positive and negative aspects of such movement. Conflict between cultures creates a natural tension between the majority and minority groups which is often stressful for a child or adolescent, especially one who is bused to a school in another district or who is biracial or bicultural. Besides intergroup conflicts, cultural conflicts between generations within a cultural group also exist. The younger generation tends to acculturate at a faster rate than the older generation. For example, as Asian youngsters begin to adopt such American values as independence, self-determination and self-fulfillment, they are forced to confront the fact that these values are often in opposition to those held by their parents and grandparents, leaving emotional scars with all generations.

A second sociocultural issue is the difference in family structure between the minority and the dominant culture. This is reflected by heavy reliance on extended family structures in all four major minority groups, the authority and deference given to male heads of households in Asian families, and the need for special support of single parent and teenage families within the black community. These are not reflected in currently provided mental health services.

The impact of the use and abuse of alcohol and drugs, especially among Native American and black youngsters and their families, is another issue. Substance abuse substantially complicates the environmental and sociocultural problems that minority children face and is recognized as a major contributing factor to their difficulties in school and their overrepresentation in the juvenile justice system. Alcohol has been identified as a key contributing factor in the high incidence of suicide and accidental deaths among Native American youth, and the children of alcohol and drug users have both psychological and biological problems attributable primarily to the abuse of substances by their parents. All of these factors have a tremendous impact on the development of positive self-concepts and feelings of competence among minority youth.

In addition to these environmental and sociocultural issues, the negative perceptions of "mental health" services held by all four major minority groups must be addressed. These perceptions about "mental health" and "mental illness" determine whether minority families will even seek mental health services or use them for their children when those services are available.

In the Hispanic community, for example, mental health services are viewed as either irrelevant or oppressive and to be avoided at all costs. Many Hispanics come in contact with a mental health professional only when they are forced by the court, welfare department or other government agency to accept services. Consequently, their experiences with the mental health system have generally been negative. Furthermore, because they stress individualization as an indication of normalcy, American mental health programs are perceived to be in conflict with Hispanic culture, and involvement in a mental health program is therefore viewed as a step closer to pathology, not mental health, by many Hispanics. In addition, many Hispanics view mental health services as incongruent with the Hispanic culture, in which, especially among first-generation Hispanics, the family is seen as the source of problem solving while individual values are de-emphasized. Elders function in the role of problem solvers, and sufficient supports are expected to be available within the hierarchy of the extended family without having to resort to mental health programs. Involvement in such a program is therefore viewed by the family and the client as an affirmation of serious dysfunction. It is perceived as evidence that the client is cut off from the family support system, which is an embarrassment to the family. Similar views are also held by many Asians, blacks and Native Americans.

Community Level Solutions

In attempting to overcome these environmental, sociocultural and service delivery barriers, "informal" support systems have developed in many communities. However, the formal mental health system tends to overlook these important, culturally relevant resources, which can be extremely valuable allies. Even when the formal mental health system is used, it is often augmented by these informal support systems.

In many minority communities, churches are among the strongest institutions that offer support outside of the mental health system. For example, "Project Image" in Chicago is an ecumenical, community-based effort designed to stimulate church-based programs that can meet the recreational, social, educational and spiritual needs of boys growing up in homes without positive male role models. Programs are centered in participating churches of various denominations located in the black community.

Other informal resources outside the mental health system which are used in seeking solutions to mental health problems include extended family members; friends; folk healers (mediums, shamans, medicine men, etc.); tribal elders, grandparents or other older persons in the community who are viewed as having "wisdom"; community ceremonials and rituals; merchant/social clubs; and self-help organizations.

Principles for Designing Mental Health Service Systems for Minorities[3]

In order to facilitate the development of mental health services, programs and systems relevant to minority populations, policy makers and program planners should be aware of the following:

- Environmental factors and the influence they have on intrapsychic conflicts.
- The level of acculturation (defined as a process of adjustment to the dominant culture). This factor may have a great impact on the type of mental health programs needed. Definitions of particular mental illnesses or disorders should be clarified and a consensus developed between parents, agency, community and treatment staff. Similarly, the goals and specific methods for ameliorating problems must be agreed upon.
- The minority culture's patterns of family systems, communications, language, values, morality and learning.
- The view that mental distress can have physical manifestations. Thus, linkages with local medical doctors and children's clinics, hospitals and other facilities that might treat the young are important. While this is a need for all populations, it is particularly important in working with minority groups—Asians, for example, tend to deny the existence of emotional problems and often manifest these as headaches or stomach problems. Treatment must be based on a holistic approach that deals simultaneously with the mental, physical and spiritual components of the individual.

Other principles to observe in developing services for minority populations include:

- Maintaining and incorporating the network of natural support systems that recreates the feeling of community for the client. Services must allow for a validation of the client's self and his or her respect for the community.
- Outreach, networking and linkages with churches and indigenous healers in the community, including bringing

lay referral services together with professional ones.

- Development of neighborhood-based services that are geographically accessible and which provide a wide variety of services, including advocacy, education, training and counseling, in a single site, such as a multiservice center.
- Linking service delivery with other systems, such as education, child welfare and substance abuse programs, to meet the multiple needs of many minority youth.
- Supporting community ownership of the problem and self-determination of the solution by involving a grassroots constituency of community members in planning, monitoring and acting as advisers for programs. For example, the support of tribal elders and tribal leadership is essential for services to American Indians.
- Provision of services by bilingual and bicultural staff, or by staff from the same cultural background.

There are also certain factors that are more important for some minority groups than others. For example, program development responsibility for American Indians must be clarified, since there are a number of poorly integrated groups responsible for various services, including state and local agencies, the Bureau of Indian Affairs, Indian Health Services, urban Indian organizations and tribal governments. For African-Americans, an understanding and assessment of responsibilities of various members (especially black males) are important determinants of needed programs. Among Asian Americans, the shame and guilt often associated with mental illness is an additional factor that should be taken into account. As a result, family therapy, group therapy and confrontational techniques are often contraindicated with Asian American clients.

In addition, it is critical that the traditional client-therapist relationship be modified to accommodate supporting the network of intimate personal relationships and extended family ties found in many minority communities. One workshop participant noted, "The traditional psychotherapy model describes motivation, self-will and the ability to control one's behavior as a prerequisite to behavior change in therapy. Thus, a cultural value system that emphasizes interdependency and the Latin's spiritual beliefs must be taken into account when developing mental health programs."[4]

Technical Assistance Program

The CASSP Technical Assistance Center provides assistance to states receiving CASSP funds in a variety of ways. Periodic mailings share relevant materials and information, and individual consultation is provided in an effort to problem-solve and identify helpful providers and trainers. As each CASSP state further develops its projects and expertise, status updates will be shared with other states. The Center also maintains a list of individuals—nominated by participants at the 1986 workshop—who can serve as resources to the states in their work with minority communities. These individuals are called upon as state technical assistance needs are defined.

In addition, the Center and NIMH planned a working group composed of workshop participants, recommended professionals and CASSP project directors to focus on mental health/special education linkages for minority emotionally disturbed children. The group met for the first time last March and generated a number of recommendations and strategies that will have an impact on research, policy, service delivery and/or training and will provide a framework for future exploration. A summary of these findings is being prepared for dissemination to state and local mental health and education agencies.

The Center is also planning a training and technical assistance session for CASSP project directors and other staff which will focus on consciousness raising as well as practical planning and monitoring of the state's minority goals and objectives.

Ongoing technical assistance will be increasingly available to all states as they continue to influence the development, delivery and effectiveness of mental health services to severely emotionally disturbed minority children and their families.

State Activities

In March 1986, all CASSP states were required to include in their project at least one major goal related to service system improvement for minority emotionally disturbed children. These objectives reflect a broad spectrum of interest areas, ranging from research on the characteristics and service system contact histories of minority children in out-of-state placement to the development of state and local task forces charged with recommending policy changes. Ideally, these state objectives should be well integrated into the overall CASSP plan and not viewed as an appendage, addressed in isolation.

Several states have sponsored local demonstration projects that are based in areas with large minority populations and use community members in many aspects of program planning and operations. One such effort, in Alaska, is described in the following article. Other states are very involved in the development of family support and advocacy groups that include targeted outreach to minority groups. The scope of CASSP's involvement with minority children and families varies in each state, depending primarily upon the size of the minority population as well as the clarity of project goals, the involvement of minority community members and the importance placed on the overall objective.

State activities include training, technical assistance, collaboration, advisory groups, parent involvement, service projects and research. In Delaware, for example, a training program addresses the needs of Hispanic youth. A Latin American community center that serves mainly Spanish-speaking people asked CASSP for help with staff training and consultation. Many of the children served by the Center have multiple problems, such as hyperactivity among the preschool children and substance abuse and emotional and behavioral disorders among the older youths. Two Hispanic clinicians under contract to CASSP act as consultants to the Center to provide case conferences and staff training and to develop family involvement outreach plans.

Mississippi is providing in-service training and workshops for mental health professionals, parents, Head Start staff and service providers focusing on recognizing and responding to the service needs of minorities. Advocacy and support networks are being formed at a local level through interagency councils.

Other states are also including minority representation on task forces, councils and committees. In Pennsylvania, the state Urban League and affiliated chapters are working with CASSP to organize local minority forums. In addition, a statewide minority concerns committee will be comprised of representatives from the Urban League and other minority groups. This will insure minority representation on decision making and advisory bodies to CASSP.

Pennsylvania, New York, Kansas and Louisiana are among those states that have new demonstration grants focusing on minority seriously emotionally disturbed children and families. In Brooklyn, CASSP project staff are working closely with community leaders and consumers to insure that the project addresses the concepts and attitudes about mental illness and youth that affect appropriate service delivery.

Reaching out to minority families is a focus that all states are addressing as a part of their overall "Families as Allies" efforts. In Illinois, CASSP staff are working with Spanish-speaking staff at a county health department and local hospital to assist them in developing a support group for Spanish-speaking parents of emotionally disturbed children. Staff members have contacted minority sororities, fraternities, churches and other agencies to identify parents who might be interested in a support group, potential group leaders and bilingual speakers to address the group.

Those states with large rural areas share the problems of too few services, isolated families, the perceived stigma of mental illness and a lack of coordination among service providers. A task force of representatives from CASSP states serving rural areas is examining some of these problems and will be looking at innovative ways to reach minority seriously emotionally disturbed children living in isolated areas.

Services to Native American children are among those specifically addressed by this task force, and a number of states have initiated innovative projects. For example, the Children's Companion Program in Idaho is designed to provide support and individual advocacy for Native American children and adolescents with severe psychiatric disorders through the use of one-to-one indigenous "natural helpers" trained and supervised by CASSP staff. This program provides prescriptive, supportive services to a child in an effort to keep him or her in the community, thus avoiding residential placement. A variation on this model has been developed in Alaska and is described elsewhere in this issue (see "Helping Our Children" by Sophie Polk).

CASSP states have adopted a wide variety of activities, strategies and resources to address the needs of specific minority and ethnic groups. Some states have well-developed, integrated plans, while others are in the beginning stages of gathering data and assessing community needs. However, the commitment to improving mental health services for culturally diverse, severely emotionally disturbed children and their families is one that is embraced by all CASSP states, and it is through such commitment that sensitivity, awareness and community involvement will increase: Small demonstration programs will serve as examples for other community programs; collaboration among agencies will spawn more appropriate services; data and demographic information on institutionalized minority children and those in the juvenile justice system will promote early identification and less restrictive placement; the development of family support and advocacy groups for minorities will reduce the stigma of mental illness as well as the isolation of families; and, finally, the visibility of representatives from minority groups in decision making issues will allow for ongoing program, legislative and system change.

NOTES

1. See "Parents and Mental Health Program Leaders: Working Together in Kansas" by John VanDenBerg and Richard Donner, *Children Today*, May–June 1986.
2. The full workshop report, *Developing Mental Health Programs for Minority Youth and Their Families* by Mareasa R. Isaacs, Ph.D., is available through the CASSP Technical Assistance Center, Georgetown University Child Development Center, 3800 Reservoir Rd., N.W., Washington, D.C. 20007.
3. Ibid.
4. Ibid.

Human Rights Review of Intrusive Behavioral Treatments for Students with Severe Handicaps

ABSTRACT: A rationale for the establishment of human rights review procedures within local educational agencies is presented. School personnel who work with students served under P.L. 94-142 who have severe behavior problems with or without mental retardation should be familiar with the legal and educational foundations for human rights review processes, especially when intrusive behavioral treatments are considered.

GEORGE S. SINGER
LARRY K. IRVIN

GEORGE S. SINGER *is Research Scientist, Oregon Research Institute, and* LARRY K. IRVIN *is Research Scientist, Oregon Research Institute and Associate Professor, University of Oregon, Eugene.*

■ Recently there has been public controversy over school-based treatment of severe problem behaviors of students served under P.L. 94-142. Disputes involving teacher liability and alleged violations of students' rights have surfaced in court, in state education agency rulings, in state protection and advocacy legal efforts, and in local news media ("Child's salvation," 1983; Martin, 1983; *Milonas v. Williams*, 1982). Our purpose here is to present a conceptual basis for development of public school policy for protecting these students who have severe aberrant behaviors and the school personnel who provide educational services to them.

Concerns about safeguarding procedures have been emphasized recently because the number of severely disordered students is increasing in public schools. There are several related reasons for this trend. First, the policy of zero exclusion, enacted into federal law with P.L. 94-142, has led to the inclusion of large numbers of children who were previously excluded from public education. Court decisions and prompting from the U.S. Department of Education are encouraging states to identify and serve these students more actively (Noel & Haring, 1982).

Another reason for the increasing numbers of severely behaviorally disordered students in public schools is that schools have less and less power to expel students. Several recent court decisions have interpreted P.L. 94-142 in such a way as to limit the school's power to remove severely disordered students. Courts have ordered due process proceedings before a handicapped child could be expelled, and warned that expulsion could not be used if it circumvented the right to an education in the least restrictive environment (*Doe v. Koger*, 1979; *S-1 v. Turlington*, 1981; *Sherry v. N.Y. State Education Dept.*, 1979; *Stuart v. Nappi*, 1978).

A third reason for the increase in numbers of students with severe problem behaviors is the national trend toward deinstitutionalization (Bruininks, Meyers, Sigford, & Lakin, 1981). Children in institutions have a higher prevalence of severe problem behaviors than similar children in the community (Eymann & Call, 1977). As states place institutionalized children in community living arrangements, more public school programs are needed to serve children with severe problem behaviors.

SAFEGUARDING STUDENT AND TEACHER RIGHTS

The need for administrative procedures to safeguard students and teachers arises most clearly in the development and implementation of appropriate educational programs for students who exhibit severe maladaptive behaviors. Severe behavioral excesses are consistently reported by regular and special educators as the most unacceptable school behaviors (Walker & Rankin, 1982). These behavioral excesses include self-abusive behavior, aggression against others, destruction of property, masturbation, extreme noncompliance, tantrums, and stealing. These extreme behaviors are likely to set the stage for strong negative reactions from teachers and school personnel.

Some students with severe maladaptive behaviors also exhibit serious deficits in those social and personal skills that would allow them to behave more appropriately in school (McClannahan & Krantz, 1981). For example, students with severe mental retardation and/or autistic and "psychotic" disorders, are often deficient in language skills. They are thus unable to seek help verbally when they are subject to misunderstanding or abuse. Their communication deficits may be integrally related to their problem behaviors (Carr & Durand, 1985). Similarly, many other handicapped students do not readily acquire basic school social behaviors such as staying in their seats, paying attention, and asking for help. The absence of these basic skills that are often taught only incidentally can provoke frustration and aggression in both teachers and students (e.g., Greenwood, Hops, & Walker, 1977). Safeguards are also required in programs for students with serious behavior problems because of the widespread use of behavior modification techniques and restrictive practices which involve removal of positive stimuli, application of aversive stimuli, or removal of the student from integrated environments (e.g. Foxx, 1983). Even though many extreme maladaptive behaviors have been successfully reduced through the provision of enriched community environments (Singer et al., 1984), communicative alternatives (Carr & Durand, 1985), positive reinforcement strategies (Deitz & Rep, 1983), and/or benign cost response procedures (Walker, 1983), many more intrusive procedures are widely used in school programs (Irvin & Lundervold, 1985). Intrusive is defined here as "causing physical or psychological distress to the recipient of the treatment."

Some special education professionals and advocates have urged that the use of all intrusive procedures be banned (e.g., The Association for Persons with Severe Handicaps, 1985), and that "positive" approaches be implemented to treat almost all maladaptive behaviors (e.g., Evans & Meyer, 1985). This "educative" approach to behavior modification stresses skill acquisition and the use of nonintrusive procedures to treat aberrant behavior. Other experts have asserted that decelerative (behavior reduction) procedures may, in some cases, be needed at least on an emergency basis (Carr & Durand, 1985). Still others have argued that intrusive, decelerative procedures may be, in some cases, the best hope for helping some severely behaviorally disordered persons (Matson & DiLorenzo, 1984; Pickering & Morgan, 1985). Because the science of behavior change is young and many techniques are of recent origin, the empirical literature offers little guidance as to which of these assertions is most valid for guiding decisions about treatment of individual severely handicapped students in school settings.

In spite of the apparent professional disagreement and lack of clear-cut empirical data, educators must increasingly serve individuals who exhibit extreme aberrant behaviors. As a result, treatment decisions must be made under conditions of great uncertainty. In such situations in which there are no hard and fast decision rules, the process of decision making takes on great importance (Beauchamp & Childress, 1983). One way to achieve a balance between a student's rights to least restrictive treatment and freedom from intrusion is to estabish a formal process that requires educators and knowledgeable external observers to carefully consider the often conflicting issues of restrictiveness, safety, skill acquisition, risk of treatment, and risks of nontreatment. The foundations for such a process are proposed here.

THE LEGAL BACKGROUND OF A SAFEGUARD SYSTEM

The major mechanism for safeguarding students with severe problem behaviors has been the requirement of P.L. 94-142 that informed consent be obtained from parent(s) or guardian(s) for all components of educational programs for their children.

Informed Consent

Full informed consent includes detailed description of problem behavior(s); previously attempted treatment(s); proposed treatment(s); risks and expected outcomes; data collection procedures; alternative treatment(s); and statements of consent including the right to withdraw consent at any time (Irvin & Singer, 1985). Though informed consent is certainly a necessary safeguard, it may not be sufficient to ensure the required due process when intrusive procedures are considered and/or implemented. Parents often do not even understand the language used in an IEP meeting (Yoshida, 1982), do not remember the outcomes of the meeting (Hoff, Fenton, Yoshida, & Kaufman, 1978), do not feel prepared for the IEP meeting (Brightman & Sullivan, 1980), and do not ask many questions or make many comments during the meetings (Goldstein, Strickland, Turnbull, & Curry, 1980).

Additionally, parental consent may not be sufficient when basic human rights are at stake. In *Milonas v. Williams* (1982), the court affirmed the principle that constitutional rights are in jeopardy with intrusive and restrictive behavior modification programs, such as isolation and corporal punishment, and held that parental permission, though necessary, was not sufficient to establish that such treatments were required. The court held that a school for emotionally disturbed students violated the civil rights provision of the Rehabilitation Act of 1973 by using highly intrusive methods dubbed "behavior modification." In this case, the court balanced the constitutional rights of the students with the school's duty to maintain order and security. It found that practices such as prolonged isolation, physical punishment, and the use of a polygraph were excessive and that parental consent was not sufficient as a rationale for waiving constitutionally guaranteed liberties.

All of these considerations collectively serve as a prompt for creating an additional mechanism for safeguarding students with severe problem behaviors. One such mechanism is specific review of proposed intrusive treatments. This can be accomplished by a Human Rights Committee or within expanded IEP procedures (Brakman, 1985; Irvin & Singer, 1984). The primary purpose of human rights review is to provide sufficient and adequate due process and safeguards for students and to ensure that appropriate educational treatment is accomplished. Such a review is also concerned with protecting educational administrators and teachers (Miller & Fuoco, 1981; VanBiervliet & Sheldon-Wildgen, 1981).

Committee Review

Committee review was first required by the courts in a case that established minimum standards of care and protection for mentally retarded persons in institutions (*Wyatt v. Stickney,* 1972). At present, such review is recommended in guidelines for the use of behavior modification by parent groups (National Association for Retarded Citizens, 1975; National Society for Autistic Children, 1975), professional groups (Association for Advancement of Behavior Therapy, 1977), accrediting agencies (Accreditation Council for Services for Mentally Retarded and Other Developmentally Disabled Persons, 1980) and by some state laws (e.g., Connecticut General Statutes, 1976) governing state institutions for persons with mental illness or mental retardation.

Overall, though, human rights review procedures are rare or nonexistent in most public schools (Irvin & Lundervold, 1985). As a result, specific guidelines for conducting such reviews in public schools need to be developed. Case law, or precedents from legal decisions can indicate legally appropriate and useful guidelines. In fact, two major guidelines have emerged from case law: the global concept of due process and the more specific concept of the least restrictive alternative treatment. The relevance of each of these for human rights review procedures in school settings is presented here.

Due Process

The legal concept of due process derives from the Fourteenth Amendment to the Constitution. It holds that the state may not deprive a citizen of liberty or property without due process of law. Due process has been extended beyond these basic rights to cover situations in which the state creates an "entitlement." An entitlement exists when a legislature provides a right to goods or service and a means whereby people can realize this right. For example, the U.S. Congress created an entitlement to a free appropriate education for handicapped children with P.L. 94-142.

Legislatures, regulatory agencies, and local school boards can establish due process procedures. There is no set of specific, formal, legislative, or court-mandated standards for such procedures. As a result, due process takes many forms. For example, in the area of suspension from school for nonhandicapped students, due process has ranged from simply telling a student why she or he is suspended to providing hearings with right to legal council and judicial review. In the absence of legislative mandate or court direction, school boards can choose which due process procedures are best in a given situation.

The Supreme Court has given some guidance on how to choose due process procedures. In *Mathews v. Eldridge* (1976), the Supreme Court explained that due process requires consideration of three factors: (a) the private interest affected by an official action; (b) the risk of erroneous deprivation of this interest through the procedures that are used and probable value of additional procedural safeguards; and (c) the fiscal and administrative costs of additional procedural requirements. The Court has generally ruled that the more serious the risk of interfering with a person's basic rights, the greater the need for rigorous due process procedures:

> In many cases, the amount of process that was due varied directly with the Court's assessment of the weight of the interest at stake. The greater the interest, the more errors matter to the affected people, the more society should be willing to spend, the more the Constitution requires it to spend. (Easterbrook, 1983)

The courts attempt to produce a balance between the cost to an agency and the risks to a person. How does this balance of interests apply to public school students who exhibit severe aberrant behaviors? Case law concerning nonhandicapped students' rights, handicapped children's rights and the use of intrusive behavior modification offers some guidance. In regard to nonhandicapped students, educators have wide leeway in exercising disciplinary powers without seeking formal approval from school officials (Overcast & Saks, 1983). However, the courts have placed limits on these powers. These limits become particularly relevant the more an individual student may be said to experience a handicapping condition. For example, a student may not be disciplined for the breach of a regulation that is beyond his or her power of compliance. Based on recent research on compliance training, it is arguable whether some students with severe handicaps possess minimal powers of compliance without special training (Engelmann & Colvin, 1983).

Similarly, schools are given wide discretion in using corporal punishment (*Ingraham v. Wright*, 1976). Again, though, there are important limits on this discretion that are particularly relevant to handicapped children. Teachers in general may use corporal punishment to enforce order at school (*Ingraham v. Wright*, 1976), but the punishment must be reasonable and within the "bounds of moderation." The "bounds of moderation" are defined by community and professional standards.

Many people, however, are not familiar with intrusive behavior modification techniques such as exclusionary time-out, restraint, and overcorrection. It is quite possible that such procedures will not always be viewed as being "within the bounds of moderation." The Supreme Court has held that if a punishment is found to be excessive, the teacher or school officials responsible for administering the punishment may be held liable for damages to the student. And if malice on the part of the teacher or officials is demonstrated, they may be subject to criminal penalties for assault and battery.

Other Restrictions

In regard to handicapped students, there are more restrictions governing discipline. P.L. 94-142 mandated that each handicapped child must have a written Individualized Education Plan (IEP). The IEP is intended to describe the major goals of a handicapped child's educational program. For a child with severe problem behaviors, an appropriate education must certainly include remediation of behavioral excesses and deficits *and* opportunities to learn new adaptive behaviors. This latter point cannot be overemphasized. The courts have ruled that for severely handicapped students, adaptive behaviors are the avenue to the educational benefit required of school programs by P.L. 94-142 (e.g., *Fialkowski v. Shapp*, 1974; *Campbell v. Talledega Co. Board of Ed.*, 1981; see Laski, 1985).

A teacher who repeatedly uses "disciplinary" methods to change a handicapped child's maladaptive behavior is implementing treatment toward a major educational objective. The teacher is not free simply to implement any program that seems necessary. Formal IEP processes must be used if disciplinary methods of any kind are a regular part of a handicapped child's educational program.

Case law concerning behavior modification also offers some guidance regarding due process in the planning and implementation of appropriate programs for students with severe behavior problems (Martin, 1979). These precedents from legal decisions suggest that intrusive treatment approaches require a level of review beyond the regular IEP procedures. More process is due to a person as the potential for violation of basic rights increases (Easterbrook, 1983).

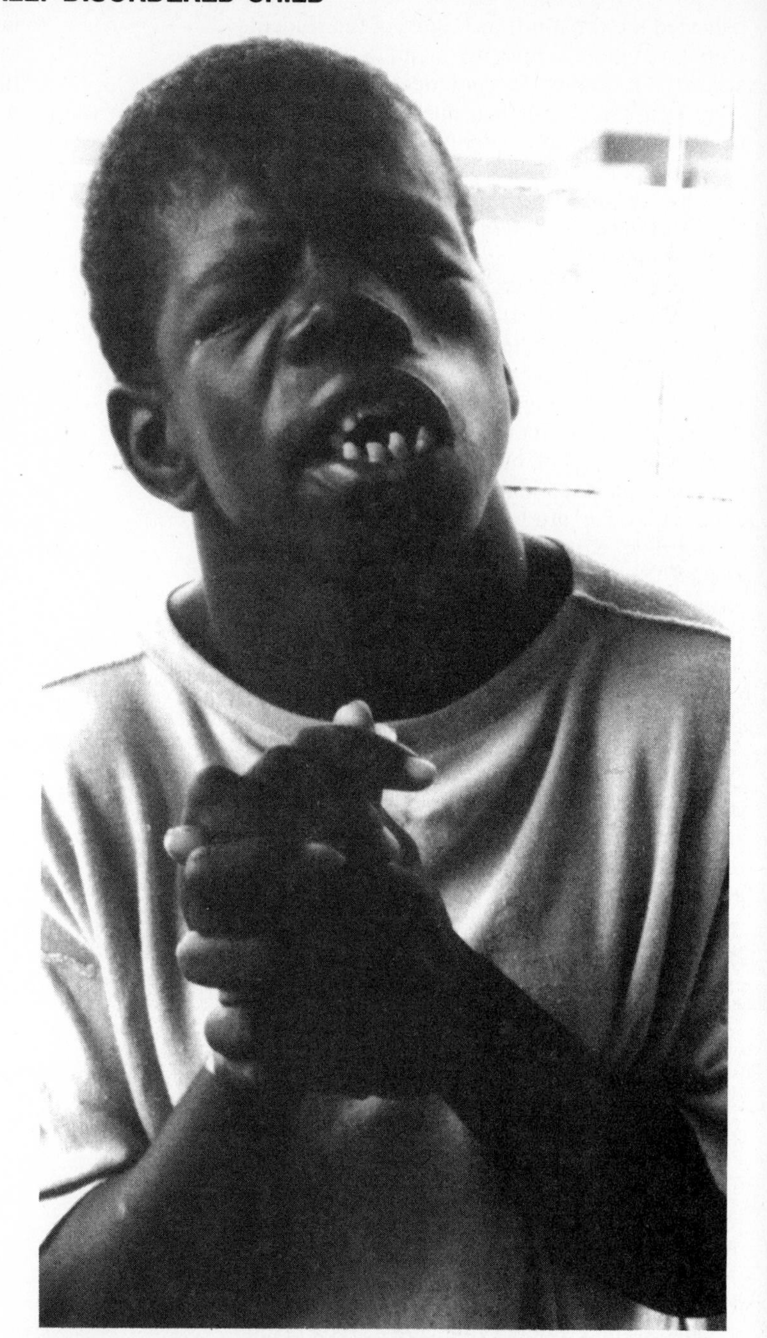

With the enactment of PL 94–142, a large number of children who were previously excluded from public education have been "mainstreamed." Simultaneously, there has been a national trend toward deinstitutionalization, resulting in an even higher number of students with severe behavior problems. The question arises as to what rights these children have in school.

Case law on behavior modification has generally held that constitutional rights are at stake when an agency of the state uses intrusive behavior modification and that, consequently, three procedural protections are necessary: informed consent, human rights review, and use of the least restrictive alternative treatment. The cases on which these findings are based arose in institutional settings. The facts usually involved flagrant misuse of behavioral treatments. Nonetheless, they set precedents that have been applied when similar treatment techniques were used with similar persons in school settings (*Milonas v. Williams*, 1982). The likelihood of such application in other special education settings is increased by the fact that the courts have already extended unusual safeguards to handicapped children in school settings.

Several constitutional rights have been invoked by the courts in behavior modification cases including First Amendment protection of free speech (e.g., *Stanley v. Georgia*, 1969; *Kaimowitz v. Department of Mental Health*, 1963), Eighth Amendment right to freedom from cruel and unusual punishment (e.g., *Wheeler v. Glass*, 1973); and Fourteenth Amendment protections against loss of life, liberty, and privacy. As a result, professionals who use behavior change must follow certain rules and afford clients or students due process of law.

In some cases, the courts have ordered review by a Human Rights Committee. *Wyatt v. Stickney* (1972) was a landmark case in treatment of retarded persons. The Court established minimal standards for the care and treatment of mentally retarded persons in Alabama's state hospital. The hospital was ordered to establish a review committee for intrusive behavioral treatments and to use least restrictive alternative treatments. These standards have been widely adopted by professional and parent advocacy organizations and written into some state laws. The court has extended most of the *Wyatt* standards to the care and treatment of developmentally disabled persons residing *in the community* (*Wuori v. Zitnay*, 1978).

The Wyatt standards offer sound guidelines for development of processes for protection of human rights of special education students in public school programs. Although human rights review of intrusive behavioral treatments in school settings is not specifically required by any legislative or judicial action, concerns for adequate due process appear to be most effectively addressed via such review. Guidelines for the development and implementation of human rights review processes are presented by Brakman (1985) and by Irvin and Singer (1984). They have been drawn from best practice procedures recommended by professional behavioral practitioners (Foxx, 1983; Miller & Fuoco, 1981; Sheldon-Wildgen & Risley 1983; Singer & Irvin, 1982) and legal authorities (VanBiervliet & Sheldon-Wildgen, 1981).

Least Restrictive Treatment

The second set of guidelines to emerge from case law for conducting human rights review in public schools derives from the concept of least restrictive alternative treatment. The courts have established some standards for making treatment decisions. The most specific of these is the standard of the least restrictive alternative treatment. In one case, the Supreme Court ruled that:

> In a series of decisions, this court has held that even though the government purpose be legitimate and substantial, that purpose cannot be pursued by means that broadly stifle fundamental personal liberties when the end can be narrowly achieved. (*Shelton v. Tucker*, 1960)

This standard was originally applied to placement or sentencing decisions for prisoners, juvenile offenders, and patients with mental disorders. The least restrictive alternative referred to treatment settings. For example, a maximum security prison was more restrictive than a halfway house.

The concept of least restrictive alternative was then extended to treatment techniques. This extension was clearly explained in a case in which a patient in a psychiatric ward refused treatment with a psychotropic drug (*Rennie v. Klein*, 1978). The court found that process was due to the patient before such an intrusive treatment could be implemented. In addition, it said:

> As a final consideration, many courts and commentators have employed the concept of least restrictive alternatives in regard to the choice of custodial setting. The court feels that this concept should be extended to the choice of medications. (*Rennie v. Klein*, 1978)

The courts have often equated medication-based treatment and behavior modification (Martin, 1979).

The doctrine of the least restrictive alternative is useful when applied to situations in which intrusive behavior modification treatments are being considered or implemented. Its greatest contribution may be that it requires issues of human rights to be considered by the professionals who provide treatment. The courts have made it clear that treatment decisions can and will be reviewed in terms of human rights.

SUMMARY

Public special education programs should establish safeguard mechanisms to protect staff and students when students' severe aberrant behavior must be controlled. To accomplish this, schools need to establish administrative policies and procedures for treatment of severe maladaptive behaviors. Court decisions suggest that new levels of scrutiny and public review are recommended. The general principles of informed consent, sufficient due process, and least restrictive treatment alternative can be used to guide the development of tthese policies and procedures. School systems may elect to institute these policies by improving existing mechanisms and/or creating new ones. For example, safeguards might include improved inservice training on behavioral techniques for teachers, improved staff supervision, more extensive due process review as part of the IEP process, and more thorough informed consent procedures. Schools may also benefit, though, by creating some new service system components such as behavioral specialist teams and district-wide human rights review committees.

Regardless of the approach, though, decisions about the use of intrusive procedures in an educational context must be guided by the perceived educational value of treatments (as opposed to their pure "discipline" value). For intrusive or restrictive procedures to be used, they must be aimed at educational objectives, and must clearly be the least restrictive alternatives. Given the risks of misuse of intrusive, decelerative, and restrictive procedures, the burden of proof must be on the proposers of an intrusive procedure or restriction to demonstrate that there is compelling evidence that less intrusive means are not the best approach and that the proposal represents the least restrictive alternative. A prima facie rule must be established against a potentially deleterious intervention. Compelling evidence must be required to override the rule. The use of intrusion and restriction should be viewed as highly unusual, never as commonplace or routine.

REFERENCES

Accreditation Council for Services for Mentally Retarded and Other Developmentally Disabled Persons (1980). *Standards for services for developmentally disabled individuals*. Washington, DC: Author.

Association for Advancement of Behavior Therapy (1977). *Ethical issues for human services*. New York: Author.

Association for Persons with Severe Handicaps (1981). *Resolution on Intrusive Interventions*, Seattle, WA: Author.

Beauchamp, T., & Childress, J. (1983). *Principles of biomedical ethics*. NY: Oxford Univ Press.

Brakman, C. (1985). A human rights committee in a public school for severely and profoundly retarded students. *Education and Training of the Mentally Retarded, 20*(2), 139-147.

Brightman, A. J., & Sullivan, M. B. (1980). A developmental perspective on stress and coping in families of autistic children. In J. Blacher (Ed.), *Severely handicapped young children and their families: Research in review* (pp. 91-142). New York: Academic Press.

Bruininks, R., Meyers, C., Sigford, B., & Lakin, K. (1981). *Deinstitutionalization and community adjustment of mentally retarded people*. Washington: Amer Assn on Mental Deficiency.

Carr, E., & Durand, V. M. (1985). Reducing behavior problems through functional communication training. *Jrnl of Appld Bhvr Analysis, 18*(2), 111-126.

A child's salvation or brainwashing. (October 2, 1983). *Register-Guard*, Eugene, OR.

Connecticut Gen Statutes (effective October 1, 1976). *Rights of persons under supervision of commissioner of mental retardation*. Section 19-575a.

Deitz, D. E., & Repp, A. C. (1983). Reducing behavior through reinforcement. *Exceptional Education Quarterly, 3*(4).

Easterbrook, F. H. (1983). *Substance and due process*. Chicago: Univ of Chicago Press.

Engelmann, S., & Colvin, G. (1983). *Generalized compliance training*, Austin, TX: ProEd Pub.

Evans, I., & Meyer, L. (1985). *An educative approach to behavior problems*. Baltimore: Paul Brookes.

Eymann, R., & Call, T. (1977). Maladaptive behavior and community placement of mentally retarded persons. *American Journal of Mental Deficiency, 82*, 137-144.

Foxx, R. M. (1983). *Decreasing the behaviors of severely handicapped and autistic persons*. Champaign, IL: Research Press.

Goldstein, S., Strickland, B., Turnbull, A., & Curry, L. (1980). An observational analysis of the IEP conference. *Exceptional Children, 46*, 278-286.

Greenwood, C. R., Hops, H., & Walker, H. M. (1977). The program for academic survival skills (PASS): Effects on student behavior and achievement. *Journal of School Psychology, 15*, 25- 35.

Hoff, M., Fenton, K., Yoshida, R., & Kaufman, M. (1978). Notice & consent: The school's responsibility to inform parents. *Jrnl Schl Psych, 16*, 265-273.

Irvin, L. K., & Lundervold, D. (1985). *Social validation of decelerative procedures: Perspective of multiple service providers*. Association for Behavioral Analysis Symposium, Columbus, OH.

Irvin, L. K., & Singer, G. S. (1984). *Human rights review manual*. Eugene: OR Research Institute.

Irvin, L. K., & Singer, G. S. (1985). *Informed consent for intrusive behavioral treatments*. Eugene, OR: Oregon Research Institute.

Laski, F. (1985). Judicial address of education for students with severe mental retardation. In D. Bricker & J. Filler (Eds.), *Severe mental retardation: From theory to practice*. Reston, VA: Division on Mental Retardation of CEC.

Martin, R. (1979). *Legal challenges to behavior modification*. Champaign, IL: Research Press.

Martin, R. (1983). *Special education litigation*. A survey of 94-142 and 504 cases, 1978-1983. Champaign, IL: Research Press.

Matson, J., & DiLorenzo, T. (1984). *Punishment and its alternatives*. New York: Springer Pub Co.

McClannahan, L. E., & Krantz, P. J. (1981). Accountability systems for protection of the rights of autistic children and youth. In R. T. Hannah, W. P. Christian, & H. B. Clark (Eds.), *Preservation of client rights*. New York: The Free Press.

Miller, D. N., & Fuoco, F. J. (1981, May). *Due process in treatment: Human right reviews and peer reviews*. Paper presented at Association for Behavior Analysis Convention, Milwaukee, WI.

National Association for Retarded Citizens (1975). *Guidelines for the use of behavioral procedures in state programs for retarded persons*. Arlington, TX: Author.

National Society for Autistic Children (1975). *White paper on behavior modification with autistic children*. Washington, DC: Author.

Noel, M., & Haring, N. (Eds.). (1982). *Progress or change: Issues in educating the emotionally disturbed*. Seattle: Program Development Assistance System, Univ of WA.

Overcast, T. D., & Saks, B. D. (1983). The legal rights of students in the elementary and secondary public schools. In C. R. Reynolds & T. B. Guthin (Eds.), *The handbook of school psychology*. New York: John Wiley & Sons.

Pickering, D., & Morgan, S. (1985). Parental ratings of treatment of self-injurious behavior. *Jrnl of Autism & Dev Disorders, 15*(3), 303-314.

Sheldon-Wildgen, J., & Risley, T. R. (1983). Balancing clients' rights: The establishment of human rights and peer review committees. In A. Bellach, M. Hersen, & A. Kazdin (Eds.), *International handbook of behavior modification*. New York: Plenum.

Singer, G. S., Close, D. W., Irvin, L. K., Gersten, R., & Sailor, W. S. (1984). An alternative to the institution for young people with severely handicapping conditions in a rural community. *Jrnl of Assn for the Severely Handicapped, 9*(4), 251-261.

Singer, G. S., & Irvin, L. K. (1982). *Behavioral Treatment and Review System Project Proposal*. Eugene, OR: Oregon Research Institute.

VanBiervliet, A., & Sheldon-Wildgen, J. (1981). *Liability issues in Community-based programs*. Baltimore, MD: Paul H. Brookes.

Walker, H. M. (1983). Applications of response cost within school settings: Guidelines, outcomes, issues, and recommendations. *Exceptional Education Quarterly, 3*(4), 47-55.

Walker, H. M., & Rankin, R. (1982). Assessing the behavioral expectations and demands of less restrictive settings. *Schl Psychlgy Review, 12*.

Yoshida, R. K. (1982). Research agenda: Finding ways to create more options for parent involvement. *Excptnl Educ Qurtrly, 3*(2), 74-80.

COURT CASES

Campbell v. Talledega Co. Board of Education, 518 F. Supp. 47 (N.D. Ala. 1981).

Doe V. Koger, 480 F. Supp. 225, N.D. Ind. 1979.

Fialkowski v. Shapp, 405 F. Supp. 960 (E.D. Pa. 1974).

Ingraham v. Wright, 430, U.S. 651, 1976.

Kaimowitz v. Dept. of Mental Health, 42 U.S.L. Week 2063, July 0, 1963.

Mathews v. Eldridge, 424 U.S. 319, 1976.

Milonas v. Williams, 691 F. 2d 931, 1982.

Rennie v. Klein, No. 77-2629, 1978.

Shelton v. Tucker, 364 U.S. 479 (1960)

Sherry v. N.Y. State Education Dept., 479f Supp. 1328 W.D., N.Y., 1979.

Stanley v. Georgia, 394 U.S. 557, 1969.

Stuart v. Nappi, 443 F. Supp. 1235, D. Conn., 1978.

S-1 v. Turlington, 635 F. 2nd 342, 1981.

Wheeler v. Glass, 473 F. 2nd 983, 984, 7th Cir., 1973.

Wuori v. Zitnay, No. 75-80-SD, D. Maine, July 14, 1978.

Wyatt v. Stickney, 344 F. Supp. 387, 1972.

Principles for A System of Care

Beth A. Stroul and Robert M. Friedman

Beth A. Stroul is Vice-President, Management and Training Innovations, Inc., McLean, Virginia, and a consultant to the CASSP Technical Assistance Center, Georgetown University Child Development Center. Robert M. Friedman, Ph.D., is Director, Florida Research and Training Center for Improved Services for Seriously Disturbed Children, Florida Mental Health Institute, University of South Florida, Tampa.

There is broad agreement in the United States that comprehensive, coordinated "systems of care" must be developed for severely emotionally disturbed children and youth. Such systems should include a wide array of mental health and other services in order to meet the multiple needs of these children and their families.[1] The concept of a system of care for severely emotionally disturbed children and adolescents, however, represents more than individual service components. Rather, it embodies a *philosophy* about the way in which services should be delivered to children and their families. While the actual components and organizational configuration of the system of care may differ from state to state and from community to community, it should be guided by a set of basic values and philosophies. These values must be clearly articulated so that they may be used to guide the character and quality of the system of care. Through a project sponsored by the National Institute of Mental Health's Child and Adolescent Service System Program (CASSP), two core values and a set of 10 principles have been developed to provide a philosophical framework for such a system of care.[2]

The two core values are central to the system and its operation. The first is that the system must be driven by the needs of the child and his or her family. It must be child-centered, with the needs of the child and family dictating the types and mix of services provided. This focus is seen as a commitment to adapt services to the child and family, rather than expecting them to conform to pre-existing service configurations. It is also a commitment to providing services in an environment and a manner that enhance the personal dignity of children and families, respect their wishes and individual goals, and maximize opportunities for involvement and self-determination in the planning and delivery of services.

Implicit in this value is a commitment to serving the child in the context of the family. In most cases, parents are the primary caregivers for severely emotionally disturbed children, and the system of care should support and assist them in this role as well as involve them in all decisions regarding service delivery. The system should also have a strong and explicit commitment to preserving the integrity of the family unit whenever possible. In many cases, intensive services involving the child and family can minimize the need for residential treatment.

The second core value holds that the system of care for emotionally disturbed children should be community based. Historically, services for this population have been limited to state hospitals, training schools and other restrictive institutional facilities. However, there has been increasing interest and progress in serving children in community-based programs, which provide less restrictive, more normative environments. While "institutional" care may be indicated for certain children at various points in time, in many cases appropriate services can be provided in less restrictive settings within or close to the child's home community.

In addition to these two fundamental values for the system of care, 10 principles have been developed which enunciate other basic beliefs about the optimal nature of the system.

1. *Emotionally disturbed children should have access to a comprehensive array of services that address the child's physical, emotional, social and educational needs.*

While emotionally disturbed children require specialized mental health services, these services alone are insufficient to promote proper growth and development. Mental health services can be effective only within the context of a larger child-caring network which is responsible for meeting the child's health, educational, recreational, family support and vocational needs. Thus, the scope and array of services included in the system of care must be sufficiently broad to account for the diverse and multidimensional needs of the developing child.

From *Children Today,* July/August 1988, pp. 11-15. Reprinted by permission of the authors and *Children Today* magazine.

2. *Emotionally disturbed children should receive individualized services in accordance with the unique needs and potentials of each child and guided by an individualized service plan.*

Since each child and family served by the system of care has unique and changing needs, the types, mix and intensity of services must be determined individually for each child and family. Hence, a comprehensive diagnostic and assessment process must be an integral part of service delivery. This assessment process should examine the child's problems and strengths, as well as any special needs, and consider the child in the context of the family, school and other relevant environments. It should be noted that the assessment process does not necessarily precede treatment or occur apart from service delivery. In some cases—particularly for children and families in crisis, or where resistance is high—it may be more important to first engage the child and family in the therapeutic process, deferring a thorough assessment or gathering information more informally as services are provided.

The culmination of the assessment process should be an individualized service plan which identifies problems, establishes goals and specifies appropriate interventions. The plan should be developed with the full participation of the child, family, providers and significant others. Service goals and plans should be reassessed regularly and revised based on the dynamic nature of the strengths, weaknesses and needs of the child and family. An ideal system of care allows the child opportunities to progress and to move to less restrictive settings as well as to use more intensive forms of services when indicated.

3. *Emotionally disturbed children should receive services within the least restrictive, most normative environment that is clinically appropriate.*

An implicit goal of the system of care is to maintain as many children as possible in their own homes by providing a full range of family-focused services and supports. In too many cases, children are removed from their homes or placed in environments that are more restrictive than they actually need. While out-of-home or protective placements may be indicated some of the time, frequently they are used because less restrictive, community-based alternatives are not available. Accumulating evidence indicates that when a comprehensive system of care is available, many severely emotionally disturbed children can be maintained in their own homes and communities.[3]

In a small percentage of cases, it may not be in the child's best interest to remain with the family, and residential services should be considered. Residential services should be employed only when more normative, nonresidential options are not effective in meeting the therapeutic needs of the child and family. In these situations, residential services should be provided in the least restrictive setting possible—in therapeutic foster homes or family-style group homes, for example—with the goal of rapid reintegration into the family or achievement of a stable, permanent placement.

Residential services, when indicated, should be located as close as possible to the child's home in order to cause the least disruption of the child's links to family, friends, agencies, school and community. Services located close to home maximize the possibility of family involvement in the treatment process and are more likely to prepare the child for successful reintegration into the natural environment.

In some cases, a child may need highly specialized services which are not reproducible in a community setting, and treatment in hospitals, residential treatment centers and other such settings may be appropriate. However, data from North Carolina (where less than seven percent of the most difficult target population is in secure treatment settings considered appropriate to the youths' needs) suggest that the vast majority of severely emotionally disturbed youth can be served in less restrictive, community-based settings given the appropriate continuum of services and supports.[4]

4. *The families and surrogate families of emotionally disturbed children should be full participants in all aspects of the planning and delivery of services.*

In order to establish parents or surrogate caregivers as partners in the system of care, they should be involved in all phases of service delivery. In addition, an array of services and supports, including parent education, counseling, respite and home aid services, should be offered to parents and families to enhance their coping skills and their ability to care for their children effectively. When adequate support is available, many families are able to maintain severely emotionally disturbed children at home and avoid placement in residential or institutional settings.

Even when children are in out-of-home placements, the participation and involvement of parents should be encouraged. In fact, family needs are most often neglected when children are in residential settings, either due to distance or other factors. Efforts should be made to reach families and engage them constructively in the service delivery process. By involving and providing supports to families, the opportunities for successful return of the child to the family are enhanced.

While family involvement is the goal, no child should be denied services because he or she has no traditional family or the family refuses participation. Where the natural family is not involved, the system of care should engage the surrogate or substitute family in services.

5. *Emotionally disturbed children should receive services that are integrated, with linkages between child caring agencies and programs and mechanisms for planning, developing and coordinating services.*

While states and communities may be developing more comprehensive services for severely emotionally disturbed children and adolescents, this does not ensure coordination of services or continuity of care. Nor does it ensure that the system will be able to respond to the changing service needs of children and their families. Coordination, continuity and movement within the system are critical for severely emotionally disturbed youth who have multiple needs that cut across agency boundaries. In order to best meet the needs of children and families, integrated, multiagency networks are needed to blend the services provided by mental health, education, child welfare, health, mental retardation, juvenile justice and other agencies. In short, the various components must be interwoven into a coherent and effective system. In addition to coordinating service delivery, a number of functions should be shared by the various agencies and programs linking together to serve severely emotionally disturbed children and their families including planning, developing, funding and evaluating services.

6. *Emotionally disturbed children should be provided with case management or similar mechanisms to ensure that multiple services are delivered in a coordinated and therapeutic manner and that they can move through the system of services in accordance with their changing needs.*

Case management has been called the backbone of the system of care, and is essential to the success of the service system. Case management, therapeutic case advocacy, and a variety of similar approaches are intended to ensure that children and families receive the services they need, that services are coordinated, and that services are appropriate to their changing needs over time.

The organizational location of the case manager or service coordinator cannot be predetermined. This should be determined by the needs of individual children and families and by the structure and resources of the system of care within a particular community. The role of the case manager, however, has been more clearly articulated and includes a number of essential functions, such as coordinating the comprehensive interagency assessment of the child's needs; planning, arranging and monitoring needed services; linking the various parts of the child's system; advocating for the child and family; and establishing linkages with the adult service system to facilitate transition. These functions are essential, unifying factors in service delivery.

7. *Early identification and intervention for children with emotional problems should be promoted by the system of care in order to enhance the likelihood of positive outcomes.*

One of the goals of the system of care should be to reduce the prevalence and severity of emotional disturbance through effective early identification and intervention. While there is increasing interest in screening and intervention programs to identify and assist high risk children and families, these services are often neglected in favor of much needed services for children who are already demonstrating serious problems. One of the challenges to the system of care is to achieve an appropriate balance between early identification and intervention services and services designed for youth with severe and persistent problems.

While family involvement is the goal, no child should be denied services because he or she has no traditional family or the family refuses participation.

8. *Emotionally disturbed children should be ensured smooth transitions to the adult service system as they reach maturity.*

Children who "age out" of the system of care become young adults who are often in need of long-term mental health care, vocational services and a range of other support services. However, a number of factors complicate their transition to the adult service system and make it difficult for these young adults to receive appropriate services. Identifying, applying to and becoming established with an entirely new set of agencies and programs may be a complex and cumbersome task. Moving from school to the world of work may also be difficult. Many of these youths have no prevocational or vocational skills, and they may not be viewed positively by vocational rehabilitation agencies which look for substantial promise of a successful outcome. They may, therefore, be left with a void without school, a job or opportunities to enhance their employability.

Moreover, adult agencies may be ill-prepared to serve many of these youths. While the adult agencies have been developing programs to serve persons with chronic mental illness, only a small percentage of the aging out youth would fit the definition of chronically mentally ill adults. Many have not met the hospitalization criteria, and many evidence conduct disorders rather than overt psychotic disorders. Their problems often include drug and alcohol usage. The programs offered by the adult mental health and other agencies may be inappropriate to the needs and characteristics of the "youth in transition" population.

Clearly, the system of care for severely emotionally disturbed youth cannot address all the issues related to transition to the adult service system. Nevertheless, it should establish functional linkages with relevant adult agencies to ensure continuity of services.

9. *The rights of emotionally disturbed children should be protected, and effective advocacy efforts for emotionally disturbed children and youth should be promoted.*

The "child advocacy" function of the system of care should be evident in several respects. First, the system of care should adopt such mechanisms as statutes, statements of the rights of children, grievance procedures and case review committees to ensure the protection of client rights. These mechanisms are needed to protect the rights of children in several respects. For example, one basic right of all children is to be treated in the least restrictive, appropriate setting. Safeguards may be necessary to ensure that this right is upheld as well as rights upon admission to hospitals and other facilities, rights of children within facilities, rights related to removal from home, etc. A complicating factor in protecting the rights of children occurs when the rights of the child and the rights of the parents may be in conflict.

In addition to rights protection, the system of care should actively promote advocacy activities on behalf of emotionally disturbed children and adolescents. Both case advocacy and class advocacy are vital to the success of the system of care. A strong and vocal network to advocate for the needs of emotionally disturbed children has been notably lacking in the past.

10. *Emotionally disturbed children should receive services without regard to race, religion, national origin, sex, physical disability or other characteristics, and services should be sensitive and responsive to cultural differences and special needs.*

The system of care should uphold a policy of nondiscrimination in the delivery of services. All emotionally disturbed children and families should have access to quality services, including minority children and children with special needs such as physical handicaps. Special efforts and arrangements may be indicated in order to be responsive to the special needs of children and families. Without such efforts, the system of care could not be truly child-centered. The President's Commission on Mental Health emphasized this principle: "Clearly services should respect ethnic differences and preferences. Quality of services should be independent of the socioeconomic or ethnic groups being served. Services should be adapted to suit the lifestyles, language, and expectations of the children and families being served."[5]

The task of developing a comprehensive system of care for severely emotionally disturbed children is both complex and difficult. These principles attempt to lay the groundwork by describing the characteristics of such a system of care and the values on which it is based.

---

[1]*Joint Commission on the Mental Health of Children, Crisis in Child Mental Health*, New York, Harper & Row, 1969; President's Commission on Mental Health, *Report of the Subtask Panel on Infants, Children, and Adolescents*, Washington, D.C., U.S. Government Printing Office, 1978; U.S. Congress, Office of Technology Assessment, *Children's Mental Health: Problems and Services—A Background Paper*, Washington, D.C., U.S. Government Printing Office, 1986; B. Stroul and R. Friedman, *A System of Care for Severely Emotionally Disturbed Children and Youth*, Washington, D.C., CASSP Technical Assistance Center, Georgetown University Child Development Center, 1986.

[2]Stroul and Friedman, op. cit.

[3]See L. Behar, "Changing Patterns of State Responsibility: A Case Study of North Carolina," *Journal of Clinical Child Psychology*, Vol. 14, 1985; L. Behar, "A Model for Child Mental Health Services: The North Carolina Experience," CHILDREN TODAY, May–June 1986; and R. Friedman and S. Street, "Admission and Discharge Criteria for Children's Mental Health Services: A Review of the Issues and Options," *Journal of Clinical Child Psychology*, Vol. 14, 1985.

[4]Behar, 1985, op. cit.; Behar, 1986, op. cit.

[5]President's Commission on Mental Health, op. cit.

Teaching the Communication Disordered Child

Communication disorders include both language impairments and speech disorders. As with all other areas of exceptionality, the category covers a diverse set of problems. Children may be language impaired due to aphasia (loss of language ability) or dysphasia (impairment of language ability). Both of these problems are usually acquired after brain injuries. They may also have delayed language ability due to brain injury or dysfunction, lack of language stimulation, bilingual or multilingual stimulation, hearing impairments, learning disabilities, cerebral palsy, cleft palate, or elective mutism. Speech disorders often involve articulation disorders such as vowel or consonant substitutions, distortions, omissions, or additions. Fluency disorders—such as stuttering or cluttering—and voice disorders—such as problems with pitch, loudness, or nasality—are also considered speech disorders.

The current emphasis on effective schools and excellence in education has created high expectations for public school students in the areas of language and communication. Teaching "correct" speech is often viewed as a regular classroom teacher's responsibility. Both students and teachers are often judged by students' language proficiencies. This can place unrealistic demands on teachers who have not been appropriately prepared to provide special speech and language services to children with communication problems.

Since the 1975 passage of PL 94-142, there have been dramatic increases in the number of children who have been assessed to have communication disorders. They are the second largest group of exceptional children, after those assessed to have learning disabilities. Often there are problems in defining a student's problem as either a learning disability (developmental aphasia) or a speech and language impairment (acquired aphasia). A communication disordered child may have problems in just one, or in two or more, of the speech and language areas. He or she may also have problems in other classifications of exceptionality (e.g., mentally retarded, gifted, emotionally disturbed, orthopedically impaired). Each communication disordered child can also be expected to have his or her own unique differences in personality, motivation, coordination, etc. These interindividual and intraindividual differences make individualized educational programs (IEPs) very important. They also increase the types of services necessary for these exceptional children.

Speech-language clinicians, special educators, regular classroom teachers, administrators, and support staff have a shared responsibility to assist communication disordered children in getting an appropriate education in the least restrictive environment. Most students with speech or language problems are integrated into regular classrooms and experience pull-out for special services. In the early grades, articulation problems and language delays are the impairments for which special services are most frequently provided. Stuttering is a more prevalent problem by middle school. Acquired aphasia, dysphasia, elective mutism, or functional aphonia are also more common in older children, especially after physical or emotional traumas. These conditions also require speech language remediation and related services (sometimes psychological services or counseling).

The first article of this unit discusses communication disordered children who may be mislabeled as emotionally disturbed because of their bizarre behaviors. The authors suggest that their behaviors serve as a form of communication. By analyzing the messages behind the behaviors, we can help such children to find better ways of communicating what they want to say. The second article discusses culturally and linguistically diverse children with limited English proficiency. It focuses on four specific groups: black children, Hispanic children, Asian children, and American Indian children. Next, Thelma Zirkelback and Kathryn Blakesley give several suggestions for enhancing the communication skills of language-deficient children in the classroom. Frequently, according to the authors, teachers do not recognize that academic failure may be primarily due to some language deficiency. The fourth article, by Beatrice Jimenz and Dee Ann Iseyama, describes a model program to train parents, aids, and other supportive personnel to help provide speech and language services in schools. The use of communication assistants can increase the frequency of therapeutic intervention for students in schools faced with large numbers of communication disordered children and a shortage of funds for special services. The final article discusses the problem of aphonia, or no voice, in adolescents. The authors describe the psychophysiological nature of the disorder, and present ways to quickly return students to full voice by referring to five actual case studies.

Unit 7

Looking Ahead: Challenge Questions

Can bizarre behaviors really be a means of communication? Can children who exhibit them be helped in a regular school setting?

How can school personnel assess the communication needs of children from culturally and linguistically diverse groups?

What are some behavioral characteristics of speech-language impaired children? How can their communication skills be enhanced in the classroom?

Can parents, aids, and other personnel help to provide speech and language services in public schools?

Can adolescents without laryngitis lose their voices? Why?

SEE ME, HELP ME

In some children, bizarre behavior is a way of communicating. Understanding the message helps.

EDWARD G. CARR
AND V. MARK DURAND

Edward G. Carr, Ph.D., is a professor of psychology at the State University of New York at Stony Brook and a research psychologist at the Suffolk Child Development Center in Smithtown, Long Island, New York. V. Mark Durand, Ph.D., is an assistant professor of psychology at the State University of New York at Albany.

BOB IS A 14-YEAR-OLD autistic boy. As part of his therapy, he attends lessons to learn how to dress himself, but he gets little from this instruction. He repeatedly throws tantrums and tries to kick, scratch and bite his teacher. The attacks are so violent that the teacher has to wear protective clothing, including gloves and a heavy coat. After 10 minutes the teacher usually gives up, puts away the lesson materials and moves the work desk aside. Within seconds, Bob calms down and begins softly humming to himself.

Jim is a 10-year-old mildly retarded child who scratches himself so badly that he has ugly sores all over his body. Other students in his school shun him and call him names. The family physician can find no medical reason for the scratching, so the boy's parents conscientiously nag at him whenever they see him scratching. But, oddly enough, when they are absorbed in other matters and say nothing about his scratching, Jim hardly ever scratches himself.

For the past 11 years, these and other puzzling cases have fueled our research at the Suffolk Child Development Center in Long Island. That research has convinced us that severe behavior problems are often not senseless acts but primitive attempts to communicate. Indeed, aggression, self-injury and tantrums are often the only effective ways some children have of making their needs known.

The notion that bizarre behavior may be a form of communication has a long history. Over 2,300 years ago, Plato suggested that newborns communicated with their caregivers by crying and screaming. The 18th-century French philosopher Jean Rousseau wrote that "When children begin to speak, they cry less. This is a natural progression. One language is substituted for another."

The ideas of these philosophers are supported by recent studies of normal child development. Harvard psychiatrist Peter Wolff, for example, found that infants cry in different ways for different purposes. They cry one way if they are hungry, another way if they are uncomfortable, yet another if they merely crave company. The differences are subtle, but by the time a baby is a few weeks old, many mothers can tell one kind of cry from another. When babies are older, they will fuss and cry when given foods they don't like; withdraw the foods and the crying stops. In a sense the baby is saying, "Take that stuff away. I don't want it." In a related study, psychologists Silvia Bell and Mary Ainsworth found that the more skillful a 1-year-old was at communicating by means of facial expression, gesture and speech, the less the baby cried.

Although most of the children we study are autistic or retarded, their behavior problems also seem to be means of communicating. We have found that these children are most likely to be aggressive or injure themselves when seeking adult attention or attempting to escape from unpleasant situations. Their strange behavior is a way of saying, "Please pay attention to me" or "Please don't ask me to do this."

Our ideas owe much to an important study conducted in 1965 by Ivar Lovaas, a psychologist at the University of California, Los Angeles, and his colleagues. The 9-year-old schizophrenic girl with whom they worked banged her head against objects such as the edge of a desk top or a wall. The more adults pleaded with her to stop, the harder she hit her head. Apparently, she had learned that hurting herself was an effective way of getting attention. (Most adults find it very difficult to ignore a child who is deliberately injuring herself.) When the adults paid no attention to her self-destructive behavior, however, but attended to her when she played in a normal way, she rarely hurt herself.

Lovaas's work showed that self-destructive behavior is often simply an abnormal way of getting something that all children normally crave: attention. Since 1965, researchers have found that many forms of bizarre behavior are often ways of asking for attention. Jim, the retarded boy who constantly scratched himself, is an example.

A chance observation in 1975 led to the conclusion that attention-seeking is not the only reason children behave abnormally. In collaboration with psychologists Crighton Newsom and Jody Binkoff, one of us (Carr) studied an 8-year-old schizophrenic boy named Tim who screamed and punched himself in the face whenever anyone tried to teach him anything. At the end of each lesson the teacher would say, "Tim, that's it for today." The boy would immediately stop hitting himself and say, "That's it, that's it," as he ran smiling for the exit. In a matter of minutes, the rate at which he punched himself fell from 30 times a minute to zero. This sudden change in behavior made us realize that bizarre behavior sometimes expresses a desire to escape an unpleasant situation. It is a way of saying, "I don't want to do this. If you try to make me do this, I'll act crazy until you stop."

In the 11 years of research that followed this discovery, we came across many children who behaved oddly as a way of escaping unpleasant situations. These situations were often those in which demands were placed upon the children. Asked to practice a speech lesson or learn how to dress themselves, for example, they would punch, bite, kick or scratch themselves—or their teacher—or scream and throw tantrums. Under these circumstances, children can often force adults to let them have their way. Bob, the autistic boy who attacked his teacher, is an example.

It now seems so obvious that bizarre behavior can be a way of communicating that it may be hard to see why this wasn't understood long ago. There are three reasons. First, such behavior used to be (and in some quarters still is) attributed to things going on inside of the person. It is only when you look to events in the environment that the communicative function of the behavior becomes clear.

Second, until 1975 most disturbed children languished in institutions where they received little more than custodial care. Since few demands were placed on them, there were few opportunities to notice that demands triggered bizarre behavior. Then, in 1975, Congress passed a law requiring that all handicapped children must be educated. This meant that the children were required to do things, and some expressed their displeasure by behaving strangely.

The third reason that we did not see the message in abnormal behavior is that the relationship between bizarre behavior and things going on in the environment is often more complex and subtle than our examples suggest. For instance, the same behavior may mean different things in different situations. One moment a child may bang his head against a wall because he objects to a demand someone has made, but in another moment he may do the same thing to get attention. And a child may have a number of different ways of "saying" the same thing—scratching or hitting, screaming, throwing objects around a room. Often the purpose of the behavior becomes clear only when the circumstances under which it occurs are carefully studied.

Scratching, hitting, screaming, throwing things—all can be different ways of saying the same thing.

The notion that abnormal behavior is a form of communication has important implications. For one thing, it means that we must understand the meaning of the behavior to treat it successfully. For example, when a child misbehaves, we sometimes use "time out" as a form of punishment. We isolate the child in an area from which he or she can't see or hear others. Usually 10 minutes is enough to discourage attention-seeking behavior. But if the misbehavior is a way of asking to get out of a demanding situation, time out can backfire. When we used time out to punish aggressive behavior in one boy, for example, he became more aggressive when he returned to his lesson. We realized that what we were asking him to do was too difficult for him. When we simplified the task, aggression practically disappeared.

Another implication of the communication approach to bizarre behavior is that if we teach children normal ways of conveying their needs, they might give up their abnormal behavior. This idea is supported by the research of psychologists Margaret Shodell and Henry Reiter with autistic children. Some of these children had good language skills and some of them did not. Their parents and teachers were asked how often the children bit themselves, banged their heads or scratched themselves during a 10-day period. The results showed that while only 19 percent of the good communicators engaged in such self-injurious acts, 47 percent of the poor communicators did so.

A second study, this one by L.W. Talkington and colleagues, compared institutionalized retarded children who had language skills with similar children who lacked such skills. Adults who worked with these children rated their tendency to behave aggressively by, for example, destroying property. On several categories, those who lacked linguistic skills were rated more aggressive than those who could communicate more or less normally.

For the past five years, we have conducted studies to see if teaching disturbed children how to communicate their needs reduces their bizarre behavior. We work with children in educational settings, since bizarre behavior is particularly troublesome there. Our first step is to determine whether the behavior is an effort to receive attention or to escape an unpleasant situation. We do this by instructing the disturbed child and one other child at the same time. At first, the teacher interacts exclusively with the problem child and then, after a few minutes, begins directing attention to the other child. If the bizarre behavior suddenly increases, we know that attention is what the child is after.

If we suspect that the behavior is a way of objecting to frustrating demands, then we ask the child to perform a series of tasks. The first is something easy, such as naming the animals in a series of pictures. Then we try something harder, such as asking the child to say how many animals are shown in a picture. If abnormal behavior suddenly increases, then we know the child is telling us the task is too difficult.

Once we understand the message in the behavior, we attempt to teach the child better ways of communicating. Children who seek attention are taught various ways of asking for praise. For example, they learn to show their teacher a completed assignment and ask, "Am I doing good work?" or "Look at what I've done!" We teach children frustrated by difficult tasks to say, "Help me" or "I don't understand." This way the children can avoid repeated failure by speaking to the teacher rather than by, for example, hitting the teacher. We teach sign language to children who are unable to speak, and signing can be just as effective as speech in getting a message across.

Teaching children new ways of communicating is more difficult than it sounds. For instance, the teacher who is working with a child who screams when frustrated must be alert to the first signs of frustration, which may be only a slightly wrinkled brow or a faint whimper. If the teacher acts too quickly, the child may be annoyed by the assistance. If the teacher waits too long, the child may progress to a full-scale tantrum. The teacher's role is made more difficult by the fact that the children sometimes appear indifferent or confused at first. Gradually, however, the children learn that the new methods work better than the old ones.

We have worked with several dozen children in this way and all have shown marked reductions in, or the elimination of, severe behavior problems. The children appear eager to use their new communication skills, perhaps because for the first time they can reliably influence another person.

The benefits seem to persist long after the training is over. We studied three children for two years and found that two of them continued to use their new linguistic skills throughout the period. Their behavior problems during this period were also negligible. In the case of the third child, however, the teacher did not respond to normal requests for attention and the child reverted to the face slapping and hand biting he had used earlier. Once the teacher learned to respond to normal requests, the problem behavior diminished.

So long as adults are sensitive to attempts to communicate normally, the children use those methods. They do not abandon their new techniques even when faced with a substitute teacher or other stranger. Perhaps we should not be surprised by this. After all, most adults know how to respond when a child says, "Help me."

For many years psychologists considered the bizarre behavior of disturbed children to be either meaningless or the expression of mysterious unconscious conflicts. We believe instead that such behavior is often a primitive way of communicating needs. By carefully analyzing the message behind the behavior, therapists, parents and teachers can help the children in their care to find better ways of communicating what they want to say.

Culturally and Linguistically Diverse Children

Bruce A. Ramirez

The United States is experiencing a pronounced shift in demography. In 1986, Black students comprised 16% of the public school enrollment, Hispanics 10%, Asians and Pacific Islanders 3%, and American Indians approximately 1% (DBS Corporation, 1987). By the turn of the century, it is projected that 40% of public school students will be from these and other ethnically diverse backgrounds. This multicultural trend is not a regional phenomenon; it is evident in states, cities, neighborhoods, and schools across the country. There are at least 6 states with a Black, Hispanic, Asian, and American Indian public school enrollment of 35% or more and another 12 states in which these students make up between 25% and 34% of the enrollment. The number of minority students in many large city school systems approaches or exceeds 80% (Plisko and Stern, 1985). In Texas, approximately half of all kindergarten students are Hispanic (Yates, 1986).

These student populations are heterogeneous in terms of native language, degree of acculturation, country of birth, immigration experience, and socioeconomic status. They are disproportionately represented among school failures, and their lack of success in school is frequently compounded by other circumstances such as poverty, poor health care, or unstable home environment. Many of these students are at risk for poor school achievement; having their education interrupted; dropping out; falling prey to drugs, teenage pregnancy, or crime; or chronic unemployment.

Need for Appropriate Instruction

Both the literature and practical experience continually remind us of the importance of understanding the cultural, linguistic, and socioeconomic backgrounds of students. Inaccurate perceptions, stereotypes, and lack of familiarity with ethnic groups, their culture and history, and contemporary experiences can lead to low expectations and unwarranted generalizations about their educational potential.

Disproportionate representation of culturally diverse students in certain programs for exceptional children is a recurring concern in special education (Chinn and Hughes, 1987; Reschly, 1988). While overrepresentation has received the most consideration, underrepresentation in some programs for handicapped children as well as for gifted and talented children also requires our attention (DBS Corporation, 1987). Teachers play a central role in the referral process for children at risk, and they are key to any effort to institute prereferral strategies emphasizing curricular and instructional adaptations for students from different cultural and linguistic backgrounds.

Many culturally and linguistically diverse students may also be eligible to participate in programs for disadvantaged children and youth, those with limited English proficiency, recent immigrants, American Indians, and migrants. Joining such programs with special education requires improved relationships and better cooperation among educators. Distinguishing among individual needs related to culture and language, poverty, mobility, or exceptionalities and providing appropriate services may require a combination of services and personnel.

Family and Community Involvement

Ethnically diverse parents tend to be less knowledgeable about and involved in their children's education programs than other parents (Marion, 1980; Lynch & Stein, 1987). Therefore, schools must find ways to encourage families from diverse cultural and linguistic backgrounds to participate to a much greater extent. Such efforts should involve various cultural groups and organizations in the community.

In striving to improve services for culturally and linguistically diverse students at risk, we cannot be content with a system that serves only a proportion of the students well. The articles that follow provide additional information on Black, Hispanic, Asian, and American Indian children who may be at risk for learning difficulties. Suggestions regarding prereferral, assessment, curriculum, parental involvement, and program coordination are presented. They have in common a commitment to appreciating cultural diversity and improving educational opportunities for culturally and linguistically diverse children and youth.

References

Chinn, P. C., & Hughes, S. (1987). Representation of minority students in special education classes. *Remedial and Special Education, 8*, 41-46.

DBS Corporation (1987, December). 1986 Elementary and Secondary School Civil Rights Survey National Summaries (Contract Number 300-86-0062). Washington, DC: Office of Civil Rights, U. S. Department of Education.

Lynch, E. W., & Stein, R. (1987). Parent participation by ethnicity: A comparison of Hispanic, Black, and Anglo families. *Exceptional Children, 54*, 105-111.

Marion, R. L. (1980). Communicating with parents of culturally diverse exceptional children. *Exceptional Children, 46*, 616-623.

Plisko, V. W., & Stern, J. D. (Eds.) (1985). *The condition of education: A statistical report.* Washington, DC: U. S. Government Printing Office.

Reschly, D. J. (1988). Minority MMR overrepresentation and special education reform. *Exceptional Children, 54*, 316-323.

Yates, J. R. (1986). Current and emerging forces impacting special education. In H. J. Prehm (Ed.), *The future of special education* (pp. 13-74). Reston, VA: The Council for Exceptional Children.

Black Children

Gladys Clark-Johnson

At-risk children have been defined as students whose poverty, family instability, or social background make them likely candidates for school failure—often falling victim to crime, drugs, teenage pregnancy, or early entry into the ranks of the unemployable (Vobejda, 1987). Black children often fall into the "at-risk" pool because of an impoverished quality of life over which they have no control. Compound this with handicapping conditions manifested as deficits in perceptual, motor, language, and attentional skills—which are prerequisites for success in the traditional school setting—and Black exceptional children are placed in double jeopardy.

The National Black Child Development Institute (1986), the Children's Defense Fund (1987), and other sources have described the status of Black children as follows:

- Nearly one of every two Black children lives in poverty.
- Almost two-thirds of young Black children live in homes relying on some form of public assistance.
- Black children generally receive poorer health care than White children.
- Blacks are three times as likely as Whites to be placed in classes for educable mentally retarded students.
- An affluent suburban White child is more likely to participate in a gifted and talented program than a Black child in the inner city.
- Nationally, the dropout rate for Black youth is almost 28%, approaching 50% in some areas.

These statistics are bleak; they may even be startling to some.

Assessment Bias

Black children who perform adequately in a variety of roles in the family and community often experience difficulty in school and are misclassified as handicapped. There is still an unresolved problem of bias in the content of the tests we use, which calls into question the validity of our entire process of determining some handicapping conditions. While due process procedures are designed to serve as safeguards, more remains to be done in the area of nondiscriminatory assessment. School personnel routinely locate the cause for academic failure in the *child* rather than in the curriculum or the school environment.

Studies such as those conducted by Clark (1983) on school achievement and Black children suggest that the conditions for high achievement cut across family income, education, and whether the family is a two-parent or single-parent household. Clark suggested that school personnel can acquire a better understanding of the "hidden curriculum" of the home, which results in children reaching school years with different levels of preparation, by looking at the Black family socialization *process* and not its compositional properties. This research could be useful to special educators who work with Black exceptional children.

Parent and Community Involvement

Schools would have added resources and allies in meeting the needs of Black exceptional children at risk if parents were not intimidated or excluded. Special educators must make parent participation in the IEP process meaningful. Parents must be encouraged to share their knowledge of the child.

More districts are taking the position that successful schools depend not only on the work of their teachers, parents, and administrators, but also on the support and involvement of their communities. A wide variety of partnerships with resources such as school volunteers, local businesses, and community leaders are being created to provide opportunities for Black exceptional children to increase job awareness and self-esteem through on-the-job training and career shadowing experiences. This experiential learning approach seems to be successful in special education transition programs.

School Programs

Culturally specific curriculum models and teaching strategies must be employed to make the educational process meaningful to Black exceptional children and compatible with the culturally influenced behavior they bring to school. The major task is to provide them with adaptive behaviors that will permit normalization of the activities of daily living, release of latent creativity, and acquisition of technical skills that will permit maximum independence in the community (Johnson, 1976). Curriculum components should include a high degree of affective support, self-concept development, and opportunities for creative expression. Teaching strategies should include sensitivity to learning styles, use of body language, provision of equal teacher:pupil talking time, and group learning experiences (Hale, 1986).

School staffing must reflect the diversity of racial and ethnic groups in our society more accurately. We must find and train more Black special educators, perhaps by strengthening preparation programs at historically Black colleges. Preservice and inservice programs must address problems of racism and ignorance of cultural differences straightforwardly to effect attitudinal change.

Conclusion

Special educators must be committed to empowering all children to achieve to their fullest potential. Children at risk are capable of success in school; educators must refuse to participate in making self-fulfilling prophesies, and faulting parents, the community, or any of the societal ills so frequently cited as the cause of schools' failures with Black children. While it is not implied that schools alone can resolve all the problems of these children, special education in particular must become committed to a central role in the ongoing effort to reverse the effects of institutional racism that perpetuate the problem of school failure. Schools can make a difference for Black exceptional children, including those who are gifted.

References

Clark, R. (1983). *Family life and school achievement: Why poor black children succeed or fail*. Chicago: University of Chicago Press.

Children's Defense Fund. (1987). *A children's defense budget: An analysis of the FY'87 federal budget and children*. Washington, DC: Author.

Hale, J. E. (1986). *Black children: Their roots, culture, and learning styles (2nd ed.)*. Salt Lake City: Brigham Young University Press.

Johnson, J. L. (1976). Mainstreaming Black children. In R. L. Jones (Ed.), *Mainstreaming and the minority child* (pp. 159-180). Reston, VA: The Council for Exceptional Children.

National Black Child Development Institute, Inc. (1986). *1986 NBCDI annual report*. Washington, DC: Author.

Vobejda, B. "Children At Risk," *Washington Post*, 11 October 1987, p. 1, 22-23.

Hispanic Children

Eda Valero-Figueira

By the turn of the century, Spanish-speaking individuals are expected to constitute the largest minority group in the United States. Not only do they immigrate in massive numbers, as a group they are significantly younger and have a higher birth rate than any other American ethnic group (Banks, 1987).

A report by the Congressional Research Service discussed by Rice (1985), indicated that in 1984 Hispanic children were the only minority group for which the poverty rate had increased. The 1984 Census, according to this article, reported that 38.7% of all Hispanic children live at the poverty level, with 71% living in homes in which a female is head of the household. Further, lack of prenatal care is especially common among Puerto Rican and Mexican women (Colburn & Melillo, 1987).

If we consider poverty and health care to be pivotal factors in the determination of high risk, Hispanic children should be overrepresented among children so identified. Unfortunately, this is not the case, as evidenced by the National Children's Center report that *no* Hispanic children are among their client groups (J. Garrett, personal communication, August 25, 1987). Rather, what we find is a negative cycle wherein Hispanics, as a group, are not seeking appropriate health services (Colburn & Melillo, 1987; Thompson, 1987), which means that Hispanic children are rarely identified as being at risk, and thus they rarely receive appropriate intervention.

Educational Outreach

Given the emphasis on early intervention, it is the responsibility of the schools to seek out Hispanic children who may be at risk through child-find activities that target non-English-speaking populations.

In order for child-find programs to be effective, traditional school methods must be abandoned and new alternatives sought out. Child-find activities must be directed through agencies known by the Hispanic community, for example, churches, adult English-as-a-second-language programs, and social clubs. Appealing to cultural values is an effective child-find technique because young children are highly valued in Hispanic households. Explaining to parents the damage they could be inflicting on their children by not seeking appropriate care often is sufficient. If this explanation is done through a highly respected figure such as a church pastor, teacher, or community leader, so much the better.

Joining forces with social welfare and other community agencies, schools can contribute to efforts to improve health and nutrition education. Programs must be designed to focus on increasing the family's understanding of and capacity for preventing disabilities. This can be achieved through such basic means as flyers; information used in both regular and adult English-as-a-second-language classes; and radio, television, and other media accessible to illiterate individuals. Prevention of disabilities and early identification of children at risk can be accomplished by families and others in the community if they have the correct information and are aware of their support systems.

A New At-Risk Population

Although we normally speak of infants and toddlers when talking about children at risk, there is among Hispanic and other linguistically and culturally different groups a new and not-so-young population that must be considered. They are the immigrant children from countries at war, who come to the United States and are expected to attend school and learn the language and subject matter just as any other child would. Many of these children are not performing well in school. They have survived experiences that are beyond our comprehension. They have experienced violence at its peak, seen their families killed or mutilated, and lived in fear for their own lives. Those who have lost their parents have realized a child's greatest fear, the fear of being abandoned by one or both parents. They cannot understand their own survival, let alone their arrival in a different culture, where a different language is spoken and things are done in a way that is foreign to them.

This new group of immigrants is at risk for "post-traumatic stress disorder" (APA, 1980, p. 137). One of the characteristics of this disorder is the lack of "responsiveness to or reduced involvement with the external world" (APA, 1980, p. 137), which is often accompanied by problems with memory and concentration. Children suffering from post-traumatic stress disorder have difficulty in school. They are physically there but are not in touch with what transpires in the classroom. Learning very little, if anything, they are lost in our world.

We do not have much experience dealing with children who are war victims. Even special educators trained to work with emotionally disturbed children do not have the skills to work with this complex problem. Referral to special education is not the solution for this group; they should be referred to mental health agencies as well.

Since these children are often found in foster or adoptive homes, parent intervention becomes critical. It is fair to assume that the parents are also having difficulties dealing with their behavior. Thus, once again, our concern must extend beyond the walls of the school.

Classroom teachers should not exert undo pressure on these students, and they should pace their work so that new knowledge is given in very small doses. Teachers can also be understanding when bizarre behaviors emerge, for example, when a child is unusually startled by a loud noise or retreats under a table or behind a cabinet. Rather than confront the child presenting these behaviors, the teacher needs to find creative ways in which to renew the child's involvement with the group and minimize the effect of the child's extreme reaction. Being sensitive to the child's confusion and pain and providing opportunities for self-expression through activities such as art, role-playing situations, narratives, and bibliotherapy could also be helpful.

Conclusion

The time has come for the disciplines of mental health and education to place Hispanic children as a priority and cooperate in the endeavor to help this at-risk population. These children need not only intensive psychological treatment, but treatment that is supported at home, at school, and in the community at large.

References

American Psychological Association (APA) (1980). *Quick reference to the diagnostic criteria from DSM-111*. Washington, DC: Author.

Banks, J. A. (1987). *Teaching strategies for ethnic studies* (4th ed.). Boston: Allyn & Bacon.

Colburn, D., & Melillo, W. (1987, June 16). Hispanics: A forgotten health population. *Washington Post*, p. 16.

Rice, S. (1985, September 15). More Hispanic origin children living in poverty. *Washington Post*, p. A7.

Thompson, L. (1987, August 11). AIDS and minorities: As the disease claims more Blacks and Hispanics, leaders struggle for solutions. *Washington Post*, p. 7.

Asian Children

Leland Y. Yee

Since the passage of Public Law 94-142, the Education for All Handicapped Children Act of 1975, there has been an increasing awareness of the needs of exceptional children. However, such heightened sensitivity has not been applied to Asian exceptional children. Past stereotypes that Asians are model minorities have reappeared in the consciousness of many, resurfaced with the characterization of Asians as hard-working, successful, and without problems (Kim & Harh, 1983). Teachers consider Asian children ideal students: studious, high-achieving, and never a discipline problem (Huang, 1976). Holding such perceptions makes it difficult to accept that Asian children can be handicapped in any way. Thus, the misperception that Asian children uniformly and regularly perform extremely well in school and therefore never require special education services is only one of many factors that place an exceptional Asian child's psychological development at risk for further deterioration.

When school personnel do acknowledge that an Asian child may require special education services, there are additional barriers to such services that may further aggravate the developmental difficulties of the child. For example, Asian parents often have tremendous difficulty accepting their child's disability (Lim-Yee, 1983). The child represents the preservation and enhancement of the family's good name for the next and future generations. Any detraction, such as the child's handicap, is undesirable and therefore denied.

Finally, the lack of bilingual special education personnel and culturally and linguistically appropriate assessment and instructional materials contributes to misunderstanding and misdiagnosis of the child's problems and inappropriate intervention. The aforementioned variables—the inappropriate stereotypes of Asians; the hesitancy of Asian parents to accept their child's handicapping condition; and the lack of culturally and linguistically appropriate special education staff, assessment instruments, and instructional materials—lead to delayed or inappropriate services and expose the child to further liability from the handicapping condition.

Given these "at-risk" conditions, what can educators do to minimize their effects on Asian children? A beginning step is to help parents understand and accept their child's disability. The balance of this article will present information and strategies for working with Asian parents.

What Teachers Can Do

The teacher is an invaluable asset to the parents. Because teachers are accorded great respect in Asian cultures, parents often will follow much of their advice. To that extent, teachers can make a tremendous impact on parents' treatment of their handicapped children and their understanding of the handicapping conditions. However, despite the high esteem Asian parents hold for teachers, not *all* parents will trust and accept a teacher's recommendations. Thus, teachers need to be prepared for some resistance. Part of this resistance stems from the parents' disappointment in a child who, rather than enhancing the family's good name, is tarnishing it through the shame brought by disability.

When parents realize that their

child may never fulfill his or her "purpose" in life, there may be tremendous energy invested in avoiding such a prospect. Parents might deny the existence of a disability and attempt to handle the problem alone. Seeking professional help, even in the community, would be an open admission of the problem, bringing shame and disgrace to the family name. When confronted with help, parents may react in a passive-aggressive fashion (Lim-Yee, 1983) such as causing teachers to wait for them at a meeting. Such a response should be interpreted in the cultural context and should not be personalized.

Parents who avoid acceptance of the problem will delay the child's receiving adequate professional help, thereby making remediation much more difficult. Thus, teachers need to continue meeting with them to share concerns. Since these parents need to come to terms with the problem, they must be allowed to cope with their reactions in their own ways. At the same time, teachers should provide support when needed, and they should provide information about the disability and available services to the parents when they are ready. Once parents are prepared to receive information about their child, they will expect teachers to establish an active, supportive, and directive relationship.

Parents often feel inadequate in addressing their child's developmental needs, particularly when the child is also handicapped. Consequently, they often will relinquish some of the parental responsibility for their children to the teachers. This "dumping" needs to be recognized and addressed when it occurs. Helping the parents understand that their efforts are integral to the child's development and learning will be important. Giving them suggestions on what to do at home with their child will lessen this practice of "dumping."

If at all possible, teachers should work with both parents. In Asian families, the father is usually the head of the household. This position is often solidified not only by virtue of cultural customs, but also because he is usually the primary wage earner. Consequently, family decisions are often deferred until he provides his input. Thus, without his investment, decisions by or agreements with the mother may later be contradicted or sabotaged by the father.

Conclusion

Asian parents' unfamiliarity with the English language and with services for exceptional children often leaves them feeling overwhelmed when deciding how best to provide for their child. They may also feel immobilized by cultural constraints. The local education agency often becomes the first and only human service agency interfacing with the child and the parents. Teachers must be prepared to provide the best information for the child and family. School staff must understand the rights of the child, parents, and family in the special education context. They must be able to explain in a culturally sensitive, linguistically appropriate, and technically sound fashion the origin and nature of the child's problems and the interventions required. Finally, educators must serve as an advocate for the child and family regarding other human services available to address the child's handicapping condition.

References

Huang, L. J. (1976). The Chinese American family. In C. H. Mindel & W. Haberstein (Eds.), *Ethnic Families in America: Patterns and variations* (pp. 124-147). New York: Elsevier.

Kim, K. C., & Harh, W. M. (1983). Asian Americans and the "success" image: A critique. *Amerasia Journal, 10*, 3-21.

Lim-Yee, N. (1983, April). *Parental reactions to a special needs child: Cultural differences and Chinese families.* Paper presented at the Annual Convention of the Western Psychological Association, San Francisco, CA.

Young American Indian Children

Jacqueline L. Walker

Indian tribes, organizations, and communities are now playing pivotal roles in the provision and improvement of educational opportunities for young American Indian children. More than 100 tribes operate Head Start programs serving 16,548 American Indian children, 11.5% of whom have handicaps (Head Start Bureau, 1986). Many public, Bureau of Indian Affairs (BIA), and tribal schools also have undertaken efforts to meet the special educational and culture-related learning needs of American Indian children through a variety of developmental and early education options.

While many young American Indian children may fall into the at-risk category due to poverty, cultural and linguistic differences, and other related health and social problems, early labeling or placement in programs that separate children from their peers inappropriately should be avoided as much as possible.

Identification

Identification of the learning needs of American Indian children must focus on the "whole" child. Too often, children who exhibit difficulty in only one developmental area and within what might be considered a normal range, albeit a lower level of the range, are referred for services or placement that may not be warranted. Immaturity and a divergent experiential background due to cultural or language differences can contribute to a lower level of skill development as measured by many commonly used instruments.

Comprehensive screening and educational assessment should encompass all developmental domains and cultural and linguistic influences, as well as familial and community information such as the following:

1. Socioeconomic status.
2. Variations in family membership and style.
3. Variations in cultural and ideological style (O'Connell, 1985).

Parent or caregiver involvement in gathering this information is essential.

A child may be targeted for referral as the result of demonstrating a 6-month delay in expressive language when all other domains of development are at or above an appropriate level of development. In this instance, cultural and linguistic influences should be considered as strong factors in the performance results. Providing the child with an opportunity for exposure and maturation in a setting with normally achieving peers may be the most appropriate instructional strategy.

Cultural factors that teachers should keep in mind when considering other program options include the following:

1. Family or cultural expectations for child behavior may differ from the expectations of the educational setting. For example, levels of independence in decision making might be greater for American Indian children.
2. Identification of a child with his or her peer group may be more important than selection or recognition as an individual, thus inhibiting performance in noncompetitiveness.
3. Cultural and family expectations for verbal interactions with adults may be contradictory to teacher expectations.

Service Delivery

Family and community involvement is critical to providing developmental and educational services to young, at-risk American Indian children. Practitioners and administrators must recognize that parent involvement may include not only the natural parents, but also other extended family members. It is not uncommon among American Indian families for the child's primary caretaker to be the grandmother.

Simply making opportunities available to families will not always be sufficient. Effective planning and persistence will be required to involve families and caregivers. Practitioners should:

1. Encourage family-oriented activities such as holiday potluck dinners that fit the community and cultural mores.
2. Be prepared to deal with the entire family unit when planning parent and family activities.
3. Conduct home visits, maintaining an objective, nonjudgmental perspective toward family interactions and lifestyle.
4. Be careful to avoid overwhelming parents with a great deal of information or jargon during any one interaction.

At-risk American Indian children may require services other than those available through early education centers or schools. This will necessitate the collaboration and coordination of federal, state, and tribal agencies such as public, BIA, and tribal schools; the Indian Health Service; tribal and federal social service agencies, and other state and local human services agencies. Care must be taken in accessing such services to ensure that the complexities of shared services do not needlessly frustrate and confuse parents or teachers.

Conclusion

A great deal more must be done to enhance the efforts of teachers to ensure that at-risk young American Indian children are provided an optimal and equitable start at the onset of their educational experiences. Programs that focus on preventive practices in areas such as fetal alcohol syndrome are needed to ensure that future generations will be less likely to be at risk. Personnel also should be provided with training in cultural and linguistic diversity.

References

Head Start Bureau, U.S. Department of Health and Human Services (1986). *The status of handicapped children in Head Start programs.* Washington, DC: Author.

O'Connell, J. C. (1985). A family systems approach for serving rural, reservation Native American communities. *Journal of American Indian Education, 24*(2), 1-6.

Bruce A. Ramirez *(CEC Chapter #192) is Special Assistant for Ethnic and Multicultural Concerns, The Council for Exceptional Children, Reston, Virginia.* **Gladys Clark-Johnson** *(CEC Chapter #49) is Director, State Diagnostic and Placement Functions, Division of Special Education and Pupil Personnel Services, District of Columbia Public School District, Washington, DC.* **Eda Valero-Figueira** *(CEC Chapter #192) is Professor, Department of Curriculum and Instruction, Bilingual Special Education Program, George Mason University, Fairfax, Virginia.* **Leland Y. Yee** *(CEC Chapter #119) is Psychologist, Oakland Unified School District, California.* **Jacqueline L. Walker** *(CEC Chapter #318) is Early Childhood Education Specialist, Rhode Island Department of Education, Providence.*

Some Ways to Help the Language-Deficient Child in the Classroom

THELMA ZIRKELBACH and
KATHRYN BLAKESLEY

Thelma Zirkelbach and Kathryn Blakesley, speech-language pathologists, are Co-Directors, Associated Speech and Language Services, Houston, Texas.

WHEN teachers see weak academic performance, it is difficult to separate the contribution of oral-language deficiency from that of low intelligence, perceptual dysfunction, or lack of motivation. We must observe the language itself to determine its adequacy; however, a careful observer can learn to recognize even subtle manifestations of oral-language deficiency. Following are some behavioral characteristics of language-deficient children, along with methods and materials to enhance these youngsters' language skills.

1. *Children with deficient oral language have difficulty learning new vocabulary.* They may use the same words over and over. For example, the word *big* may also be used to denote items that are tall, wide, long, or heavy.

Words may be learned in specific contexts, almost as if they were proper names, and not generalized to other appropriate contexts. Eric's first-grade teacher prepared strips with sentences from a basal reader story and told the children to paste them on paper in order. Eric pasted the strips on his paper neatly, but in the wrong sequence; his mistake could have been avoided if the teacher had elaborated on the meaning of *in order*. Explaining what is meant in another way, using synonyms, or relating new ideas to familiar ones will enhance the language-deficient child's understanding.

Children with language deficits, like all of us, learn best through experience. Vocabulary teaching that focuses on looking up word definitions is ineffective with these youngsters; they need to participate actively in the learning task. In "Vocabulary Scavenger Hunts," teams of students are asked to find meanings of lists of words—for examples, names of clothing. Students who find an example of clothing earn more points for their team than those who bring in pictures or definitions of clothing items. Certainly, children who rummage through closets to find a piece of clothing will remember its name more easily than students who simply look the word up in the dictionary.

A second choice is to provide multisensory learning. The child with a language deficit may not process well auditorily. Seeing pictures of models, manipulating objects, watching films, or acting out word meanings can help in learning and retaining new vocabulary. Further, words must be resurfaced and reinforced many times before they become permanently embedded in these children's lexicons.

Multiple Meanings

2. *Multiple meanings of words may confuse these children.* They may know the common meanings of words but not the less familiar ones. They may acquire one meaning of a word and use it in all circumstances, even inappropriate ones. Andrea announced that Reagan was our leader: "He stands at the front of the line, and everyone else gets behind him."

Again, teaching through experience is the most effective way to familiarize children with multiple meanings of words. The teacher might select a word such as *spring* and ask youngsters to bring in various examples of its meanings: One child might bring in a metal spring, another might demonstrate how a cat springs at a mouse, a third could bring in a glass of spring water, and still another might display spring flowers.

Youngsters who are weak in language need ready access to vocabulary materials. Placing them on the bulletin board or resource table helps students remember and use new words.

3. *Word definitions or explanations of similarities and differences may be poor.* Missy, age 9, defined puddle as "a little group of water"; Jeremy, age 6, using in his definition the word to be defined, stated that *fall* means "to fall down." Language-deficient youngsters tend to produce immature or lower-level definitions or explanations—given in terms of attributes or functions rather than synonym or category names.

A game that focuses on defining or explaining can be played in the classroom. The teacher puts two words (e.g., *cat* and *dog*) on the board and asks how they are alike. Answering with common parts or attributes ("They have tails" or "They are furry") earns one point; giving common functions ("They both eat") earns two points; category names ("They are animals") are worth three points; more defin-

From *The Educational Digest*, January 1986, pp. 52-55. Condensed from *Academic Therapy* XX (May 1985), pp. 605-12. Reprinted by permission.

itive categories ("pets," "mammals") earn five points. The first team to earn 20 points wins. This game provides models and strategies; practice alone is not effective. These youngsters need explicit instruction in how to produce acceptable responses.

In another technique, to be used when students use the word to be defined in their definitions, the teacher may substitute a nonsense word: "Do you know what *glong* means? It means 'to glong.' That doesn't make sense, does it? But if I say that *glong* means to make a noise like an angry lion, then you can understand."

4. *These youngsters may have difficulty thinking of an appropriate word when speaking; they exhibit "word finding" problems.* When describing a birthday party, Jonathan said, "You wrap the present with the—the wrapping thing." As utterances become longer, difficulty in retrieving words may increase; children may even appear to be stutterers.

Aid to Retrieval

Word association exercises help these youngsters gain proficiency in retrieving appropriate words. Students should be encouraged to organize their responses in some logical way, a strategy that language-deficient youngsters may not use. For instance, when asking children to think of animals, the teacher can suggest that they first name zoo animals, then farm animals, then pets.

In brainstorming, the teacher provides a word or idea, and students think of as many associated words or phrases as they can. Children's memories for words may be stimulated by hearing their classmates produce related words. Brainstormed words should be prominently displayed in the classroom; language-deficient children profit from quick and easy access to new words.

5. *The quality of these children's verbal expression may be poor.* They "talk around" a subject, never seeming to come to the point. They use vague terms such as "that thing" and "you know."

Structuring by the teacher enables these youngsters to communicate more effectively. Before show-and-tell period, the teacher might say, "Tell us three things about your toy: its name, where you got it, and how it is used." One set of materials provides structured language activities for upper elementary students. For example, before giving directions for playing a game, they listen to the teacher give examples of good and poor directions. Next, they receive a format sheet listing information they should include: name of game, number of players, etc. After the activity, the students evaluate their presentations.

Describing Pictures

Referential communication tasks, which require children to give explicit descriptions, are useful for language-deficient children. Using another set of materials, students must describe pictures of unusual "creatures" clearly enough for their listeners to select the correct one from a group. Children may be told (i.e., given strategies) that they must tell how the creature they have in mind differs from other similar ones. Referential communication tasks provide immediate feedback: If a "creature" was not clearly described, the listener will not be able to identify it.

6. *These children do not use verbal information to make inferences or draw appropriate conclusions.* Mark, age 10, studying for a test, read that the settlers in Virginia named their town Jamestown in honor of the English king. "What was the king's name?" Mark's mother asked. Mark thought for a while and then offered, "Henry?" Language-disordered children can profit from models of *how* to infer, predict outcomes, or identify missing information, and from experience in defending or proving their reasoning.

Breaking Tasks Down

Reasoning tasks may be broken down into smaller steps when a child is having difficulty. The following techniques have been suggested: Repeat the question; rephrase the question using simpler words; modify the task to highlight specific components; offer relevant comparisons; present didactic information; and relate the unknown to the known.

7. *These children may exhibit grammatic errors in oral or written language.* Andy, seven years old, described a family fishing trip, saying, "I catched the biggest fish."

Extensive drill is needed to correct such errors. Materials available include exercises for modifying errors, and activities for introducing all children to the grammar of their language.

8. *These children may exhibit defective interpretation of and response to social situations.* Since socialization is largely dependent on language, these youngsters are at a substantial disadvantage in social situations. Often, they are unaware of how much information a listener requires and will "jump into the middle" of a topic, confusing the listener.

Language-deficient children may have difficulty processing rapid conversation and frequent topic shifts, and so may withdraw from conversation instead of trying to participate. They may not have mastered the conventions of turn taking, and may monopolize a conversation or interrupt other children. They may have limited ability to talk about subjects of interest to their classmates or may misinterpret others' remarks because of their own limited comprehension. When another child mentioned that his father arrived home from work at five o'clock, Bryan, age 8, commented, "I haven't even gotten up then. It's still dark."

Language-deficient youngsters may need explicit instruction in techniques of social communication. One set of materials lets children role-play situations such as extending invitations, making phone calls, or responding to remarks of others. Role playing takes place in a nonthreatening environment with strong teacher support, and provides youngsters with the opportunity to discuss and discover appropriate behaviors in social situations.

These suggestions and materials can help teachers enhance the abilities, not only of language-deficient youngsters, but of all their students.

A Model for Training and Using Communication Assistants

Beatrice C. Jimenez and Dee Ann Iseyama

Beatrice C. Jimenez is an associate professor at California State University, Chico, CA 95929-0222. Requests for reprints may be sent to her at this address. Dee Ann Iseyama is a bilingual speech-language pathologist with the Butte County Office of Education.

The article describes a model for training and using communication assistants to provide services to students with speech and language disorders. The steps include: Orientation, Demonstration, Participation, and Implementation. These steps are explained and examples are provided.

The importance of early identification and intervention of communication disorders has been acknowledged for many years. More recently, this notion was incorporated into the definition of the word "prevention" developed by the American Speech-Language-Hearing Association (ASHA) Committee on the Prevention of Speech, Language, and Hearing Problems (1982). Currently, many preschool programs recognize the importance of early identification and treatment of communicative disorders, and various strategies have been used to obtain the needed assessment and remediation services. For example, some preschools employ speech-language clinicians, others receive services from area school districts, and yet others obtain services from university speech and hearing centers. Regardless of the service delivery system used, the frequency of therapeutic contact with preschool students is often limited. Public schools also recognize the importance of early identification and intervention; however, due to caseload size, the clinician is often able to provide only limited remedial contact.

The frequency of therapeutic intervention in preschools and public schools may be increased through the use of communication assistants. Parents, aides, and other personnel have been effective in providing services to communicatively handicapped children in the past. Studies have demonstrated that, with training, paraprofessionals can successfully remediate speech and language disorders.

Parents have been incorporated in service delivery models by several researchers in recent years. MacDonald, Blott, Spiegel, Gordon, and Hartman (1974) reported language improvements in six Down's Syndrome children when parents implemented language therapy programs. Improvement was noted in both utterance length and grammatical complexity. Success was also reported by Carpenter and Augustine (1973), who trained four mothers to work with a variety of communication disorders. The authors found three of the four mothers were able to modify their children's speech in a positive manner. Similarly, Fudala, England, and Ganoung (1972) reported improved articulatory performance in 46 children who received parent-implemented therapy.

Communication aides and other supportive personnel have also delivered services successfully in a number of investigations. Braunstein (1972) found that trained communication aides could implement language therapy with positive outcomes. Similar findings were reported by Scalero and Eskenazi (1976), and successful language therapy was provided by aides in a study by Lynch (1972). Thirty-nine paraprofessionals were trained to provide articulation therapy to 134 students in an investigation by Galloway and Blue (1975). The authors found that misarticulations were corrected at a success rate of 83.5%. In addition, Costello and Schoen (1978) noted very good improvement in the articulation of /s/ by students who received therapy by trained paraprofessionals.

Various amounts of training were reported across studies. For example, Galloway and Blue (1975) provided 70 hours of preservice training; whereas, Carpenter and Augustine (1973) trained mothers an average of only 3 hours. Fudala et al. (1972) found no significant difference in the success of therapy provided by a group of parents who observed an average of 3.5 therapy sessions and a group that observed an average of 13 sessions. However, both did significantly better than a group that observed no sessions.

This article will describe a model for training and using

Reprinted from *Language, Speech, and Hearing Services in Schools*, April 1987, pp. 168-171.

communication assistants to provide services to students with speech and language disorders. The model includes the following steps: Orientation, Demonstration, Participation, and Implementation.

The Model

In the proposed model, all students are screened and assessed by the speech-language pathologist (SLP). Any necessary referrals to other professionals are made at this point. A therapy program is then designed by the SLP for each student diagnosed as having a speech and/or language disorder. Prior to implementing the designed program, selected assistants participate in pre-service training.

Orientation

In this step, the SLP provides the assistant with necessary information pertaining to behavior modification, techniques for charting responses, guidelines for following lesson plans, and maintaining daily records. Further, the SLP describes the nature and causes of the identified disorders, the specific therapy program designed for each student, and the rationale for the therapy plan. For example, an explanation for a vocal disorder might include a description of the parameters of voice, normal and abnormal functioning of the vocal mechanism, abusive and nonabusive vocal behaviors, and the purpose for the therapy procedures.

Demonstration

During the Demonstration phase, the SLP conducts therapy with the student while the assistant observes. Throughout each session, the SLP describes and demonstrates the previously discussed techniques and identifies correct and incorrect target responses. Discussions follow each session to provide information and to answer questions regarding the therapy session. The number of demonstration sessions is determined jointly by the SLP and the assistant. When both agree that the assistant has an adequate understanding of the therapy procedures, the Participation phase begins.

Participation

In the third step, the assistant and the SLP both actively participate in the therapy process, and the students' responses are charted by both, independently. The SLP provides feedback, instruction, and modeling of specific techniques during the session. Additional evaluation and discussion follow each therapy session, at which time a point-by-point comparison is made of charted responses. Training continues until the assistant and the SLP agree on 85% of the responses. In addition, students should meet minimal performance levels. For example, a student with an articulation disorder should be able to produce the target phoneme(s) in isolation spontaneously with at least 80% accuracy in a minimum of 50 persons before the assistant is given responsibility for conducting such therapy. Specific criteria should be determined on a case-by-case basis by the SLP.

Implementation

In the final step of the model, the therapy program is implemented by the assistant who actively conducts the sessions, while the SLP serves primarily in a supervisory capacity. The assistant is responsible for carrying out the procedures designated in the therapy plan, charting target behaviors, and maintaining daily logs. Any necessary consultation, follow-up procedures, report writing, conferences, referrals, and determination for student dismissal are the responsibility of the SLP.

Application in a Migrant Head Start Program

The model described above was used to train communication assistants in Migrant Head Start centers. This section describes the initial training of two such assistants. In the first case, a communication assistant was trained to work with two Spanish-speaking students, a voice case and an articulation case. Following seven hours of training, the first three steps of the model were completed; the communication assistant and both children met required performance levels for proceeding to the implementation phase of the model. One hour was spent on orientation; 2 hours were spent in the demonstration step; and 4 hours were spent in the participation phase. Shortly after the implementation step began, both students relocated and were no longer enrolled in the center; therefore, follow-up data were not available.

In the second case, a communication assistant was trained to deliver services to an articulation-disordered Spanish-speaking student. The first three steps were completed after 7½ hours of training. One hour was spent on orientation; 3 hours were spent on demonstration; and 3½ hours were spent on participation. Performance levels were met by both the assistant and student; the implementation phase then began and continued for approximately 10 weeks. Therapy was successful; during the trial period the child improved from production of the phoneme /s/ in isolation, to its production in the initial position of words. In this case, the student received 13 hours of additional therapy through the use of a trained communication assistant.

Summary

A review of the literature indicates that trained parents, aides, and other supportive personnel have successfully provided speech and language services. By using communication assistants, the frequency of therapeutic contact can be increased. In an attempt to better prepare communication assistants for work with children enrolled in speech and/or language therapy, a training model was developed. The model includes orientation, demonstration, participation, and implementation phases. Training steps are linked to performance and skill levels of the assistant, rather than being time-based.

The model was applied successfully in a clinical setting. In the two cases cited, communication assistants were successfully trained to implement therapy programs for three students. These aides could easily be trained to work with additional students. The use of such a model should lead to improved quality and quantity of services to students with communication disorders.

Acknowledgment

The authors wish to thank Judith Brasseur for her assistance in the preparation of this manuscript.

References

American Speech-Language-Hearing Association Committee on Prevention of Speech, Language, and Hearing Problems. (1982). Committee on the prevention of speech, language, and hearing problems report. *Asha, 25*, 425, 431.

Braunstein, M. (1972). Communication aides: A pilot project. *Language, Speech, and Hearing Services in Schools, 3*, 32-35.

Carpenter, R.L., & Augustine, L.E. (1973). A pilot training program for parent-clinicians. *Journal of Speech and Hearing Research, 38*, 48-58.

Costello, J., & Schoen, J. (1978). On the effectiveness of paraprofessionals and speech clinicians as agents of articulation intervention using programmed instruction. *Language, Speech, and Hearing Services in Schools, 9*, 119-128.

Fudula, J.B., England, G., & Ganoung, L. (1972). Utilization of parents in a speech correction program. *Exceptional Children, 38*, 407-412.

Galloway, H., & Blue, G. (1975). Paraprofessional personnel in articulation therapy. *Language, Speech, and Hearing Services in Schools, 6*, 125-130.

Lynch, J. (1972). Using paraprofessionals in a language program. *Language, Speech, and Hearing Services in Schools, 3*, 82-87.

MacDonald, J.D., Blott, J.P., Gordon, K., Spiegel, B., & Hartman, M. (1974). An experimental parent-assisted treatment program for language-delayed children. *Journal of Speech and Hearing Disorders, 39*, 395-415.

Scalero, A.M., & Eskenazi, C. (1976). The use of supportive personnel in a public school speech and language program. *Language, Speech, and Hearing Services in Schools, 7*, 150-158.

FUNCTIONAL APHONIA IN THE CHILD AND ADOLESCENT: THERAPEUTIC MANAGEMENT

Sharon L. Murray, Mary E. Carr, Virginia Jacobs

Sharon L. Murray, Mary E. Carr, and Virginia Jacobs are affiliated with the Children's Hospital National Medical Center and with the Department of Child Health and Development, George Washington University, Washington, DC. Requests for reprints should be directed to Sharon L. Murray, Children's Hearing and Speech Center, Children's Hospital National Medical Center, 111 Michigan Avenue, NW, Washington, DC 20010.

Five cases of adolescents with functional aphonia are presented. The cases include four teenaged girls and one teenaged boy. Each was referred with the presenting symptom of "no voice." Indirect laryngoscopic examinations were normal. Therapeutic management is described which followed the symptomatic voice therapy approach. Four cases returned to use of full voice within two sessions, the fifth after five sessions. A consistent theme for four of the adolescents was stressful family environment, academic failure, and inadequate peer support. Referral for psychotherapeutic counseling was necessary for all but one.

Background

Functional aphonia occurs when the vocal cords appear normal but the patient uses no speaking voice, typically abducting the cords farther apart when asked to phonate (Boone, 1977). It may occur as the result of acute stress, prolonged stress (Aronson, Peterson, & Litin, 1966), or be related to an experience of laryngeal pathology (Aronson, 1969; Boone, 1966). Although functional aphonia may occur at any age (Brodnitz, 1969), it is found predominately in women during middle age.

The occurrence of functional aphonia in the young child and adolescent is acknowledged but is not well documented in the literature (Aronson, 1973; Boone, 1966). Single case studies have been reported by Bangs and Freidinger (1949), Wolski and Wiley (1965), and Boone (1966). Overall management, including the use of psychotherapy, varied in each of the cases described. Bangs and Freidinger provided voice therapy with no psychiatric intervention for their client, a 13-year-old girl. Wolski and Wiley's client was a 14-year-old boy. They used a nondirective therapy approach concurrent with ongoing psychiatric treatment. Boone's client, a 7-year-old girl, readily achieved normal voicing from a symptomatic voice therapy approach.

The adolescents presented in this paper were seen at the Children's Hearing and Speech Center Voice Clinic, Children's Hospital National Medical Center, Washington, DC. The following case summaries indicate rapid progress in voice therapy with the symptomatic approach. They also illustrate the existence of environmental stress in the lives of these adolescents and a tendency toward academic difficulties. These two factors emerged as a pattern after four of the five cases were seen. Academic testing and in-depth interviews *prior* to voice therapy were not conducted routinely, because initially these were not considered essential to successful return of voice. Information regarding stress in each subject's life, therefore, was obtained informally during therapy. However, because of the experience with these five cases, such testing and interviewing have become routine at the onset of contact with each new child. An overview of the therapeutic management employed at this Center's Voice Clinic are described, followed by illustrative case summaries.

Therapeutic Management

The therapeutic management of clients closely follows Boone's suggested symptom-modification approach (1966. 1977). Phonation is achieved first through a nonverbal function, specifically a cough or throat clearing. The client then is asked to extend a vowel from the cough, followed by chaining vowels (following a cough, if necessary). The next step adds meaning to utterances using a vowel-consonant format, as in "I . . . I eat . . . I eat apples . . . I eat apples every day. . . ." Rote tasks then are introduced, such as counting or naming the days of the week. The use of rote tasks reduces the need to formulate language, thus avoiding a potential source of anxiety associated with

Reprinted from *Language, Speech, and Hearing Services in Schools*, October 1983, pp. 260-265.

speech discourse. Next, words and eventually imitated sentences are elicited. Finally, language formulation is emphasized and tasks are presented in which there is progression from a question-answer format to spontaneous conversation. Vocabulary and phrases used during voice therapy are taken from the client's daily communication needs (e.g., names of family members, hobbies).

Throughout the therapeutic process the speech-language pathologist makes every effort to (a) support the client's efforts; (b) recognize how "hard" it is to regain voice; (c) remind the client to "try" because normal voice is possible. The clinician also establishes a time frame for expected progress. The clients are told that using voice following the first therapy session is not anticipated; however, full use of the voice would be expected in a few days. This counseling gives the clients an opportunity to mentally adjust to abandoning their symptom. The clients also need a reason for "recovery," so that aphonia followed by a sudden voice return is not construed by others as faking. Clients usually are told "your muscles got tired and they forgot what they were supposed to do."

Parents are advised about the need for preserving the client's self-esteem. They are told that their child is not malingering and undoubtedly is not aware of why the voice loss occurred. The parents are instructed to be as supportive as possible, particularly following the first few days of voice return. The client's parents, siblings, and teachers are counseled to offer encouragement by indicating that the new voice is very pleasant.

The clinician schedules an especially long initial session with each client. This time frame provides an opportunity to "wait-out" the symptoms if necessary. The clinician also imparts absolute confidence to the client that voice will return soon with time, patience, and work.

Cases

An indirect laryngoscopic examination revealed normal appearance and motility of the vocal cords in each of the cases described below.

Subject No. 1. CM was an 11-year-old girl brought to the Voice Clinic by her mother. According to the mother, CM became aphonic 6 months prior to the initial clinic visit. There was no apparent precipitating illness, although CM had a history of fevers.

During the first therapy session, the following factors were identified as having the potential to produce excessive stress on CM:

1. Her father was deceased.
2. Her mother had remarried but was in the process of a divorce.
3. There were six siblings.
4. The child's mother was employed and CM was expected to care for her younger siblings.

Educationally, CM was repeating the sixth grade due to academic failure. The feelings and attitudes of CM were not explored by the speech-language pathologist since referral for counseling was anticipated. However, CM told the clinician that she stopped seeing her "three best friends because they had betrayed [her] confidence." She also expressed the feeling that adults and peers were lying to her and about her.

CM successfully regained complete use of her voice following only one therapy session and has maintained normal voice for 3 years. There has been no recurrence of functional aphonia. CM's mother was advised to contact the Children's Hospital Adolescent Clinic for counseling because of the combination family, peer, and school stress factors. Recent follow-up revealed that the entire family is being seen for counseling.

Subject No. 2. ES, a 14-year-old girl with aphonia, was referred for evaluation following approximately 3 weeks of hoarseness. Her history was otherwise negative except that she claimed to experience occasional difficulty breathing.

Results of the case history obtained at the onset of therapy did not reveal any apparent stress within the family or at school. However, further probing revealed that the father did not live at home, the mother worked, and ES was responsible for the care of her younger brother. Although ES was in the 10th grade (which was appropriate for her age), she reportedly received help in math and reading during previous school years. In an attempt to assess her academic levels, ES was tested at this Center using the *Peabody Individual Achievement Test* (PIAT; Dunn & Markwardt, 1970) and found to have severe deficits. Her subject scores in reading, spelling, and math were at the fourth-grade level.

ES attained normal voicing during the first session and was seen for two additional follow-up sessions to stabilize this achievement. She has remained asymptomatic for 3½ years. ES was referred for counseling at the time of voice therapy to assess how family, educational, and emotional stress contributed to the original loss of voice and to provide any necessary support.

Subject No. 3. DT, a 15-year-old girl, experienced one episode of temporary voice loss about a year before she came to the Voice Clinic with aphonia. Her health history showed frequent uncomplicated illnesses, including colds, dizziness, and throat irritations.

Assessment of DT's family, peer relationships, and school history highlighted a number of factors contributing to stress in her life. Family information revealed a mother working full time, an absence of the father in the home, eight siblings (five younger than DT), a run-away older sister, an imprisoned older brother, and a teenaged nephew living in the home. Further, the burden of younger sibling care rested heavily on DT. Because of the need to meet family and household responsibilities, she reported having no friends except one male peer.

DT was in the ninth grade at the time of her initial clinic visit. However, she had repeated the eighth grade because of multiple absences necessitated by family responsibilities. Although the only remedial educational services she had received was help with reading, testing for academic levels at this Center revealed a probable school stress situation. Test results using the PIAT showed reading (recognition and comprehension) and math to be at the fourth-grade level, while spelling was at the fifth-grade level.

DT achieved normal voice following the second therapy session and a third visit confirmed continuous use of normal voice. Three months after the last therapy session at the Voice Clinic, DT reported the recurrence of voice loss in conjunction with a cold. However, normal voice returned in a few days without voice therapy. She has remained asymptomatic for 2½ years. DT was referred for counseling because of the probable sources of stress.

Subject No. 4. HS, an 11-year-old girl, became aphonic several months before her initial Voice Clinic visit. The voice loss reportedly occurred after she experienced a sore throat. When her voice did not return following this illness, the school speech-language pathologist initiated the referral to the clinic.

Information obtained during the initial therapy session suggested there was a prolonged history of emotional and financial stress in this child's family. Because of the family-financial problems, HS's mother returned to full-time employment about 6 months prior to the initial Voice Clinic visit. When she did, HS assumed the total care of her 8-month-old sibling. This responsibility resulted in a considerable number of school absences, and her academic performance was reportedly poor. Additional history information indicated inadequate and probably stressful peer relationships. HS stated that she only played with one friend at a time because she did not like participating in groups. HS and her family were referred for counseling immediately after the first Voice Clinic visit. Counseling for the entire family was provided concurrent with the voice therapy sessions.

Subject No. 5. BB, a 13-year-old boy, was the only child among this group of subjects whose loss of voice was precipitated by a traumatic accident. He ran into a wire, was hospitalized for three days with a swollen neck and was unable to produce a loud voice. His neck and thyroid cartilage were bruised from the accident. BB regained complete use of his voice after discharge from the hospital, but 1 day later he became aphonic.

When BB was initially seen at the Voice Clinic, an indirect laryngoscopy revealed normal appearance and motility of his vocal folds. During the parent interview, no apparent family or social stress was highlighted. However, his mother indicated that BB liked to be babied and that his voice problem might reflect his desire for the special attention he received while hospitalized. BB was in the eighth grade and doing well academically, although he had received remedial help in the early elementary grades. Academic testing at this Center using the PIAT showed his reading, spelling, and math to be at grade level.

BB achieved normal voice in three sessions. No referral for counseling was initiated. There has been no recurrence of aphonia, and BB has maintained normal voice quality for 5 years.

TABLE 1. Summary of history and therapy for each case of adolescents with functional aphonia.

	History			*Therapy*			
Case	*Onset*	*Stress*	*Learning problems*	*# Of sessions*	*Success*	*Referral for counseling*	*Repeat episode*
CM	?	X	X	1	100%	X	–
ES	Hoarseness	X	X	2	100%	X	–
DT	Colds—one prior temporary loss	X	X	3	100%	X	one temporary
HS	Sore throat	X	X	4	100%	X	–
BB	Trauma to neck	–	X	3	100%	–	–

Since HS had to travel quite a distance to Children's Hospital, she was seen once a month for a total of four sessions. Little progress was made during the first three voice therapy sessions except for an extension of vowels elicited from a cough. However, upon arrival for the fourth therapy session, HS used a normal voice. She explained that upon awakening one morning, she was able to use her voice again. When these circumstances were explored with the family's counselor, it was learned that HS's mother began to remove privileges, such as watching television, contingent upon the child's use of voice. Apparently the use of such contingencies by her mother precipitated the return of HS's voice. Follow-up contact with this child and the family's counselor reveals continued use of normal voice to date, a period of 4 years. The absence of substantive voice change in this girl over a 3-month period underscores the need for intensive voice therapy, once it is initiated.

Summary

Four of the five aphonic adolescents in the group of children reported in this paper displayed similar characteristics. A pattern emerged from their histories and vocal behaviors (Table 1). All four subjects were girls, consistent with previously reported findings (Brodnitz, 1969). Each female adolescent had assumed significant caretaking responsibilities for younger siblings, each had pronounced academic problems, and three of the four had difficulty with peer relationships.

The stressful family, peer, and school circumstances highlighted by these children emphasize the need for careful history taking on the part of clinicians. When such stress factors become apparent, referral for counseling services in conjunction with symptomatic voice therapy seems warranted. Further, educational testing should be undertaken if learning deficits are implicated. Depending on the outcome of such testing, educational recommendations may be a necessary part of the total management of adolescents with aphonia.

References

Aronson, A.E. Speech pathology and symptom therapy in interdisciplinary treatment of psychogenic aphonia. *Journal of Speech and Hearing Disorders*, 1969, *34*, 321-341.

Aronson, A.E. *Psychogenic voice disorders*. Philadelphia: W.B. Saunders, 1973.

Aronson, A.E., Peterson, H.W., & Litin, E.M. Psychiatric symptomatology in functional dysphonia and aphonia. *Journal of Speech and Hearing Disorders*, 1966, *31*, 196-227.

Bangs, J.L., & Freidinger, A. Diagnosis and treatment of a case of hysterical aphonia in a thirteen year old girl. *Journal of Speech and Hearing Disorders*, 1949, *14*, 312-317.

Barton, R.T. The Whispering Syndrome of hysterical dysphonia. *Annals of Otology, Rhinology, and Laryngology*, 1960, *69*, 156-164.

Boone, D.R. Treatment of functional aphonia in a child and an adult. *Journal of Speech and Hearing Disorders*, 1966, *31*, 69-74.

Boone, D.R. *The voice and voice therapy* (2nd ed.). Englewood Cliffs, NJ: Prentice-Hall, 1977.

Brodnitz, F.S. Functional aphonia. *Annals of Otology, Rhinology, and Laryngology*, 1969, *78*, 1244-1253.

Dunn, L.M., & Markwardt, F.C., Jr. *Peabody Individual Achievement Test*. Circle Pines, MN: American Guidance-Service, 1970.

Wolski, W., & Wiley, J. Functional aphonia in a fourteen year old boy: A case report. *Journal of Speech and Hearing Disorders*, 1965, *30*, 71-75.

Teaching the Hearing Impaired Child

PL 99-457, the amendments to the Education for All Handicapped Children Act, mandates special services for handicapped children between the ages of 3 and 5, before they begin their public school education. Early assessment of hearing impairments is very important to the development of language and to social development. Once a hearing impairment is diagnosed, remediation should begin. While PL 99-457 provides free and appropriate educational services at age 3, parents or caregivers should get a hearing aid (if appropriate) for their child much earlier, and/or should learn sign language with the child. Both receptive language (understanding what is said) and expressive language (speaking) are better among hearing impaired children who begin intervention programs early.

The National Technical Institute for the Deaf takes the position that teaching hearing impaired children in regular public school classrooms, without providing appropriate supportive services, is tantamount to child abuse. Teachers of mainstreamed classes are often very confused as to what constitutes appropriate supportive services. Must they wear a microphone connected to the hearing impaired child's FM auditory training device? Do they have to know how to service the child's hearing aid? Should they control background noises and room reverberations when a child in their class is wearing a hearing aid? Is it sufficient to have the hearing impaired child pulled out for a portion of the day for special services provided by a speech-language clinician or a special education teacher?

Even when very appropriate special services are provided by professionals trained to work with hearing impaired students, teachers must also provide an appropriate environment in which the hearing impaired student can learn in the regular classroom. This includes wearing a microphone if the child has an FM auditory trainer, checking the hearing aids of younger children on a daily basis, providing preferential seating, giving all directions and assignments in writing, not standing in front of windows or bright lights, remaining stationary while talking, keeping mouth movements visible for lipreading, sharing notes or providing a note taker, and, in some cases, allowing an interpreter to sign in the classroom or learning sign language oneself.

Teachers must be aware of the communication problems which hearing impaired children often exhibit. Failure to respond, or an inarticulate response, is not necessarily a sign of low intelligence or a lack of understanding. The hearing impaired child may need a longer time, or a more supportive climate, in which to respond. The hearing-speech disability, however, should not become an excuse for remaining silent. Hearing impaired children should be continually challenged to both learn and communicate up to their potential. They should receive positive reinforcements for their best efforts, but should not be praised for less. The handicap should not be allowed to engender pity or understimulation.

Not all hearing disabilities are diagnosed before a child enters school. Some hearing disorders are acquired during the school years as a result of otitis media or injuries to the ear. Often the teacher is the first person to suspect a hearing loss. If so, he or she should request that an audiologist examine the child. The teacher should then have a follow-up visit with the audiologist to discover the degree and nature of the loss. In addition to reporting the suspicion of a loss and requesting hearing assessment procedures, the teacher should confer with the parents of any newly diagnosed hearing impaired child. Parents, the teacher, a special education expert, perhaps the audiologist, perhaps a physician, and the child (if appropriate) should plan an individualized education program (IEP) to be provided in the least restrictive environment. If medical treatment such as surgery is involved, the teacher should confer with the physician in order to understand the medical care which must be provided during school hours, and the prognosis for recovery of hearing abilities.

Unit 8

The first article of this unit provides a checklist for teachers so that they will know how to recognize and respond to children who have hearing impairments. The second article provides information about hearing aids. Regular education teachers must determine, on a daily basis, whether or not the aids worn by their younger mainstreamed students are functioning properly. The third article provides information about frequency modulation (FM) auditory training devices. These are increasingly being used by hearing impaired children mainstreamed into regular classrooms. The following selection by Diane Brackett and Antonia Brancia Maxon offers three case studies to illustrate "Service Delivery Alternatives for the Mainstreamed Hearing-Impaired Child" and presents data on 162 other hearing impaired students who attended public schools. Finally, in the last article, David Martin discusses the negative attitudes often directed toward hearing impaired students in regular classrooms. Teachers have a responsibility for reducing ethnocentrism in any form, whether it is directed against a cultural group or a handicapped group.

Looking Ahead: Challenge Questions

How can hearing impairments be distinguished from other learning problems?

What is a typical teacher's knowledge of, exposure to, and attitude toward a hearing aid and hearing aid wearer?

What is an FM auditory training device? What must a classroom teacher know in order to wear the microphone and check the receiver worn by the student?

What are the most appropriate options in services for mainstreamed hearing impaired children?

Can teachers recognize ethnocentrism when it takes the form of prejudice against hearing impaired students? What strategies can be used in the classroom to reduce it?

Poor Learning Ability . . . or Poor Hearing?

Lawrence B. Mollick and Kenneth S. Etra

Lawrence B. Mollick and Kenneth S. Etra are practicing ear, nose and throat specialists in Great Neck and Glen Cove, N.Y.

Jennifer, in many respects, is an ideal pupil. She sits quietly in class, paying close attention to what is being said. She almost never misbehaves. Her good conduct, however, does not result in good grades. Jennifer's test scores are surprisingly low.

Timmy is less of a mystery. He, too, is not doing well in school, but it's not hard to see why. He simply doesn't pay attention. Despite all efforts to draw him out, he ignores most of what is going on in class, preferring to daydream or to draw pictures (which he does extremely well) in his notebook.

Jennifer's and Timmy's problems appear to be altogether different. But, in fact, they stem from an identical source: both children are hard of hearing.

We often think of hearing loss as a problem of the elderly. But current statistics indicate that approximately *half a million* American children between the ages of six and 12 suffer from hearing loss to some degree (Office of Demographic Studies, Gallaudet College, Washington, D.C.). And in the past 10 years it has been shown again and again that poor hearing is the cause often unsuspected—of a wide range of childhood problems, from bad grades to inadequate social adjustment. For example:

- In a 1969 test, American children with impaired hearing were found to be badly delayed in their language development ("Effect of Chronic Otitis Media on Language and Speech Development" by V.A. Holmes and L.H. Kunze, *Pediatrics,* Vol. 43, 1969, p. 833).

- In 1972, a study of 14,000 seven-year-olds in Great Britain showed that those with hearing loss were not only poorer in reading ability, but also "more clumsy" and "less stable" than other children ("School Attainment of Seven-Year-Old Children With Hearing Difficulties" by C.S. Peckham, M. Sheridan and N.R. Butler, *Developmental Medicine in Child Neurology,* Vol. 14, 1972, p. 592).

- In 1973, Eskimo boys and girls with impaired hearing scored "significantly lower" than others in tests of verbal skills ("Long-Term Effects of Otitis Media: A 10-Year Study of Alaskan Eskimo Children" by G.J. Kaplan, J.K. Fleshman and T.R. Bendman et al, *Pediatrics,* Vol. 52, 1973, p. 577).

During the elementary school years children pass through a crucial period of cognitive development. It is the concluding phase of what psychologist Jean Piaget termed the "concrete operations period." In this period the child masters the thought patterns that prepare him or her to move ahead into mature conceptual thinking. To be hard of hearing at such a time is a handicap that may result in lifelong damage. Yet the condition frequently goes undiagnosed, largely perhaps because the signs of hearing loss are not always what you might suppose.

In Timmy's case, an alert teacher or parent might suspect that his inattentiveness was the result of poor hearing and ask that auditory testing be done. But how many would guess that a "model student" like Jennifer had the same problem . . . that her extreme attentiveness was due to the fact that she had to watch her teacher's lips in order to know what was being said?

Recognizing a Problem

You, the teacher—admittedly already overburdened with non-teaching tasks—will be in a good position to recognize this problem. And in many ways you are the person best able to do so. On school days, you actually spend more hours with children than their parents do. And even more important, you work with the children at a higher level of awareness. You often need to focus your attention directly on a particular youngster, as a parent may not do. Hence you are more likely to notice subtle differences in response. Here are some questions to ask yourself:

• Is the child abnormally attentive like Jennifer or abnormally inattentive like Timmy? Either extreme can be a sign of trouble.

• Is the child behind in speech development? Distorted or immature speech may be the result of distorted hearing. By the age of six a youngster should be able to pronounce clearly such blends as *th, tl, gr, br* and *pr*. More difficult sounds, such as *thr, sk, st, shr, z, sh, ch* and *j*, may not be mastered until age seven or eight.

• Does the child have frequent colds and ear infections? If the answer is yes, then you should watch this child closely for signs of impaired hearing. Approximately 80 percent of all hearing loss in children is *conductive*—that is, it comes from an impediment of some kind that interferes with the transmission of sound inside the ear. Infections often produce such impediments. Fluid in the middle ear is a common cause of problems.

• Is the child subject to allergies? They can produce swollen tissues in the nose and ear area, leading to faulty hearing. Signs of allergies, however, can vary widely. Among the more visible ones are dark circles under the eyes (possibly indicating presence of fluid in the tissue and middle ear), red eyes, a chronically runny nose or frequent sneezing. A teacher also should watch for what is known as the "allergic salute"—rubbing the palm of the hand upward over the mouth and nose. In children with allergies, this gesture sometimes become habitual.

• Has the child had measles, mumps or rubella, either recently or in the past? Despite the existence of preventive vaccines, these diseases are still around, and all three can lead to impaired hearing. It is not uncommon to discover a boy or girl who had one of these diseases as a small child, and whose hearing loss remained unsuspected until he or she started school.

• Does the child rely on gestures when speech would be more effective? Some hearing-impaired children develop gestures into a virtual sign language. One child we know became almost a mime—and the class clown—before it was finally realized that, far from being a natural show-off, he was a partially deaf child.

• Does the child come to school with bruises about the face? The battered child suffers many forms of damage, both physical and psychological. Not infrequently, there is a loss of hearing due to blows on the head which displace delicate bones inside the ear.

• Does the child often ask you to speak louder or give inappropriate answers to your questions? These, of course, are the most obvious of indications that he or she hasn't heard well.

The Need for Prompt Action

As these questions suggest, many cases of hearing loss come from conditions that produce pressure inside the ear—allergies, infections, even enlarged adenoids.

This means that many cases are frequently temporary in nature and often respond readily to treatment. (Even the stubbornest cases of fluid in the middle ear—the commonest cause of hearing loss in children under 10—can be relieved by a simple operation that creates a tiny hole in the eardrum. An inserted tube allows the fluid to drain.) This does *not* mean, however, that you can disregard danger signs, or that it is safe to "wait and see" before speaking to the school doctor or to the parents.

Some of the conditions, if left untreated, will worsen, so that what might have been a temporary loss of hearing becomes a permanent one.

An equally important reason for prompt action is the child's own urgent need not to be out of touch with the world, even for a short time. During the next 12 months, you, as an adult, will take in only a limited amount of new information compared to the child, with so much more to learn. He or she will be taking in new information at an incredibly rapid rate. Interfere with this learning for even a few months and you can create a serious handicap in terms of misunderstood lessons and social isolation.

In guarding against this danger you, the teacher, are the child's first line of defense.

If there's a child in your class who is hard of hearing . . .

Due to the growing implementation of mainstreaming, more and more classroom teachers have hearing-impaired children in their classrooms. For such youngsters, school can be a pleasant experience—and a far more productive one—if you observe the following rules:

1. Always turn and face the class when you have something to say. Don't "teach to the chalkboard." It may seem easy and natural while you're writing on it, but avoid it at all times.

2. Use preferential seating. Seat youngsters with hearing losses near the front of the classroom, close to your desk. A child with a bad left ear should be seated on your right as you face the class, a child with a bad right ear on your left.

3. Pay attention to your diction. Actors know that voices are projected not by speaking louder but by emphasizing the consonants. Sounds like "h" and "th" require special emphasis to be understood by a hearing-impaired person.

4. Be vigilant to make certain you're "getting through." A student's degree of participation in class is one index of good hearing. The child who appears disinterested simply may not be hearing everything that is said.

5. Stay in close touch with the parents. They can tell you whether medical treatment is improving the child's condition and what the long-term outlook is.

6. Help the child overcome any self-consciousness. If it is necessary to refer to the child's handicap, always do so in private, never in front of the class.

7. Allow the child to participate in appropriate activities. Being overprotective when there is no need stifles a child. There's no reason for a youngster who wears a hearing aid not to take part in active sports—keeping the aid on—if he or she wishes. Never compel a youngster who wants to join in a game to remain on the sidelines if there is no medical reason for it.

8. Schedule regular private conferences with the children. Some youngsters talk freely about their problems, others do not. Handicapped children, especially, should always have the opportunity to speak up. In listening, you may discover new ways to be helpful.—*L.B.M. and K.S.E.*

Teachers' Knowledge of, Exposure To, and Attitudes Toward Hearing Aids and Hearing Aid Wearers

Norman J. Lass, John E. Tecca, and Charles M. Woodford

Norman J. Lass is in the Department of Speech Pathology and Audiology, West Virginia University, 805 Allen Hall, P.O. Box 6122, Morgantown, WV 26506-6122. Requests for reprints may be sent to him at this address. John E. Tecca is with the Constance Brown Hearing and Speech Center, Kalamazoo, MI. Charles M. Woodford is in the Department of Speech Pathology and Audiology, West Virginia University, Morgantown, WV.

A questionnaire concerned with various aspects of hearing aids and hearing aid wearers was completed by 113 teachers employed in county school systems in West Virginia. Results of their responses indicate some deficiencies in knowledge of, academic and experiential exposure to, as well as attitudes toward hearing aids and hearing aid wearers. Implications and suggestions for preservice and continuing education programs for teachers are discussed.

With the implementation of Public Law 94-142 and the inherent concept of provision of a least restrictive environment, increased numbers of hearing-impaired children are being placed in regular classrooms in the schools. As a result, classroom teachers have the responsibility for assessing, counseling, and educating these children and thus become a critical link in the effort to place these students into the mainstream of American society. Moreover, PL 94-142 requires that "Each public agency shall insure that the hearing aids worn by deaf and hard of hearing children in school are functioning properly" (Federal Register, 42, (163), p. 42488, August 23, 1977). This regulation is interpreted by the State of West Virginia (West Virginia Department of Education, *Standards for the Education of Exceptional Children,* September, 1977) as "A daily hearing aid check by teacher (regular or special) under procedures for compliance with PL 94-142, Section 121a. 303." Consequently, teachers' knowledge of, exposure to, and attitudes toward hearing aids and hearing aid wearers may influence the progress and integration of their hearing-impaired pupils and, consequently, their own professional effectiveness with the hearing-impaired population.

The purpose of this survey was to determine the knowledge of, exposure to, and attitudes toward hearing aids and hearing aid wearers by teachers employed in county school systems in West Virginia.

Method

A 20-item questionnaire was constructed by the authors. The questionnaire contained questions on respondents' knowledge of various aspects of hearing aids, their attitudes toward hearing aids and hearing aid wearers, as well as their academic exposure to hearing aids and their experiences with hearing-aid wearers. True-false and fill-in-the-blank questions were employed to assess respondents' knowledge and exposure while agreement-disagreement judgments applied to statements on hearing aids and hearing aid wearers were used to evaluate respondents' attitudes. The standards for scoring the informational items on the questionnaire came from research reported in the literature (Bebout, 1985; Bess & McConnell, 1981; Hull, 1977; Mahon, 1985; Pollack, 1980; Public Citizens' Retired Professional Action Group, 1973; Ross, 1975; Schow & Nerbonne, 1980; Walsh, 1979.)

Reprinted from *Language, Speech, and Hearing Services in Schools*, January 1987, pp. 86-90.

The questionnaire was distributed to classroom teachers employed in county school systems in West Virginia in the following manner. Teachers who were enrolled in on- and off-campus classes in the Division of Education of the College of Human Resources and Education at West Virginia University served as respondents. The instructors of these classes were asked to determine who in their classes were teachers, to distribute copies of the questionnaire to them, ad then to collect and return all completed questionnaires to the investigators. A total of 113 teachers employed in county schools primarily in north-central West Virginia completed the questionnaire.

Results

The following is a summary of the major findings of the survey.

Exposure to Hearing Aids and Hearing Aid Wearers

1. Only 4.4% of the respondents had a hearing loss, and of those with a hearing loss, none wore a hearing aid.
2. More than one third of all respondents (37.2%) had not known anyone who wore a hearing aid.
3. The overwhelming majority of respondents (80.5%) had never had a course that included the topic of hearing aids.

Knowledge of Hearing Aids

4. Almost all respondents (98.2%) knew that a hearing aid does not improve a person's hearing in such a manner so that after extended use, he/she eventually does not have to wear it anymore.
5. Almost all respondents (96.5%) knew that hearing aids can be worn by children under 5-years-old.
6. The overwhelming majority of respondents (88.5%) knew that hearing aids are powered by batteries.
7. The overwhelming majority of respondents (85.8%) knew that not everyone with a hearing loss can benefit from a hearing aid.
8. Almost all respondents (97.3%) knew that the size of the hearing aid is not related to the amount of amplification that it provides.
9. Almost all respondents (98.2%) knew that the statement, "Hearing aids are not useful for individuals who are over 65 years old," is false.
10. Almost all respondents (94.7%) knew that the cost of a hearing aid is not related to the degree to which it improves a person's hearing.
11. When asked where hearing aids can be purchased, almost half of all responses (47.3%) were incorrect.
12. Almost half of the respondents (46.9%) did not know that the nonmedical professional who tests people's hearing and makes recommendations regarding the use of hearing aids is called an *audiologist.*

Attitudes Toward Hearing Aids and Hearing Aid Wearers

The following findings are based on respondents' agreement or disagreement (using a forced-choice Likert scale) with statements on the questionnaire concerning hearing aids and hearing aid wearers.

13. Almost one fifth of all respondents (19.5%) indicated that they feel uncomfortable when talking to people who wear hearing aids.
14. Almost all respondents (97.3%) agreed that hearing aids are a worthwhile expense.
15. The overwhelming majority of respondents (81.4%) did not believe that people who wear hearing aids tend to feel sorry for themselves.
16. More than 40% of all respondents (43.4%) agreed with the statement, "People who wear hearing aids tend to be embarrassed about their hearing aids."
17. More than one-fourth of all respondents (29.2%) believed that hearing aid wearers are socially more restricted than those who do not wear hearing aids.
18. The overwhelming majority of respondents (91.2%) disagreed with the statement, "People look older when they wear hearing aids."
19. Almost all respondents (95.6%) agreed that hearing aid wearers are equally intelligent as those who do not wear hearing aids.
20. Almost all respondents (97.3%) indicated that they would wear a hearing aid if it were recommended for them.

Discussion

The findings of this survey indicate some deficiencies in teachers' knowledge of, exposure to, and attitudes toward hearing aids and hearing aid wearers. In view of the potential impact of PL 94-142 on the education and mainstreaming of hearing-impaired children in the schools, including the law's requirement of the assurance that the hearing aids worn by deaf and hard-of-hearing children in school are functioning properly, the results of this survey indicate a need for more information on and exposure to hearing aids and hearing aid wearers in preservice academic training programs as well as in continuing education programs for teachers.

In regard to the content of these programs, it is suggested that the following topics be included:

1. The general structure and function of hearing aids and their use with hearing-impaired children.
2. Troubleshooting principles involved in checking the functioning of hearing aids.
3. The cost of and purchase locations for hearing aids.
4. The hearing aid evaluation process in determining the need for and selection of a hearing aid.
5. The role of the audiologist in assessing hearing and making recommendations regarding the use of hearing aids.
6. Facts versus myths about hearing aids and hearing aid wearers.
7. General principles of aural rehabilitation.

Suggested formats for presenting the above topics include the following:

1. The offering of academic coursework on hearing disorders and hearing aids. In addition to classroom discussions and reading assignments, it is suggested that opportunities be provided for observation and direct practicum experiences with hearing-impaired children who wear hearing aids.
2. The inviting of teachers to observe the clinical ses-

sions of speech-language pathologists and/or audiologists working with hearing-impaired children who wear hearing aids.

3. The establishment of conference and consulting times for speech-language pathologists and/or audiologists to discuss with classroom teachers the role of hearing aids in the learning process of specific hearing-impaired children in their classes.

4. The presentation of in-service workshops to teachers.

5. The preparation of fact sheets for distribution to teachers.

6. The construction of posters and exhibits for display in schools.

7. The preparation of a brochure, perhaps in a question-and-answer format, that would include examination questions to determine if the reader understood its contents.

8. The preparation of a list of published resource materials (books, pamphlets, catalogs, etc.) on hearing aids and their use with hearing-impaired children.

9. The preparation of a list of community human resources (professionals and parents) regarding the use of hearing aids with hearing-impaired children.

Continuing education programs should also include professional information and awareness programs sponsored by state and national education organizations. Suggested formats for these programs, many of which are similar to those listed above, include special seminars and workshops, fact sheets, brochures, slide shows, posters, and exhibits at state, regional, and national meetings, in-service programs, speakers' bureaus, and articles in state and national publications. These programs should provide teachers with a heightened awareness and understanding of hearing aids and hearing aid wearers as well as a positive attitude toward them that will increase the efficiency and effectiveness of their educational services to hearing-impaired children and thereby facilitate their communication and learning processes in the schools.

Acknowledgments

The authors wish to thank Patricia Holden, Evelyn Boyle, Sandra Olexa, Sharon Santilli, Brenda Knight, Vonnia Harris, Jacqueline Barnett, Susan Baker, and Calvin Willson, III for their assistance in the construction of the questionnaire as well as in the collection and analysis of data in this survey. Thanks are also extended to the instructors in the Division of Education of the College of Human Resources and Education at West Virginia University for distributing, collecting, and returning questionnaires, as well as to the teachers who completed the questionnaires. A paper based on the results of this survey was presented at the 1985 Annual Convention of the American Speech-Language-Hearing Association in Washington, DC.

References

Bebout, J.M. (1985). The Vienna Hearing and Speech Center. *The Hearing Journal*, 19-21.

Bess, F.H., & McConnell, F.E. (1981). *Audiology, education, and the hearing impaired child.* St. Louis, MO: C.V. Mosby.

Hull, R.H. (1977). *Hearing impairment among aging persons.* Lincoln, NE: Cliff Notes.

Mahon, W.J. (1985). The M.D. in hearing aid dispensing. *The Hearing Journal*, 13-17.

Pollack, M.C. (1980). *Amplification for the hearing-impaired.* (2nd ed.). New York: Grune & Stratton.

Public Citizens' Retired Professional Action Group (1973). *Paying through the ear: A report on hearing care problems.* Washington, DC.

Ross, M. (1975). Hearing aids for young children. *Otolaryngology Clinics of North America, 8,* 125-141.

Schow, R.L., & Nerbonne, M.A. (1980). *Introduction to aural rehabilitation.* Baltimore, MD: University Park Press.

Walsh, S. (1979). A guide for the person considering hearing aid dispensing. *Hearing Instruments, 30,* 12-35.

HEARING FOR *Success* IN THE CLASSROOM

JoAnn C. Ireland
Denise Wray
Carol Flexer

JoAnn C. Ireland *is Communication Specialist/Audiologist, Special Education Regional Resource Center, Cuyahoga Falls, Ohio.* **Denise Wray** *is Assistant Professor of Speech Pathology, Department of Communicative Disorders, University of Akron, Ohio.* **Carol Flexer** *is Associate Professor of Audiology, Department of Communicative Disorders, University of Akron, Ohio.*

Frequency Modulation (FM) auditory training devices are designed to solve the problems of noise, distance, and reverberation that hearing aids cannot solve alone. Here a student, on the far end of the classroom, is repeating vowel sounds that the teacher spoke into her microphone.

An FM device consists of a teacher wearing a microphone and a student wearing a receiver situated up to approximately 200 feet away.

■Increasing numbers of hearing-impaired children are being mainstreamed, causing educators to express legitimate and realistic concerns. Many of these concerns are in regard to the assistive listening devices needed by hearing-impaired children. Although this equipment can be intimidating, it is essential; hearing-impaired children cannot function in the classroom setting without it (Berg, 1986; Ross, Brackett, & Maxon, 1982). This article answers questions that are typically asked about the technology necessary for children with any degree of hearing loss, from mild to profound, to participate actively in *any* educational environment.

A Prerequisite for Achievement

Hearing is pivotal to academic achievement. Hearing loss is an initial step in

From *Teaching Exceptional Children*, Winter 1988, pp. 15-17.

a detrimental progression of cause and effect. Loss of hearing sensitivity acts as an acoustic filter that hinders a child's normal language development due to inappropriate sensory input (Ling, 1976). The hearing loss subsequently impacts expressive language as well as reading, writing, attending skills, social interaction, and, ultimately, overall academic achievement (Ross, Brackett, & Maxon, 1982). Since reading and writing are built on verbal language skills, they suffer as a direct result of hearing loss. Until the problem of auditory reception is addressed, the pervasive effects of hearing loss will persist and escalate. Therefore, anything that can be done to maximize hearing will have a positive impact on the child's academic performance.

Hearing aids are typically worn to augment auditory reception. Unfortunately, however, the problems of distance, room reverberation, and background noise can greatly interfere with the wearer's ability to discriminate a preferred auditory signal such as a teacher's voice (Berg, 1986; Bess & McConnell, 1981). In fact, speech discrimination is significantly reduced, even when the child is only 1 foot away. A signal must be 10 times louder than the background noise in order to have a signal-to-noise ratio that will allow for intelligibility of speech (Hawkins, 1984; Ross & Giolas, 1978). A typical classroom could not possibly provide a preference signal (teacher's voice) that is loud enough to be intelligible over the background noise (Berg, 1986).

When the signal-to-noise ratio is poor, an auditory signal may be audible to a hearing-impaired child, but not necessarily "intelligible" (Boothroyd, 1978). In other words, the child may respond in a seemingly appropriate way but not really understand what he or she has heard. The child may actually be responding only to intonation patterns and not truly comprehending the specifics of the utterance.

Lipreading is an ineffective substitute for hearing, because visual cues do not provide enough information for identifying the many homophenous words in the English language, for example, "pan," "man," and "ban" (Jeffers & Barley, 1971). These words look alike on the lips and cannot be discriminated without the addition of some auditory information. Therefore, lipreading is considered important, but only as a complement to auditory reception (Boothroyd, 1978).

Preferential seating, even with the use of hearing aids, is not enough! Neither lipreading skills nor hearing aids can substitute for a learning strategy that incorporates the use of an optimal auditory signal.

FM Assistive Listening Devices

Frequency Modulation (FM) auditory training devices are one of the many systems available as personal listening devices. According to Zelski and Zelski (1985), assistive listening devices are products designed to solve the problems of noise, distance, and reverberation that cannot be solved with a hearing aid alone. They do not replace hearing aids, but augment them to more fully meet the needs of hearing-impaired individuals in group listening situations.

An FM auditory trainer is comprised of a microphone, which is placed near the desired sound source (e.g., teacher, loudspeaker, etc.), and a receiver worn by the listener, who can be situated anywhere within approximately 200 feet. These devices can often be coupled to the child's own hearing aid for appropriate individual amplification. There are many models of FM equipment on the market (Van-Tasell, Mallinger, & Crump, 1986). It is important to obtain a model that can be worn by both the teacher and the child in an inconspicuous fashion (Flexer & Wood, 1984). The multiple FM fitting and setting options require visits to the audiologist for appropriate selection and adjustments.

The FM device creates a listening situation that is comparable to the teacher's being only 6 inches away from the child's ear at all times. Ideally, if the unit is fitted and adjusted correctly by an audiologist, its use promotes speech intelligibility and not simply audibility. For example, a child might hear the teacher's voice through a hearing aid alone, but might not be able to distinguish the differences between words such as "wade/wait," "can't/can," "invitation/vacation," and "kite/kites." Such confusions are detrimental to the child's concept and vocabulary development, and they influence the child's potential for success in a regular classroom.

Unfortunately, the FM system is not a panacea for classroom management of hearing-impaired students (Ross, Brackett, & Maxon, 1982). One successful supplement to the regular class curriculum with FM use is to provide tutoring, which can be offered on a pre- and postlesson basis. Teachers can also employ other facilitating strategies such as repeating and rephrasing information and using the cue word "listen" prior to presenting instructions.

Incorporating FM into the Classroom

The Ling Five Sound Test offers a quick and easy way to check, on a daily basis, whether or not a hearing-impaired child can detect the necessary speech sounds (Ling, 1976). This information is vital for instruction. The test can be administered with the child at the far end of the classroom, wearing the FM device and facing away from the teacher. The child repeats each sound as the teacher says it 6 inches from the microphone. The sounds used are /a/, /oo/, /e/, /sh/, and /s/ and are representative of the speech energy contained in every English phoneme. If the child can detect these five sounds, he or she can detect every English speech sound (Ling, 1976). Responding to the sounds may take some practice for children who have not been encouraged to use their residual hearing to its fullest extent.

If the Ling Five Sound Test reveals absent or abnormal FM function, the teacher should always check the battery first. Some 90% of breakdowns reportedly are due to problems with the battery (Ross, 1981). The charge should be checked with a battery tester, because even a new battery or one that has been plugged in may not be fully charged. The teacher should make sure the battery is in the compartment properly and check to see that the poles match. A contact person should be available to take care of quick repairs. Many repairs such as replacing cords or receivers can be done inhouse by an audiologist, speech-language pathologist, or other trained personnel.

As soon as a hearing-impaired

child enters any kind of classroom situation, even preschool, an FM device is necessary and appropriate. The child will need to wear the FM unit throughout the school day, since it provides vital assistance any time instructions or information are presented (e.g. gym rules, art, lunch, speech therapy, etc.).

Children never outgrow their need for FM units; even college students find them invaluable. Hearing-impaired people use the devices any time they wish to hear in public or group situations such as lectures, movies, or church services (Leavitt, 1985).

Summary

It is evident that FM auditory trainers are an integral part of educating hearing-impaired students. These units improve speech intelligibility by reducing the effects of background noise and reverberation and providing an adequate signal-to-noise ratio. There are no substitutes for the efficient use of residual hearing. Therefore, all hearing-impaired children mainstreamed into regular classrooms need FM units. If such a device is not provided, both teacher and child are made to function at an unnecessary disadvantage. The classroom teacher may need to serve as the child's advocate in order to maximize his or her potential for academic success and minimize the frustration often encountered when hearing-impaired pupils are mainstreamed.

References

Berg, F. S. (1986). Classroom acoustics and signal transmission. In F. J. Berg, K. C. Blair, S. H. Viehweg, & J. A. Wilson-Vlotman (Eds.), *Educational audiology for the hard of hearing child* (pp. 157-180). New York: Grune & Stratton.

Bess, F. H., & McConnell, F. E. (1981). *Audiology, education, and the hearing-impaired child.* St. Louis: C. V. Mosby.

Boothroyd, A. (1978). Speech perception and severe hearing loss. In M. Ross & T. G. Giolas (Eds.), *Auditory management of hearing-impaired children* (pp. 117-144). Baltimore: University Park Press.

Flexer, C., & Wood, L. A. (1984). The hearing aid: Facilitator or inhibitor of auditory interaction? *Volta Review, 86,* 354-355.

Hawkins, D. B. (1984). Comparisons of speech recognition in noise by mildly-to-moderately hearing-impaired children using hearing aids and FM systems. *Journal of Speech and Hearing Disorders, 49,* 409-418.

Jeffers, J., & Barley, M. (1971). *Speechreading (lipreading).* Springfield, IL: Charles C Thomas.

Leavitt, R. (1985). Counseling to encourage use of SNR enhancing systems. *Hearing Instruments, 36,* 8-9.

Ling, D. (1976). *Speech and the hearing-impaired child: Theory and practice.* Washhington, DC: The Alexander Graham Bell Association for the Deaf.

Ross, M. (1981). Classroom amplification. In W. R. Hodgson and R. H. Skinna (Eds.), *Hearing aid assessment and use in audiologic habilitation* (2nd ed., pp. 234-257). Baltimore: Williams & Wilkins.

Ross, M., Brackett, D., & Maxon, A. (1982). *Hard-of-hearing children in regular schools.* Englewood Cliffs, NJ: Prentice-Hall.

Ross, M. & Giolas, T. G. (1978). *Auditory management of hearing-impaired children.* Baltimore: University Park Press.

VanTasell, D. J., Mallinger, C. A., & Crump, E. S. (1986). Functional gain and speech recognition with two types of FM amplification. *Language, Speech and Hearing Services in Schools, 17,* 28-37.

Zelski, R. F. K., & Zelski, T. (1985). What are assistive devices? *Hearing Instruments, 36,* 12.

Photographs, by Mark A. Regan, were taken in cooperation with the Kendall Demonstration Elementary School, a part of the Precollege Program at Gallaudet University, Washington, DC.

Service Delivery Alternatives for the Mainstreamed Hearing-Impaired Child

Diane Brackett and Antonia Brancia Maxon

Diane Brackett is a speech-language pathologist affiliated with the New York League for the Hard of Hearing, New York, NY. Antonia Brancia Maxon is an audiologist in the Department of Communication Sciences, University of Connecticut, Storrs, CT 06268. Requests for reprints may be sent to her at this address.

During a 6-year in-service training program demographic and correlational data were obtained on 162 hearing-impaired children in public schools. A discussion of these data and specific case histories of three children are used to describe a set of appropriate service delivery options which may be used by direct service personnel.

Public school personnel have been given the responsibility of serving the needs of hearing-impaired children who are mainstreamed into regular classrooms. Consequently, they are expected to provide appropriate educational programs, but may not have the necessary information to assist them in developing individual plans. The lack of available information reflects the type of research which has been conducted to date. Due to the availability of subjects, most studies have been conducted with hearing-impaired children in self-contained settings. (Jensema, 1975; Jensema & Trybus, 1978). Typically, these studies describe children with severe to profound hearing losses placed in restricted educational settings based on their inability to handle the extensive communicative demands of regular classes. This narrowly defined subject pool makes it difficult to develop management strategies from those data which can be applied to children who are functioning in a public school setting. Several studies (Kennedy, Northcott, McCauley, & Williams, 1976; Kodman, 1963; McClure, 1977; Reich, Hambleton, & Houldin, 1977; Ross, Brackett, & Maxon, 1982) demonstrated academic, communicative, and social differences between the two populations of hearing-impaired children, mainstreamed and self-contained. However, a more comprehensive description of mainstreamed hearing-impaired children is crucial, if the public school educator is expected to effectively address the unique needs of this population.

Method

Through a federally funded grant (The UConn Mainstream Project, 1977-1982) the authors were able to collect demographic information on over 200 hearing-impaired children in the Connecticut public schools. This paper presents a discussion of that demographic information. Specific case histories of three children will be used to describe appropriate service delivery options which may be used by direct service school personnel. Some of the children included in the Mainstream Project were not in fully mainstreamed programs, however, 162 of them were receiving all of their academic preparation in the regular classroom from regular educators. Some of the children who fell within this group were not in placements deemed appropriate by the authors, but are being included to more accurately reflect the wide skill level present in mainstreamed hearing-impaired children. One of the goals of the Mainstream Project was to assist direct service personnel in assessing the relationship between a child's needs and the services being provided, and modifying the existing program when indicated. Due to the voluntary nature of the Project, the Project Directors were presented with a wide variety of child and school-related conditions, which made it difficult to apply a "programmed" approach to modifying the service delivery. Child-related conditions included (a) socioeconomic background, (b) previous educational placement, and (c) parental support. The school's population density, ethnic composition, and attitude towards special

TABLE 1. Means and standard deviations for the demographic data compiled on the 164 public school hearing-impaired children.

Variable	$\bar{x}$	*SD*
PPVT*	−42.44 months	36.93
Pure-tone average**	65.15dB HTL	25.65
PBK Look***	47.11%	25.35
PBK Listen~	53.30%	29.30
PBK Look + Listen~~	84.78%	17.57

*Peabody Picture Vocabulary Test (Form A or B) with scores calculated to represent deviation from chronological age in months.
**Average of 500, 1,000, 2,000, & 4,000 Hz thresholds in the better ear.
***Speech reading discrimination of kindergarten-level monosyllabic words.
~Auditory discrimination of kindergarten-level monosyllabic words.
~~Auditory and speech reading (face-to-face) discrimination of kindergarten-level monosyllabic words.

needs had an impact on the effectiveness of the Project personnel. In summary, this Project allowed the authors to obtain information on the mainstreamed hearing-impaired child and define appropriate service delivery models, while providing in-service training to direct service personnel. The information obtained and material developed on that Project form the basis of the present paper.

Variable 1	*Variable 2*	*Correlation coefficient*	*Significance level*
PPVT	Pure-tone average (PTA)	−0.2612	.003
PPVT	PBK Listen	0.4716	.000
PPVT	PBK Look + Listen	0.4519	.000
PTA	PBK Listen	−0.5630	.000
PTA	PBK Look + Listen	−0.3341	.000
PBK Listen	PBK Look + Listen	0.6414	.000

Results

Table 1 displays the means and standard deviations of audiological and communication data most readily available on the 162 children studied. It should be noted that these data are limited to those which the Project participants were willing and able to provide. Table 1 indicates that, in general, the children were able to receive orally presented information quite readily. That is, they could repeat the phonemes, syllables, and words, but they experienced considerable difficulty in extracting the meaning of those words due to reduced vocabulary levels. However, large standard deviations of each variable listed indicate that this population of hearing-impaired children in regular schools was quite heterogeneous.

A comparison between chronological age and present grade placement (Figure 1) demonstrated that below grade 5, most of the children were in appropriate classes for their ages. Apparently the upper elementary levels required a level of language complexity and abstract thinking which put an extra burden on the already over-extended communication skills of the hearing-impaired child. This age/grade discrepancy is corroborated in the literature (Kodman, 1963).

In addition to the descriptive data, correlational analyses were conducted to inspect the relationships between degree of hearing loss, speech reception mode, and vocabulary competency. A portion of this data pool was described in a previous publication (Maxon & Brackett, 1983). Table 2 shows the expected relationship between degree of hearing loss (pure-tone averages of 500, 1,000, 2,000 and 4,000 Hz in the better ear) and use of residual hearing (PB-K Listen), that is, as hearing loss increased the ability to correctly perceive speech in an auditory only condition decreased. Although such a relationship exists, it does not mean that children with reduced hearing levels cannot make use of auditory information. On the contrary, Maxon (1982) demonstrated that, when speech discrimination ability is scored by phonemes and/or acoustic cues rather than by entire words, one sees the extensive use of acoustic information made by even the most severely impaired children. The ability to perceive speech in a combined (auditory-visual) mode also decreased as hearing-loss increased. Presumably, those results reflect the influence of the inclusion of the auditory information because visual perception of words (PB-K Look) did not vary with the extent of hearing loss. The positive relationship between degree of hearing loss, use of residual hearing, and vocabulary can also be seen in Table 2. The children with milder hearing losses and/or better use of their hearing were more likely to acquire vocabulary skills which more closely approximated those of their normally hearing peers.

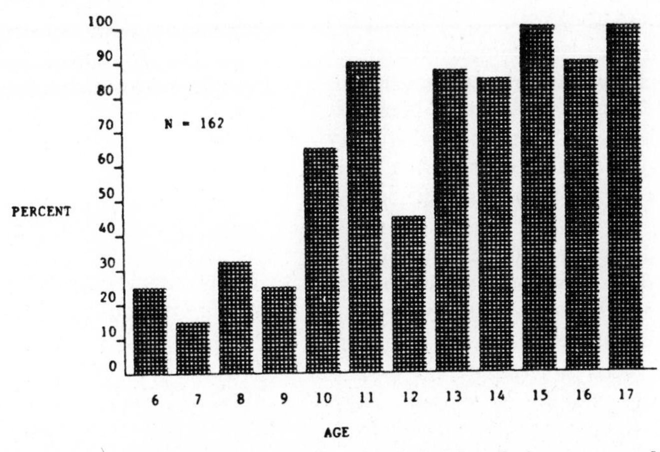

FIGURE 1. Percent of hearing-impaired children below expected grade placement from age 6–17 years.

For these mainstreamed children who are dependent upon using their residual hearing, it is expected that noise and distance factors in a classroom would be especially detrimental to their reception of speech. Yet, that was not manifest in increased usage of FM systems which would facilitate listening at distances of more than 0.91 m (3 ft) and in noise (see Table 3). The use of FM systems in the classroom was distributed across grades with the greatest usage occurring from first to seventh grades. The high percentages in 11th and 12th grades can be attributed to the low number of hearing-impaired children in those classes.

Although there were some instances in which a high percentage of hearing-impaired children were benefitting from improved listening conditions afforded by FM systems, a closer look at Table 3 indicates that there were a large number of children who could have benefitted from FM use, but were without the systems. It is not possible from these data to determine if the fault lies with the lack of awareness by direct service personnel or administrative inflexibility.

Although it is not possible to describe a "typical" mainstreamed child from the data, one can generalize the difficulties peculiar to many of the hearing-impaired children in regular schools from those data. They have trouble in receiving, understanding, and producing spoken language which has a negative effect on their academic performance.

The service delivery models used to address the deficits of the children studied were often quite varied. Through the Mainstream Project the authors were able to isolate and integrate factors within those models which were most effective in supporting the regular classroom program. Factors related to the physical en-

TABLE 3. Percentage of hearing-impaired children in each grade who were using wireless FM systems as classroom amplification; as well as a percentage of children who were candidates, but were not using the FM systems.

Grade (number)	*% using*	*% not using*
Preschool (9)	33	67
Kindergarten (7)	14	86
First (9)	88	12
Second (14)	57	43
Third (9)	66	34
Fourth (19)	27	73
Fifth (21)	42	58
Sixth (17)	47	53
Seventh (18)	44	56
Eighth (11)	18	82
Ninth (7)	43	57
Tenth (4)	25	75
Eleventh (2)	50	50
Twelfth (1)	100	0

vironment, classroom instruction, and communicative strategies were determined to have the most influence on academic performance. A service list has been developed which includes all factors to be considered for each hearing-impaired child in regular schools. The list does not include specific tests, procedures, or materials in order to make it generalizable. Concepts have been listed giving leeway to the informed professional to decide which specific materials best fit the child's needs. The use of this rather exhaustive list will allow for the inclusion of factors which may otherwise be overlooked by school personnel.

Case Studies

To illustrate the flexibility inherent within the service list given, three cases are presented. The descriptions of the children contain summaries of their existing programs. In the Discussion section suggestions for modifications of each program are given to demonstrate ways in which to better meet each child's individual needs.

BF is a 6-year-old boy with a bilateral moderate high-frequency sensorineural hearing loss. He wears binaural ear level hearing aids and uses a wireless FM auditory trainer in school. BF is fully mainstreamed into the first grade (i.e., receives all of his academic subjects in the regular classroom). Academically, BF is performing in the upper 25% of his class with formal testing indicating even greater potential. His only support service is speech-language remediation five times a week which primarily consists of vocabulary enrichment. The form and use of his language are presently age-appropriate. BF is a child who is able to make good use of his residual hearing when listening conditions are good, that is, in quiet and/or in a one-to-one situation. When confronted with typical classroom conditions (noise, distance from the speaker/teacher, and poor room acoustics) BF's ability to receive speech is severely hampered. Through the use of his FM system, BF is able to have access to all classroom presentations by maximizing the use of his residual hearing. He lives in a rural area which does not allow him any socialization with peers except in school, resulting in his difficulty establishing peer relationships. Academic achievement is not encouraged in the home.

JM is a 12-year-old girl with a congenital severe-to-profound sensorineural hearing loss. Personal amplification consists of binaural ear level hearing aids which are used in conjunction with a teleloop FM system in school. Even though she has a significant hearing loss, JM does not rely primarily on visual cues for receiving information, but is able to effectively interface the auditory and visual modalities. JM is presently placed in the seventh grade where instruction is conducted by a variety of subject-specific teachers. She is performing at grade level in nonlanguage-based subjects (i.e., math and spelling) and as much as 2 years below grade level in those subjects which require language facility. Teachers' reports and formal testing indicate that JM needs supportive services in order to reach her potential. Her support system consists of daily preview/review tutoring and intensive communication management. She is one of several hearing-impaired children in this small city school system and has both normal-hearing and hearing-impaired friends. Parental support is excellent.

ER is a 15-year-old boy with a bilateral severe sensorineural hearing loss for which he wears binaural ear level hearing aids. The school has provided a traditional wireless FM auditory training system (cords and snap-on transducers) which he has refused to wear since his entrance this year into the 10th grade. He is capable of using his hearing as the primary modality for speech reception, but because of the rejection of school amplification, he is falling behind his peers in all subject areas. His academic difficulties are further exacerbated by the language interference from his bilingual (Hispanic) background. ER attends a resource room which uses a prestructured curriculum for the hearing-impaired rather than materials designed to address the deficits he demonstrates in his mainstreamed classes. No speech-language services are provided. ER is well socialized into the large inner city school which he attends. Because he is so "normalized" he is especially resistant to any efforts to provide him with the remedial services he may need. His parents are concerned about his school performance, but because they are non-native English speakers, they find it difficult to communicate with the special education personnel in this inner city school.

Discussion

This section describes the services which are required to modify the mainstream setting for any hearing-impaired child. Following those general items are the specific adaptations for the individual cases described above.

Summary

Every year the child's educational placement should be reevaluated and, through a team decision, future programming should be determined. The specific members of the team may vary across school systems, but it is essential that at least one member has expertise in the limitations and needs of the hearing-impaired child. In addition to the requisite presence of the parents, participation of adolescents should be considered since their involvement increases the chances of success. Decisions regarding placement and/or remedial programs should be based on up-to-date evaluations. Specifically, audiological, communication, and achievement assessments should be conducted on an annual basis and psychological evaluations carried out minimally every 3 years. In order to design the individualized program, it is crucial that the team have well-interpreted test results available which directly translate into the child's classroom performance. If outside agencies/professionals are used for any of these evaluations, a communicative exchange must occur between direct service personnel and the evaluator. The individualized program that is generated from the team will be specific to the needs of each of the hearing-impaired children. There are, however, certain commonalities that exist in the programming for this population. Regardless of the extent of the hearing loss, every child should be considered a viable candidate for classroom amplification. That FM system should be specifically set for the child's hearing loss in an arrangement that reflects both the teacher's and the child's preference. Because it is assumed that all of the children will have some form of amplification (personal and school-worn) there must be a school staff member designated to troubleshoot the equipment on a daily basis.

The negative effects of external and internal classroom noise sources on the child's performance should be considered every time a change of room is anticipated. Although FM systems help to overcome some of these negative influences, acoustic treatment of a room may further enhance the listening condition.

Having discussed the obvious factors related to the hearing loss itself, what remains is the communication deficit and its effect on academic performance. The necessity of communication management for this population is always assumed with the intensity and focus dependent upon the individual child's communication needs. While improvement in articulation may be one of the management goals, it is more than likely that it is not the area which most directly impacts on the child's educational success. In an effective management program, emphasis on speech intelligibility and communicative competence should be balanced according to the child's specific needs.

An underlying assumption of mainstreaming is that the hearing-impaired child will benefit from exposure to and participation in the curriculum of the regular classroom. There are minor modifications in the classroom presentation and teacher's style which can make the educational setting more accessible to the hearing-impaired child. The use of visual support techniques, such as writing key words on the chalkboard, benefits the entire class while allowing the hearing-impaired child an equal opportunity to receive the pertinent content material. Instructional support can be carried out without changing the curriculum or imposing unreasonable constraints on the classroom teacher. By simply designating the speaker or restating a comment during class discussion the teacher can make the orally presented information available to the hearing-impaired child. Although these modifications may appear obvious to experienced professionals, the team should ensure that the regular school personnel are apprised of the benefits that such changes generate.

One of the ways in which this information may be transmitted is through an organized in-service training program. Since the regular school placement results in the child having a new teacher(s) every year, in-service programming should be conducted on at least an annual basis. It is also beneficial to provide information to the normally hearing classmates in order to increase their awareness of and sensitivity toward hearing impairment. A hearing-impaired child's self-image may influence his/her desire to be an integral part of any in-service programming.

Individual Items

It can be noted that BF's individualized program provides him with the services which enable him to work up to his potential. Of major concern at this time are his difficulties in peer interaction. Extracurricular activities, such as scouts or sports, may give him the exposure he needs to develop appropriate interactive skills. Because this is not necessarily considered the school's responsibility, the "case manager" may want to encourage BF's mother to make these social situations available to him. As the academic demands increase BF may need more of the support services in order to continue at his present rate of progress. An annual reevaluation of his program and his skill level will ensure that such services are available when necessary.

The need for extensive service is evident in JM's case. Her difficulty in the language-based subject areas (language arts, reading, social studies, and science) is obviously related to her decreased language proficiency. Therefore, the personnel providing the academic support and the communication management should coordinate their services to target those areas which bear the greatest relationship to JM's classroom needs. Aside from these remedial services, JM will need assistance in receiving the information presented in the classroom. Her classroom teachers will need the expertise of the support service personnel in discerning the communication strategies that will best enhance the classroom presentation. Since this is JM's first year in a departmentalized program, different teachers for each subject, the possibility exists that she may need the services of a notetaker in the classroom. The fact that JM relies on both auditory and visual cues for reception of speech results in her being unable to take notes during a lecture to which she is listening. This problem is likely to be exacerbated by her entry into high school.

When a team annually reviews a child's program the members must take into consideration, not only the extent of services provided, but the appropriateness of those services. ER's programming is quite extensive with the provision of an FM system and academic support, but it fails to meet his specific needs as a bilingual socially well-integrated high-school student. ER has demonstrated that he will use amplification when he does not find it cosmetically unattractive. His refusal to use the traditional FM system is not unusual at his age and should be considered when selecting the appropriate model, for instance the use of a teleloop with his personal hearing aids. Similarly, the use of a separate curriculum in the resource room has not provided him with the preview/review tutoring he needs to function in the regular classroom. If the resource room service better met his academic needs, he might be less reluctant to be singled out and attend on a daily basis. ER's involvement in designing the support program, increases the likelihood of his acceptance of the remedial assistance. The issue of bilingualism and its effects on ER's programming must be handled with sensitivity by school personnel. It is not a situation that is easily accommodated. All of ER's programming is designed and conducted by English speaking school personnel. This fact precludes the involvement desired by ER's parents who feel alienated because of the language barrier.

Summary

Due to the heterogeneity of this mainstream population, it is difficult to "plug in" an already existing program and have it meet the children's needs. There are, however, a sufficient number of commonalities that make it possible to generate a list of services that should be considered for all hearing-impaired children. An annual evaluation of the child's audiological, communicative, academic, and social skills in conjunction with a review of the service list should aid in the development of an appropriate individualized program.

Acknowledgments

The activities described in this paper took place during the course of several grants funded by the Office of Special Education of the US Department of Education. We particularly thank Dr. Mark Ross for his continuing support and sharing of knowledge throughout the course of the UConn Mainstream Project. We also thank the public school personnel who participated in the Project.

The Project's Principal Investigator, Dr. Mark Ross, was the first to recognize the need to support public school personnel in their work with hearing-impaired students and to design the specific format of the in-service training program. His efforts on behalf of the hearing-impaired children in the schools are the foundation of the present article. The UConn Mainstream Project was housed in the Department of Communication Sciences at the University of Connecticut.

References

Jensema, C.J. (1975). *The relationship between academic achievement and demographic characteristics of hearing-impaired children and youth.* Office of Demographic Studies, Gallaudet College, Series R, No. 2.

Jensema, C.J., & Trybus, R.J. (1978). *Communication patterns and educational achievement of hearing-impaired students.* Gallaudet College, Series T, No. 2.

Kennedy, P., Northcott, W., McCauley, R., & Williams, S. (1976). Longitudinal sociometric and cross-sectional data on mainstreaming hearing-impaired children: Implications and preschool programming. *Volta Review, 78,* 71-82.

Kodman, F. (1963). Educational status of hard of hearing children in the classroom. *Journal of Speech and Hearing Disorders, 28,* 297-299.

Maxon, A.B. (1982). *Speech acoustics: A model for management of hearing-impaired children.* Miniseminar presented at the American Speech-Language-Hearing Association Convention, Toronto, Ontario, Canada.

Maxon, A.B., & Brackett, D. (1983). Inservice training for public school speech-language pathologists in the management of mainstreamed hearing-impaired children. In I. Hochberg, H. Levitt, & M.J. Osberger (Eds.), *Speech of the hearing-impaired: Research, training, and personnel preparation.* Baltimore, MD: University Park Press.

McClure, A.T. (1977). Academic achievement of mainstreamed hearing-impaired children with congenital rubella syndrome. *Volta Review, 79,* 379-384.

Reich, C., Hambleton, D., & Houldin, B.K. (1977). The integration of hearing-impaired children in regular classrooms. *American Annals of the Deaf, 122,* 534-543.

Ross, M., Brackett, D., & Maxon, A.B. (1982). *Hard of hearing children in regular schools.* Englewood Cliffs, NJ: Prentice-Hall.

REDUCING ETHNOCENTRISM

David S. Martin

David S. Martin *(CEC Chapter #264) is Associate Professor of Education and Dean of the School of Education and Human Services, Gallaudet University, Washington, DC.*

■Misunderstanding, miscommunication, and negative attitudes—problems of *ethnocentrism*—are common in the day-to-day contact between any two different cultures. They can occur regularly when deaf and hearing children interact in schools.

What is classroom ethnocentrism? It includes negative attitudes exhibited toward other culture groups being studied in the classroom or toward groups represented in the school itself. How will a teacher recognize ethnocentrism when it is expressed? There are two kinds of ethnocentrism, which anthropologists label *cultural absolutism* and *cultural relativism* (Guggenheim, 1970):

1. **Cultural absolutism: When children respond to some foreign cultural behavior with a statement such as, "How awful—how could anyone do that?", they are looking at their own culture as superior.**
2. **Cultural relativism: If the same children look at the same foreign behavior and say, "Well, we have our ways, and they have theirs," they are missing the idea of the unity that underlies all human behavior.**

The problem of reducing ethnocentric behavior in educational settings is complex because it involves both thinking and feeling. For example, a hearing person who looks down on a deaf peer's sign language may be expressing ethnocentrism toward the deaf population rather than merely judging their method of communication.

The Deaf Population and Ethnocentrism

How can we be sure that the misunderstandings between deaf and hearing people are forms of ethnocentrism? We know that there is a deaf "subculture." Meadow (1975) has explained its characteristics as (a) intermarriage among deaf people, (b) membership in certain voluntary organizations, (c) membership in special religious organizations, (d) special opportunities in the arts for deaf people, (e) traditional residential schooling, and (f) use of American Sign Language.

Other research has found that people who are deaf believe that hearing people are more negative toward them than they really are (Schroedel & Schiff, 1972) and that hearing students' attitudes toward deaf students can become more negative after a period of months of going to school together (Emerton & Rothman, 1978).

Methods for Reducing Ethnocentrism

Researchers have found some ways to reduce ethnocentrism between different cultural groups. We can apply some of these findings to the specific goal of increasing understanding, positive attitudes, and clear communication among both deaf and hearing children in mainstreamed school settings and adults in the workplace. The following six areas of research can be helpful in revealing ways to accomplish this goal.

Prejudice Reduction

Pate (1981) has reported that facts alone are not enough to reduce prejudice toward another group, so teachers need to focus on attitudes, too, by asking children to openly discuss how they *feel* toward another group.

People who have high self-image tend to have a low degree of prejudice. Therefore, teachers need to help *all* children feel positive about themselves so that they will feel positive toward those who are different from them.

The thinking, feeling, and behavioral components of prejudice are not necessarily related. Therefore, teachers may see children expressing kind *words* but prejudiced *feelings* toward children of different groups. To uncover their true attitudes, teachers should confront children individually when their behavior does not match their expressed words. The first step toward changing attitudes is for individuals to *admit* what they feel *now*.

Films and other media also tend to improve intergroup attitudes. In schools, multimedia lessons on deafness may go further than books and discussion to help improve attitudes of hearing students.

Social contacts among members of different groups may reduce prejudice, whereas isolation of deaf children may foster prejudice toward them. Therefore, the more direct contact between deaf and hearing children, the better. Classes of hearing children should experiment with joint field trips and other activities with special classes of deaf children.

Expression of Negativism and Cultural Contact

Another study looked at attitude changes between deaf and hearing people after an 8-week period in which deaf student teachers taught full-time classes of hearing public school students (Martin, 1983). The study showed a clear improvement in attitudes of the hearing children toward the deaf teachers, supporting the idea that regular contact between the two cultures can reduce ethnocentrism.

If a regular public school has a special day-class of deaf children, those children need to have regular, supervised interaction with hearing children. Recess is not enough; lunch periods, joint projects, and paired reading activities could help develop more positive attitudes.

But what do these studies mean for hearing learners who have *no* opportunity to interact with deaf learners and vice versa? The data suggest two other instructional conditions for reducing ethnocentrism: (a) providing sufficient time for in-depth study of both deaf and hearing cultures in social studies and (b) a classroom climate that allows open expression and discussion of students' initial negativism toward other cultures. Teachers need to encourage students to express their negative attitudes so that they can be discussed openly.

Process of Stereotyping

The work of Glock, Wuthnow, Piliavin, and Spencer (1975) showed that "cognitive sophistication" is also important in reducing negative attitudes toward other groups. This sophistication requires that children understand the mental process of stereotyping and labeling as well as the other culture's life experience and history. Therefore, teachers should teach both deaf and hearing children about how stereotypes are formed. Activities could include showing how a picture of one poor beggar in tattered clothes in New Delhi could make us wrongly generalize that *all* Indians are poor if we do not know all the facts.

Countering Stereotypes

Freedman, Gotti, and Holtz (1981) built on Glock's work by teaching elementary students about this stereotyping process and then showing them some examples of "counter-stereotypic" behavior by members of ethnic groups (e.g., Puerto Rican celebrities in the United States). Students demonstrated reduced stereotypic attitudes after the use of these two techniques.

Pecoraro (1970) also found that exposing children to the positive contributions to the American heritage by an ethnic subgroup (Native Americans) could improve their attitudes toward that subgroup. In this vein, teachers of hearing and deaf students could teach about the contributions of famous deaf persons to American society, both now and in the past.

Three books that would be useful for this purpose are *Fastest Woman on Earth* by A. M. Thacher (1980); *Works of James O'Connor, the Deaf Poet* by J. O'Connor (1882); and *Representative Deaf Persons of the United States of America*, edited by J. E. Gallagher (1898).

Simulating the Other Culture

The Hawaii State Department of Education (1981) developed a framework for studying another culture that included the following activities:

- exploring an "arranged" or artificial cultural environment in the classroom,
- raising questions about that culture, and
- observing and analyzing each other's behaviors.

Thus, the classroom could become a kind of anthropology "lab." Teachers could set up a "deaf" environment for hearing children by having them carefully insert cotton in their ears and list their feelings and sensations for a period of 5 minutes. They would then remove the cotton and share the insights they gained about being "deaf."

Some teachers have also taught hearing children some basic sign language and helped them to understand how the use of a manual language assists some deaf persons to distinguish between sounds that take similar shapes on the lips (e.g., "m" and "b"). Without some visual cue, a deaf person cannot distinguish such pairs.

Teaching Logical Categorization

Still another method may be worth testing: teaching children how to find underlying *similarities* as well as the more obvious differences among peoples. The program *Instrumental Enrichment* (Feuerstein, 1980) teaches students how to compare and categorize on a logical basis. Teachers can also teach children better categorization skills by having them look at a randomly organized collection of pictures of objects, such as tools arranged on a flannelboard, then listing the criteria for sorting them (color, size, shape, number, etc.), sorting them into categories, and labeling the categories. Then, teachers can ask, "What is the same about all the pictures, even though they are in separate labeled groups?" (They are all still tools.) These same categorization skills can be applied to pictures of people. No matter how many separate groups and labels one might invent (skin color, eye shape, face shape, hair color, etc.), they are all still people, and people are all similar in needing food, shelter, clothing, beliefs, and love.

Summary

These research studies suggest the following classroom strategies for the teacher who wants to reduce ethnocentrism among deaf and hearing students:

1. Provide multiple opportunities for deaf and hearing students to interact on a regular basis, preferably on joint projects or activities.
2. Give deaf and hearing children the opportunity to discuss openly why they react positively or negatively toward each other.
3. Encourage children to express in what ways their own culture might appear strange to a person from the other group. For example, hearing children should imagine which aspects of spoken language might appear bizarre to a deaf person.
4. Discuss the fundamental ways in which *all* human groups are similar (kinship, division of tasks, language, prolonged childhood dependency, belief system, use of symbols, tool systems, etc.). Deaf and hearing people are equally "human" because each group has

established its own specific responses to those *same* needs.

5. Teach children about the processes by which humans develop -stereotypes and have them list the ways in which they have seen themselves follow those processes in judging or misjudging deaf or hearing children.

6. Teach students that there is a wide variation of behavior *within* any culture; thus, stereotyping is bound to be false (e.g., some deaf people use sign language, while others do not).

7. Point out some nonstereotypic behaviors of both groups. For example, numerous deaf persons today have earned Ph.D.'s and teach in universities.

8. Teach about the positive contributions to human life by both groups. For example, focus on well-known deaf actors or athletes.

9. Help students to create and analyze a written description of a model culture in order to develop their thinking tools for understanding the deaf or hearing culture.

The teacher's yearly plan for using these methods would include the following activities:

1. Working at the beginning of the school year with the principal and other teachers to plan joint activities for deaf and hearing children.
2. Working with the Parent-Teacher Association to schedule their fall meeting around the topic "Improving Children's Attitudes Toward Handicaps," in which parents of handicapped and nonhandicapped children would share their own experiences and positive suggestions.

3. Inviting a guest speaker into the classroom to tell about deafness, teach some sign language, and describe the problems of being deaf.

4. Planning at least one social studies unit on deaf culture to teach children about the traditions of the deaf community and sign language in America. This would be the place for multimedia presentations and teaching about the stereotyping process.

5. Incorporating into the reading program some biographies of famous deaf persons in history.

6. Inviting deaf and hearing children to tell each other, in pairs, about experiences, problems, and solutions they have in communication. This could take place once a week, perhaps on Friday afternoons during a special activity period. A sign language interpreter would be important in ensuring communication among these children.

7. Invite a skilled parent to visit the classroom twice a week throughout the year to teach the hearing children basic sign language, which they could use during the regular interaction times with deaf children.

A local teacher of deaf children can also serve the regular classroom -teacher as a valuable resource and support person in learning to employ these and other ideas and in solving problems that may arise between deaf and hearing students.

Conclusion

Teachers have a responsibility to take advantage of what is known about ways to intervene in the tendency toward ethnocentrism. If teachers and administrators truly believe that positive interaction between handicapped and nonhandicapped persons can lead to a better world for everyone, then they must employ the techniques available to them for fostering such interaction on a regular basis.

Only as educators take advantage of these useful procedures can they hope to promote a world where the word "handicap" will lose its original negative connotation and instead be seen as merely another manifestation of the amazing variation in human characteristics. It is not *bad* to be different; it is only *interesting* to be different. At the core, we are all human.

References

Emerton, R. G., & Rothman, G. (1978). Attitudes toward deafness: Hearing students at a hearing and deaf college. *American Annals of the Deaf, 123,* 588-593.

Feuerstein, R. (1980). *Instrumental enrichment.* Baltimore, MD: University Park Press.

Freedman, P. I., Gotti, M., & Holtz, G. (1981, February). In support of direct teaching to counter ethnic stereotypes. *Phi Delta Kappan,* p.456.

Gallagher, J. E. (Ed.). (1898). *Representative deaf persons of the United States of America.* Chicago: J. E. Gallagher.

Glock, C. Y., Wuthnow, R., Pilievin, J. A., & Spencer, M. (1975). *Adolescent prejudice.* New York: Harper & Row.

Guggenheim, H. (1970). The concept of culture: Talks to teachers. In *Man: A course of study.* Washington, DC: Curriculum Development Associates.

Hawaii State Department of Education. (1981, June). A framework for culture study with special focus on the study of Hawaii. *Resources in Education.* (ERIC Document Reproduction Service No. ED 198 031).

Martin, D. S. (1983). Preparing hearing-impaired teachers of hearing children. *Teacher Education and Special Education, 6,* 143-150.

Meadow, K. (1975, July-August). The deaf subculture. *Hearing and Speech Action.*

O'Connor, J. (1882). *Works of James O'Connor, the deaf poet.* New York: N. Tibbals.

Pate, G. S. (1981, January). Research on prejudice reduction. *Educational Leadership* , 288-291.

Pecoraro, J. (1970). *The effect of a series of special lessons in Indian history and culture upon the attitudes of Indian and non-Indian students.* (ERIC Document Reproduction Service No. ED 043 556).

Schroedel, J. G., & Schiff, W. (1972). Attitudes toward deafness among several deaf and hearing populations. *Rehabilitation Psychology, 19*(2), 59-70.

Thacher, A. M. (1980). *Fastest woman on earth.* Milwaukee: Raintree Publishers.

Teaching the Visually Impaired Child

Visually impaired and blind children are no longer usually segregated from sighted children in educational settings. PL 94-142, with its mandate for least restrictive environments for education, has initiated a multitude of changes in programs for low vision students. While students with visual impairment currently constitute the smallest category of exceptional children for whom special educational services are provided in the public schools, it is becoming a more conspicuous category. Increasing numbers of blind students are leaving residential schools, special day schools, or self-contained special classes to enroll in mainstreamed public education programs. Assessments of visual handicaps are improving as well. Increasing numbers of low vision children are now qualifying for special education services because of their impairments.

Legal blindness does not always connote no vision. A person is considered legally blind when he or she can only see at 20 feet, with the best eye, what a normally sighted person would see from 200 feet away. Most blind people have some perception of light and some residual vision that can be utilized. A person is considered visually impaired when he or she can only see at 20 feet what a normally sighted person would see from 70 feet away. Thus, the best corrected vision one can have in the best eye to be labeled blind or visually impaired, respectively, is 20/200 and 20/70. Between 20/70 and 20/200, there can be many degrees of visual impairment in one or both eyes. In addition, there are many degrees of legal blindness from 20/200 in both eyes to no vision or light perception at all in either eye.

Despite the relatively smaller numbers of blind or visually impaired students in regular classes in the public schools, educators need to know how to meet their needs, provide supportive services, alter the least restrictive environment to make education appropriate, and annually update their individualized education plans (IEPs). Like all other exceptional children, blind or low vision students should be challenged to do as much as they are capable of doing for themselves. To this end, teachers should be both encouraging and supportive.

Adapting a regular classroom and teaching materials to a blind or low vision student depends not only on the degree of impairment, but also on other characteristics of the student (e.g., hearing, coordination, intelligence, emotional maturity). Each blind or visually impaired child will have his or her own prescription for, or access to, other technological aids (e.g., glasses, magnifier, large-type books, sonic guide, reading machine, Optacon, braille writer, typewriter, microcomputer). The classroom teacher will need to become familiar with the uses (and abuses) of such aids. Students must be challenged and motivated to make use of all such supportive devices. The teacher should respond to legitimate requests for assistance with them, but should not give unwanted help, nor do the work for the student.

Microcomputer technology for visually impaired children is profoundly changing their education. The temptations are great for computer literate teachers to want to use the students' computers. Rather, each child with a personal computer, or access to one, should be encouraged to use it as independently as possible. Microcomputers allow blind and low vision children to function as capable, competent students. As they are able to learn more efficiently and keep up with nonhandicapped students, they become more self-confident and their self-esteem improves. Concurrently, other students develop more positive attitudes toward them. Non-computer literate teachers will need to learn enough about the use of these computers to assign work, grade work, assure continual progress, and praise self-direction and independence.

The first article of this unit differentiates between the learning abilities and needs of children with different degrees of visual impairment. It also addresses the needs of children with other classifications of handicaps. About 50 percent of visually impaired children do have other co-existing disabilities. The next article discusses the need for early intervention for newborn to 3-year-old infants with visual impairments. It describes a program for both infants and parents to facilitate effective interactions. Next, Randall Jose, Stephanie Labossiere, and Marsha Small present "A Model for Integrating Low Vision Services into Educational Programs." They address the issues of assessment, rehabilitative activities, educational programs, and multidisciplinary coordination of services. In the next selection, Geraldine Scholl discusses creative placements for low vision students, the writing of IEPs, and the use of special equipment such as the Optacon, Kurzweil reading machines, large-type books, braille writer, type-

Unit 9

writer, or microcomputer. In the final selection of this unit, Sandra Ruconich outlines the advantages and disadvantages of several kinds of microcomputer programs. She addresses considerations such as cost-benefit ratios, how the device is to be used, how portable the microcomputer must be, and the user's capabilities, preferences, speed, and opinions.

Looking Ahead: Challenge Questions

How does a visual impairment affect learning abilities? Are other physical disabilities common in low vision children?

Can parents of visually impaired infants and toddlers provide intervention services for their children before the advent of special services in preschool or public school?

What constitutes an appropriate educational program and related services for low vision students? How can the services of several disciplines be coordinated to optimize the program?

What special techniques can be used in individualized education plans for children with visual impairments?

How are computers changing the education of visually impaired students? What are the limitations of computers in this regard?

The Visually Handicapped Child

Infancy through Pre-school Age The importance of vision stimulation

William V. Padula, O.D.
Susan J. Spungin, Ed. D.

The majority of children who are visually handicapped are not blind but have useable vision. Unfortunately, there are visually handicapped children treated as if they are blind and never given the opportunity to function as sighted individuals. Since vision is learned, all children must develop it through use. A child with a visual handicap may have difficulty developing it and have special needs that require types of aids and techniques to allow the child the opportunity to use his/her vision.

Why is vision so important?

Simply considering the physiology of the eyes, 70% of all the sensory nerves in the entire body come from the eyes. These nerves give information that not only enable us to see, but also reinforce our ability to coordinate movement, maintain balance, think, problem-solve and many other actions. For the child, vision is an extremely important process and greatly affects and influences the child's development.

When a child has an impairment to his or her sight, this means that the child's ability to function and perform in the environment has been affected because of either a reduction in acuity (reduced ability to see clearly) and/or a restriction in the child's field of vision (scope or peripheral extent of sight) and that is not correctable with ordinary eye glasses.

A child is considered **visually impaired** if he/she has 20/70 acuity or less in his/her best corrected eye. The child is considered **legally blind** if he/she has 20/200 acuity or less in the best corrected eye or a 20° field of vision or less. Visual acuity is a measurement used to describe the smallest size detail that a person can see at a particular distance. For example, a child with 20/200 acuity would have to be within 20 feet of the same object that another child with so-called normal acuity (20/70) could see from 200 feet away.

A child who is visually handicapped may qualify for federal or state funding to provide a special education program designed to meet his/her visual needs.The definitions of visual impairment and legal blindness are not functional ones. These definitions only use acuity and/or field measurements as a means to determine eligibility for services. Both of these measurements (visual acuity and visual field) do not indicate how the child uses his or her vision to function in their environment. A child may have better than 20/70 acuity (ie. 20/40) but have a significant interference with processing and understanding what they are seeing. In turn, that child's performance and functional abilities are affected.

Although the standard criteria used for classification (ie. legal blindness, visual impairment, etc.) is based on acuity and field measurements, the child's ability to use his/her vision effectively depends on many other factors. These classifications are a means to identify groups of people, however, generalizations about whether a person can or cannot function must be avoided. For example, two children who are the same age, may function quite differently. This is because their ability to use their remaining vision may vary. Therefore, the impairment is not the diminished acuity level or the field restriction, it is rather the interference with how the child uses his/her remaining vision. The acuity and field measurements do not relate function and performance. Function and performance relate to a complex interaction between the senses, the motor system, and the child's ability to perceptually manipulate these processes to establish meaningful relationships.

When there is a visual handicap, the child's performance and learning abilities will often be affected. This is because the child's dominant means for learning has been interfered with. In turn, delays in the child's development may result because the learning process has been interfered with. This doesn't mean that the child can't utilize other senses to learn with. If the child can compensate for his/her visual loss through high intelligence and a suitable environment to learn of other means, then a developmental delay may not occur. However, for the majority of visually handicapped children, visual interferences can greatly interrupt and delay their development.

Even before the child is born, the visual system is matching information received through other senses regarding position and balance to establish basic experiences which the child, after birth, will utilize to develop new relationships. After birth, the visual process leads in establishing perceptual experiences and learning necessary for normal development. Through the visual process, the child actively probes the environment, matching information through motor and sensory functions. In early development,the infant monitors all sensory and motor information and attempts to relate all information to his/her visual world. Once the information is matched visually, the infant develops a relationship and, in turn, a perceptual experience that is stored as a reference base to compare to new situations. In this way,development proceeds by the establishment of perceptual experiences and because of the general physiology and nature of the child, development progresses primarily as a function of vision with the strong support from the other senses.

This does not mean that the totally blind child, who has lost the ability to see, will not develop. The totally blind child, depending on factors of other physical abilities, intelligence, and environmental surroundings will compensate for the loss of vision by utilizing other senses to match information to develop the relationship to establish perceptual experiences. However, delays in development will occur because the child must wait for other physiologic sensory-motor functions and perceptual processes to mature to a level that meaningful relationships can be established.

For the visually impaired child, delopment will progress depending on the amount of interference created by the impairment. It is important to note that the amount of visual impairment (ie., acuity and/or field loss) is not directly proportional to delay in development. This is because the child will attempt to maximize his or her residual vision and depending on factors of other physical abilities, intelligence, and environmental surroundings may not demonstrate consistent development delays. The acuity loss (lowered ability to see clearly) or the field loss (constriction to the scope of a vision) does not mean that the child has a lesser ability to function. Function and development will depend on the three factors previously mentioned and how the child can adapt and compensate for the impairment.

The Multi-handicapped child

Over 50% of visually impaired children have additional physicial handicaps. These may range from severe gross motor impairments to minor impairments of fine motor control. Just because a child is physically impaired, it must not be taken for granted that the child is retarded or lacks the potentials for advanced learning. Again, the physical impairment (sensory and/or motor) is not directly related to an inability to develope the skills needed for learning. The latter depends upon the child's ability to adapt and compensate for the physical impairment by utilizing other motor and sensory processes to experience with. Therefore, delays in developement depend on whether the child can adequately manipulate his/her environment motor and sensory function to grasp meaningful relationships.

When a child has a visual handicap together with other physical impairments, delays in development become more predictable. The child will require comprehensive plans of care from a multidisciplinary team of professionals to help the child adapt, compensate and overcome his/her physical restrictions. It is important that one member of this multi-disciplinary team be a vision specialist (optometrist and/or opthalmologist) who understands low vision and the developmental needs of the child. The vision specialist should also work with other members of the team (ie. educator, physical therapist, speech and hearing specialist, etc.) to design therapy programs and prescribe whatever may be needed to improve the child's visual abilities to improve visual functioning. In this way, the child will be maximizing use of his or her vision which can then be used for learning and supporting normal development.

What can be done? – Low Vision

By understanding the importance of vision for the development of the child, when a visual impairment is suspected, the child should be taken, without delay, for a complete visual examination to a qualified optometrist or ophthalmologist. It may be determined that the child only needs glasses to improve his/her vision. In this case, glasses will be extremely important to support the development and the factors mentioned previously. A visual examination can be performed at any age, including early infancy. If a visual impairment is diagnosed, plans should then be made for the child to have a low vision examination. This examination is different from a routine visual examination, for this form of examination determines what can be done for the child beyond conventional glasses such as prescribing special optical aids that will improve the child's ability to see.

Optical aids vary in type. They range from simple hand held magnifiers to special types of telescopes and microscopes small enough to be mounted on glasses or even a closed circuit TV. The purpose of these aids is to magnify what the child is looking at so that he/she may be able to utilize his/her residual vision effectively to read, watch TV, spot signs, and street lights at a distance, and otherwise function visually. The optical aids vary in type and power, and the doctor specializing in low vision will be able to evaluate the child's vision and determine which type and power optical aid will be most effective.

Low vision services do not end with the prescription of an optical aid but begin there. A low vision examination performed as early as possible allows a team of professionals from many fields (low-vision specialists, educators, therapists, orientation and mobility specialists, etc.) to plan ahead for what the child's needs will be. Special programs can be designed to enable the child to maximize use of his/her vision. As previously discussed, some visually handicapped children are unable to use their residual vision effectively and, in turn, the impairment actually interferes with their development. The reason for this is that the child has never learned how to use his or her vision and, in turn, has suppressed it. For this child, a program of vision stimulation designed specifically for the child's needs and abilities, could be developed. Vision stimulation can be developed for children of any age. Of course, the younger the child the earlier his/her vision can be habilitated, thereby causing less of an interference with development.

According to Faye, Hood and Sprague (1975), all children whose vision measures light perception or better are candidates for a low vision evaluation and for utilization of low vision instruction and should receive both as long as they have vision problems. However, since vision is learned, a child will sometimes appear totally blind but actually have useable vision because that child has never learned to use his/her vision. Therefore, every child, regardless of whether it is believed the child is blind or not, should be given the opportunity to receive a low vision examination. Low vision services offer a comprehensive, multi-disciplinary approach toward affecting and improving the child's vision. Prescribed low vision optical aids together with other specially designed programs can allow the child to function visually to his or her maximum potential.

The next article will examine specific needs of the visually impaired child. Also, we will discuss the roles of professionals serving these children and various other resources in the U.S. for materials.

The Parent and Toddler Training Project for Visually Impaired and Blind Multihandicapped Children

Abstract: Numerous clinical reports have shown that many families with visually impaired or blind multihandicapped children have problems of social and emotional adjustment and that the development of seriously handicapped children is enhanced by early intervention. This article describes the Parent and Toddler Training (PATT) Project—research-based early intervention program—that serves visually impaired and blind multihandicapped infants and toddlers and their families. The purpose of this project is to 1) increase the social responsiveness of handicapped infants, 2) implement a psychoeducational intervention program to develop adequate parenting skills, 3) initiate specific treatment approaches with parents to reduce psychological distress and improve the quality of family life, and 4) collect quantifiable data that permit the assessment of the progress of all participants.

B. Klein; V.B. Van Hasselt; M. Trefelner; D.J. Sandstrom; P. Brandt-Snyder

Barbara Klein, M.S.W., former project coordinator and social worker (PATT Project), Western Pennsylvania School for Blind Children, 201 North Bellefield Avenue, Pittsburgh, PA 15213; Vincent B. Van Hasselt, Ph.D., former project director (PATT Project), and presently assistant professor of psychiatry, Department of Psychiatry and Human Behavior at the University of California-Irvine Medical Center, 101 City Drive South, Orange, CA 92668; Mary Trefelner, child development specialist (PATT Project); Dorothy Sandstrom, M.S., senior child development specialist (PATT Project); and Patrice Brandt-Snyder, M.S., former senior child specialist (PATT Project).

In recent years, special educators, psychologists, and child development specialists have directed increased attention to social functioning in young children (see reviews by Gresham, 1981; Strain & Kerr, 1981; Van Hasselt, Hersen, Whitehill, & Bellack, 1979). The heightened activity in this area is attributable, in part, to research that has found that problems in social adaptation may be associated with the quality of interpersonal relationships formed as early as infancy. A major developmental task for the first two years of life is to establish effective social interactions with others. This process is facilitated by the formation of a strong attachment (reciprocal relationship) between infants and their caregivers, usually their mothers (see the review by Campos, et al., 1983). The social interactions of handicapped infants, however, may be severely impaired (Odom, 1983). As Walker (1982) posited, "the handicapped infant may have qualities that affect his [or her] abilities as initiator, elicitor, responder, and maintainer of synchrony in the interactive bout. He or she may be less reinforcing,

Preparation of this article was facilitated by Grant No. G008302245 from the Handicapped Children's Early Education Program, U.S. Department of Education. The authors thank Judith A. Lorenzetty and Mary Jo Horgan for their assistance in preparing the manuscript.

less interesting, and more difficult as a social partner."

The potential for the disruption of the social relationships of handicapped infants and their caretakers is perhaps more clearly illustrated by the behavior of blind children. For example, smiling is regarded as potent behavior for promoting infant-adult interactions (Odom, 1983) and is considered an "indicator of the infant's participation in a social relationship. . . and of the strength of the developing attachment bond" (Warren, 1977). However, blind infants, in comparison to their sighted counterparts, have a low rate of smiling and the quality of their smiles is different (Fraiberg, 1970, 1977). Another elicitor of infant-adult interactions is the ability of infants to establish eye contact and then a gaze. The role of eye contact as a "releaser of appropriate and personal maternal responses" has been discussed in the developmental literature for many years (Bakeman & Brown, 1977; Robson, 1967). Although empirical data regarding the amount of eye contact established by blind infants is limited (see Als, 1985; Als, Tronick, & Brazelton, 1980a; 1980b). Warren (1977) suggested that this response is also deficient in blind infants. Moreover, Fraiberg (1974) found that mothers were disturbed by the absence of gaze in their blind infants. Thus, the blind infants' minimal smiling, eye contact, and absent gaze may affect their ability to engage in social interactions.

In addition, parental behaviors and difficulties in adjustment have a direct impact on the quality and quantity of infant-adult social exchanges and, hence, may adversely affect the parent-child relationship (Lowenfeld, 1971; Sommers, 1944). For example, parents who feel angry, sad, guilty, or depressed about their handicapped child may not be able to identify and appropriately interpret their blind infant's signals. Their difficulties in adjustment are underscored by early case studies that found psychiatric symptomatology (primarily maternal depression) in some parents of blind children (see, for example, Catena, 1961; Fraiberg & Freedman, 1964).

To prevent problems in the social and emotional adjustment of visually impaired and blind multihandicapped infants and their families, the Parent and Toddler Training (PATT) Project was developed in October of 1983 at the Western Pennsylvania School for Blind Children in Pittsburgh. PATT was initiated through a grant from the Handicapped Children's Early Education Program of the U.S. Department of Education. The purpose of the project is to 1) enhance the social responsivity of visually impaired and blind multihandicapped infants and toddlers; 2) provide a psychoeducational training program that develops adequate parenting skills in families with a handicapped infant; 3) initiate specific interventions with distressed parents to improve their overall psychological adjustment and the quality of family life; and 4) conduct comprehensive assessments that yield quantifiable data regarding patterns of interaction and adjustment in participating families.

Population served

The population served by PATT includes newborn to 3-year-old visually impaired and blind multihandicapped infants and toddlers from Western Pennsylvania and the surrounding tri-state area. The major criterion for eligibility is legal blindness or suspected legal blindness, as determined by ophthalmological evaluations. In addition to legal blindness, the multihandicapped population served by PATT includes infants with neurological conditions, cerebral palsy, and metabolic or endocrine diseases. Referrals to PATT are made by ophthalmologists, pediatricians, health care agencies, friends, or parents. Direct involvement by at least one significant caregiver (the mother, father, or foster parent) is required. When families are intact, efforts are made to include both parents; when the parents have separated or divorced, a significant other (a relative or close friend) is recruited as a support person. The project consists of four phases: assessment, training, booster sessions, and follow-up.

Assessment

Assessments of infants and families are carried out using a variety of procedures. First, parents complete a number of self-report measures to evaluate their level of social and emotional functioning, including the Beck Depression Inventory (Beck, 1967), Minnesota Multiphasic Personality Inventory (Dahlstrom & Welsh, 1960), Questionnaire on Resources and Stress (Holroyd, 1974), and the Hopkins Symptoms Checklist (Derogatis, et al., 1974). In addition, parents answer questions about their level of marital satisfaction on the Locke-Wallace Marital Satisfaction Scale (Locke & Wallace, 1957) and of family support on the Family Support Scale (Dunst & Jenkins, 1983). Their perceptions of their handicapped child are evaluated by their answers on the Infant Temperament Scale (Carey & McDevitt, 1978), the Toddler Temperament Scale (Fullard, McDevitt, & Carey, in press), Vision-Up (Wright, 1980), and their perceptions of any nonhandicapped children in the family are evaluated by the Child Behavior Checklist-Parent Form (Achenbach, 1978). When age-appropriate, the handicapped child's siblings complete the Youth Self-Report Inventory (Achenbach & Edelbrock, 1979) to determine possible behavioral problems. The handicapped infant is assessed via the Adaptive Performance Instrument (Consortium on Adaptive Performance Evaluation, 1978).

Second, behavioral observations of parent-child interactions (mother-infant, father-infant, and mother-father-infant combinations) in play- and task-oriented situations are conducted for each family. These interactions are videotaped and retrospectively rated using guidelines developed by Wilcox and Campbell (1986) to examine such factors as the type of behavioral cues exhibited by infants during interactions, the consistency of responding, reciprocity, and the engagement of the infants.

Third, both physical and occupational therapy consultants complete an evaluation of each infant to examine gross and fine motor development, respectively. During these assessments, parents are encouraged to ask questions about their child's gross or fine motor development and are instructed by the therapists in specific remedial activities.

Fourth, the social worker and the assessment specialist make a home visit to observe the infant in a natural environment. At this time, the mother is administered the Home Inventory (Caldwell & Bradley, 1978), for additional information about the child's home life.

All assessment data are reviewed by PATT staff and utilized to design an appropriate individualized treatment plan for each family. Families are reevaluated after they complete the training program and at a six-month follow-up. This information allows PATT staff to monitor any significant changes that may occur in the infant and the family and to address them accordingly.

Training

The PATT curriculum is implemented after reviewing the assessment data. PATT cotrainers (a social worker and a senior child development specialist) sequentially address the following topics: 1) early childhood development, 2) social development, 3) the family members' reactions, 4) behavioral management, 5) enhancing the infant's development, and 6) family communication and problem-solving. The components of the curriculum were selected on the basis of our previous clinical work and areas of need that have been identified in recent investigative efforts involving handicapped infants and their families (see Bricker, 1982). The project's curriculum offers parents information, training in a number of skills, and support to help them cope with current problems, as well as those that may arise.

Families participate in two-hour weekly sessions over a six-month period. They generally spend three to four two-hour sessions on each topic in the curriculum. Training includes a variety of components: didactic presentations, direct instruction, behavior rehearsal, feedback on performance, modeling, and role playing. In addition, homework assignments, in the form of self-monitoring and record-keeping of specific areas targeted in training, are used to monitor the progress of the infants and parents and to provide ongoing feedback to parents and staff.

The curriculum

As was noted, the PATT curriculum includes six topic areas designed to address the unique needs and difficulties of families with visually impaired or blind multihandicapped infants. These are outlined in the following sections.

Early child development

Visually impaired or blind multihandicapped infants may differ from nonimpaired infants in that they often exhibit significant, albeit not necessarily permanent, delays in most areas of development (Adelson & Fraiberg, 1974; Fraiberg, 1968, 1977; Scholl, 1986; Warren, 1977, 1984). Such delays may produce considerable stress in parents. Providing parents with adequate knowledge about development and responding to their questions and concerns, therefore, are important initial steps in diminishing their distress. This topic area presents an overview of the 1) normal sequence of development, 2) nature of developmental delays typically found in visually impaired or blind multihandicapped infants, and 3) similarities and differences between handicapped and nonhandicapped infants in attaining developmental milestones. Parents are encouraged to assist their infants to maximize their potential for development. When developmental delays occur, parents come to understand that with practice and adapted environmental experiences, their baby can make progress. Parents of multihandicapped infants are helped to understand the nature of the handicapping conditions, their synergistic effects, and their possible impact on their infants' overall development.

Social development

Parents' early interactions with their baby, their attitudes toward his or her disability, and the opportunities they provide are crucial to their child's short- and long-term adaptive functioning. As was previously noted, certain interactions foster the attachment between infants and their parents. When these behaviors are absent, deficient, or misunderstood, attachment may be delayed or seriously disrupted. This topic provides information on the social development of infants, the relationship of synchrony and reciprocity as they relate to parent-infant interactions, atypical or alternative cues that the visually handicapped infant may provide to parents, the types of decreased social responsiveness demonstrated in many visually handicapped infants (such as the lack of eye contact, delayed smiling, the tendency to be quiet and less mobile at the approach of a parent), and the impact of blindness on an infant's social development. To promote a healthy and reciprocal social relationship, parents are taught to identify their baby's interactive cues and to respond appropriately and consistently with the same (or even greater) quantity and quality of attention as they would give to a nonhandicapped infant.

Family reactions

As was mentioned earlier, numerous reports have described negative reactions, including stress, grief, anxiety, and depression, of parents to the diagnosis of a handicapping condition in their child (Beckman, 1983; Breslau, Staruch, & Mortimer, 1982; Catena; 1961; Fraiberg & Freedman, 1964; Froyd, 1973). The acknowledgement of these reactions and the realization of their commonality in many families can be of considerable therapeutic value to parents. Furthermore, a conceptualization of each member of the parental dyad as the primary support for the other helps to underscore the vital role of reciprocity in their relationship. In this topic, these issues are discussed to facilitate the couple's examination of their feelings, reactions, and attitudes and to help them begin to explore new ways of perceiving their infant and their relationship.

The reactions of the extended family can also have a significant impact on the family. For example, siblings of the handicapped child are a group that has received surprisingly little attention (see review by Skritic, Summers, Brotherson, & Turnbull, 1984). According to Clay (1961) and Bentovim (1972), the time and energy directed to the handicapped child often results in the neglect of other children in the family. The social isolation of the families also has a limiting effect on the breadth and scope of siblings' interpersonal behavior. Bentovim (1972) argued that the presence of a handicapped child may lead to the following responses of siblings: 1) aggressive, attention-seeking behavior, 2) anxiety, 3) depression, and 4) jealousy. These problems are discussed to help parents understand the various reasons for the reactions of siblings and extended family members and to encourage parents to seek alternative ways to elicit more understanding and support.

Behavioral management

Most parents use some techniques (for instance, positive reinforcement and punishment) that are based on learning principles in dealing with their children. However, such approaches often are ineffective because they are applied incorrectly or unsystematically. An understanding of fundamental learning principles and the use of behavioral interventions enables parents to manage problems related to their infants, as well as other children in the family, more effectively. In this topic, parents are trained to use specific behavioral managment strategies and to implement behavioral intervention programs at home. In one case, parents were taught to plan and execute a behavioral management program for their visually impaired toddler who displayed high rates of eye pressing. They were asked to keep a record for two weeks of the number of times the problem behavior occurred. The staff charted these baseline (pretreatment) data (Figure 1), and then directed the parents to begin a program of positive reinforcement and contingent hands restraint in the following manner. First, each time the toddler pressed his eyes, the parent was to give a loud verbal cue ("Stop!") and restrain the toddler's hands in front of him for 30 seconds. At the end of this interval, the parent released the toddler's hands and continued with regular activities. The parents were also instructed to provide positive reinforcement in the form of verbal praise when the toddler was engaged in appropriate motor activities. As Figure 1 shows, one week of this treatment procedure resulted in a significant suppression of eye-pressing behavior. The parents reported that when the child's hands started in the direction of his eyes, all they eventually had to do was use the verbal cue and he would immediately put his hands down.

Enhancing the infant's development
Mothers often report feeling stressed and overwhelmed by the increased burden and responsibilities of caring for their handicapped infants. Although the role of fathers in these families has only recently been the focus of investigation, the research has indicated that the level of the father's involvement may have a significant effect on 1) the infant's overall development, 2) effectiveness and satisfaction of both the father and the mother, and 3) the quality of the marital relationship (Meyer, 1986; Meyer, Vadasy, Fewell, & Schell, 1982; Vadasy, Fewell, Meyer, & Greenberg, 1985; Vadasy, et al., 1986). This topic provides strategies for increasing the father's role in care giving activities with the handicapped child. A skills-training format is used to enhance the fathers' ability to perform certian daily routines, such as bathing and feeding, with their handicapped child.

A second aspect of this topic involves instructing parents in a variety of infant-stimulation techniques and play skills that are relevant to their handicapped infants. Some of these procedures involve showing parents how to use 1) hand-over-hand skills to teach visually impaired children to wind up a toy, drink from a cup, or feed themselves, 2) objects to elicit motor and verbal responses from their infants, and 3) tactile and kinesthetic stimulation to compensate for diminished sensory input. Parents are taught that play stimulation activities should include practice in movement, communication, and a variety of sensory experiences. They then begin to identify appropriate skills that can be shaped to become part of the handicapped children's behavioral repertoire.

Family communication and problem solving
The birth of any baby requires the devotion of substantial time and energy to the tasks and demands of caregiving. In the case of handicapped infants in general and the visually impaired infants in particular, the commitments of time, energy, and responsibilities are even greater and often place a tremendous strain on the marital relationship (Blacher, 1984; Gath, 1977; Jan, Freeman, & Scott, 1977; Tavormina, et al., 1981). Studies have found that parents of handicapped children spend less time together and often decrease the extent of their individual social activities. The well-documented association between marital satisfaction and parental effectiveness underscores the need for intervention in this area (Emery, 1982; Long, Forehand, Fauber, & Brody, 1987; Margolin, 1981).

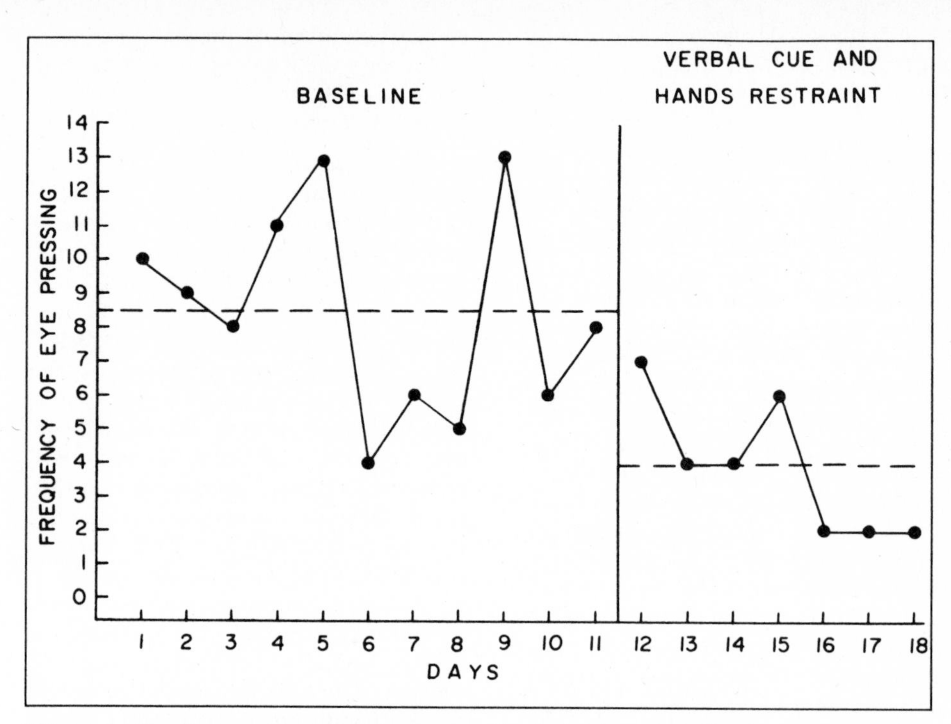

Figure 1. Baseline and treatment phases of a behavior modification program implemented to reduce eye pressing in a visually impaired toddler.

The concept of marital partners as mutual support persons is emphasized in this topic. Parents are trained in specific skills to increase the efficacy of their efforts to effect changes in their relationships. The primary aim is to resolve conflicts through behavioral and cognitive changes. Role-play and problem-solving tasks are utilized to give parents the opportunity to practice requisite skills. Parents are provided with guidelines for simplifying the process of decision-making and then assigned the task of solving relevant family or marital problems. When parents return for their next session, they discuss the specific steps taken at home to resolve conflicts or diminish distress.

Booster sessions and follow-up
Booster sessions are reviews of areas in which the parents were trained. They take place after the families' participation in the PATT program has formally ended. In this phase, parents meet monthly with staff for about three to six months. The topics that are covered in the booster sessions depend on the problems, deficits, concerns, and questions that have arisen in the preceding period. The purposes of booster sessions are to 1) consolidate the gains made during the project's training phase, 2) facilitate the maintenance and generalization of intervention effects, and 3) provide parents with continued support, information, and feedback.

During the next six months, booster sessions are faded to bimonthly meetings. During this follow-up period, the PATT staff provides ongoing coordination and consultation with community-based agencies in an effort to maintain a consistent overall program.

Other parental activities
With the multitudinous tasks that are inherent in the care of a visually impaired or multihandicapped infant, it is not unusual for parents to feel isolated from the mainstream of normal life. Throughout the course of the PATT project, various social activities (for example, birthday parties for infants, holiday celebrations, and visits to the zoo) are scheduled for families. Siblings are always included and grandparents often participate as well. Opportunities are also provided for parents to meet and network with other parents of visually impaired or multihandicapped children through their participation in such voluntary activities as a parent support group that meets once a month. In the group, the parents are responsible for planning and conducting their own meetings, and guest speakers are invited to discuss pertinent issues concerning handicapped children and their families.

Conclusion
By providing efficacious early intervention

to families with visually impaired or blind multihandicapped infants and toddlers, PATT is attempting to prevent possible social and emotional difficulties in these children later in life. A more immediate goal is to decrease the stress of and improve adaptation in families. A major impetus for PATT is the realization that few such models are available to address the complexities of parenting a young blind or multihandicapped child.

Observational and self-report data are providing important information about the deficits and strengths of families who have visually impaired and multihandicapped infants. We believe that the evaluation and training components developed in this project will be of considerable value to families with such infants or toddlers. Furthermore, the PATT project is replicable and compatible with a variety of special education systems. Indeed, PATT already is being replicated in a rural setting to contrast the experiences of an urban-based program with that of a less densely populated area in which services are scarce.

The impact of PATT on participating children and families has yet to be empirically determined. However, preliminary analyses and anecdotal reports from families seem to suggest the utility of this effort. Data pertaining to the assessment of infant and family functioning and treatment outcome will be disseminated soon.

References

Achenbach, T. (1978). The child behavior profile: I. Boys age 6–11. *Journal of Consulting & Clinical Psychology,* **46,** 478–488.

Achenbach, T., & Edelbrock, C. (1979). The child behavior profile: II. Boys age 12–16 and girls age 6–11 and 12–16. *Journal of Consulting & Clinical Child Psychology,* **47,** 223–233.

Adelson, E., & Fraiberg, S. (1974). Gross motor development in infants blind from birth. *Child Development,* **45,** 114–126.

Als, H. (1985). Reciprocity and autonomy: Parenting a blind infant. *Zero to Three,* **5,** 8–10.

Als, H., Tronick, E., & Brazelton, T.B. (1980a). Affective reciprocity and the development of autonomy. *Journal of the American Academy of Child Psychiatry,* **19,** 22–40.

Als, H., Tronick, E., & Brazelton, T.B. (1980b). Stages of early behavioral organization: The study of a sighted infant and a blind infant in interaction with their mothers. In T.M. Field, D. Stern, A. Sostek, & S. Goldberg (eds.). *High-risk infants and children: Adult and peer interactions.* New York: Academic Press.

Bakeman, R., & Brown, J.V. (1977). Behavioral dialogues: An approach to the assessment of mother-infant interaction. *Child Development,* **48,** 195–208.

Beck, A.T. (1967). *Depression: Causes and treatment.* Philadelphia: University of Pennsylvania Press.

Beckman, P.J. (1983). Influence of selected child characteristics on stress in families of handicapped infants. *American Journal of Mental Deficiency,* **88,** 150–156.

Bentovim, A. (1972). Handicapped pre-school children and their families: Effects on child's early emotional development. *British Medical Journal,* **9,** 634–637.

Blacher, J. (ed.) (1984). *Severely handicapped young children and their families: Research in review.* New York: Academic Press.

Breslau, N., Staruch, K.S., & Mortimer, E.A. (1982). Psychological distress in mothers of disabled children. *American Journal of Diseases of Children,* **136,** 682–686.

Bricker, D.D. (ed.) (1982). *Intervention with at-risk and handicapped infants: From research to application.* Baltimore: University Park Press.

Caldwell, B., & Bradley, R. (1978). *Home observation of the environment.* Unpublished manuscript, University of Arkansas at Little Rock

Campos, J., Barrett, K., Lamb, M., Goldsmith, H., & Stenberg, C. (1983). Socioemotional development. In P. Mussen (ed.). *Handbook of Child Psychology, 4th ed., Vol. 2: Infancy.* New York: John Wiley & Sons.

Consortium on Adaptive Performance Evaluation (1978). *Adaptive assessment for evaluating the progress of severely profoundly handicapped children functioning between birth and 2 years.* Annual report of a field-initiated research project funded by the Bureau of Education for the Handicapped.

Carey, W.B., & McDevitt, S.C. (1978). Revision of the Infant Temperament Questionnaire. *Pediatrics,* **61,** 735–739.

Catena, J. (1961). Pre-adolescence: The caseworker and the family. *New Outlook for the Blind,* **55,** 297–299.

Clay, F. (1961). Social work and the blind child. *New Outlook for the Blind,* **55,** 321–325.

Dahlstrom, W.G., & Welsh, G.S. (1960). *MMPI handbook.* Minneapolis: University of Minnesota Press.

Dunst, C.J., & Jenkins, V. (1983). *The family support scale: Reliability and validity.* Morganton, NC: Family, Infant and Preschool Program, Western Carolina Center.

Derogatis, L.R., Lipman, R.S., Rickels, D., Uhlenhuth, E.H., & Covi, L. (1974). The Hopkins Symptom Checklist (HSCL): A self-report symptom inventory. *Behavioral Science,* **19,** 1–15.

Emery, R.E. (1982). Interparental conflict and the children of discord and divorce. *Psychological Bulletin,* **92,** 310–330.

Fraiberg, S. (1968). Parallel and divergent patterns in blind and sighted infants. *Psychoanalytic Study of the Child,* **23,** 264–300.

Fraiberg, S. (1970). Smiling and stranger reaction in blind infants. In J. Hellmuth (ed.). *Exceptional infant.* New York: Brunner-Mazel.

Fraiberg, S. (1974). Blind infants and their mothers: An examination of the sign system. In M. Lewis & L. Rosenblum (eds.). *The effect of the infant on its caregiver.* New York: John Wiley & Sons.

Fraiberg, S. (1977). *Insights from the blind.* New York: Basic Books.

Fraiberg, S., & Freedman, D. (1964). Studies in the ego-development of the congenitally blind child. *Psychoanalytic Study of the Child,* **19,** 155–169.

Froyd, H.E. (1973). Counseling families of severely visually handicapped children. *New Outlook for the Blind,* **67,** 251–257.

Fullard, W., McDevitt, S.C., Carey, W.B. (in press). Assessing temperament in one to three year old children. *Journal of Pediatric Psychology.*

Gath, A. (1977). The impact of an abnormal child upon the parents. *British Journal of Psychiatry,* **130,** 405–410.

Gresham, F.M. (1981). Social skills training with handicapped children: A review. *Review of Educational Research,* **51,** 139–176.

Holroyd, J. (1974). The Questionnaire on Resources and Stress: An instrument to measure family response to a handicapped member. *Journal of Community Psychology,* **2,** 92–94.

Jan, J.E., Freeman, R.D., & Scott, E.P. (eds.) (1977). *Visual impairment in children and adolescents.* New York: Grune & Stratton.

Locke, H.J., & Wallace, K.M. (1957). Short marital adjustment and prediction tests: Their reliability and validity. *Marriage & Family Living,* **42,** 118–123.

Long, N., Forehand, R., Fauber, R., & Brody, G.H. (1987). Self-perceived and independently observed competence of young adolescents as a function of parental marital conflict and recent divorce. *Journal of Abnormal Child Psychology,* **15,** 15–28.

Lowenfeld, B. (1971). *Our blind children: Growing and learning with them.* Springfield, IL: Charles C Thomas

Margolin, G. (1981). The reciprocal relationship between marital and child problems. In J.P. Vincent (ed.). *Advances in family intervention, assessment and theory: An annual compilation of research* (Vol. 2). Greenwich, CT: JAI Press.

Meyer, D.J. (1986). Fathers of children with mental handicaps. In M.E. Lamb (ed.). *The father's role: Applied perspectives.* New York: John Wiley & Sons.

Meyer, D.J., Vadasy, P.F., Fewell, R.R., & Schell, G. (1982). Involving fathers of handicapped infants: Translating research into program goals. *Journal of the Division for Early Childhood,* **5,** 64–72.

Odom, S. (1983). The development of social interchanges. In S. Garwood & R. Fewell (eds.). *Educating handicapped infants: Issues in development and intervention.* Rockville, MD: Aspen.

Robson, K.S. (1967). The role of eye-to-eye contact in maternal-infant attachment. *Journal of Clinical Psychiatry,* **8,** 13.

Scholl, G.T. (1986). Growth and development. In G.T. Scholl (ed.). *Foundations of education for blind and visually handicapped children and youth: Theory and practice.* New York: American Foundation for the Blind.

Skritic, T.M., Summers, J.A., Brotherson, M.J., & Turnbull, A.P. (1984). Severely handicapped children and their brothers and sisters. In J. Blacher (ed.). *Severely handicapped young children and their families: Research in review.* New York: Academic Press.

Sommers, V.S. (1944). *The influence of parental attitudes and social environment on the personality development of the adolescent blind.* New York: American Foundation for the Blind.

Strain, P.S., & Kerr, M.M. (1981). Modifying children's social withdrawal: Issues in assessment and clinical intervention. In M. Hersen, R.M. Eisler, & P.M. Miller (eds). *Progress in behavior modification* (Vol. 2). New York: Academic Press.

Tavormina, J.B., Boll, T.J., Dunn, N.J., Luscomb, R.L., & Taylor, J.R. (1981). Psychosocial effects on parents of raising a physically handicapped child. *Journal of Abnormal Child Psychology,* **9,** 121–131.

Vadasy, P.F., Fewell, R.R., Meyer, D.J., & Greenberg, M.T. (1985). Supporting fathers of handicapped young children: Preliminary findings of program effects. *Analysis and Intervention in Developmental Disabilities,* **5,** 151–163.

Vadasy, P.F., Fewell, R.R., Greenberg, M.T., Dermond, N.L., & Meyer, D.J. (1986). Follow-up evaluation of the effects of involvement in the fathers program. *Topics in Early Childhood Special Education,* **2,** 16–31.

Van Hasselt, V.B., Hersen, M., Whitehill, M.B., & Bellack, A.B. (1979). Social skill assessment and training for children: An evaluative review. *Behaviour Research and Therapy,* **17,** 413–437.

Walker, J. (1982). Social interactions of handicapped infants. In D.D. Bricker (ed.). *Intervention with at-risk and handicapped infants: From research to application.* Baltimore: University Park Press.

Warren, D.H. (1977). *Blindness and early childhood development.* New York: American Foundation for the Blind.

Warren, D.H. (1984). *Blindness and early childhood development* (rev. ed.). New York: American Foundation for the Blind.

Wilcox, M.J., & Campbell, P.H. (1986). Interaction patterns of mothers and their infants with severe handicaps. Paper presented to Division of Early Childhood Conference on Children with Special Needs, Louisville.

Wright, F.J., (1980). Project Vision-Up Assessment, validity and reliability. Unpublished doctoral dissertation, Brigham Young University, Provo, UT.

A Model for Integrating Low Vision Services into Educational Programs

Randall T. Jose, Stephanie Labossiere, and Marsha Small

Randall T. Jose is director, University of Houston/Lighthouse of Houston Low Vision Clinic and a member of the faculty, University of Houston College of Optometry. Stephanie Labossiere is supervisor, Services for Visually Handicapped Students, Region IV Education Service Center, Houston, Texas. Marsha Small is supervisor, Programs for the Visually Handicapped, Houston Independent School District, Houston, Texas.

ABSTRACT: The need for routine annual low vision services for visually impaired children is gaining acceptance in most educational systems. However, the questions of costs, cost-effectiveness, professional responsibilities for various aspects of the low vision service, and delivery of this special vision care are begging for answers. This article discusses a model for integration of low vision services into a child's educational program.

The accepted definition of low vision service is "a professional evaluation(s) in which assessment, prescriptive, instructive and/or rehabilitative activities are provided in a coordinated, multidisciplinary setting for the visually-impaired child" (Johoda, 1981). Handing out optical aids, even if they improve the acuity, is not a low vision service. Prescribing an optical aid in a doctor's office without educational input is also not considered an appropriate low vision service.

A low vision assessment includes a behavioral assessment, which takes the child's psycho-social, cultural, socio-economic and psycho-physical needs into consideration. A clinical assessment is a quantitative measurement of the visual impairment that results in the dispensing of prescriptive low vision aids. The actual service is delivered as a series of comprehensive, interrelated, multi-disciplinary diagnostic tests and assessments/evaluations for the child who has low vision. The goal of the service is the prescription of low vision aids and/or training programs to enhance the child's visual performance.

Frequently, resistance must be overcome before low vision services can be provided to all visually handicapped children in a particular educational system. Such services are seen as too expensive as an immediate "add on" to already strained budgets. Classroom teachers and teachers of the visually handicapped will require specialized training. Schools will need to find a source from which to purchase the low vision aids. School personnel argue that these services will disrupt other educational activities the child is involved in, that the information gained through the low vision assessment is difficult to integrate into the child's educational activity and goals, and that there is no proof that the services are cost effective and/or will impact positively on the child's education.

Despite these reservations, teachers realize the importance of low vision service to a child's educational program. In order to provide low vision services, a model of care compatible with these concerns needs to be developed. Designing an educational program for visually handicapped children without the benefits of low vision care is comparable to designing an educational program for a deaf child without evaluating the use of hearing aids or providing auditory testing. The designers of Project D.O.V.E.S. (Delivering Optimal Vision and Educational Services) had all of those considerations in mind in designing a service model which provided low vision evaluations to visually impaired students while developing skills to encourage cooperation between the teacher of visually handicapped students and low vision clinicians.

The premises underlying this service model were (1) low vision services are of value to the visually handicapped student; (2) there is an optimum delivery system for low vision services; (3) there is a unique and a shared role for the teacher of visually handicapped children and the low vision clinical team in the delivery of low vision services to the visually handicapped student; (4) on-going support and training to the teachers and the members of the clinical team are vital to the success of this effort; (5) effective communica-

Reprinted with permission from *Education of the Visually Handicapped,* Vol. XIX, No. 4, Winter 1988, pp. 157-166.

tion is vital to the ultimate impact of low vision services: (6) through interactions in this optical delivery system, the prescribing practices of the low vision clinician can be changed to benefit the student more effectively.

An informal survey of teachers indicated that transportation, finances, time out of school, lack of knowledge regarding optical systems, lack of follow-up in the school system, and a history of prescriptions ending up in desk drawers were the factors which dissuaded individuals from seeking low vision services. By utilizing the resources of the University of Houston College of Optometry, Region IV Education Service Center, Houston Independent School District, and the Lighthouse of Houston, the D.O.V.E.S. project was able to address those problems.

THE PROJECT

Because certified teachers of visually handicapped students were critical to the success of the project, only school districts with such teachers were chosen to participate. Each selected district designated one or more teachers who participated in four days of low vision training, provided a completed functional vision evaluation on each student, and attended the clinic examination with the selected student. Training took place over an eight-month period. In addition an administrator from each participating district attended the first day of training to ensure the cooperation and commitment of the district.

The project had four components: teacher training, a pre-clinical functional vision evaluation done for each child by a teacher, a clinical examination, and follow-up visits.

Teacher Training

Teachers in the program were pretested to determine the level of their familiarity with various aspects of low vision services and with the visual system of the impaired child. Having this information about teachers' knowledge made it possible to design a curriculum that would meet the specific needs of the participants.

During the first day of training the doctors and teachers developed a functional vision evaluation to be completed on each child before the clinic visit. Eye specialists conducted the training sessions, which consisted of a review of the optical functions of the eye, eye diseases and disorders, review of the examination process, and most importantly, basic techniques for training students in the use and care of low vision aids.

The last day of training was devoted to a posttest to measure changes in knowledge as a result of the workshops and clinical examinations. Clinician scores on the posttest also indicated an increase in awareness of students' educational programs. Also at the last session all participants critiqued the program and made suggestions for changes.

Functional Assessments

A functional assessment of the child by the teacher was required before the child could be examined by the low vision clinician. The correlation between clinically measured visual acuities and performance is well known to be poor. Either clinical or functional data are misleading when taken in isolation from other measurements and observations. The service model presented was organized to provide two indications of functional and clinical acuity. In the clinical measurements the actual loss of resolution due to an ocular disorder is measured. This is the child's impairment. How that loss of acuity or field, color vision, depth perception, etc., affects the child's ability to function normally in the classroom is the handicap. The handicapping effect of the impairment cannot be measured in the clinic. A functional evaluation of the child's ability to perform specified representative tasks in the home, school, and play environment is needed to determine the handicap. There are numbers of such functional assessments available (Barraga, 1980; Corn, 1983; Smith, 1982). These were reviewed and modified for this service model.

The Project D.O.V.E.S. functional vision evaluation addressed the following areas of visual functioning on an educational level:

1. *Reason for referral.* What problems does the student have? How is the student visually affected in school and at home? Does the student understand his visual diagnosis?
2. *Parent and teacher expectation.* What do the parents and/or the teacher expect to learn from the evaluation? What is their understanding of the visual problem?
3. *Medical history.* All eye medical information and other handicapping conditions.
4. *Observation of the student.* How the student functions in the classroom. The location of the student's seat in the room. How close the student is to objects such as a textbook or a toy. What type of lighting is preferred.
5. *Visual response.* Any abnormal appearance of the eye, head turn or tilt; scanning and tracking skills. Gross field checks will determine if further testing is indicated at the clinic.
6. *Near visual tasks.* The size of print for short term and long term reading. The distance at which the student is reading the material. Working distance for writing tasks. Type of paper and writing instrument.
7. *Intermediate tasks.* With the importance of technology affecting younger children, visual impairment problems should be checked for all school age children. If the student has a hobby, certain low vision aids may make the leisure activity more enjoyable.
8. *Distant visual tasks.* Optimal seating for the student

in the classroom, taking into consideration glares, size of print on chalkboard, color of the chalkboard or chalk, or the position in the room from which the teacher instructs. This area would screen for any obvious mobility problems within the school or outside.

With the information above, the strengths and weaknesses of the child's functional vision can be noted. The teacher would use his or her judgment to determine if other problems, such as behavior or attention span, affected the child's vision problem.

Clinical Examination

The optometrist received the functional assessment information prior to making the examination. This assessment plus discussions with the teacher at the time of the examination made the clinician somewhat familiar with the child. More importantly, specific educational goals for the examination were established.

The clinical examination consisted of (1) a review of available material and a completion of the child's history; (2) measurement of distant and near acuities utilizing special low vision charts; (3) trial frame refraction; (4) assessment of binocularity and quality of eye movement/fixation; (5) assessment of visual fields including Amsler Grid; (6) color vision evaluations; (7) assessment of illumination needs; (8) evaluation of low vision aids; (9) training in the use of tentatively prescribed aids for distant and/or near systems; (10) if necessary, provision for two to three weeks of loaner aids with appropriate training material; (11) discussion of the case with the teacher and the parent, if available, followed by a written letter; and (12) scheduling of follow-up examination(s).

Follow-up Visits

The teacher worked with the child in the classroom during the two or three week loaner period to determine the benefits and limitations of the device. Concerns of the student, teacher of the visually handicapped student, parents, and classroom teachers and reports of the successes and failures of the aid were discussed with the clinician.

At the second visit the optometrist reviewed all the information with the teachers, made necessary additional tests/evaluations, and initiated a final treatment plan or dispensed the prescribed low vision aid. In other situations further evaluations, assessments, or training regimens were recommended.

These follow-up visits became so important that an additional feature was added to the original model. The optometrists conducted follow-up visits in the classroom to evaluate the low vision systems prescribed. This visit gave the doctor the opportunity to work directly with teachers in the child's environment and to make effective modifications in the prescription based on the on-site evaluation. Teachers were given one-on-one time with the doctor to develop more in-depth understanding of the prescribed aids or a child's performance with the particular system. The experience gave the clinician greater insight into the needs of the student and teacher. This experience in the classroom allowed the doctor to prescribe more effectively for the educational setting. The exchange of information between educator and practitioner made both professionals more aware of each other's needs and responsibilities and led to more comfortable and frequent dialogue.

CHARACTERISTICS OF PROJECT D.O.V.E.S. CHILDREN

The program evaluated 110 children aged 6 to 18 years old, 80 in the Houston Independent School District and 30 in other districts. The children represented a broad socio-economic sample.

Completed records were available on 107 of the students. The highlights of these records are as follows:

Refractive Error. Only 11 of the 107 children were not able to have a refractive error determination made. This means that the number of "not testable" on reports should be at a minimum in any vision care program, if properly organized to allow coordinated evaluations between doctor, teacher, and parent.

Prescriptions. No recommendations were made for 13 of the children evaluated. They were functioning well with present glasses or with their habitual vision. Conventional prescriptions were provided for 23 children (21%), which points to the importance of a good refraction as part of the low vision service. An additional 20 children were sent to the contact lens clinic to determine the feasibility of utilizing special contact lenses to improve their functional vision. Sunfilters (sunglasses) were provided for 17 children after they demonstrated significant improvements in their independent travel skills with the filters. Since most of the children experienced good near acuity by holding materials close to their eyes, bifocals or reading lenses were not a significant treatment option.

Pathologies. The most prevent conditions causing visual impairment in this young population were cataract/aphakia (21), albinism (14), and optic atrophy (11).

A significant incidence of congenital nystagmus, glaucoma, retintis pigmentosa, micro-ophthalmus, RLF or ROP, myopic retinal detachment, and coloboma were noted. Only 5 of these children needed additional medical care as the school systems were helping the families maintain medical appointments.

Distant Acuity. Four children had acuities better than 20/40. Two of these had significant field losses causing their impairment. A total of 67 children (63%) were partially sighted or had acuities better than 20/200. This statistic clearly demonstrates the significance of the inappropriate use of 20/200 as a guideline for services. Only 6 children had acuities of light perception/form perception or less. This figure closely agrees with the commonly accepted statistic that 85% of the legally blind population has useful residual vision.

Near Acuity. These acuities were taken with the children holding the material at any distance they preferred. By using their own accommodation and holding the material close, 37 students (35%) could *see* magazine size print or smaller.

Seventy-four or 69% of the children seen in the clinic had the ability to function easily in the medium of print without optical intervention. The 37 children with 1.0M to 1.6M acuities (large print) are excellent candidates for the use of optical aids to allow them to function with regular print text at least for the majority of their classes. Only 89 children responded to a near acuity chart or printed symbol. Of these 89, only 6 had an acuity of 5M or less. These 6 are probably the only ones who would be considered for full-time CCTV use. We found a large percentage of the children relying heavily on the CCTV in their educational program instead of utilizing more practical optical systems, with the CCTV as a back-up system for specific tasks.

Additional data derived from the clinical evaluations of the students in this program are presented in Table 1.

Table 1. Additional Data for 107 Children in Project D.O.V.E.S.

Status	Number
Color vision	15 children had color vision defect.
Binocularity	22 children were binocular. 10 children were bi-ocular.
Visual fields	2 children showed significant central field losses. 34 children showed significant peripheral field losses. 12 children could not be tested with reliable results.
Illumination	23 children were photo-phobic. 17 children were recommended to use additional lighting.
Optical aids	32 children were using optical aids at the time of examination.
Large print	5 children were known to be using large print and were removed from this medium (option).

EDUCATIONAL IMPLICATIONS OF THE PROJECT

As expected, many students could now sit with the rest of the class and see the blackboard. The use of telescopes allowed viewing at a further distance. The students preferred sitting among their peers rather than in front of the class at the board. Likewise, near aids allowed many of the students to eliminate or reduce the use of large-print texts. Use of regular text allowed them to do extra reports and readings and to submit this work on time. They felt more like the "rest of the kids." The low vision aid offers a much better system of viewing pictures because photographs often are poorly enlarged in large-print books. Also an optical aid is a more portable system and is not as obvious to sighted peers. Most importantly, the students seemed to enjoy a higher level of independence. The teacher for the visually handicapped needed to intervene less because this aid did not necessitate the need for large-print materials or audio tapes. Many students progressed from a resource room program to an itinerant teacher program, which promoted mainstreaming.

The low vision reports were written in educational rather than medical terms. This broadened the support system available to the child by making more people aware of the child's abilities and limitations.

The doctor's reports also confirmed the teacher's observations of the child's performance in the functional evaluation. This gave the teacher more confidence in designing educational programs for the individual child.

The responses were generally positive. As with any program, there were misunderstandings and lack of follow-up on specific cases. These situations were also reflected in the comments from teachers. It is encouraging to note that because of the open and positive communication channels the program developed, almost all of these situations have now been addressed.

EVALUATION

All participants in the program received an evaluation questionnaire that supplemented the critique of the program at the final training session. The purpose of these evaluations was to highlight the positive aspects of Project D.O.V.E.S. and point out areas of weakness that can be addressed for later programs.

In delivering low vision services, participants agreed that clinic visits should be shortened for younger students and broken into two visits if necessary. A preliminary letter to parents describing their child's involvement in the program might have encouraged parents to accompany their child to the clinic, thus providing better follow-up care and acceptance by the family when low vision aids were prescribed. Additional clinic visits would have been beneficial in some cases where the student's vision was unstable and when follow-up was necessary.

To provide these follow-up services in the school setting, an optometrist and educator visited the student to determine if the recommendations made in the clinic were correct or the environmental conditions and optical aids prescribed in the clinic were the best system for the student in the classroom. In many cases the student was ready to be given a stronger optical aid after some practice with initial aid prescribed.

A team approach was designed between the teacher and low vision clinician to assess and prescribe the aids that would provide the most support to the student. Descriptive written reports followed the student's visit. Prior to the examination the teacher and clinician had the opportunity to discuss the functional vision results and goals of the teacher for the student. If more time for the pre-clinic visit had been available, the clinician might have been able to individualize the examination based on questions and concerns of the teachers. More doctor/teacher discussions throughout the examination were needed to discuss results. These discussions could have resulted in more active participation by the teacher in the decision-making process.

The training and support aspect of Project D.O.V.E.S. was designed to provide materials and training in low vision and optical aids. The teachers interviewed agreed that the two days of low vision training were invaluable in providing instruction to the student in the classroom. In addition, there were some problems with the loaner system, and students did not always get loaners at the time of the examination. It would been best for students to leave the clinic with the loaner aid while enthusiasm was fresh. In addition, better coordination between agencies was needed for more timely purchase of aids for students.

FUTURE IMPLICATIONS FOR DELIVERING LOW VISION SERVICES

Based on analysis of the project and teacher responses, anyone designing a program similar to Project D.O.V.E.S. should consider the following:

1. Providing shorter functional vision evaluations to the clinician and allowing five to ten minutes before the examination to discuss the evaluation.
2. Shortening the clinic visits and allowing two or three visits per child.
3. Providing the child with the low vision aid when it is prescribed and giving the teacher or Orientation and Mobility instructor procedures for instruction in the classroom and outdoors.
4. Having follow-up by an optometrist in the educational setting will reinforce the diagnosis or provide an opportunity to make changes in the original prescription.

By encouraging parent participation and interagency coordination, all people involved in the welfare of the student will be informed about the low vision services. It is a cost-effective program that can be maintained with modest expenditures as a continuing service to children.

Organizing and sustaining such a program of vision care takes constant attention and nurturing. It is a lot of work, but the results can be overwhelmingly successful! Enjoy the children; they are the best part of the program.

NOTES

This project was made possible through funding from the Texas Education Association. The authors appreciate the support of Dr. William Baldwin, dean, College of Optometry, University of Houston; Mrs. Vassar Dickerson, director, Deaf and Visually Impaired Program, Houston Independent School District; and Dr. Frances Stetson, coordinator for special education, Region IV Education Service Center, Houston.

REFERENCES

Bachman, O., & Inde, K. (1975). *Low vision training*. Malmo, Sweden: Liber Hermods.

Barraga, N. C., & Morris, J. (1980). *Program to develop efficiency in visual functioning*. Louisville, KY: American Printing House for the Blind.

Beliveau, M., & Smith, A. (1980). The interdisciplinary approach to low vision rehabilitation. *Proceedings From the 1980 Interdisciplinary Low Vision Workshop*. New York: American Foundation for the Blind.

Corn, A. L. (1983). Visual function: A theoretical model for individuals with low vision. *Journal of Visual Impairment & Blindness, 77*, 373–77.

Faye, E. E. (Ed.). (1984). *Clinical low vision (2nd Ed.)*. Boston: Little, Brown.

Goldie, D., Gormezano, S., & Raznik, P. (1986). Comprehensive low vision services for visually impaired children: A function of special education. *Journal of Visual Impairment & Blindness, 80* (7), 844–848.

Jahoda, M. A., Bleeker, R. W., & Collingwood, H. (1981). Low vision service standards. *National Accreditation Council for Agencies Serving the Blind and Visually Handicapped*, New York.

Jose, R. T. (Ed.). (1983). *Understanding low vision*. New York: American Foundation for the Blind.

Jose, R. T., Cummings, J., & McAdams, L. (1975). The model low vision clinical services: An interdisciplinary vision rehabilitation program. *New Outlook for the Blind, 69* (6), 249–54.

Overbury, O., & Brass, M. (1978). Improvement in visual acuity in partially and fully sighted subjects as a function of practice, feedback and instructional techniques. *Perceptual and Motor Skills, 46*, 815–22.

Smith, A., & Cote, K. (1982). *Look At Me*. Philadelphia: Philadelphia College of Optometry.

Watson, G., & Brug, R. V. (1983). Near training techniques. In R. Jose (Ed.), *Understanding low vision* (pp. 317–362). New York: American Foundation for the Blind.

Appropriate Education for VISUALLY HANDICAPPED STUDENTS

Geraldine T. Scholl

Geraldine T. Scholl *(CEC Chapter #551) is Professor of Education at the School of Education, The University of Michigan, Ann Arbor.*

■ The provisions of Public Law 94-142 (Education for All Handicapped Children Act of 1975) present many challenges to school administrators and teachers as they strive to implement appropriate educational programs for visually handicapped pupils. Three major challenges are assessment, placement in the least restrictive environment, and planning an appropriate program. Who are visually handicapped pupils? What special educational needs do they have that are unique to them because of their visual impairment? Finally, what should be included in their individualized education programs (IEP's) to assure them equal educational opportunities? This article will explore these questions, focusing on pupils whose only special education needs are those that accompany a visual impairment. (Additional adaptations are necessary when other handicapping conditions are present.)

Who Is Visually Handicapped?

Pupils with visual impairments constitute a relatively small portion of the total school population—approximately 1 in 1000—and they make up only about 1% of all handicapped pupils served in special education programs and services (Kirchner, 1985). Thus, a school district with 20,000 pupils might expect about 20 to have moderate to severe visual impairments that will require special educational programs and services. However, because of the heterogeneity of this population, it might not be possible to group those 20 pupils for educational purposes. Some of the reasons are as follows:

- They might represent the entire age span from birth through high school.
- They are very likely to have other impairments that may be more educationally handicapping than their visual impairments.
- They have a broad range of visual abilities.
- They have a broad range of intellectual abilities.
- They have educational needs that might require different service delivery systems.
- They may come from families with a wide variety of socioeconomic and cultural characteristics.
- They may have a minimal support system provided by their families.
- They may reside in geographical locations that preclude having a full continuum of services available to them.

Thus, teachers typically have limited opportunities to become familiar with the special educational needs of this small but heterogeneous population. A commitment by school administrators to provide appropriate educational programs for *all* children is required to assure equal educational opportunities.

Special Educational Needs

A visual impairment can modify the normal patterns of growth and development, creating barriers to learning. Visually handicapped students may have delayed concept development, must learn through other sensory channels, (e.g., touch and hearing), need specialized skills and equipment for learning, are limited in learning through observation and incidental learning, often require individualized instruction to learn specialized skills, and require unique strategies or adaptations to acquire necessary skills (California Leadership Action Team for the Visually Impaired, 1985).

The impact of these barriers will differ for each individual pupil, depending on the variables associated with the visual impairment (age of onset, degree of vision, etiology of the visual impairment); the presence of other educationally handicapping conditions such as mental retardation or emotional disturbance; attitudes of family, school, and community; and the social and cultural characteristics of the family.

From birth onward visual impairments limit or deprive pupils of a valuable source of sensory input. This may have an impact on cognitive development, causing delays and deficiencies that interfere with social, emotional, psychomotor, academic, and vocational development. Learning by visual imitation often is not possible and incidental learning is limited. Some concepts, for example, color and three dimensions, may never be acquired. To compensate for these deficits, pupils must be provided with specialized media, materi-

From *Teaching Exceptional Children*, Winter 1987, pp. 33-36.

A partially sighted volunteer (l) helps a totally blind student (r) develop her manual dexterity in the Work Activity Center.

als, equipment, and instruction in compensatory skills to learn to use their limited vision effectively and efficiently and to maximize the use of other sensory channels in the learning process, primarily hearing and touch. In implementing such a compensatory education program, school and family must cooperate to teach skills that other pupils learn naturally by visual observation.

The Educational Program

Modifications in assessment procedures, creative placement practices, and IEP's specifically designed to meet their unique educational needs are essential ingredients of educational programs designed to assist visually handicapped pupils overcome barriers to learning.

Modifications in Assessment

Identification of these pupils presents the first challenge to school personnel. Young children have no frame of reference to let the adults in their environment know that they have a vision problem. Routine vision screening programs may not be adequate since most screen only for distance vision. Therefore, parents and teachers must be aware of the signs of possible eye trouble, as shown in Figure 1. Teachers of pupils with other handicapping conditions especially must be aware of possible unidentified visual impairments that may hinder the progress of their pupils.

After visual impairment has been identified, the next step is to assess whether or not the impairment is educationally handicapping. Eligibility for special education programs and services usually is based on an eye examination by an ophthalmologist or optometrist. While this is a necessary component of a comprehensive assessment, the results often have little relevance for educational planning. A qualified teacher of visually handicapped pupils should be requested to administer a functional vision assessment.

Instruments designed for this purpose usually consist of checklists based on observation of the pupils performing visual tasks (see Jose, 1983; Swallow, Mangold, & Mangold, 1978). Functional vision assessments coupled with medical eye examinations are helpful in determining what pupils see and how well they are using the vision they have. For pupils who retain some vision, an optometrist may be consulted to determine whether or not a low-vision aid might be useful.

Although an assessment of the visual impairment is the critical component for determining eligibility for services, other areas such as intellectual functioning, emotional-social skills, and career-vocational skills should also be assessed in order to develop the IEP. Tests specifically designed for pupils with visual impairments are few in number; yet they are critical since the use of instruments standardized on other populations is questionable (Warren, 1984). (See Bauman & Knopf, 1979; Hall, Scholl, & Swallow, 1986; Scholl & Schnur, 1976; Swallow, 1981 for lists.)

Teachers of visually handicapped pupils should participate in planning the assessment and should function as consultants to school psychologists so that the comprehensive assessment of the pupil's abilities can lead to an appropriate IEP (Morse, 1975; Spungin & Swallow, 1977). Informal or nonstandardized assessment procedures such as observation, interviews, and curriculum-based approaches may yield more meaningful educational information. (See Hall et al., 1986; Oka & Scholl, 1985; Swallow et al., 1978; and Tucker, 1981 for descriptions of these alternatives.)

Creative Placement Practices

Selecting an appropriate placement probably presents the greatest challenge to administrators. A full continuum of

Figure 1

SIGNS OF POSSIBLE EYE TROUBLE IN CHILDREN

Behavior

- Rubs eyes excessively
- Shuts or covers one eye, tilts head or thrusts head forward
- Has difficulty in reading or in other work requiring close use of the eyes
- Blinks more than usual or is irritable when doing close work
- Is unable to see distant things clearly
- Squints eyelids together or frowns

Appearance

- Crossed eyes
- Red-rimmed, encrusted, or swollen eyelids
- Inflamed or watery eyes
- Recurring styes

Complaints

- Eyes itch, burn, or feel scratchy
- Cannot see well
- Dizziness, headaches, or nausea following close eye work
- Blurred or double vision

Adapted from NSPB (1978).

services for pupils with visual impairments as required by P.L. 94-142 is not likely to be available in the typical school district, resulting in school administrators sometimes considering placement in another special class or program in the school district or in a residential school. However, these options may not be appropriate for many pupils. The decision should be based on what is most appropriate for each student, and this often requires creative planning.

Education of visually handicapped pupils in integrated settings can be successful only with the specialized help of professionals qualified to understand and interpret the educational needs unique to the visual impairment and regular teachers who are provided with the support they need to work effectively in meeting those needs. Cooperation with local agencies and organizations, making use of all available community resources, pooling resources to encompass a wider geographical area, and professional development for all regular school personnel may help the school district with few visually handicapped pupils create the multiple program options necessary for appropriate placements. Several states use the intermediate school district organizational structure effectively to serve low-prevalence groups with, for example, one district operating the program for hearing impaired students and another for the visually impaired populations of both districts.

Individualized Education Programs

All components of the regular curriculum offered to nonhandicapped pupils should also be available to visually handicapped pupils, even including the classroom activities that accompany driver education. The IEP should detail which of these instructional areas a particular pupil should study with nonhandicapped peers.

To meet their special education needs, visually handicapped pupils require instruction from specialists and use of special techniques in certain areas. In the communication skills area, they need instruction in the following:

- Reading-tactile forms (braille and Optacon).
- Reading-auditory forms (readers, talking books, Kurzweil Machine, and cassettes).
- Reading-print forms (large type and low-vision aids).
- Writing (Braillewriter, slate and stylus, handwriting, and typewriter).
- Computer literacy.

Visual efficiency training should include nonverbal communication, science/mathematics, social studies, map reading, and reference skills. Additional instructional areas include concept development, orientation and mobility, and independent living skills.

Substitutes for the typical visual materials used in classrooms are essential, including textbooks—in braille for some, in large print for others—and recorded materials. The Optacon should be provided for tactile readers. The Optacon is a device that enables blind students to read regular print; images on the retina of a miniature camera activate tiny pins to vibrate in the shape of the letters so that they can be perceived by the finger. Volunteer readers can be recruited from local agencies or the nonhandicapped student population to help out when materials in these media are not accessible. For some pupils with very limited vision, low-vision aids can provide access to visual materials. These aids may include hand-held magnifiers, telescopes, or closed-circuit televisions.

Teachers of the visually handicapped or the state department of education consultant for the visually handicapped are the best resourses for locating such materials. Some instructional materials resource centers provide valuable assistance in procuring needed materials. Additional teaching suggestions include the following:

- Braillewriters, slates, and styli to facilitate written communication for pupils who are tactile learners.
- Felt tip pens and wide lined paper for those who are visual learners.
- Cassettes for pupils with physical disabilities that inhibit the use of their hands or whose vision loss is recent.
- Typewriters for all visually handicapped pupils.
- Microcomputers with large print, braille, and voice output options.

Pupils with visual impairments often are limited in their ability to move about safely, gracefully, and easily. Qualified teachers can provide instruction in orientation and mobility skills. Additional work in physical education is helpful to improve posture, fitness, orientation, and mobility skills.

Because visual impairment may prohibit students from learning by visual imitation, their independent living and social skills such as self-care in dressing and eating are often limited and must be taught, frequently through individualized instruction. Social skills areas such as getting along with peers, engaging in turn taking in conversation, and other social graces often require direct

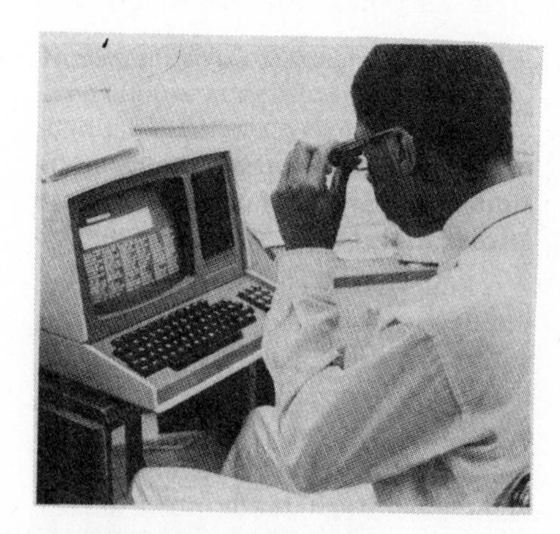

A student uses a prescription telescopic lens to help him read the screen of a computer.

instruction. These areas are the joint responsibility of parents and both regular and special education teachers.

Except for those who have no vision, all pupils with visual impairments should be instructed in techniques that will help them use their vision more effectively and efficiently. This includes special instruction in visual efficiency as well as the proper use of specialized materials and equipment and appropriate low-vision aids. Again, teachers of visually handicapped pupils are the best suited to help pupils in these areas.

Nonacademic or extracurricular experiences, including clubs, recess, and athletics, should not be neglected. Play is an important part in the life of all pupils and provides experiences in social learning. Visually handicapped pupils may need help in joining into games and other physical activities on the playground. Skill in indoor games should also be developed to provide future leisure activities. When age-appropriate, participation in community activities such as Scouts should be introduced.

Conclusion

Visually handicapped pupils are a small group of handicapped pupils who are more similar to than different from their nonhandicapped peers. Their visual impairment is, in general, little known and understood, so that they are often considered more different than they actually are.

They have the same educational needs as all other pupils. The major difference lies in their need for compensatory education to meet their unique educational requirements. School administrators and teachers must work in concert with parents and other professional personnel qualified in the area of visual impairments to ensure that the IEP includes the full range of instructional areas: those studied with their nonhandicapped peers, those that require special instruction, and those outside of the school curriculum that are essential to enable them to compete with their nonhandicapped peers when they move into the adult world.

References

Bauman, M. K., & Knopf, C. A. (1979). Psychological tests used with blind and visually handicapped persons. *School Psychology Digest, 8,* 257-270.

California Leadership Action Team for the Visually Impaired. (1985). *Statement of educational needs of visually impaired students in California.* San Francisco, CA: American Foundation for the Blind.

Hall, A., Scholl, G. T., & Swallow, R. M. (1986). Assessment. In G. T. Scholl (Ed.), *Foundation of education for blind and visually handicapped children and youth: Theory and practice* (pp.187-214). New York: American Foundation for the Blind.

Jose, R. T. (1983). *Understanding low vision.* New York: American Foundation for the blind.

Kirchner, C. (1985). *Data on blindness and visual impairment in the U.S.* New York: American Foundation for the Blind.

Morse, J. L. (1975). Answering the questions of the psychologist assessing the visually handicapped child. *The New Outlook for the Blind, 69,* 350-353.

National Society to Prevent Blindness (NSPB). (1978). *Signs of possible eye trouble in children.* (Pub. G-102.) New York: Author.

Oka, E., & Scholl, G. T. (1985). Non-test-based approaches to assessment. In G. T. Scholl (Ed.), *The school psychologist and the exceptional child* (pp. 39-59). Reston, VA: The Council for Exceptional Children.

Scholl, G. T., & Schnur, R. (1976). *Measures of psychological, vocational, & educational functioning in the blind and visually handicapped.* New York: American Foundation for the Blind.

Spungin, S. J., & Swallow, R.-M. (1977). Psychological assessment: Role of psychologist to teacher of the visually handicapped. In Swallow, R.-M. (Ed.) *Assessment for visually handicapped children and youth* (pp. 67-82). New York: American Foundation for the Blind.

Swallow, R.-M. (Ed.). (1977). *Assessment for visually handicapped children and youth.* New York: American Foundation for the Blind.

Swallow, R.-M. (1981). Fifty assessment instruments commonly used with blind and partially seeing individuals. *Journal of Visual Impairment and Blindness, 75,* 65-72.

Swallow, R.-M., Mangold, S., & Mangold, P. (1978). *Informal assessment of developmental skills for visually handicapped students.* New York: American Foundation for the Blind.

Tucker, J. A. (1981). *Non test-based assessment: A training module.* Minneapolis, MN: National School Psychology Inservice Training Network, University of Minnesota.

Warren, D. (1984). *Blindness and early childhood development* (2nd ed.). New York: American Foundation for the Blind.

Evaluating Microcomputer Access Technology for Use by Visually Impaired Students

Sandra Ruconich

Sandra Ruconich is the director of educational technology at the Hadley School for the Blind in Winnetka, Illinois.

ABSTRACT: A variety of devices exist which enable visually impaired students to gain access to microcomputers. In an effort to provide guidance for students, professionals, and others in the field who may be called upon to evaluate the merits of such devices, this article outlines the advantages and limitations of each generic kind of microcomputer access technology used by visually impaired persons. Factors such as how the device is to be used are also considered.

The computer revolution is here. There are computers and microprocessors everywhere—in grocery-store checkout lines, microwave ovens, cars, drink vending machines, and a host of other places. This special issue of *Education of the Visually Handicapped* is evidence that computers are being used by visually impaired students as well as by their seeing peers.

Many kinds of technology—electronic braille, paper braille, Optacon, synthetic speech, and enlarged print—currently enable these visually impaired students to access computers. Each possesses unique advantages as well as unique limitations, and it can be difficult to identify them all. This article is therefore an attempt to outline the advantages and limitations of each kind of computer access technology in order to enable professionals, students, and others in the field to make a more informed choice of the technology which best meets their needs.

Electronic Braille

Visually impaired students who use braille as their primary reading medium have had the most difficulty gaining access to microcomputers. One way students who read braille are now able to gain such access is through electronic braille devices. These microprocessor-based devices use magnetic audio cassette tapes or disks to store and retrieve information written in braille. The six keys ordinarily employed in braille-writing devices allow the user to send information to the computer. Information sent from the computer is displayed to the user through a refreshable braille display of 20 or more characters in a line of movable pins representing braille dots. An example of such an electronic braille device is the VersaBraille, manufactured by Telesensory Systems, Inc.

Advantages

One of the greatest advantages of electronic braille devices is the ability to send as well as receive information through a single instrument. As will become apparent later in this article, not all kinds of computer access technology used by visually impaired persons are so versatile. A second advantage of electronic braille is its extensive and compact storage capability. Whereas each paper braille character requires 1/4 inch of horizontal line space and each line requires 2/5 inch of vertical page space, an ordinary 60-minute cassette tape can store the equivalent of 400 pages of bulky paper braille. Disk capacity is even more extensive. In addition, electronic braille provides a one-to-one print-to-braille representation at a high rate of accuracy. By

Reprinted with permission from *Education of the Visually Handicapped*, Vol. XV, No. 4, Winter 1984, pp. 119-125.

contrast, synthetic-speech computer access devices may correctly pronounce a misspelled word or incorrectly—and perhaps misleadingly—pronounce a correctly spelled word. Another advantage of electronic braille is the speed at which it can be read and produced. Students can generally read electronic braille significantly more rapidly than they can read tactile counterparts of print as produced by the Optacon. In addition, the VersaBraille produces characters sent from the computer at approximately 100 characters per second, a rate significantly faster than is possible with some other access devices.

Limitations

Like any access technology, electronic braille has limitations as well as advantages. Currently available electronic braille devices present information only in displays of 20 to 40 braille cells on a single line, so that only one line of information is available at any time. Thus, although it is possible to search for information, the tactile information search process is more difficult and time-consuming than it would be if an entire screenful of information was immediately accessible for scanning and searching. An additional constraint is that all information is provided in computer braille, a combination of grade 1 (uncontracted braille), Nemeth code numbers, and selected punctuation marks and other symbols unique to the computer braille code. This fact, together with the short line length of electronic braille devices, means that users read computer information more slowly and with a different style of touch reading than they do when reading paper braille. The single-line format also precludes the display of tactile graphics (drawings composed of raised dots or lines) which are essential to many computer programs and games. A further disadvantage is that the stored information is not interchangeable among different brands of electronic braille devices. A tape made on an electronic braille device from one manufacturer will not necessarily be readable on an electronic braille device from another manufacturer. Furthermore, not all devices use precisely the same computer braille code. The "carriage return" message, for example, is not sent in the same way from all electronic braille devices. The lack of portability of such devices is an additional problem. Even the smallest and lightest electronic braille machine is heavy (about 9 pounds) and difficult for a young student to transport. Finally, electronic braille devices are expensive, ranging in price from $4,850 to $13,000. Since the low incidence of visual impairment precludes quantity production, a price decrease is not likely. Thus, it may not be possible for every braille-reading student who needs computer access to use electronic braille devices.

Paper Braille

Until the advent of electronic braille, computer access through braille was limited to paper braille provided on large paper-braille printing devices such as the LED-120 printer from Triformation Systems, Inc. Now the Cranmer Modified Perkins Brailler (CMPB) allows students to send information to the computer using a Perkins-brailler-style keyboard and to receive information from the computer in paper-braille form on the page inserted into the machine.

Actually a modification of the conventional Perkins brailler, the CMPB simply adds electronics (housed in a box beneath the brailler) which enable the device to provide computer access. The CMPB incorporates solenoid-operated keys, an electronically driven carriage return, and line-spacing functions. The braille embossing head writes while moving right to left as well as left to right, embossing at the approximate speed of 10 characters per second.

The CMPB includes a standard RS-232C connector, so that it may be linked to peripheral devices. It utilizes conventional cassette tape equipment to store and retrieve information. Word processing, the ability to change control parameters from the keyboard so that the device can be connected to a wide variety of computers, and other features similar to those available on electronic braille devices are also included. Perhaps one of the CMPB's most exciting features is its ability to produce tactile graphics. The CMPB is manufactured by Maryland Computer Services, Inc.

Advantages

Foremost among the CMPB's advantages is its full-page display capability. It is highly desirable, particularly when comparing lines of computer programs, to have easy and immediate access to an entire page, as opposed to a single line, of information. This full-page display capability also means that material in columns can be read rapidly and efficiently. Priced at $2,750, the CMPD is significantly less expensive than presently marketed electronic braille devices. Since braille-reading students are accustomed to using the Perkins Brailler, the transition to the CMPB can be made easily. Finally, the device can draw and label curves, graphs, maps, and other graphic displays, increasing the number and variety of programs available to braille users. Since this capability has not been available on other braille computer terminals, its use and potential have yet to be explored.

Limitations

A significant limitation of the CMPB is its slow printing (embossing) speed of 10 characters per second—far slower than the VersaBraille's approximately 100 characters per second. This speed limitation becomes important when many pages are to be brailled. The CMPB's use of braille paper presents two limitations. First, braille paper is a much bulkier and more costly storage medium than is an audio cassette or a disk. Second, the device cannot currently utilize continuous fan-fold or a roll of paper as do conventional inkprint printers. Thus, each page must be inserted and removed by hand, necessitating virtually constant monitoring and time-consuming paper handling. Care must also be taken to keep the pages in usable order. In addition, the CMPB is hampered by some of the limitations of electronic braille terminals. Computer braille code output further reduces reading speed. The device is heavier than desirable and does make some noise. CMPB tapes cannot be read on other braille devices and vice versa.

Optacon

Because of its early availability, the Optacon is at present probably the most widely used computer access technology. Introduced in 1971 (Bliss & Moore, 1974), the device is currently priced at $4,295. The Optacon uses an array of 144 electronically activated pins to translate printed material into raised vibrating print readable by touch. A computer paper printout can be read using the regular lens of the Optacon camera. A cathode ray tube lens which can be easily attached to the Optacon camera makes it possible to read computer video displays.

Advantages

The Optacon's primary advantage is its versatility. A computer's output can be read either from a printed version generated by a computer printer or from an electronic version on the computer's video display. As is true of paper braille devices, the Optacon allows the user immediately to access any information on a full page of computer output. Thus, immediate search capability is not limited to a single line as with electronic braille devices, and material in columns can be scanned easily. In addition, the Optacon can provide access to graphics.

Limitations

Perhaps the Optacon's chief limitation is the speed at which material is generally read. Average Optacon reading speeds range from 20 to 60 words per minute (Telesensory Systems, Inc., 1978). In addition, the Optacon is a one-way communication medium. Although information received from the computer can be read directly with the Optacon, information cannot be sent to the computer via the Optacon but must be entered from some separate device with a keyboard. The Optacon also requires the user to know how or to learn to read various styles of upper case letters, lower case letters, and numbers, necessitating a higher level of training than that required simply to master the mechanics of using the device. Good bimanual coordination is necessary to orient the Optacon camera properly and to move it straight across the line of print. Faulty camera alignment and poor tracking produce slanted, hard-to-read letters and slow or preclude Optacon use by some otherwise capable students.

Synthesized Speech

Voice-synthesis devices have become widely and inexpensively available. They provide a very promising means of access to microcomputers for visually impaired persons. Although digitized (pre-recorded) speech is used in some applications, the most popular type of speech access technology uses synthetic speech to enable the computer to talk. Synthetic speech involves the putting together (concatenation) of electronically generated sounds to form words. Some methods of producing synthetic speech use a computer program to generate the speech. Others employ a special terminal and computer hardware for this purpose. In general, all information received from the computer can be spoken as words, spelled letter by letter, and/or reviewed. Synthetic speech devices range in price from $150 (Echo II speech synthesizer, manufactured by Street Electronics) to $8,000 (the Information Through Speech computer, manufactured by Maryland Computer Services, Inc.).

Advantages

A significant advantage of computer access through synthetic-speech technology is speed. One manufacturer claims that users of its synthetic-speech terminals and computers routinely read at 360 words per minute (Gilson, personal communication, 1982). Equally important, synthetic-speech users may include but are not limited to the braille-reading population. Those who find computer braille output frustratingly slow, partially seeing students who want an alternative to enlarged print, and students with normal vision can all benefit from this technology and can use it to work on games and assignments together.

Limitations

Probably the primary limitation of current synthetic-speech devices is the limited information review capabilities of the equipment. Some synthetic speech devices have no review capability, so that information is completely ephemeral; other devices retain less information in memory than do electronic braille devices. A second limitation is the relatively low quality of speech output which requires a period of learning and accommodation to understand. New devices promising higher speech quality continue to be developed, but current quality remains unacceptable to some users. As noted earlier, words can be pronounced correctly even though they are spelled incorrectly. Alternatively, some correctly spelled words are incorrectly pronounced. However, some devices allow users to make program changes which correct particularly troublesome mispronunciations. In addition, like the Optacon, synthetic-speech devices provide only one-way communication. Information can be received but not sent using synthetic speech. Finally, as is true of other kinds of access technology, synthetic speech is incapable of displaying graphics.

Enlarged Print

Since about four-fifths of those who come within the accepted definition of blindness for legal purposes retain some useful vision, enlarged print is an important means of computer access. Enlarged print is, of course, a particularly helpful medium for partially seeing and low vision students. On a computer it can be generated through read only memory (ROM) or by using a program (RAM). Enlarged print can also be made available by means of computer terminals, computers which employ closed-circuit television, or hand-held or stand-mounted magnifying devices. The cost of enlarged print can be as inexpensive as the price of the program which generates it or as costly as the price of a closed-circuit television computer system.

Advantages

Since such a large proportion of visually impaired students have useful vision, enlarged print's chief advantage is the high percentage of the visually impaired population it can serve. Enlarged print can also be a comparatively inexpensive access technology, since it already comes as a part of some computers and requires only the purchase of computer programs to provide the capability for others. Finally, graphics in standard size—or, in some cases, enlarged—can be displayed using this medium.

Limitations

Enlarged print's variety of presentation formats is a mixed blessing. Computers equipped with enlarged print capability may generate only one size print. Thus, the needs of those who find it easiest to read some other size print might remain unmet. If a program is used to enlarge the print, every piece of material to be enlarged requires initial modification. Finally, extremely enlarged print is virtually impossible for Optacon users to read because it is so much larger than the Optacon camera's zoom lens can handle.

Conclusion

No single mode or medium of access technology is ideal or meets the needs of all visually impaired users. Indeed, a user might ideally choose to use one device for one task and a different device for another. A braille reader, for instance, might like to read columnar material using the Optacon or a full page of braille produced on the CMPB, but use synthetic speech to read textual material because of its greater speed. Thus, in addition to the careful evaluation of the advantages and limitations of each device, other factors must also be considered if realistic choices of access technology are to be made. Factors which deserve consideration include how the device is to be used, the cost-benefit ratio, how portable the device must be, user speed, and other requirements. Wherever possible, the user's capabilities, preferences, and opinions should be taken into account. In summary, the technology which can provide visually impaired students access to computers now exists. It is likely to exist in even greater abundance and variety in the future. Our task as educators is to be certain that lack of computer access—and, by implication, lack of computer literacy—do not make our students multiply handicapped in this increasingly technological era.

References

Bliss, J. C., & Moore, M. W. 1974. The Optacon reading system. *Education of the Visually Handicapped*, 6(4), 98–102.

Telesensory Systems, Inc. Efficient Optacon reading. In *Optacon Teacher Seminar*. Palo Alto, Ca.: Author, 1978.

Teaching the Physically or Health Impaired Child

There are so many forms and varied consequences of physical and health impairments that it is difficult to envision this category as a single topic. PL 94-142 differentiates between orthopedic impairments and other health impairments. Orthopedic problems affect mobility (e.g., cerebral palsy, muscular dystrophy, brittle bone disease, accidentally sustained paraplegia, hemiplegia, or quadriplegia). Other health impairments can affect vitality (e.g., asthma, rheumatic heart disease, cystic fibrosis), multiple structures and functions (e.g., leukemia, AIDS, pregnancy), or may have no apparent effects unless medications are forgotten or insufficient (e.g., diabetes, epilepsy, rheumatoid arthritis).

Orthopedic impairments are no longer sufficient cause for placing a child in a residential school, a special day school, or a self-contained, special class. PL 94-142 addressed the problem of architectural barriers within public schools. It authorized monetary grants to state education agencies to pay for alterations to existing educational facilities to make them accessible to orthopedically handicapped students. Section 504 of the Amendments to the Vocational Rehabilitation Act had as one of its principle objectives the termination of discriminatory practices against the physically handicapped. Section 504 did not order totally barrier-free schools, but it did order full accessibility to educational programs conducted in schools. Schools which fail to comply with Section 504 may have their federal aid to education withheld until they conform to full program accessibility.

As students with severe orthopedic disabilities move into public school settings, a major responsibility for the educational staff is to assure a smooth transition and help instill positive attitudes toward the disabled student in his or her nondisabled peers. The teacher must become acquainted with the limitations imposed on the student by the orthopedic handicap. The room and desks may need to be rearranged for a wheelchair user. As with other exceptional conditions, the teacher must challenge the child to do all he or she is capable of doing. Learning must be encouraged, supported, and evaluated to assure continual progress without "sympathy grading."

Chronically ill children are often more challenging to integrate into regular classrooms than those with orthopedic impairments, because they do not appear as disabled. Nevertheless, they need to be challenged, supported, and evaluated for continual progress as well. Many need supportive medical, psychological, or other related therapies.

In 1979, in *Tatro v. Texas*, the Supreme Court ruled that life support services that are not strictly the province of a physician are, alternatively, required duties of schools. For example, if a child with spina bifida needs urinary catheterization during the school day in order to allow him or her to benefit from school, someone on the school staff must do it. School nurses are frequently not available full-time in many public schools. As a consequence, teachers are usually asked to learn to provide whatever special life support services are required. They may also be asked to give medicines or provide counseling, once strictly viewed as the responsibilities of health care providers. Increasingly, teachers are being asked to watch for side effects of medicines or possible exacerbations of a disease. When such symptoms are recognized, prompt reporting and follow-up are necessary.

Educators should provide nondisabled peers in the classroom with some information about each orthopedically or otherwise health impaired child's specific condition. The impaired student should choose whether or not to be present during the discussion. A teacher may elect to have a qualified speaker provide some facts or answer questions. Classmates should be encouraged to be supportive of the disabled child but not to provide too much assistance. The goal should be to increase compassion while reducing fear, pity, rejection, or obsequiousness.

The first article in this unit gives advice to regular education teachers who have mainstreamed young children with chronic illnesses in their classes. It includes a medical management information form which is helpful for the teacher to have. It suggests several ways to work with the chronically ill child, health care providers, parents, and healthy classmates. The second selection offers advice on IEPs, classroom modifications for physically or health impaired students, and remedial work in cooperation with hospital teachers when and if students are forced to miss school. The last two selections are concerned with orthopedically impaired students. "Project PAIRS" describes a program in which nondisabled students tutor physically

Unit 10

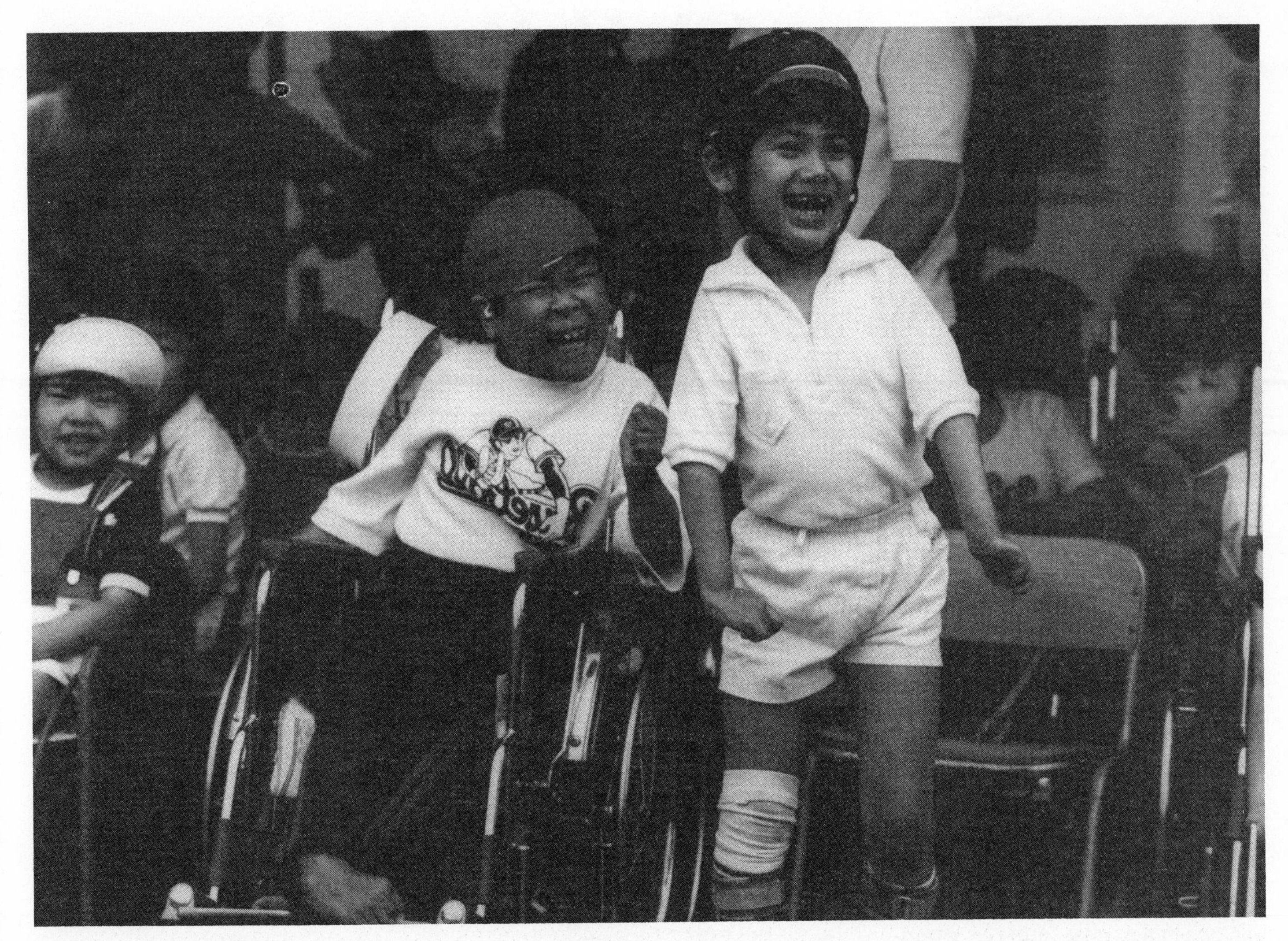

impaired peers in water safety and swimming techniques. This is designed to increase positive interactions between the students. The last article describes the many ways in which microcomputers can be used to enhance the education of physically disabled students.

Looking Ahead: Challenge Questions

Can teachers trained in regular education learn to include children with life-threatening chronic illnesses in their mainstreamed classrooms?

How do educators plan for students with special health care needs? Of whom can they ask assistance?

Does peer teaching improve relations between disabled and nondisabled students?

What new benefits can computer technology offer to children who have severe physical handicaps?

Including Young Children With "New" Chronic Illnesses in an Early Childhood Education Setting

Mary Fauvre

Mary Fauvre, *Ph.D., Educational Psychologist/Parent Liaison in the Department of Pediatrics at UCLA Medical Center, has taught nursery and elementary school as well as college. Her young son had chemotherapy and radiation for leukemia 1982–1985; she has always kept his teachers informed of his health status.*

The effects of modern medical science and technology are being felt in places far beyond the hospital, and early childhood educators may soon have more experience with some of these medical successes. Children born with serious birth defects have been treated successfully with surgeries and modern drugs. Children who develop cancers of various types now undergo strenuous but successful treatments of chemotherapy and radiation. Organ transplants have become more available for children whose livers or kidneys have not developed properly, and congenital heart defects often now can be corrected by intricate surgeries. These conditions, previously thought to be terminal, have recently been shifted to the "life-threatening chronic illness" list (Ruccione, 1983). These children often lead quite normal lives, perhaps punctuated by trips to clinics or hospitals. The children are often part of regular school and community programs.

Unfortunately, very few nonmedical professionals have received the training to feel comfortable with this new population. They may feel unable to help identify the needs of these children and their families (Hobbs, Perrin, & Ireys, 1985).

Although this is a new group to plan for in programs and schools,

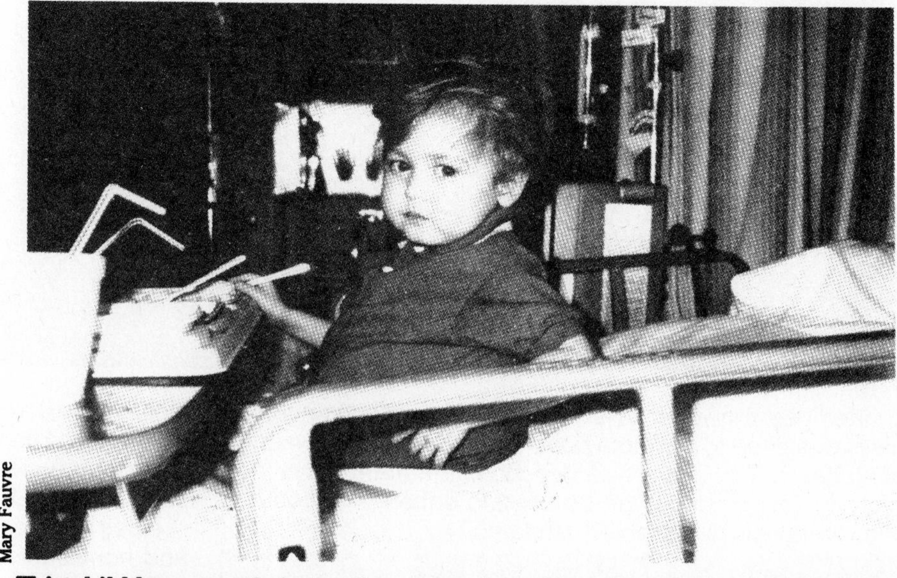
Mary Fauvre

This child has recently had a liver transplant. Soon he will be in a family day care home. It is imperative that there be close, trusting communication between Christopher's parents and caregiver.

From *Young Children,* Vol. 43, No. 6 (September 1988), pp. 71-77.

children with other specialized medical needs have been included in programs in the past. For years children with chronic asthma conditions, sickle cell anemia, and juvenile diabetes have been successfully included in regular school settings. There is every reason to expect that these children with "new" chronic illnesses will also be included. PL 94-142, the Education of Handicapped Children Act, recognizes "health impaired" as a category of children to whom services must be offered in the least restrictive environment—by law, they must be included.

Interdisciplinary collaboration imperative

Careful communication and collaboration among parents, school officials, and health care providers are factors critical to the successful schooling of seriously health-impaired children. There must be a high level of trust and understanding on the part of all. Although most parents are overwhelmed by the initial diagnosis of their child's condition, by the time the child is ready for school, they have usually developed a certain level and style of coping with their child's health problem. A teacher, on the other hand, may feel quite frightened or disconcerted about the presence of a young child with a "weak heart," who may tire easily, become slightly blue, or need specific medication on a predetermined schedule. If the parents can explain the circumstances carefully so that the teacher can feel comfortable with the child, then there is every reason to expect successful school entry.

A sick child is first and foremost a child

Teachers need to remember that a child with a health condition is first and foremost a child, like all other children; the health problems are secondary. With this philosophy, we should be able to include the child as a normal member of the group. All children, after all, have individual needs and peculiarities, not just children with chronic health problems. The following specific suggestions have come from working with both parents and teachers who have had children with chronic life-threatening illnesses in their classes. The presentation is not meant to be exhaustive, but rather to aid in raising further questions and in raising the awareness of teachers and other nonmedical professionals who work with these children.

The first concept is perhaps the most important, so I will repeat it: The needs and successes of children with chronic life-threatening illnesses are similar to those of other children. Even though they may have been through extremely difficult medical procedures, and there may be restrictions on their regular activities, they are children above all.

Parents may be in a quandary as to how much to tell teachers.

Discipline as usual

Parents often complain that it is difficult to discipline their young child when they know he is being treated for leukemia because they fear that his condition may in fact be terminal rather than chronic. Teachers face a similar dilemma. Although it is tempting to "give in" and to be "softer," in reality this special treatment is a disservice to the child.

Specifics of warning signals teachers should be alert to must be clearly spelled out.

Limit special privileges to essentials

Siblings become jealous of favors or privileges, and classmates, too, will resent a child who receives too much special attention. This is similar to any circumstance that makes one child different from others. The frequent snacks a diabetic child requires or the extra attention given to an asthmatic child may be appropriate for the child's medical condition. However, the handling of the treatment must be considered carefully as it will affect both the child's and the class's social and emotional environment.

Exploration and mastery are crucial

Classroom experience and socialization opportunities are important for all children and are particularly important for children with chronic illnesses. In a classroom, a child has the opportunity to explore and try out new skills, and to achieve mastery or recognize limitations. Parents of a child with health problems frequently are overprotective and do not allow their child to attempt new activities independently (Lansky, Cairns, & Zwartzes, 1983; McCollum, 1981). Once enrolled in a school program, however, the child ought to have numerous opportunities for exploration and discovery. The child will benefit from being in a group and will have an opportunity to develop independence and self-sufficiency, so important between the ages of 3 and 8 (Adams & Deveau, 1984; Deasy-Spinetta & Spinetta, 1980).

But be watchful. A problem opposite that of the teacher minimizing health problems and remembering that the child is first a child is that, since many of these children do not look sick, the teacher will forget that they are slightly more fragile or may require extra attention to energy levels or medication needs. For example, children who have had successful heart surgery may look perfectly healthy and may in fact *be* perfectly healthy, but they may be at risk of overtiring with exertion and so need restricted activity levels for a period of time after their surgery. Children undergoing chemotherapy may look no different from other members of their class, unless they have temporarily lost hair, but their immune systems are more vulnerable—they catch colds, flus, and other common childhood illnesses more easily (Deasy-Spinetta & Spinetta, 1980). The same is true for children who have received organ transplants or who are taking certain medications. The healthy-looking chronically ill child may require only slightly more vigilance than classmates, and only at certain vulnerable times, but the extra attention to potential trouble may protect against other, more serious, setbacks.

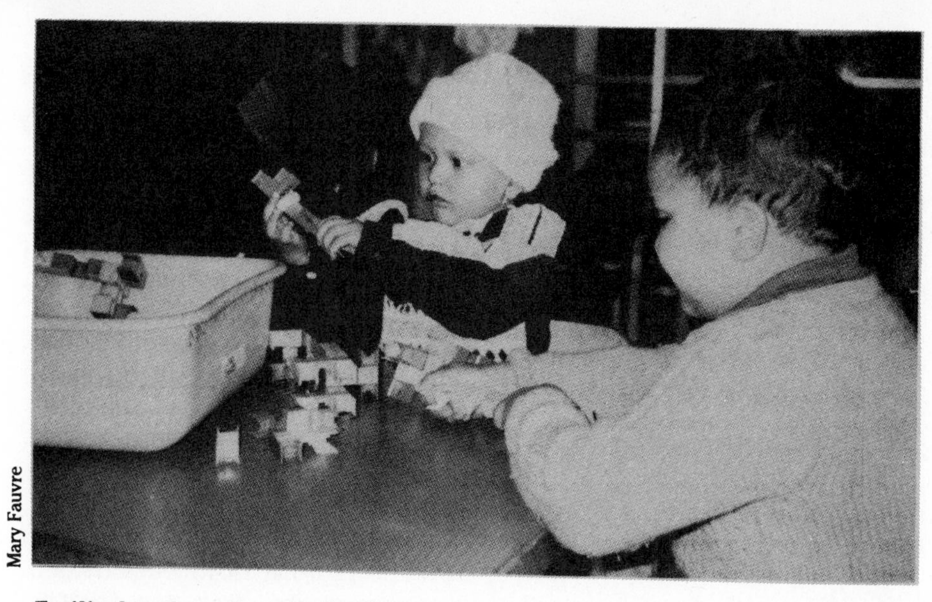

Mary Fauvre

Emilia has been hospitalized for a long time and has had many head surgeries. Her number one need now that* that *is over is to be part of a group of normal children and to be regarded as a normal child.

Parent-teacher communication key

The key element to successful integration of these children into school settings is communication among parents, teachers, the school nurse (if available), and health care providers, as has been said, *but* information sharing is a sensitive event (Chekryn, Deegan, & Reid, 1987; Schulz, 1978). Parents may feel that once they have explained their child's condition, the teachers understand it as much as they do. Or teachers may feel that the medical details are more than they need. They may feel uncomfortable hearing about things that have become routine for parents.

Special health forms are helpful

Some families and clinics have found it helpful to start with a form similar to the one shown on the next page, which lists more details than the normal school record charts (Hansen & Jeppson, 1986). Other parents have written detailed descriptions of their child's condition, explaining exactly what occurs at monthly clinic visits. Children make references to experiences that teachers cannot understand without these careful explanations. What does a child mean when she comes to school after a day's absence, proudly shows her three or four Band-Aids, and announces, "It took four sticks this time"? The teacher might not recognize her reference to the IV chemotherapy and may not know how to respond. Often the child will elaborate or explain if the teacher questions; but just as often, the child is not interested in further discussion, and the teacher is left feeling rather inadequate.

Conferences are crucial

Conferences are another important way to communicate information about a child's condition or treatment. It is probably a good idea for the teacher to take notes during such conversations and not rely solely on memory for details. Because parents have become the experts on their child's health status and are so involved with and concerned about their own child's welfare, they may make assumptions about a teacher's understanding of the problem even as they are trying to communicate what they think is important. A teacher of a child with sickle cell anemia should be told directly to pay careful attention to complaints of a specific localized pain. It is something to be taken seriously. Similarly, a teacher may not realize from conversation that a child who is *immunosuppressed,* from cancer treatments or organ transplant medications, is highly susceptible to any contagious germs and that exposure to some common childhood illnesses, like chicken pox, may be life threatening. Parents who ask to be informed if there is an exposure to chicken pox really mean that they want immediate information, because an antidote is available if a child is treated within 72 hours after exposure. Such specifics are important and must be spelled out clearly to ensure that what the parents have told has been thoroughly understood. Occasionally, a teacher's misconception or experience with an adult with the same illness may need to be addressed or dispelled in order to facilitate complete understanding of the child's health.

Medical Management Information Form

(Physician's Directions)
(adapted from Hansen & Jeppson, 1986)

child's name ______________________ birth date ______________________

address ______________________ parent or guardian ______________________

Diagnosis: ______________________
Symptoms: ______________________
Prognosis: ______________________

Management information for the school:

1. Will medication or treatment be administered at school? Yes/No
   If yes, by whom? ______________________
   At what times? ______________________
   Any special instructions or precautions? ______________________
2. What considerations affect this child's ability to participate in the classroom?
   Special place in classroom due to hearing, vision, or mobility problems? ______________________
   Special physical assistance? ______________________
   Help with toileting? ______________________
   Help with eating? ______________________
3. What considerations affect this child's ability to participate in physical education or playground activities?
   Endurance? ______________________
   Activity restrictions? ______________________
   Need for special monitoring? ______________________
   Can the child judge his/her exertion level appropriately? ______________________
4. What aspects of the child's condition might require preparing the other children in the classroom?
   Special equipment? ______________________
   Physical appearance? ______________________
   Speech characteristics? ______________________
   Seizures? ______________________
   Behavioral characteristics? ______________________
   Increased susceptibility to illness or disease? ______________________
5. What side effects of medications might affect the child's behavior? ______________________
6. When would you like the teacher to contact you? ______________________
   Under what special circumstances? ______________________
   At what intervals? ______________________
   In an emergency situation, must you be notified before treatment? ______________________
   What is the best time to reach you? ______________________
   Other comments: ______________________

name of physician ______________________ address ______________________

phone ______________________

Mary Fauvre

Luther is a lovely little boy. His health history has been dramatic and has left him very fragile. His parents' anxiety is high; they hate to leave him at the child care center, but the demands of life and the work place do go on. The teachers, too, are nervous. Moreover, Luther will probably continue to be in and out of the hospital, and in and out of the center. Perhaps more than most children, Luther needs the sensitive care of a teacher, firm limits, and playmates. The adults will need to get their alarm under control.

Health professionals as consultants

There are times when teachers may want more information than parents can give, and it may be appropriate for school personnel to consult with the doctors or medical staff treating the child (Chekryn et al., 1987; National Cancer Institute, 1984). Of course, such discussions must be held only with the consent of the parents, and all information must be recognized as confidential. After a child has been through a medical crisis, or has finished a series of treatments, some parents feel it is important not to share information or prejudice others who will be working with their child. This is often true for children who have been treated for any of the childhood cancers. A child may have had chemotherapy for 2 or 3 years, and the teachers may have been included and informed thoroughly; but, once treatment is over, new teachers may not be told anything. Understanding the child's behavior could be difficult for teachers who may know a little about the child's history but have not been informed about current status. That is an issue for parents and teachers to work through together. Parents are often in a quandary as to how much to discuss and as to what information is important to which staff members. It may be an appropriate time for a school nurse or administrator to step in to screen such information.

Perhaps the child's pediatrician would be willing to confer with teaching staff. This would be particularly likely and helpful if the child has a "behavioral pediatrician." This is a pediatrician who specializes in childrearing and educational aspects of patients with serious health problems.

With good communication, parents and teachers can work together, building a sense of trust and respect that works to the child's best interests.

Resting up for a big school event

If a special school event is planned for the future, a teacher might be able to alert the parents of a child who has low energy levels. Perhaps the parents could limit other activities for a few days to help the child prepare for the school occasion.

Preparing teachers for a new treatment

If a child will be starting a new treatment or medication that may have noticeable side effects, the teacher will welcome warning and information to help interpret behavior in light of medical circumstances. Teachers also need to have ready access to emergency information and to know how to recognize the onset of a crisis—whom to call and what to do should there be an unusual situation involving the chronically ill child. Is there any reason that the local hospital should be informed before treating a child's broken arm or suspected concussion? Such information is better learned ahead of time than in crisis circumstances.

Will other children ask questions?

A different aspect of information

sharing is anticipating questions that may be raised by other children in the class. Teachers must first be comfortable with their own understanding of the medical details and should have support from the parents before answering or anticipating the questions of other children (Chekryn et al., 1987; American Cancer Society, 1980). Sometimes the medical center where the child is treated will have a nurse or psychologist who specializes in school visits and can explain the medical aspects to the children. Issues commonly raised include causes of the illness or changes in appearance, especially hair loss or other side effects of medication (National Cancer Institute, 1984). Children in classes with a chronically ill child often need reassurance that they will not catch the same germ. Is having a heart condition contagious?

Parents of other children might also need reassurance and might have questions of their own. The growing awareness of AIDS and AIDS Related Complex has sensitized many to the issue of communicable germs, but the chronic, life-threatening illnesses discussed here (cancer, heart disease, kidney disease, or liver disease) are not contagious. Depending on the circumstances, the teacher and parents of the chronically ill child can work together to offer relevant information, with help from the medical center if appropriate.

Teachers need to emphasize the positive

The importance of parents working with teachers when planning for a chronically ill child cannot be overemphasized. Parents have been through major events concerning their child's health and will appreciate a teacher's support. Parents' anxiety levels may be extremely high, and an apparently minor problem can raise stress levels to greater heights than might seem appropriate. Teachers can be sensitive to parents' needs by making an effort to include positive topics in conversations without letting the "problems" become the dominant or exclusive theme. Another potential pitfall is parents' tendency to feel instantly guilty in reacting to many situations. Teachers can alert parents to opportunities to become involved in the program, without letting them feel inadequate or unsupportive if they are unable to spend more time at school.

Patience with parents pays off

A final area of advice for teachers is to allow parents of chronically ill children a little extra time in making decisions about plans regarding their child's education (Hansen & Jeppson, 1986). The parents have so many variables to consider, and are often so fearful about anticipating the future, that school-related decisions may take on heavier meaning than they would in other circumstances.

* * *

It is a tribute to modern medical technology that information such as that touched upon here is even necessary. As recently as 10 or 15 years ago, no one worried about the early school experiences of a child with leukemia, or a defective liver, or certain heart conditions, because such diagnoses were virtual death sentences. Now opportunities for normal education experiences are available to many children with life-threatening chronic illnesses or conditions. Parents of these children look anxiously for staff people they trust, where their children can be part of the regular program but will also receive gentle understanding. As one parent said, "After all he went through as a baby, he *deserves* a little extra attention, but I don't want him to be different from the others." Clearly, this dichotomy presents both a dilemma and a challenge for parents and educators to address together.

For further reading

Hanline, M. F. (1985). Integrating disabled children. *Young Children, 40*(2), 45–48.

Souweine, J., Crimmins, S., & Mazel, C. (1981). *Mainstreaming: Ideas for teaching young children.* Washington, DC: NAEYC.

White, B. P., & Phair, M. A. (1986). "It'll be a challenge!": Managing emotional stress in teaching disabled children. *Young Children, 41*(2), 44–48.

References

Adams, D. W., & Deveau, E. J. (1984). *Coping with childhood cancer: Where do we go from here?* Reston Publishing, 200 Old Tappan Rd., Old Tappan, NJ 07675.

American Cancer Society. (1980). *When you have a student with cancer* [80–(100m)–No. 2613–LE]. American Cancer Society, 777 Third Ave., New York, NY 10017.

Chekryn, J., Deegan, M., & Reid, J. (1987). Impact on teachers when a child with cancer returns to school. *Children's Health Care, 15,* 161–165.

Deasy-Spinetta, P., & Spinetta, J. J. (1980). The child with cancer in school: Teacher's appraisal. *American Journal of Pediatric Hematology/Oncology, 2,* 89–94.

Hansen, J. P., & Jeppson, E. S. (1986). *Seasons of caring: Curriculum guides for parents, educators, and health professionals.* Association for the Care of Children's Health, 3615 Wisconsin Ave., N.W., Washington, DC 20016.

Hobbs, N., Perrin, J. M., & Ireys, H. T. (1985). *Chronically ill children and their families.* San Francisco: Jossey-Bass.

Lansky, S. B., Cairns, N. U., & Zwartzes, W. (1983). School attendance among children with cancer. A report from two centers. *Journal of Psychosocial Oncology, 1,* 75–82.

McCollum, A. T. (1981). *The chronically ill child.* New Haven: Yale University Press.

National Cancer Institute. (1984). *Students with cancer: A resource for the educator* (NIH Publication No. 84-2086). Washington, DC: U.S. Department of Health and Human Services.

Ruccione, K. (1983). Acute leukemia in children: Current perspectives. *Issues in Comprehensive Pediatric Nursing, 6,* 329–363.

Schulz, J. (1978). The parent-professional conflict. In A. P. Turnbull & H. R. Turnbull (Eds.), *Parents speak out* (pp. 28–37). Columbus, OH: Merrill.

Students With Special Health Care Needs

Barbara Sirvis

Barbara Sirvis *(CEC Chapter #402) is Dean, Faculty of Applied Science and Education, and Professor of Exceptional Education, State University College at Buffalo, New York. She is Chair, CEC Ad Hoc Committee on Medically Fragile.*

■In Louisiana, a 9-year-old girl sustained a high cervical spinal cord injury, resulting in minimal head control and need for ventilator assistance in breathing. In her fourth grade class, she requires mechanical ventilation, suctioning, positioning, catheterization, and assistance with equipment for eating and computer writing. She also requires immediate action in the case of an equipment breakdown or a health emergency.

A 16-year-old young man sustained a closed head injury as a result of a motor vehicle accident. He was in a coma for a period of 9 weeks. When he reentered school, he was ambulatory with a walker and exhibited impaired memory, fluctuating academic skills, poor attention, poor judgment, and minimal impulse control. He requires frequent evaluations to monitor changes in his behavioral and academic status as well as modifications of conventional classroom structure, discipline, and programming.

A 3-year-old with a rare congenital metabolic disorder requires a protein-restricted diet and monitoring of vital signs and symptoms of ammonia buildup. She is in a full-day preschool program. Her teacher assists cafeteria workers in the selection of foods and carefully records food intake. (Caldwell, 1987)

Public Law 94-142, the Education for All Handicapped Children Act, and Section 504 of the Rehabilitation Act have opened classroom doors for many students who previously were unserved. Recently, a new group of students has emerged who have unique educational needs that are confounded by their extreme medical needs. The referral of these students, who are sometimes labeled *medically fragile*, and who may be technologically dependent, has raised many questions about the nature of educational and medical services for which school districts are responsible. While administrators, legislators, public health officials, and others attempt to resolve the question of who shall provide services, classroom teachers have an immediate need to understand the educational potential and needs of these students to ensure that they will not be at risk, either physically or educationally, in the classroom. This article provides a broad overview of the nature and needs of these students.

Definition Is Difficult at Best

Students who have special health care needs have survived catastrophic medical events and may need prolonged specialized health care. The CEC Task Force on Medically Fragile has provided a broad-based functional definition of this group as follows:

"Medically fragile students require specialized technological health care procedures for life support and/or health support during the school day. These students may or may not require special education" (The Council for Exceptional Children, 1988).

Students may have a variety of specialized health care needs including ventilator dependence, tracheo stomy dependence, oxygen dependence, or nutritional supplement dependence, congestive heart problems, long-term care, high-technology care, apnea monitoring, and/or kidney dialysis (GLRRC, 1986). The Office of Technology Assessment (OTA) (1987) has defined these children as in need of "both a medical device to compensate for the loss of a vital body function and substantial and ongoing nursing care to avert death or further disability" (p. 3). Depending on the definition applied, OTA estimates that as many as 100,000 infants and children may be technologically dependent in some way.

While much of the current literature focuses on issues related to health care financing and the relative cost benefits of hospital versus home-based services, professionals have also begun to give attention to appropriate educational programs. The need for high-quality nursing care, home health services, and extensive equipment availability to facilitate successful transition to the home environment has implica-

From *Teaching Exceptional Children*, Summer 1988, pp. 40-44.

tions for the development of appropriate school-based programs. The transition of students from home to school settings will be affected by the ability of school districts and health care providers to establish guidelines for financing health care services and professional liability insurance; to organize interdisciplinary teams of professionals who will provide appropriate support and inservice training for successful integration in school settings; and to provide an appropriate educational program.

Students with specialized health care needs often can qualify for special education services if their medical diagnosis qualifies them as "other health impaired." For example, they are eligible under P.L. 94-142 if they have "limited strength, vitality or alertness, due to chronic or acute health problems, . . . which adversely affects [their] educational performance." The definition provides the potential justification for appropriate educational placement. However, issues surrounding liability and appropriate medical services that support participation in the educational environment still must be resolved, and potential barriers to educational services must be removed.

Why Are They at Risk?

Concerns of special education personnel focus on the factors that put these students at risk for learning difficulties. Students' medical needs and technological dependence must be met before they can benefit from the classroom experience. Teachers are central to classroom success, but even the most skilled special education teacher may be somewhat reticent to provide educational services for students with special health care needs. Questions about liability exposure when a student's life is dependent on special health care procedures, combined with the problem of finding time to meet the educational needs of all students in the classroom, are two of the concerns the receiving teacher might have.

Medical concerns are one of the major factors affecting learning for these students. Fatigue, limited vitality, short attention span, and limited mobility are just some of the characteristics that can accompany technological dependence. Because of them there can be a need for supplemental assistance from support personnel (e.g., physical and occupational therapists, inhalation therapists, nurses, aides). All education personnel must be familiar with the appropriate medical procedures and interventions that are part of the regular care of students with special health care needs as well as those required in emergency situations. Inservice programs such as those developed by the Milwaukee Public Schools (P. Ollie, personal communication, September 9, 1987), provide staff with the knowledge and skills they need to interact with and meet the needs of each student.

Educational Options

Historically, children with severe health problems who required careful medical attention were placed in isolated settings in institutions or hospitals. With the advent of P.L. 94-142, these children now have a right and an opportunity to receive a free and appropriate education. Students with special health care needs must have their immediate medical needs accommodated before their educational needs can be addressed. When they are medically stable, such students should participate in the educational programs that best meet their learning needs. In some cases, this means providing instruction in specialized medical settings, but in the majority of cases, students can be placed in classroom settings. Placement choices should be diverse, providing a broad continuum of opportunities. In all cases, educational placements should be made by an interdisciplinary team that includes the student's parents and physician. Decisions should take into account health care needs, appropriateness of setting, risks to the student, and training of personnel.

Hospital and Home Placement

In the most serious cases, children may reside in hospital settings, and hospital-based instruction may be most appropriate. If the transition from hospital to home is considered a significant enough change, requiring time for additional stabilization and adjustment by the student and the parent, home-based instruction may be appropriate. Some students need home-based instruction due to the physical demands of the school program or because their life support equipment cannot be made portable and adaptable to the school setting (Kaufman & Lichtenstein, n.d.). One innovative approach involves the use of teleteaching, which provides opportunities for students to participate in class discussions from their beds at home. This strategy might also facilitate transition to the school environment (Kleinberg, 1984). Home-based instruction or parent-infant education programs are also appropriate for young children for whom school programs are not available. With the advent of Public Law 99-457 (EHA Amendments of 1986), there should be an increase in the number of programs available for young children who have severe health problems.

Special Class Placement

For some students, the least restrictive and most appropriate educational environment is a special class. Nursing and related care can be provided by the school nurse, a home health agency nurse, or, in some cases, the classroom teacher or aide. It is important that placement in a special class be based on the unique educational needs of the student and *not* solely on the basis of the need for nursing care. As in the case of home-based instruction, placement in a special class can often be a transitional placement to allow time and opportunity for educational personnel to assess the child's educational potential and determine what special needs must be provided for in the regular classroom setting.

Regular Class Placement

Students with special health care needs may be able to function in regular classrooms. However, due to fatigue factors, regular class placement may need to be on a limited basis. Flexible scheduling might be needed; for example, a student might receive some instruction in the regular classroom and some in the hospital when receiving outpatient services such as dialysis. Although many medically fragile students need uninterrupted availability of support services personnel such as an additional full-time nurse or aide, in many instances, it is possible for classroom teachers and other school personnel to be trained to provide the necessary support services. Programs such as the ones at Children's Hospital in New Orleans (T. Caldwell, personal communication, September 11, 1987) and the Coordinating Center for Home and Community Care in Baltimore (N. J. Bond, personal communication, September 10, 1987) address the issues of providing care and training high-quality caregivers in schools to assure student well-being and safety.

Teacher's Roles

While administrators wrestle with the difficult issues surrounding necessary interagency agreements for provision of appropriate noneducational support services, teachers must prepare their classrooms for students who have severe health impairments, and/or are technologically dependent. The learning environment must be made hygienically safe. Teachers must be ready to adjust classroom schedules until a satisfactory system can be developed that maximizes educational benefit for these students. They must also be ready to adapt assessment and instructional procedures to foster academic success. A balanced intervention approach that recognizes the importance of quality of life should provide the basis for the delivery of high-quality services. Quality of life issues include the "importance of humor, leisure education, behavioral expectations for participation in family life, and death education" (Sirvis, 1987, p. 27).

Teachers also should be ready to spend time with students' parents. Parents are likely to have concerns about their child's medical and psychological vulnerability in the classroom. They need reassurance that their child will be cared for by well-trained personnel. Parents generally are quite knowledgeable about their child's strengths and weaknesses, and they can suggest specific techniques for maximizing performance. To allay parental fears about school placement, teachers might consider encouraging parents to observe their child in the classroom.

Classroom schedules should be adjusted for students with limited vitality to create maximum on-task learning time. Teachers should avoid "exaggerated deference to the medical implications of a child's handicap" (Hobbs, Perrin, Ireys, Moynihan, & Shayne, 1984, p. 212) to normalize the educational experience. There should be clear plans for emergencies, (e.g., fire drill procedures that allow one-to-one care for each student), but as much as possible, interruptions for medical intervention, such as suctioning and medication, should be nondisruptive to classmates. Classroom activities should maximize options for social interaction rather than isolation or a focus on limitations. For example, suctioning can be scheduled for quiet individual study times rather than group music times, or class parties can include food "treats" that meet a student's dietary restrictions.

Once the medical and related management needs of students have been addressed and appropriate assessment completed, teachers should identify or develop suitable curricula and implement appropriate educational programs. Modifications common to students with physical disabilities may be necessary (e.g., providing adaptive response modes for completion of assignments; removing timing requirements for examinations; and modifying tasks that require hand use and/or mobility). Some students can benefit from the use of specially designed adaptive positioning equipment that enhances their potential for engagement in activities and facilitates social interaction with classmates. Some may require frequent changes in position for comfort or to prevent development of deformities. Several modifications may be necessary to decrease the potential for fatigue, but in some cases the modifications may be temporary.

Teachers may have to provide remedial instruction when students are forced to miss school due to medical complications. Whenever possible, cooperative programs should be established with hospital teachers to assure continuation of educational programs while students are in the hospital.

The Challenge

The educational challenges created by the special needs of students with severe health impairments and/or technological dependence can be great. However, this group of students can participate successfully in the learning experience. Special education personnel are responding to the challenge, not in a vacuum, but in collaboration with health care and related service personnel and parents. Quality of education is an important component of quality of life. Teachers can enhance the quality of these students' lives by providing a safe and appropriate learning environment.

References

Caldwell, T. (1987). Correspondence regarding the Chronic Illness Program, Children's Hospital, New Orleans, LA.

The Council for Exceptional Children. (1988). *Final Report: CEC ad hoc committee on medically fragile*. Reston, VA: Author.

Great Lakes Area Regional Resource Center (GLRRC). (1986). *"Medically fragile" handicapped children: A policy research paper*. Columbus, OH: Author.

Hobbs, N., Perrin, J. M., Ireys, H. T., Moynihan, L. C., & Shayne, M. W. (1984). Chronically ill children in America, *Rehabilitation Literature, 45*, 206-213.

Kaufman, J., & Lichtenstein, K-A. (n.d.). The family as care manager: Home care coordinattion for medically fragile children. In *Workbook series for providing services to children with handicaps and their families*. Washington, DC: Georgetown University Child Development Center.

Kleinberg, S. (1984). Facilitating the child's entry to school and coordinating school activities during hospitalization. In *Home care for children with serious handicapping conditions* (pp. 67-77). Washington, DC: Association for the Care of Children's Health.

Sirvis, B. (1987). The medically fragile child: A response. In F. P. Connor (Ed.), *Critical issues for low-incidence populations* (pp. 26-28). Reston, VA: The Council for Exceptional Children.

U.S. Congress, Office of Technology Assessment. (1987). *Technology-dependent children: Hospital v. home care—A technical memorandum*, OTA-TM-H-38. Washington, DC: U.S. Government Printing Office.

Special credit to Nancy Jane Bond, Education Coordinator, Coordinating Center for Home and Community Care, Inc., Millersville, Maryland, and the teachers and students at James Ryder Randall Elementary School, Prince George's County, Maryland.

Project PAIRS: A Peer-Assisted Swimming Program for the Severely Handicapped

Don Compton, Patricia Goode, Bettie Sue Towns and Laine Motheral

Don Compton, Ph.D., is Program Director, Division of Program Evaluation, Texas Education Agency, Austin, Texas; Patricia Goode is Director of Special Education, Laguna Madre Cooperative; Bettie Sue Towns is Chairperson, Physical Education Department, H.M. King High School; and Laine Motheral is an Adaptive Physical Education Teacher, Kingsville Independent School District, Kingsville, Texas.

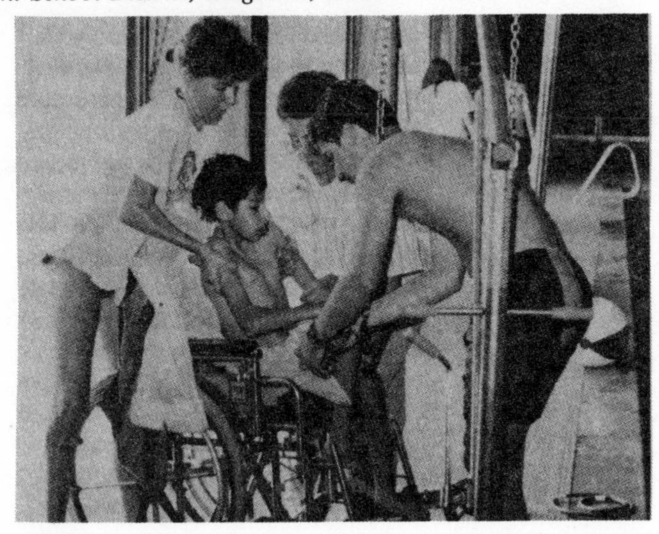

Project PAIRS (Peer-Assisted Instruction in Recreational Skills) joins special education, regular education and the peer tutoring concept to teach water safety and swimming techniques to handicapped students. In addition to teaching recreational skills, the program increases handicapped students' contact with other young people and gives non-handicapped students a chance to interact with a special population while earning American Red Cross Swimming Aide Certification.

PAIRS began, quite spontaneously, in the Kingsville Independent School District in south Texas in 1982. An adaptive physical education teacher was giving swimming lessons to students in her self-contained class for mentally retarded and multiply handicapped students at the H.M. King High School's pool. At the other end of the pool, a high school physical education class was in session, and soon the high school students began playing in the water with the handicapped youngsters. Observing their interaction, the high school physical education teacher became very enthusiastic and devised a plan for the students to earn credit for teaching their handicapped peers to swim.

After receiving administrative approval, the high school physical education teacher developed a curriculum for a class called Swim Aide Instruction, for which high school students can earn physical education credit. The course uses American Red Cross training procedures which give the peer teachers certification in Water

From *Children Today*, January/February 1988, pp. 28-30. Reprinted by permission of the authors and *Children Today* magazine.

Using a hydraulic lift, teens in Project PAIRS gently lower a youngster into the water for his swimming lesson, then work with him on developing water safety skills.

Safety Aide Instruction, cardiopulmonary resuscitation and American Red Cross Advanced Life Saving.

Also included in the curriculum is a system for evaluating the progress of each handicapped student. Part of the high school students' grade depends on their success in teaching various skills to the handicapped students.

Since the self-contained special education classes are located on a campus across town, transportation was a primary concern. Through a cooperative effort between the school district's special education and transportation departments, Special Olympics funds were used to defray transportation costs, since the swimming classes were viewed as training for the Special Olympics. The funds paid for a bus to bring the handicapped children to the high school twice a week during October, November, April and May.

The high school physical education teacher realized early in the program that the pool was too deep—four feet at the shallow end. A local charitable foundation donated money for a "Tot Dock," a portable platform that decreased the depth of the pool at the shallow end by two feet. The high school students install and remove the platform for every class. The foundation also purchased a hydraulic lift which is used to assist wheelchair-bound students in and out of the pool.

About 65 handicapped students participate in the Swim Aide Instruction class each year. They range in age from three to 19 and have varying degrees of disabilities. During one semester, for example, the group included one autistic child, a student who was blind as well as mentally retarded, several students who had physical handicaps, and some with extremely limited verbal skills. Each handicapped student is paired with a peer teacher who is assigned the responsibility for teaching water safety and basic or advanced swimming skills to the best of each handicapped student's ability.

The high school students participate voluntarily in the program. Many are actively recruited by the physical education teacher; others have returned to the program after their first or second year because of a sense of accomplishment and satisfaction with their relationship with the handicapped students.

The peer teachers must be strong swimmers, and they are very conscious of the need to be prepared to save a handicapped student in trouble. They swim numerous laps so they will be strong enough to help if necessary.

The orientation given to the high school students before they begin working with the handicapped children contributes significantly to the program's success. At the first orientation session, the high school physical education teacher reviews the program's purposes and objectives. During the second session, the director of special education discusses handicapping conditions and specific problems that may be encountered during the swimming lessons. The adaptive physical education teacher then meets with the class and demonstrates techniques for moving and holding handicapped students and for managing behavior. Video tapes made during the previous year also help to initiate the students to the program.

The peer teachers are then taken to visit the local self-contained, multiply handicapped and early childhood classes, and they observe the specific student they will be teaching. Through these observations, "they can see who can't use his right arm, who's in a wheelchair, or who can walk or crawl," explains the teacher. "It allows them to do a better job of working with the students."

New peer teachers also benefit from doing exercises with students who had been in the program the previous year. For example, a student might tie another's arms against his body and blindfold him to help him understand how a handicapped student might feel.

Currently, the handicapped participants are divided into two age groups: ages three to 12 with some water skills, and age 12 and above with good water skills. A third group is formed of non-verbal swimmers. Each group swims one day per week with the peer teachers.

One of the objectives of the swimming program is to give physically and mentally handicapped students a chance to participate in the Special Olympics District Aquatics Meet. Each spring, students in the program are grouped according to ability level and age to compete in either developmental or advanced events. Developmental events include a 15-meter walk, a 15-meter floating race or a 10-meter assisted swim, while the advanced events include a 50-meter breast stroke, a 50-meter freestyle and a one-meter dive, among other events.

First, second or third place winners in the district swim meet advance to the Texas Special Olympics State Aquatics Meet. The 1987 meet was held in Kingsville, and 45 handicapped students from three school districts participated. During the developmental events, 15 PAIRS peer teachers assisted the handicapped students in the water. They also assisted in timing the races and presenting medals and T-shirts. For many students, it was a highlight of the PAIRS program. "The best part of working with the handicapped student that I had was seeing how much he had accomplished and taking him to the meet at the end of the year," one peer teacher said.

One of the most notable aspects of the program is that the handicapped youngsters do learn to swim. This surprises many parents who attend the Special Olympics Aquatics Meet and see children who have never experienced swimming prior to the adapted aquatics classes.

Three of the young handicapped students have learned to swim with assistance, and 25 of the older students can swim by themselves. Their parents can now take them to a swimming pool and feel comfortable about letting them swim by themselves. As the special education director commented, "These children thoroughly enjoy anything that gives them a freedom of movement, which the water does."

In addition to learning to swim, the communication skills of the handicapped students have improved significantly. The adaptive physical education teacher observed, "They just seem to open up a lot more because they're having a good time. They're with the high school students and are talking to them for an hour. Kids who have been quiet for years have opened up, and they go home and talk about it. If they can't talk, they'll imitate swimming. If you watch their faces in the pool, they look so happy. The little ones especially are so pleased with themselves."

Program Evaluation

Student gains or losses from the PAIRS program, unlike many educational programs, cannot be measured through the use of standardized test scores. However, interviews with the peer teachers reveal positive attitudes toward the program. They speak of learning patience and wanting more time to work with handicapped students, and they express satisfaction in "really learning how handicapped kids act and feel."

School district staff have produced a curriculum guide, a brochure and a video tape of the program to be used in disseminating information to others interested in replicating the PAIRS project.* Because of the difficulties in documenting the tangible results of programs of this nature, perhaps the most effective way of capturing its value is through the video tape.

Conclusions

The PAIRS program is easily replicable because of its low cost and because it requires little specialized staff training. The only required certification is for both the adaptive physical education teacher and the regular physical education teacher to be certified American Red Cross water safety instructors.

Although this particular project focused on water skills, any physical activity under the supervision of an adaptive physical education teacher can be implemented using the peer teaching concept. For example, during the winter months, PAIRS classes are offered at a nearby bowling alley on the same basis as the swimming classes. The owner of the bowling alley has purchased lightweight bowling balls and a wheelchair ramp for the handicapped students.

Whether in swimming, bowling or whatever setting a peer teaching program is implemented, all participants agree that handicapped and non-handicapped students will interact and learn from one another.

*The video tape and curriculum materials may be obtained from Patricia Goode, Director of Special Education, Laguna Madre Cooperative, P.O. Box 871, Kingsville, Texas 78363.

Article 50

Comprehensive Microcomputer Applications for Severely Physically Handicapped Children

G. Evan Rushakoff
Linda J. Lombardino

G. Evan Rushakoff *is a member of the faculty in the Department of Speech at New Mexico State University, Las Cruces. His clinical research and teaching have focused on the use of microcomputers for the nonvocal, severely handicapped, and the clinical and administrative applications of microcomputers for the speech-language clinician and audiologist.*
Linda J. Lombardino *is on the faculty in the Department of Speech at the University of Florida. She has published in the area of language programming with developmentally delayed children. She teaches graduate courses in language development; assessment and intervention; parent-child interactions; and nonvocal communication.*

■ Current microcomputer technology will continue to offer increasing benefits for many exceptional populations. Microcomputers have been successfully integrated into special education programs for mentally retarded, autistic, and physically handicapped children (Carman & Kosberg, 1982; Romanczyk, 1982; Sandals, 1979; Thorkildsen, Bickel, & Williams, 1979). Children who are severely physically impaired with uncompromised or minimally compromised intellectual abilities serve to gain significantly from the myriad of benefits that the microcomputer affords. Answers to the following questions will serve to help educators better understand the potential comprehensive uses of microcomputers with severely physically handicapped children.

What are the basic component parts of the microcomputer system?

A basic system for a physically impaired child should include a microcomputer (64K RAM), disk drive, and a monitor (or TV). If the child will be using the machine for writing, a printer is necessary. If the system is to be used as a speech-output communication aid, a speech synthesizer is needed.

In our clinical programs, we have used the Apple II (now Apple IIe) for three reasons. First, the Apple system can interface with most standard televisions when an RF modulator is used to convert the television into a monitor. Second, to date, it appears that the majority of the educational software and programs developed specifically for the physically handicapped are written for the Apple systems. And finally, most devices that allow severely motorically impaired children to control a microcomputer are developed for the Apple.

Can microcomputers be adapted for children who are unable to use a standard keyboard?

While some physically impaired children will be able to use the standard keyboard, others will require keyboard adaptations or modifications. There are five alternatives to standard keyboard use: (a) software-based single and multiple switch control; (b) firmware single and multiple switch control; (c) hardware single switch access; (d) keyguard for the standard Apple keyboard; and (e) expanded keyboards.

Single switches are available for children whose physical limitations preclude them from using the standard keyboard. There are three methods available for implementing single switch operations. The first method is to modify the keyboard entry program with a scanning subroutine. The Florida Scanner (Rushakoff & Steinberg, 1982) and the Special Inputs Disk (Schwejda, 1982) are examples of software which transform some keyboard entry programs into single switch programs. In these programs, all letter or number characters are arranged horizontally on the bottom of the screen. A pointer or marker performs a step-scan process from left to right across the characters until the switch is activated to indicate a desired entry.

The second and more versatile method is to use the Adaptive Firmware Card which, when plugged into the Apple, allows single and multiple switch control of all Apple programs. There are also hardware devices such as the Tetra-Scan II, Zygo 100, Omni, and Express, which will allow single and multiple switch control when hooked to the Apple.

Individuals who are unable to use the keyboard because of erratic motor movements may still have access to all Apple keyboard entry programs. A keyguard will often be sufficient in deterring extraneous keyboard entries. Finally there are expanded keyboards available which would be useful for those children for whom the keyguard is insufficient but for whom a larger keyboard is functional.

What are some of the commonly used applications of the microcomputer for physically handicapped children?

Communication

The microcomputer can be used as an efficient, versatile, and flexible speech output communication aid for nonvocal, severely physically handicapped children. The microcomputer allows for three communication output modes: monitor display, printed material, and synthesized speech.

The specific software chosen determines the degree to which the microcomputer will serve the child's communication needs. While only limited software are presently available, the next few years should witness an increase in the availability of programs which convert the microcomputer into a communication aid. The most comprehensive source of information on communication software is the Trace Center International Software/Hardware Registry (Vanderheiden & Walstead, 1982).

TALK II (Rushakoff, Condon, & Lee, 1982) is an example of a versatile and flexible communication microcomputer program. When an Echo II speech synthesizer is interfaced with the Apple microcomputer, this program automatically converts the microcomputer into a speech-output communication system. TALK II allows for a totally customized vocabulary from 1 to 800 letters, words, and phrases all of which can be accessed from 1–2 key presses. This strategy helps increase message efficiency (the number of key presses needed to produce a message). All of the vocabulary can be deleted, added, and moved around at any time, thus rendering this system readily adaptable to the user's immediate and future communication needs. TALK II can accommodate up to 200 sentences allowing the child to speak any message up to 100 words long with a single key press. The single-key sentence feature greatly increases the speed of spoken conversation. As with the vocabulary, these sentences can be changed at any time. The following are some single-key sentences that have been used in children's communication programs.

"May I have some help please?"
"Hang on . . . it will take me a minute to respond to that."
"I heard this great joke . . . care to hear it?"

With TALK II, the message created by the user may be displayed on the monitor, spoken, and printed. Messages of any length (such as stories or jokes) can be stored for use at a later time. Once stored, messages can be spoken or printed with one or two key presses.

Academics

The microcomputer offers several potential benefits for physically impaired children who are unable to meet academic objectives without direct teacher assistance. Once the student can activate the microcomputer via the keyboard or single switch device, computer assisted instruction can provide a mechanism for independent and active learning. Several software packages currently available for academic subjects (Educational Software Directory, 1981) are interactive in nature; that is, they provide the stimulus, prompting, feedback, and reinforcement necessary for independent learning of academic skills. Further, many educational programs possess the capability to maintain ongoing data for immediate and/or future monitoring of the student's work.

Computer assisted instruction should serve to increase the speed of learning when physical rather than cognitive limitations are deterring the student from achieving a normal rate of academic progress. In addition to facilitating student learning directly, computer assisted instruction will allow classroom personnel more time to work with students whose special needs require frequent teacher assistance.

Perhaps most importantly, the microcomputer may function to improve the self-concept of physically impaired students who have not developed a strong sense of autonomy because of their constant dependence on others for even the most basic of needs. In discussing the psychosocial benefits of computer training, Goldenberg (1979) stated that

> Because it [the computer] enables these special children to affect and control their world, and because it is a tool with which they can become proficient and show their creativity, it offers them a powerful chance to develop their own feelings of self-worth and to see themselves as learners and doers. (p. 25)

Writing

Children who use either the keyboard or a single switch device can operate microcomputer word processing programs. Some programs such as the Bank Street Writer are especially appropriate for children. Word processing allows the student to produce written material, make major text changes with relative ease, and store and print that material. These basic functions provide the student with a mechanism for correcting written material before printing a final copy and storing material for continued work at a later time. Word processing programs can reduce greatly the amount of time necessary to complete a writing task.

Creative Arts

In the area of creative arts, mild and moderately physically involved children may be able to use some percussion-like instruments along with recorded music, while severely physically impaired children are often limited to passive participation in music appreciation, i.e., listening. Microcomputers and appropriate music software allow these children to bypass their motor disabilities and generate their own musical creations. They can write music one note at a time, save, edit, and play it through the microcomputer system. For very young children, participation in music might entail merely playing a note-by-note version of "Mary Had a Little Lamb." However, older children can use "music composer" software for creating, editing, and playing more complex music compositions.

In the area of art, many physically impaired children are limited to projects that require direct assistance from the teacher or to activities which require only limited fine motor coordination, such as fingerpainting. Art creation software allows for the production of color artwork and animation. As with music software, the artwork can be saved and changed at a later time.

Recreation

Microcomputers provide severely physically impaired children, including single switch users, access to thousands of recreational programs. In general the most appropriate types of programs are games of strategy, memory, and logic. Several card games such as solitaire, blackjack, and bridge are available and can be played alone or with friends. Board games that are available for two or more players include chess, checkers, cribbage, monopoly, and scrabble.

Generally, games that require fine motor movements and timed responses should be avoided. Most "arcade" games fall into this category and invariably require the use of game paddles. There are a few instances in which such games can be modified to reduce the speed of response; however, typically they are unadaptable for use with severely physically impaired children. Vanloves Software Directory (1983) is one resource available for recreational software.

Vocational

Microcomputer training holds the potential to open up a vast number and variety of employment opportunities for the physically impaired population. The increasing reliance of various sectors of industry on microcomputer technology is spawning numerous career options for physically impaired adolescents and adults who are skilled in the use of computer operations. In reference to the appropriateness of current employment opportunities for the physically impaired, Goldenberg (1979) noted that "jobs exist that depend more on the manipulation of information than on the manipulation of things" (p. 13).

How is the microcomputer currently being used with young severely physically impaired children?

The Speech and Hearing Clinic at the University of Florida has prescribed microcomputer systems for several children between the ages of 5 and 8 years. The rationale varied according to individual needs. Some children required the microcomputer for use as an efficient speech output communication aid. Others used the system primarily for writing and computer assisted instruction. All children used the system for recreational purposes. Two of the children with whom we have worked are described below. These examples were chosen to highlight the diverse communication, academic, and personal needs of this population.

Robbie is a six-year-old non-ambulatory male with cerebral palsy characterized by severe spasticity in all limbs. He is functioning at an intellectual level that is commensurate with his chronological age and is currently attending a Montessori elementary school program. After an evaluation of Robbie's cognitive and motor abilities and a discussion with his family regarding their potential plans for his future educational and vocational needs, we determined that a microcomputer system would be the most appropriate aid for Robbie because of its potential to (a) provide him with a vehicle for independent learning; (b) help improve his writing efficiency; (c) permit his active participation in art and music activities; and (d) begin to prepare him for future career activities.

Within a period of less than a month (eight therapy sessions), Robbie learned to operate independently many academic and leisure programs on his microcomputer. Because he is still learning to read, he often requires assistance with some of the more complex reading programs; however, he has no difficulty operating programs where minimal reading is required. He has learned to input information reliably into the microcomputer by using keyboard control with a single finger.

After minimal training at the clinic, Robbie's parents have assumed primary responsibility for training him to use numerous programs. His parents have indicated that their major difficulty in using the system is finding quality academic and recreational software for his age level. Eventually Robbie's system will be integrated into his classroom activities.

Jasmine is an eight-year-old female with cerebral palsy and severe mixed dysarthria which involves neuromuscular movements necessary for speech production. She is ambulatory and is functioning at an intellectual level that is nearly commensurate with her chronological age. She attends a public school program for the physically impaired.

When first seen at the clinic, Jasmine communicated primarily through vocalizations and unintelligible single-word sign productions. She quickly learned to communicate through a large repertoire of signs and soon combined them into simple telegraphic sentences. However, neither her teacher nor her fellow classmates were able to understand signs, rendering her communication minimally functional outside the home environment. Jasmine's mother and school speech-language clinician agreed that a speech output communication aid would be the most efficient and effective communication mode for classroom use. They also agreed that the other applications of the microcomputer, including writing and computer assisted instruction, would serve to facilitate Jasmine's academic and personal-social development.

Jasmine was funded through Cerebral Palsy Services, Florida Department of Health and Rehabilitative Services for an Apple II microcomputer (48K) with a disk drive, monitor, and speech synthesizer. Within a period of less than two months Jasmine was able to use the microcomputer to construct and speak simple sentences. She was also beginning to use "stock" sentences in appropriate social situations such as *"How are you today?"* and *"Goodbye, it was nice talking to you."* This training is now being accomplished in her classroom where she must contend with more than a dozen communication partners. Jasmine's school speech-language clinician is working with her classroom teacher to integrate the communication system into Jasmine's everyday academic activities.

What are some factors that educators should consider before recommending the microcomputer as an aid for physically impaired children?

A number of performance and environmental factors need to be considered when prescribing a microcomputer as a comprehensive living aid for the physically impaired child. In some cases some degree of reading ability may be necessary for the child to benefit from many of the communication, academic, writing, and leisure activities described above. The level of reading ability varies from program to program. However, some preacademic and communication programs are available which can be used by the nonreader.

An environmental support system is critical if the microcomputer system is to be successfully integrated into the child's daily activities. All persons (family members, teachers, speech-language clinicians, physical therapists, and occupational therapists) who are responsible for the child's academic, social, physical, and communication growth and development should be involved in determining the appropriateness of the microcomputer system as a comprehensive living aid for the child. In addition, the child's primary caregivers need to agree upon goals for the child's immediate and future use of the microcomputer system.

In choosing a system it is important to remember that the microcomputer should be considered a stationary aid. Although it can be moved quite easily from home to school, it does require an electrical outlet. Although a number of portable, battery operated microcomputers have been developed recently they do not have the software needed to accomplish many of the applications described here.

The clinical applications of the microcomputer are far reaching for physically handicapped children who have the potential to achieve academic and non-academic accomplishments when provided with a mode of performance that bypasses their physical limitations. Prescriptions for microcomputer systems require careful consideration of performance and environmental factors to ensure that the individual and comprehensive needs of these children are met.

REFERENCES

Carman, G. O., & Kosberg, B. Educational technology research: Computer technology and the education of emotionally handicapped children. *Educational Technology*, 1982, 22(2).

Educational software directory: Apple II Ed. Austin TX: Sterling Swift, 1981.

Goldenberg, E. P. *Special technology for special children.* Baltimore: University Park Press, 1979.

Romanczyk, R. G. The impact of microcomputers on programming for the autistic child. Paper presented at the annual meeting of The Council for Exceptional Children, Houston, 1982.

Rushakoff, G. E., Condon, J., & Lee, R. TALK II: A speech-output, customized vocabulary microcomputer program. In Vanderheiden & Walstead (Eds.), *Trace Center International Software/Hardware Registry*, 1982.

Rushakoff, G. E., & Steinberg, D. Florida Scanner: Single switch software conversion. In Vanderheiden & Walstead (Eds.), *Trace Center International Software/Hardware Registry*, 1982.

Sandals, L. H. Computer assisted applications for learning with special needs children. Paper presented at the meeting of the American Educational Research Association, San Francisco, 1979.

Schwejda, P. Special inputs disk. In Vanderheiden & Walstead (Eds.), *Trace Center International Software/Hardware Registry*, 1982.

Thorkildsen, R., Bickel, W., & Williams, J. A. Microcomputer/videodisc CAI system for the moderately mentally retarded. *Journal of Special Education Technology*, 1979, 2(3).

Vanderheiden, G., & Walstead, L. (Eds.). *Trace Center International Software/Hardware Registry.* Madison: University of Wisconsin, Trace Center, 1982.

Vanloves 1983 Applė II/III Software Directory, Vol. II. Overland Park KS: Advanced Technology, 1983.

HARDWARE RESOURCES

(*Note:* You will need to specify whether you require equipment for the Apple II Plus or the Apple IIe.)

Adaptive Firmware Card
Adaptive Peripherals
4529 Bagley Ave. N.
Seattle WA 90103

Express III

Apple Keyguard
Prentke-Romich Company
R.D. 2, Box 191
Shreve OH 44676

King Keyboard (expanded keyboard)

Apple Keyguard
Technical Aids and Systems for the Handicapped
2075 Bayview Ave.
Toronto, Ontario
M4N 3M5, Canada

Omni
Communications Research Corp.
1720–130th Ave. N.E.
Bellevue WA 98005

Expanded Keyboard
Cacti Computer Services
130 9th St. S.W.,
Portage la Prairie, Manitoba
R1N 2N4, Canada

Tetra-Scan II

Zygo 100
Zygo Industries
P.O. Box 1008
Portland OR 97207

Index

Credits/ Acknowledgments

Cover design by Charles Vitelli

1. Mainstreaming
Facing overview—United Nations photo by L. Solmssen. 20—Photo by Mark A. Regan.

2. Attitude Change
Facing overview—United Nations photo by L. Solmssen.

3. The Learning Disabled Child
Facing overview—United Nations photo by Marta Pinter.

4. The Mentally Retarded Child
Facing overview—United Nations photo by O. Monsen.

5. The Gifted and Talented Child
Facing overview—United Nations photo by Milton Grant. 120—United Nations photo by John Isaac.

6. The Emotionally Disturbed and Behaviorally Disordered Child
Facing overview—EPA Documerica. 154—United Nations photo by L. Solmssen.

7. The Communication Disordered Child
Facing overview—United Nations photo by L. Solmssen.

8. The Hearing Impaired Child
Facing overview—United Nations photo by L. Solmssen. 189—Photos by Mark A. Regan.

9. The Visually Impaired Child
Facing overview—United Nations photo by S. Dimartini. 217, 218—Courtesy of J. A. Bensel, Maryland School for the Blind.

10. The Physically or Health Impaired Child
Facing overview—United Nations photo by Jan Corash.

We Want Your Advice

Annual Editions revisions depend on two major opinion sources: one is our Advisory Board, listed in the front of this volume, which works with us in scanning the thousands of articles published in the public press each year; the other is you—the person actually using the book. Please help us and the users of the next edition by completing the prepaid article rating form on this page and returning it to us. Thank you.

ANNUAL EDITIONS: EDUCATING EXCEPTIONAL CHILDREN 90/91

Article Rating Form

Here is an opportunity for you to have direct input into the next revision of this volume. We would like you to rate each of the 50 articles listed below, using the following scale:

1. Excellent: should definitely be retained
2. Above average: should probably be retained
3. Below average: should probably be deleted
4. Poor: should definitely be deleted

Your ratings will play a vital part in the next revision. So please mail this prepaid form to us just as soon as you complete it. Thanks for your help!

Rating	Article	Rating	Article
	1. The Necessary Restructuring of Special and Regular Education		27. Educator Perceptions of Behavior Problems of Mainstreamed Students
	2. The Regular Education Initiative Debate: Its Promises and Problems		28. Suicide and Depression: Special Education's Responsibility
	3. A Social Observation Checklist for Preschoolers		29. Meeting the Mental Health Needs of Severely Emotionally Disturbed Minority Children and Adolescents: A National Perspective
	4. The Individualized Family Service Plan and the Early Intervention Team: Team and Family Issues and Recommended Practices		30. Human Rights Review of Intrusive Behavioral Treatments for Students With Severe Handicaps
	5. Parent Participation by Ethnicity: A Comparison of Hispanic, Black, and Anglo Families		31. Principles for a System of Care
	6. Special Class Placements as Labels: Effects on Children's Attitudes Toward Learning Handicapped Peers		32. See Me, Help Me
	7. Promoting Handicap Awareness in Preschool Children		33. Culturally and Linguistically Diverse Children
	8. Classwide Peer Tutoring With Mildly Handicapped High School Students		34. Some Ways to Help the Language-Deficient Child in the Classroom
	9. Educating Students With Severe Disabilities		35. A Model for Training and Using Communication Assistants
	10. Learning Disabilities: A New Horizon of Perception		36. Functional Aphonia in the Child and Adolescent: Therapeutic Management
	11. The Learning Disabled Preschool Child		37. Poor Learning Ability . . . or Poor Hearing?
	12. The Masks Students Wear		38. Teachers' Knowledge of, Exposure to, and Attitudes Toward Hearing Aids and Hearing Aid Wearers
	13. Teaching Organizational Skills to Students With Learning Disabilities		39. Hearing for Success in the Classroom
	14. Helping Disabled Readers in the Regular Classroom		40. Service Delivery Alternatives for the Mainstreamed Hearing-Impaired Child
	15. Learning Disabled Students Make the Transition		41. Reducing Ethnocentrism
	16. Changes in Mild Mental Retardation: Population, Programs, and Perspectives		42. The Visually Handicapped Child
	17. Special Talents		43. The Parent and Toddler Training Project for Visually Impaired and Blind Multihandicapped Children
	18. Autism: The Child Within		44. A Model for Integrating Low Vision Services Into Educational Programs
	19. Using Task Variation to Motivate Handicapped Students		45. Appropriate Education for Visually Handicapped Students
	20. Increasing Independence Through Community Learning		46. Evaluating Microcomputer Access Technology for Use by Visually Impaired Students
	21. Sexuality and Students With Mental Retardation		47. Including Young Children With "New" Chronic Illnesses in an Early Childhood Education Setting
	22. Our Most Neglected Natural Resource		48. Students With Special Health Care Needs
	23. Meeting the Needs of Gifted Preschoolers		49. Project PAIRS: A Peer-Assisted Swimming Program for the Severely Handicapped
	24. Training for Staff, Parents, and Volunteers Working With Gifted Young Children, Especially Those With Disabilities and From Low-Income Homes		50. Comprehensive Microcomputer Applications for Severely Physically Handicapped Children
	25. Gifted/Learning Disabled Students: Their Potential May Be Buried Treasure		
	26. Creative Underachievers: Marching to the Beat of a Different Drummer		

(Continued on next page)

ABOUT YOU

Name____ Date__________
Are you a teacher? ☐ Or student? ☐
Your School Name ____
Department ____
Address ____
City ____________________________________ State __________ Zip __________
School Telephone # ____

YOUR COMMENTS ARE IMPORTANT TO US!

Please fill in the following information:

For which course did you use this book? ____________________________________
Did you use a text with this Annual Edition? ☐ yes ☐ no
The title of the text? ____
What are your general reactions to the Annual Editions concept?

Have you read any particular articles recently that you think should be included in the next edition?

Are there any articles you feel should be replaced in the next edition? Why?

Are there other areas that you feel would utilize an Annual Edition?

May we contact you for editorial input?

May we quote you from above?

No Postage Necessary if Mailed in the United States

ANNUAL EDITIONS: EDUCATING EXCEPTIONAL CHILDREN 90/91

BUSINESS REPLY MAIL

First Class Permit No. 84 Guilford, CT

Postage will be paid by addressee

DPG **The Dushkin Publishing Group, Inc.**
Sluice Dock
Guilford, Connecticut 06437